CRIME AND POLICING CRIME

PETER JOHNSTONE

University of North Texas

Kendall Hunt
publishing company
www.kendallhunt.com
Send all inquiries to:
4050 Westmark Drive
Dubuque, IA 52004-1840

ISBN 978-1-4652-1094-4

Printed in the United States of America
10 9 8 7 6 5 4 3 2

CONTENTS

Acknowledgements v
Preface vii

CHAPTER 1 A BRIEF HISTORY OF POLICING CRIME 1

CHAPTER 2 HOMICIDE AND ASSAULTS 57

CHAPTER 3 KIDNAPPING AND ABDUCTION 93

CHAPTER 4 THEFT, BURGLARY AND ROBBERY 121

CHAPTER 5 DRUG TRAFFICKING 163

CHAPTER 6 POLICING 199

CHAPTER 7 POLICING AROUND THE WORLD 233

CHAPTER 8 LAW ENFORCEMENT IN THE USA 259

CHAPTER 9 FORENSICS AND TECHNOLOGY 285

ACKNOWLEDGEMENTS

Thanks to Zachary Powell, Joslyn Adams, James Cheney, Brittany Thompson, Shatara Turner, Britannica Scott, Sarah Standlee, Sarah Gray, Michael Dorsey and Kameron Awbrey. Special thanks to Stefani DeMoss and Jay Cavalier at Kendall Hunt for making this as painless as possible, again.

PREFACE

Since this book is in part about policing—how the police are recruited, what they do and who do we want and select to police society—I feel obliged to start with a confession. When I was an undergraduate I never read the preface to a book. It took me some time to realize that there is lots of information in the preface and frequently some insight into the author as well. Many hundreds of books later, I now look forward to reading the preface as a way of learning more about the writer of the work with which I am about to spend many hours. In fact, in reading this book some of you will spend more time with me than you do establishing a partner to have a relationship with; yes, that is a sobering thought. I agreed to write this book because I felt that many of the books about policing were rather heavy on the recruitment and training aspects of the job and a little light on the work itself. I found that a lot of the books informed me about the profile of recruits in the US and sometimes a little about policing elsewhere; they told me about basic training and about the content of these courses; and they told me about the initial year or two as a street cop. Many of the books then discuss issues such as stress, diversity and ethics. These are all very relevant. But in my experience most people who are taking a degree in criminal justice know who becomes a cop and what basic training entails; and, if they don't, they go online and look at a syllabus. What very few undergraduates seem to have knowledge of is how other countries select police officers: Do they need a degree or a high school diploma; how long is basic training; and is the focus upon the social work aspects of policing, upon crime fighting or upon providing a military style presence to make citizens feel secure? Also, few undergraduates seem to have a grasp of the link between commonly reported crimes of a minor nature and how these correlate with serious crime. If most people join a police force to fight crime—and I would contend that a significant number do join for this reason, and many police departments see this as their primary function also—then it seems to me that to attract and sustain the enthusiasm of future recruits there should be a discussion at an early stage about the range of crimes a police officer will deal with, both in early career and as their career progresses. Most of you reading this preface now will know that early career police officers do not investigate serious assaults, kidnappings, robberies and drug trafficking. They investigate the crimes that lead to these offences: minor assaults, missing persons, thefts and street drugs offences. In this book I discuss the major crimes and the lesser offences so that there is a context for the reader when later in the book there is a discussion about what the police do, early career and later, locally, nationally and internationally. So this book is about four types of crime that are commonly committed across the world—assaults, missing persons and abductions, theft offences and drug offences. It is then about the people—the municipal police, the state law enforcement, and the federal and international agencies that investigate these crimes. It is a book about a police life, not only initial recruitment and training. The first part of the book covers the history and contemporary aspects of assaults, abductions, thefts and drug offences. The second part of the book looks at the people who investigate these offences, how they are recruited, trained and supported more and more by technology. This book is a journey through time, attitudes and the development of a science of policing. Not all of the actors have been as forthright, honest or honorable as we might have wanted them to be, given the nature of the work, crime fighting. But there have clearly been significant achievements and there are incredible examples of progress in the understanding of crime, who commits crime and how we can identify and prosecute them. That story unfolds throughout the pages and in particular during the final chapter when the history of forensics is discussed. Then you will see how pioneers in many of the sciences have made such huge contributions to the identification of victims and offenders. Any author writes with a degree of trepidation as one can inadvertently offend, fail to acknowledge or just plain annoy the reader because the reader's experience is different from the authors. I served as a police officer investigating some of the crimes discussed in this book; then I took a Ph.D. and started university teaching. I admire the attempts that are being made to professionalize the police across the world, and I am frequently amazed at the advances in science that have a practical application in policing. I have found that to share my passion and respect for policing, my students want to learn about the crime side of that job, and they want to know a little history about how the crimes themselves have changed over time. If your students have the same thirst as mine I believe they will enjoy this book and you, the professor, will enjoy using it to inform your own style of delivery and as a vehicle to stimulate meaningful discussion. If I achieve these modest aims, this book will be a success in no small part due to you bothering to read the preface.

A BRIEF HISTORY OF POLICING CRIME

To commit a crime implies that the offender has participated in an act that is more than offensive or damaging to one individual person, the victim; it is an action that offends all of a given society. Consequently, over time various societies have recorded those actions that offend individual and group members and these transgressions have formed the basis of modern criminal legislation and legal systems. Initially there was little distinction between an act that was a private wrong and one that is now considered a public wrong. For many years in England a person who was the victim of theft was responsible for bringing the matter to court. In many ways this merged the idea of a private and a public action so much so that numerous offences were never prosecuted, as the victims were not in a position to pay for a trial and private arrangements

were made to compensate the victim. Eventually it was recognized that the feelings of the community were important and that sophisticated society needed a means of holding criminals accountable regardless of whether or not the aggrieved party could afford a prosecution. Once the distinction between a private action and a public action was firmly established the role of the state was clearly apparent as crimes were then, as they are today, prosecuted in the name of the crown or the state, e.g. R v Smith[1] or The People v Smith or Commonwealth v Smith.

Just as the responsibility for prosecuting a criminal act has now been transferred to the state, so too are the subsequent sentence and application of punishment. It is often considered that the defining difference between criminal law and all other forms of law is that criminal law attracts punishment. In some respects this is true, but it is not an absolute. For example, if you fail to pay your taxes and a penalty is imposed on you, is this a criminal fine or a civil fine?[2] Contemporary discussions often raise the question as to whether it is possible to apply the criminal law to corporate entities and, if this is not possible, then why have criminal laws that make certain corporate actions criminal. This discussion is beyond the scope of the introduction but it should be immediately clear that for all of the clarity the law seeks to bring to our lives the actions of real, corporate and virtual criminals will always challenge our understanding of what it is to act criminally. For this book, crimes are the actions that are brought by the state against an individual(s) in response to a formal disapproval of the individual's action or inaction, the remedy for which is punitive—a fine, imprisonment or loss of life. In addition, crime also embraces a degree of seriousness that may be minimal—a misdemeanor—or very serious, a felony. Also, crimes capture acts that may offend against the community's sense of morality.[3]

Crime is organic. No society has developed a code of conduct from its origin and retained that code without amendments and additions. The nature of human action is such that we alter our behavior over time and create new and often inventive ways of circumventing the law. In response, laws are modified and matured to accommodate societal development. For example, killing another human being may be murder or manslaughter; it may be done intentionally or through carelessness; by accident or due to the insane actions of a deranged person who does not know they are participating in the death of another person. The variables of human killing are almost infinite. The role of the criminal law is to establish those killings that are unacceptable to society at that point in time in the development of that society. As we all know, crimes change over time and an action that was criminal in the past may not be a crime today, and a criminal offense today may not have been such in the past.[4] That said, it is generally accepted that taking another person's life is an evil act that all societies find repugnant.

The Code of Hammurabi was created about 2200 BC.[5] It comprises engravings on a piece of black diorite stone about seven feet tall. The Code was found in Susa, Iran between December 1901 and January 1902 by a team of French archeologists. The original location of the code was Babylonia and it is believed that the stone was moved to Sula by a previous conqueror.[6] A carving of King Hammurabi[7] sits on top of the code. He is receiving his regal authority from the sun god. When found, the codes were in numerous pieces that were reconstructed into the original 3,600 lines of text.[8] The codes show a significant level of sophistication in terms of the rights of individual citizens. They also give us a reference point for future trial methods. For example, Code 132 states that "plunge into the sacred river" is used a test of innocence or guilt. Three thousand years later, this method of testing innocence was widely used across Europe and the US as a means of establishing innocence and punishment. It was known as Ordeal by Water. The contemporary manifestation, water boarding, is still in contentious use today. Modern day adjournments to facilitate the presentment of witnesses are also seen in the Code, number 13: "If a man has not his witness at hand, the judge shall set him a fixed time not exceeding six months, and if within six months he has not produced his witness, the man has lied: he shall bear the penalty of suit." It was not until the Middle Ages that there developed a systematic distinction between a criminal and a civil offence or a private and public matter. The practice of merging laws is apparent in Hammurabi where Code 108 states, "If the mistress of a beer-shop has not received corn as the price of beer or has demanded silver on an excessive scale, and has made the measure of beer less than the measure of corn, that beer-seller shall be prosecuted and drowned." Also, in Code 153: "If a man's wife, for the sake of another, has caused her husband to be killed, that woman shall be impaled"; and Code 196 says, "If a man has knocked out the eye of a patrician, his eye shall be knocked out." In a time of social inequality and slavery, it should be noted that Code 198 stated, "If he has knocked out the eye of a plebian or has broken the limb of a plebian, he shall pay one mina of silver."[9] The delineation of social standing was also apparent in the fees a surgeon could charge. For example, in the case of operating on a patrician, he was rewarded with 10 shekels of silver (Code 215), and for the same operation upon a plebian the surgeon could charge 5 shekels (Code 216). Unlike today, negligent surgery was not covered by insurance and lengthy court hearings. Code 218 states "If a surgeon has operated with the bronze lancet on a patrician for a serious injury, and has caused his death, or has removed a cataract for a patrician, with the bronze lancet, and has made him lose his eye, his hands shall be cut off." The actions of veterinary surgeons were also subject to the codes. When a successful operation was carried out, the veterinary surgeon could claim one-sixth of a shekel as his fee (Code 224). When the surgeon made a mistake and caused the death of an animal, he was liable to pay the owner one-quarter of the value of the dead animal (Code 225).[10]

The ability of the state to regulate moral behavior has been a feature of all legal systems and it remains prominent in most societies today, some more so than others, as the role of religion fluctuates in different jurisdictions. This is apparent in the codes where adultery, incest and marriage were strictly controlled by the monarch as a means of controlling the private as well as the public lives of citizens. The first section of the Code deals with false accusations and the second sorcery and witchcraft; the next section deals with witnesses and the role of judges, followed by matters of theft and kidnapping, burglary and robbery and harboring offenders. Next is a section that deals with ownership and responsibilities pertaining to land and animals. Sections 66–99 are missing. Section 100 then discusses trade and the liability of merchants. This is followed by a lengthy section on morality: marriage contracts, adultery, rape, divorce, separation, prostitution and inheritance, then by a section relating to the liability of surgeons, veterinarians and builders. The final part of the Codes deals with slaves and slave ownership and an elaborate series of curses that shall beset anybody who fails to adhere to the Codes.[11]

The great achievement of Hammurabi was that in creating the Code he brought together customs and judicial decisions into one body of law. This is a model that has been copied numerous times since then by leaders such as Roman emperor Justinian and French emperor Napoleon Bonaparte. Vestiges of the Code remained apparent for many centuries after the death of Hammurabi and can be seen in practice in mode of trial and punishment during the formation of the Common Law and the Civil Law with use of ordeals and purgation oaths and communal liability for criminal offences conducted within the borough.[12] Further evidence of incorporation of the Code is found in early medieval distinctions between the value of the aristocracy and serfs in terms of compensation tariffs for the loss of life or limb.[13]

The influence of Hammurabi upon the biblical laws of Israel continues to be debated today. Sin is a concept that pervades biblical laws and is believed by some to be an inherent part of any discussion about crime. Contemporary Western thought frequently excludes sin from inclusion in a meaning of 'crime'. Yet it was the case that the two were intertwined because many rulers, such as Hammurabi, believed that they had a divine right to rule and therefore the laws promulgated were a fusion of god given authority alongside a secular means to control the people. Over time the religious aspects of a criminal action were transferred into a moral issue so that now we view offences such as pornography as a moral crime, whereas in the past this would have been a crime against god and a sin. The transition from ecclesiastical dominance to secular is clearly seen in the evolution of the Common Law in England during the Middle and late Middle Ages.

Biblical Israel's legal system is recorded in the books of Exodus, Leviticus, Numbers and Deuteronomy. The much quoted 'eye for an eye' concept embraced in the *lex talionis*[14] moved away from the hierarchical principles of Hammurabi in that all people were treated equally under God's law. Under Israelite law, all crimes were an offense against god as recorded in the Mosaic codes drawn from the Ten Commandments delivered to Moses by god. Although the Ten Commandments placed an outright ban on all killing of humans, killing during war or unintentional killing was excusable. In cases of homicide though, the idea of compensation for a life, as apparent in the Hammurabic Code, was not an option under Mosaic law and a culpable death required the shedding of the blood of the offender to redress the harm caused. In cases where an offender was not traced, the village was liable to shed the blood of an animal in lieu of a culprit.[15] In instances where bloodletting was not a suitable means of redress, for example in cases of theft of property, the thief was fined to the amount of the value of the stolen items. Under Mosaic and Hammurabic law, prosecutions were brought by individuals, and the instances of state intervention were largely restricted to matters involving warfare claims. The importance of the individual claim was expressed in the rule that in cases where the death penalty was imposed the individual bringing the prosecution was liable to throw the first stone at the condemned person.[16] Four centuries after Moses, King Solomon introduced a number of legal provisions that are still evident today. Two witnesses were required to find a defendant guilty. This was subsequently followed by the Romans, who required two eyewitnesses to a crime, and in lieu of two one witness and torture could be utilized, a theme that became commonplace in France during the establishment of the Civil Law system of that country. In cases where there were not two eyewitnesses the defendant could opt for taking an exculpatory oath. This too was an option across Europe for more than 1,500 years following Solomon. Punishment fashion also followed Solomon where in cases of capital crimes when the offense was deemed particularly heinous the body of the offender was displayed at the scene of the crime to deter future offenders. This translated into use of the gibbet across Europe, as well as the displaying of the head and limbs of offenders in strategic locations around the city in which the offence took place. The influence of the Law of Moses is also still apparent in many legal systems and it impacts directly many followers of Judaism through *Halakhah,* the religion of obedience to the Word of God. Orthodox followers consider the *halakhah* to be absolutely binding; reformists do not consider the texts binding and they believe that they are open to contemporary interpretation.[17]

The Hittites established a kingdom around current northwest Syria and Lebanon between the 18th and 11th centuries, BC. They used cuneiform script, one of the earliest known forms of written expression. Due to the prevalence of recording the written word, the Hittites have provided us with a comprehensive body of treaties and legal documents. The society was highly stratified and legal rules reflected the status of slaves, serfs and an aristocracy. The Hittites were a conquering people and therefore many of the legal materials relate to the rights and status of conquered countries and their populations with specific references to 'vassals' and 'runaway slaves'. The impact of the Hittites upon our understanding of crime was enhanced by the discovery of the Hittite cuneiform tablets found at Hattusa[18] and first published in 1922. The laws, written on clay tablets, were divided into two series. The first deals with the actions of men, the second with material ownership. Apparently the death penalty was not favored and an elaborate system of monetary compensation existed rather than the later *lex talionis* direct physical exchange. In lieu of a death penalty, serious crimes were punished by way of slavery and hard labor. The last 14 clauses of section one deal with sexual behavior and it is here that one sees the implementation of the death penalty for cases of bestiality and incest. Interestingly, not all cases of bestiality incurred the death penalty; it depended upon the animal chosen for the deviant act.[19]

The best known legal system from ancient Greece is the Laws of Athens. However, for many centuries Greece was not one unified nation or legal system but a cluster of city-states separated by harsh terrain and mountains. Some states, such as Corinth, were run by a group of leaders, whereas one or even two kings ruled others, such as Sparta. Athens is the city that today we associate with the birthplace of democracy, largely due to the leaders of Athens involving its citizens in some level of decision-making—the Assembly, the Council of 500 and the People's Court. Before the classical period of Athenian history, the laws resembled those of ancient Israel and protection by the state was considered the most valuable asset available to a citizen. Consequently, many criminal offences attracted the sentence of deprivation of citizenship, banishment. Homicide, intentional or negligent, was punishable with exile from both Athens and the surrounding countryside. Notwithstanding these provisions under Athenian law, some homicides were justifiable, such as execution of an exile that returned to the kingdom (also available as a sentence in England up until the 19th century for those who returned from America and Australia, having been banished). So too was killing in the height of passion or '*crime passionelle*' in instances where a male found his wife or his lover in the embrace of another. Equal rights had not yet arrived in Greece and mistresses and wives could not claim the same legal excuse if they found their husband or lover in bed with another. Other forms of sexual offences were treated with greater equity and far greater tolerance than Bible based criminal laws. In Greece, the prevalence of homosexuality was such that rape and seduction laws were the same regardless of the sex of the victim. Laws in relation to theft offences bear greater similarity to the Israelite legal system. Housebreaking at night was subject to the death penalty and also contained a 'Make my day' provision whereby the house owner was exempt from prosecution if he killed a nighttime intruder. Kidnapping was also a capital offense as were counterfeiting and forgery. The influence of the Greeks upon the Roman legal system is apparent in a number of ways. One lasting impact was the creation and use of magistrates. In ancient Greece, an aggrieved party was not solely responsible for bringing a prosecution. He could utilize the services of a city magistrate who would assist in making an arrest and completing forms and court paperwork. It was the magistrate who would hold a preliminary hearing and hold the matter over for trial. The fundamental feature of a state official taking control of the prosecution remained a mainstay of the Civil Law system. It took the Common Law until the mid-18th century to catch up and bring cases on behalf of the state or the crown. Once the Athenian period became the dominant force in the legal system, oath taking became a normal feature of establishing guilt or innocence. This era also saw the introduction of juries; sometimes up to 50 citizens sat as a jury. Each member cast a secret ballot to determine guilt or innocence. If a defendant could muster more 'oath-helpers' than the prosecution, the case was dismissed. Ordinarily it was expected that the prosecution would attract a minimum level of support, but if this fell below one-fifth of the total number of jury ballots, then the prosecution was liable to pay a fine. The purpose of fining the prosecution was to deter frivolous prosecutions, which were increasingly a problem in ancient Greece, so much so that the term sycophant,[20] understood today to mean a self-seeking person, was used to describe those who brought forward sham prosecutions. In instances where the crime was proven and attracted the death sentence, which became more prevalent than the previous use of exiling, death was most frequently by stoning. Under Athenian law, premeditated murder was always considered a special crime subject to trial before a specially appointed tribunal of magistrates, *archons,* and at a special location. Premeditated murder attracted the death penalty, which if delivered was conducted immediately after the trial. The mode of sentence varied from drinking hemlock to burial alive in an open pit to impalement. Although a number of famous Greek jurists are well known today—Draco, Lycurgus of Sparta and Solon, all of whom encouraged the writing of laws into a codified format—there is little evidence of a unified system of jurisprudence, and it would seem that the great orators of Greece were more concerned with philosophical debate than with analyzing the legal system and making concrete proposals for improvement.

The influence of Roman law remains apparent today, most notably within the Civil Law system of continental Europe and those countries influenced by the colonizing continental European nations. A significant association stems from the use of the term justice taken from Emperor Justinian, who established a *Corpus Iuris Civilis* during the 6th century: 12 books of the Codex, 50 books of the Digest, the best-known Institutes and the Novels. However, it should be remembered that by this time the Western Roman empire had collapsed and therefore the influence of Justinian's collective works would have been largely limited to the eastern empire. In the west marauding bands of Visigoths, Burgundians and Franks were establishing themselves as the dominant groups across a fragmented Europe. Nevertheless, the impact of Justinian did reach the West, initially in Italy and then throughout most of southern Europe. Prior to the collapse of the empire, Rome was the most influential and powerful democracy on earth. Its government, known as a republic, was based upon elected officials representing the people. The Greeks, via the Etruscans, naturally influenced the early era legal system, and from the basis of the Greek legal system the Romans refined and grew legislation to make many of the laws ultimately uniquely Roman.[21] Society was highly stratified and this was reflected in the legal system. Upper, protected classes consisted of those who should be treated differently by the laws than the commoners. For example, after the Christianization of Rome by Constantine, priests and clerics were included in the elite group of citizens who were not subject to the ordinary rules of trial. Those in holy orders, alongside senators, equestrians and teachers, were exempt from the requirement to appear before an ordinary tribunal when answering a criminal charge. This anomaly developed into the famous, and infamous, practice of Benefit of Clergy that allowed criminous clerks to avoid prosecution in secular courts for 1,200 years and to seek the protection and sanctity of the bishop.[22] Criminal offenses in Rome were classified in terms of severity; intentional homicide attracted the death penalty, unintentional homicide resulted in the payment of financial compensation to the aggrieved family. Sex offenses were clearly articulated in the early years of the Roman Empire, but as the status of Rome grew and it paid greater attention to the rights of citizens, so too did the law expand to capture a range of criminality that exposed the victim to abuse of a slanderous as well as of a sexual nature. Compensation was utilized far more extensively in Rome than had been the case in the biblical or the Greek legal systems. Nevertheless, the victim could kill burglars caught in the act, in flagrante delicto, if the intruder was in the premises at nighttime or if he had a weapon with him during the daytime. Slaves caught breaking into a house, regardless of the time of day or whether they had a weapon or not, were flogged and then thrown from the Tarpeian Rock.[23] In criminal cases, if the defendant was a Roman citizen, he was entitled to an appeal. Originally this was to a body of citizens. Julius Caesar changed this to be an appeal directly to the emperor. Intentional homicide, perjury, treason and accepting bribes (as a public official) were all subject to beheading. Arson was subject to death by burning. Since there was an appeal process for Roman citizens, particularly in the era prior to Caesarial intervention, many citizens of Rome escaped corporal punishment and were banished instead. Slaves were less fortunate, and with no citizenship status they were subject to corporal punishment, imprisonment and death, most frequently by strangulation.

As we look back at the early era of defining actions as criminal, certain common themes are apparent. All the civilizations discussed viewed the intentional killing of a human being as the most serious level of crime. All of the societies implemented sanctions against those found guilty of killing a superior, equal or inferior citizen, and all of the societies started to incorporate alternative sanctions so that the death penalty might be transmuted to exile or banishment for certain classes of society. Killing rulers and leaders was, and remains today, viewed as a particularly heinous crime, and punishments increased in savagery and calculated pain infliction over the next millennia as rulers continued to view themselves as divinely appointed. That said, crime cannot be viewed as an absolute in any of the early era civilization groups as a number of factors come to bear upon why certain laws were implemented and what impact those laws had upon individual societies. Essentially, crime may be a legal construct, an act punishable by law or it may be a social construct that is variable depending upon the norms or moral values of a given group of people. Reconciling these two positions is complex and features as a major factor in the division between the approaches the Common Law took when compared and contrasted with the Roman law based Civil Law.[24] As Professor of Roman Law Frank Wieacker commented, "The substantial reception of Justinian's law and the unrestricted dominance of the academically-trained jurist appointed by a sovereign did not, with certain exceptions, occur in the Anglo-American system."[25] Where we do see a resounding influence of Roman law upon the legal systems of continental Europe and the Common Law countries of England and Wales, and to some extent the United States, is in the development and impact of canon law.

Our discussion so far has centered upon the influence of major civilizations upon the meaning of crime and how various groups treated it. By the time that the Roman Empire had collapsed, the legal influence of the Babylonians, Hittites, Greeks and Romans was such that parts of their systems would inevitably feature in the new order that would be established across Europe over the next 1,000 years. England developed a system of dealing with crimes that became distinctly different from the rest of Europe. Today we call this English origin family of law, the Common Law. In France, Germany and the rest of Europe, there remained closer ties with the Roman tradition and the system of law that developed included more references to the Roman legal tradition than to the Common Law. We call the codified legal system of Europe the Civil Law.[26] Through colonization and empire building, England exported the Common Law and The Netherlands, Spain, Germany, Italy, Portugal and France exported the Civil Law. During the last 200 years, some countries that operated an individual legal system have modified their provision to now be a codified system that resembles that of the Civil Law. Examples of this include Russia and Japan.

During the Dark Ages Britain was subject to numerous attacks and invasions from tribes based in Germany, Denmark, Norway and France. Throughout Europe many regions were tribal and autonomous, with local kings and tribal leaders attempting to gain territory and power through the process of marauding warfare. Medieval Europe experienced a period of social chaos after the Romans and brute force was the ruling factor. The only unifying feature was the Christian church and to a lesser extent the Latin language. It was from the church that literacy, learning and teaching emanated. But even the church could not withstand the forces of tribalism and it too became fragmented and regionalized with power vested in local bishops rather than in one unified Holy See. Out of this patchwork of social order the definition of a crime reverted back to customary interpretation with a spattering of Roman law. Crime control was based upon local group support and a system of compensation based upon the loss of a life or a limb became the standard way of resolving criminal actions. Expulsion from the protection of the group, as we saw in ancient Greece, was viewed as one of the more serious sanctions, as exile or banishment could literally mean death. Without the protection of the group and family members, an individual was unlikely to survive long in the forests and wastelands of Europe. Although it may be hard to imagine today, what was occurring across Europe was the foundation of nation states and formal legal order. Because it was poorly recorded due to the lack of literacy, much of what was happening across Europe perpetuated the social order constructed in Babylonia, Israel, Syria, Athens and Rome. A new social order was definitely in the making, however, and with this came the need for a structured legal system that could effectively deal with criminal conduct. But the basis for the new order was a fusion of established societies, the burgeoning influence of the Christian church and a basic instinct for survival in the midst of rampaging tribes. Europe was experiencing a period of weak and unreliable government and it was individual rights and associated avenues for redress that would inevitably come to the forefront of the criminal justice system. For the next 1,000 years all of the countries of Europe would mingle legal systems into a hodgepodge of church law, customary law, tribal law and remnants of Roman law. Then as the future kings of Europe asserted authority and consolidated their powers the need for a justice system developed—one that would be designed and operated by the new rulers. If the Dark Ages were a period of legal uncertainty, the

Middle Ages were a period of growth, definition and control. A significant factor in the control of the people was control of the criminal law, and where better to start than by making the most serious of all crimes a threat upon the life of the ruler. Treason and regicide became the most serious criminal offense that any person could commit and the death penalty was designed to be both lengthy and particularly painful to ensure that nobody attempted to malign or threaten the life of the king.

By the early Middle Ages, the European Frankish kingdom was divided into three regions that today represent the nations of France, Germany and Italy. Due to geography and a longer Roman presence in these countries, Roman law is more strongly evident in the burgeoning legal systems there than in Britain. Also, there was the beginning of a divide between matters that were deemed private and those that were public, particularly with respect to criminal matters. The Roman system of appointing a magistrate to conduct criminal trials was to become a standard feature in Europe and the use of torture also became necessary and prevalent for six hundred years. With some degree of legal snobbery, the English will claim they do not mar their criminal justice system with the use of torture, but this is stretching the imagination rather far unless you are prepared to ignore one hundred years of torture inflicted by the Tudor monarchs. The reality is that the use of torture is not commonplace in the English Common Law and it is not a fundamental and necessary element in the laws of proof. In Europe, reliance upon the Roman law means that two eyewitnesses are needed to secure a conviction. Without such, then one eyewitness and persuasive accompanying evidence may suffice. In lieu of any witnesses, then torture was used in Rome and was taken up across Europe as the only alternative means to gathering sufficient evidence to hold a trial. As history has demonstrated, the lack of correlation between inflicted pain upon a person and the propensity to tell any truth whatsoever has been tragically clear for decades. Nevertheless, the developing Civil Law system of Europe bound itself to a Roman tradition that had little alternative other than to torture suspects. It has been alleged that the Enlightenment was the driving force of change, but this too is open to debate as in reality there is a considerable body of evidence to the effect that it was the adoption of a jury system under the Civil Law that collapsed the reliance upon torture and not enlightened philosophical rhetoric in an age of plenty.

Alongside the development of a separate and different legal system in Europe and England ran the church and its laws. For much of the early period, the monarchs of Europe were heavily reliant upon the church to provide scribes and lawyers. Latin was the language of the aristocracy and the courts, and training in reading and writing was the preserve of the church. Church scholars were themselves influenced by the Romans, and over time a body of canon, ecclesiastical, law developed. By the late Middle Ages, canon law and Civil Law were main subjects of study at the universities of Europe, and together the two laws formed a united body of laws applicable throughout continental Europe. The difference between England and the rest of Europe, however, was that church law in England was increasingly becoming a separate body of law, whereas in continental Europe canon law informed the development of the main body of laws. Eventually the two families of law, Common and Civil, took on distinctly different features. Ultimately both were to influence the establishment of law in the US, particularly in some individual states, notably Louisiana and a number of the Southwestern states. California is an interesting example as it has a state civil code that is a fusion of Roman law influences and Common Law. The founding fathers of the US numbered many lawyers and most of them were familiar with the Common Law and Roman Law. Thomas Jefferson possessed a copy of the leading Common Law text, Blackstone and Justinian's *Institutes*.[27]

By the 11th century universities were being established across Europe and many former theological schools were becoming universities themselves. England was behind much of Europe, but it too established the first university at Oxford in 1096. Perhaps surprisingly, England continued to move towards a legal system distinctly different from France given that a Frenchman had conquered the English in 1066. However, William the Bastard, William of Normandy, the Conqueror and King William I elected to tread his own distinct path as ruler of a new nation. He recognized the valuable influence of the previous Germanic invaders and he recognized that to implant a French model of justice in totality would undoubtedly be rejected by his new people. William was responsible for the integration of some features common to his homeland Normandy, but he also subsumed existing customs and vestiges of Romano-canon law into what was to become the Common Law. Revenge and blood feud had been commonplace in England for the four hundred years preceding William's arrival. A system of involuntary compensation existed for families that suffered loss of a family member through unlawful killing. In lieu of compensation, slavery by the culprit for the aggrieved family was an option. The church also managed to retain a prominent position in the compensation stakes; stealing from the church was compensable at a higher rate than stealing from a commoner, and if the life of a cleric was taken, this too was valued at considerably higher a rate than if one killed a serf or peasant. Society was highly stratified generally, so that a serf's life was valued at two hundred shillings and a nobleman's at twelve hundred shillings. Under Alfred the Great, an ear was valued at thirty shillings and a nose at sixty.[28] During the Dark Ages and the early Middle Ages there was no distinction between a felony and a misdemeanor. This was addressed in the Assize of Northampton 1176. William I was keen to see an end to blood feuds as they deprived the king of control over the legal system and a loss of life was viewed as a waste when that person might be needed subsequently to serve the king in peacetime or in battle. From 668 onwards, English kings had made extensive use of clerics to assist in trials. Truth finding was achieved through use of the 'compurgatory oath'. This Athenian model became a forerunner to juries, which deliberately or not would cause England to avert assumption of the Civil Law and its associated reliance upon torture. If the exchange of oaths did not result in a conviction or acquittal, then the parties moved onto the next stage, a cessation of the case or ordeal. Hot water was one common form of ordeal; water boarding, ducking, poisoning and hot oil and coals were approved variations. Remaining unscathed from the ordeal denoted God's intervention on behalf of the innocent. Death by drowning or visible injuries sustained from burning the flesh indicated guilt at which point, if you could still live long enough, you would be put to death for the crime. The ordeal process was lengthy and calculated and was run by the clergy. In time this was to prove fatally problematic as the church disassociated itself with trial procedures that resulted in the letting of blood. Well, let's agree that in principle they did. In reality, if your crime was against the church, heresy for example, then the clerics became masters of torture and non-bloodletting means until proven guilty. At that point, when it was proven you were a heretic, you were excommunicated and handed over to the secular authorities for a positively bloody death.

William I introduced a new form of trial, the Trial by Battle.[29] He extended the use of the death penalty in lieu of numerous mutilation sentences, and he precluded bishops from significant involvement in secular trials. William also created a new court system, the king's court, the *curia regis,* at which, like his forefathers in France, he periodically sat personally to administer justice. It has been suggested that William also introduced the first office of 'Constable' to England. There existed at the time a *Comte de Stable* in France who was a person with responsibility for the king's stables. It has been mooted that this term was employed in England and derivated in use to become a person with responsibility for maintaining the king's peace. William most definitely extended the role and function of the shire-reeve to become an integral part of the entire justice system. His influence upon this role is still apparent today in the sheriff in the US who can probably claim the longest direct heritage of any law enforcement official in the country. As stated, William did not create the office of shire-reeve, sheriff, or *scirgerefa;*[30] this was achieved by King Ine, King of Wessex, 688–726. What William did was to seize the opportunity to use a well-known law enforcement official and extend his authority beyond that of tax collector and prison keeper to the chief law officer for a county. In his role as the chief law officer for a shire, the sheriff held the authority to demand assistance from local village people. The 'Hue and Cry'. Additionally, over time various appointments were made to provide a level of local rudimentary protective services that from modest beginnings as watchmen and vigilantes[31] would eventually form the basis of a professional police force for England. "Within the first few years of his reign he appointed numerous fellow countrymen to the county shire-reeves position to ensure that there was a close watch upon the fiscal as well as local feudal responsibilities.[32] Whereas in the pre-Norman period the sheriff had authority to preside over hundred court hearings, to uphold the king's peace and to apprehend suspected criminals, under William these functions were formalized and positively encouraged."[33] Overall, however, one of the most decisive moves that William made during his reign was to divide church and state through the establishment of church courts with separate jurisdiction from the secular courts. His ability to dilute the power of the church in legal matters was a decisive blow to the power of the church—one, which in England it never recovered from. This was most certainly not the case in continental Europe where the influence of the church upon the establishment of the new legal order was paramount.

Perhaps stimulated by the separation of church and state started by William the Conqueror or perhaps due to a genuine concern over clerical involvement in legal procedures that resulted in the spilling of blood, by the thirteenth century the church removed itself entirely from any legal procedures that required a cleric to participate in bloodletting. Determined to reform clerical abuses that had grown over the centuries, Pope Innocent III instigated the meeting of the Fourth Lateran Council in 1215, the result of which was to effectively abolish trial by ordeal from the legal calendar. The quandary for England and the Continental European justice systems was how would they replace divine intervention, the ordeal, with a manmade judicial process? Who would believe that a human judge could or should sit in judgment of another person when for the past thousand years everybody knew that it was God who sat in judgment? For England, the substitution was to be the jury. It would henceforth be your peers that judged you, much in reality as they had done for hundreds of years anyway since the involvement of William the Conqueror. For Europe, the question was more challenging, as they had no jury system. Continental Europe had relied upon the Roman law principles of proof, which might or might not include torture. For the time being at least, Europe had no choice; it would have to formalize the use of torture and embed it into its legal culture. Serious crimes, felonies, would be subject to torture and lesser offences, misdemeanors, would not.

In addition to taking the religious high ground on involvement in the secular legal system, Pope Innocent III also wanted to extend the privileges associated with being a member of the clergy, so that they were afforded even greater protection from the expanding arms of the secular law. Clearly, if the church was not to be a part of the secular law, then its members, the clergy, should not be subject to this new legal system. Innocent was adamant that clerics should not appear before a secular court for a broad range of criminal offences. This had already caused one of the most celebrated arguments in Europe between Henry II and Thomas Beckett at the close of the 12th century. It was to prove a major stumbling block to harmony between the monarchy and the church for many years to follow. Interestingly though, although Innocent's intentions were to remove the clergy from involvement in the secular legal process, the expansion of Benefit of Clergy actually achieved the reverse but in a positive way.

Benefit of Clergy had been established with the conversion of Emperor Constantine to Christianity when he pronounced that clerics should join the list of protected persons who should not be subject to the ordinary courts in Rome. This privileged status was reinforced periodically throughout the next millennium so that by the close of the 12th century the term cleric captured a broad range of males that were associated with working for the church. The problem was that many of these 'clergymen' were common criminals who managed to escape justice by claiming their privilege. And so the system came into increasing disrepute. Henry II sought to correct this anomaly but fell afoul of his former friend, turned religious zealot, Thomas Beckett. Famously, Beckett was murdered in Canterbury Cathedral on December 29, 1170. The King was implicated in his death and excommunicated. He was subsequently allowed to return to the church after receiving the public humiliation of being flogged by monks at the scene of the murder, Canterbury Cathedral. Soon after this, Pope Innocent III came to power, and due to a number of life influences he was determined to strengthen the position of the clergy, especially in England where it was clear that the monarchy was gaining the upper hand in the power struggles. Via the vehicle of the Fourth Lateran Council, Innocent III was able to disrupt the English legal system's reliance upon trials by battle, wager and ordeal, especially ordeal, by imposing an absolute ban upon clerical involvement. He was then able to reinforce this abstention by demanding, and achieving, greater protections for the clergy through the use of the clerical privilege, Benefit of Clergy.

By a circuitous route, however, the extension of Benefit of Clergy actually helped many more people than the large number of alleged 'criminal clerics'. Over time, the process for establishing that a defendant in the secular courts was exempt from trial or sentence was by asking the 'cleric' to recite a psalm from the Bible. With the passage of time and familiarity of use, the cited psalm was always the same, Psalm 51, the misère.[34] It now became possible for genuine members of the clergy to school commoners and non-clerics in the required Bible verse so that innocent citizens could avoid the increasingly draconian English criminal law by falsely claiming they were clerics. It became so commonplace for non-clerics to claim 'their benefit' that judges routinely asked defendants if they wished to claim the privilege. After hundreds of years of use and abuse, many serious crimes that attracted the death penalty were downscaled to be subject to the Benefit of Clergy, so much so that eventually the requirement to cite the psalm was abolished and first-time offenders were routinely branded rather than executed, under the fiction that they were clerics. The high point of the system was when women too were allowed to claim they were clerics in an era when it was only men who could join the tonsured ranks of the cloth. Benefit of Clergy became such an established method of downgrading the severity of a crime and its sentence that it was transported to America and existed in this country too until the mid-19th century.[35] Perhaps not unsurprisingly, Psalm 51 became known as the 'neck verse', as it saved the neck of the person reciting it.

Henry II had taken the lead from his great-grandfather William the Conqueror and extended the role of the secular courts. He had created the circuit court system, increased the role of royal judges and formalized the 12-member jury system. He expanded the writ system as a means for the king to send sealed massages to the sheriffs, and he established a Court of

Chancery that would evolve into the Court of Equity where inequities or wrongs could be addressed. Overall, Henry II can be credited with having an influential and positive role in the formation of the Common Law—a legal system that would become the most widely adopted in the world.

The Fourth Lateran Council also impacted the development of the legal system of Europe, which as commented upon above had started to take a very different route from that of England. From 1150 onwards, the church was fighting heresies, in the criminal courts and on the battlefield. It was against this backdrop of criminal disbelief in the words of the church that the legal system for Europe evolved. Much like England during this time, responsibility for bringing a criminal action lay with the victim. Consequently, many actions were never progressed and those that were had more to do with achieving damages for a loss than protecting society from the actions of individuals intent upon usurping the law. As a result, it was difficult to determine whether an action was criminal or civil and a general system of customary law was the most common form of legal redress in existence. To establish whether or not an action was punishable at law, the victim needed to take the matter before a *Turba,* a form of custom hearing. This 'court' remained in existence until 1667 in France and consisted of 10 local men who were known to be familiar with local customs and practices. At this point in time, the developing legal system in England and Europe had certain similarities. In particular, both were accusatorial in nature as the victim brought forward an accusation against the culprit who then had to defend his position before a tribunal. However, as the church attempted to assert its authority over heretics, the mode of trial became increasingly inquisitorial in nature and form with deputized bishops attempting to avert the spread of heretical beliefs by conducting inquisitions against suspected religious transgressors. Over time these inquisitorial methods became the established mode of trial across Europe. A dominant feature of the Inquisition was that defendants were required to answer questions put to them not by a lay accuser but by a judge. Under the English model, the judge was relegated to being an impartial referee who ensured that the parties adhered to the rules of play. In Europe, the judge conducted the game of play and asked whatever questions he liked. In Europe, the accuser was the church or the state. In England, it was, and remained for many years, an individual. In England, evidence was obtained through a process of questioning witnesses and confronting the accused. In Europe, a judge who could revisit the investigation and obtain further direct evidence himself if he deemed it necessary conducted the investigation into the allegation. This evidence could be obtained in private and the defendant was not invited to be present to hear what witnesses said against him. In summation, under the English model the judge played a passive role, while under the continental European model the judge was an active participant in the entire proceedings. Under the English model, it was assumed that there are two sides to every story and these should be tested. Under the Civil Law model, one truth is attainable and that truth is achieved by drawing together all of the available evidence, and it may be necessary through torturing the accused to obtain that evidence. It is easy to see why over time it became a mainstay of the legal system that the state prosecution would need to have a confession from the defendant, as this proved guilt and was a part of the evidence. Consequently, obtaining a confession became an art form via the implementation of torture. Initially France was not disposed towards using torture in 'ordinary' procedures, that is, in cases that were not unusual or extraordinary. However, by the 14th century the use of torture had spread to most hearings and secret hearings, and trials were becoming normal practice. "By 1400, torture became a fundamental part of French criminal procedure and torture times were directly related to the time it took to recite a prayer such as the Pater Noster."[36] By the middle of the 16th century, France had formalized use of the extraordinary method of investigation into a two-stage process, examination before one judge followed by a trial before an entire bench. There was no right to representation, nor was there in England either at this time, and the accused was not permitted to confront witnesses. Largely due to the manic belief that heresy was rampant throughout the civilized world and that Satan was manifest in numerous aberrations, criminal trials were not restricted to humans and the inquisitorial process prosecuted animals as well as humans during this time. Animals, however, were not subject to torture, but they could, and did, receive the death sentence.

An important distinction between the Civil Law and the Common Law has now started to develop. Under the Civil Law the decisions of the judge are individual to each case. This is not viewed as potentially confrontational as a qualified judge runs each investigation and then another bench of judges hears the trial; there is no need to record the trial proceedings or outcomes as the process is run and administered by professional judges. Under the Common Law, the trial was essentially run by lay people who did not have expert legal training; therefore, it would be prudent to record the events and the outcome so that good practice may be replicated in the future and similar trials have similar outcomes. The very basis for the Common Law is that it is commonly applied to all participants and the decisions of trials; nowadays the decisions of judges are similar and will bind future cases. The basis of the Civil Law is that professional judges do not need to bind each other or have an unerring need to follow previous cases in succession. These two distinctly different features will be commented upon further at a later stage in the discussion, but it is worth noting now that the lasting differences between the two legal systems and the manner in which criminal trials are conducted have a history that started in the fundamentally different approach taken towards who should bring forth a prosecution and whether or not the proceedings should be recorded or not. As we shall subsequently establish, these differences have a significant impact upon the nature and form of police investigations into serious crime, particularly those offences that transcend national borders.

The advantages of having a body of legal decisions recorded for future reference need to be contrasted with the Roman law tradition of writing down the law. This model, extended by Justinian and employed by the Romano-civil lawyers of Europe, meant that a comprehensive body of rules and offences was written down for all users of the law to learn and use. Even today, lawyers of the Civil Law learn by wrote the laws and procedures of their country before selecting options for study at an advanced level. Students of the Common Law do not learn any part of the law verbatim but rather learn concepts and the importance of legal decisions that will bind future cases through the process of binding precedent. During the Early Middle Ages, many of the universities of Europe, led mostly by Bologna in Italy,[37] embraced the idea of a jurist being essential to the legal process, much as the Romans had done by creating the position more than one thousand years previously. The Middle Age version moved away from the singular role of developing rules and procedures conducted by elite members of Roman society on a *pro-bono* basis to doctors of law drawn from the ranks of the general public, who would become "the midwives in the birth of a new system of law for an emerging Europe."[38] Inevitably much of the Italian Civil Law was to influence the rest of Europe. This growth in a body of written codes occurred alongside another Italian based legal system, the rapid expansion of laws created by the Roman Catholic Church, or canon law. It should be remembered at this time that the influence of the church in virtually every aspect of everyday life was commonplace across Europe. Medical science was in its infancy and suspicion and fear was a currency utilized by the church and monarchs as a means of asserting control. This fear featured not just in life but also in the afterlife, and for centuries it was believed that a dismembered body was not eligible to enter heaven. Hence, traitors were not only executed, they were also quartered to ensure that they could not gain an afterlife. Given the powerful influence of the church, canon law was significant. It controlled many matters that today would not be viewed as religious—divorce and separation, for example. Marriage after the death of a first spouse, sexual relationships with family members, adultery, blaspheming, failing to attend church on a Sunday and even being drunk were all matters strictly regulated by the church. It therefore followed that in many instances writers of the Civil Law would look to the canon law for examples and guidance when drafting new legislation. Ecclesiastical influence was particularly noticeable with regard to the use of written documents and witness testimony being used in courtrooms. Europe was moving gradually away from the solution to a grievance being settled by battle towards a non-combative courtroom scenario. Since the withdrawal of clerics from the ordeal process in 1215, the church had developed a considerable body of evidential rules and procedures that could be replicated and modified to suit the new Civil Law courtroom. The church was clearly not averse to this copying as it meant that it maintained a leading role in the development of laws across Europe. The other major influence upon developing a comprehensive code of laws was the burgeoning middle class made up of merchants, traders and seafarers who were becoming a forceful voice in the desire for uniform rules of business and trade and international maritime regulations. Within a short period of time, a variety of specialist courts started to emerge across Europe to deal with trade disputes, commercial contract disputes, maritime rules and regulations, the licensing of fairs and markets and the establishment of craft guilds within cities. By the 14th century, Europe possessed a comprehensive body of written laws pertaining to most aspects of a citizen's life. England by comparison had a legal system that relied upon the interpretation of the law by judges even though the law itself was not written down. What was recorded was the decisions of the judges so that in future cases a judge could look at what had been decided previously and then apply the same logic to the case in front of him, so that there was continuity of the law across the country. Well, that was the theory, which eventually after a number of twists and turns became the practice.

With such a variety of sophisticated levels of redress being developed in Europe and England, it would perhaps seem unnecessary to submit citizens to torture. However, as we have established, with the removal of supernatural ordeals a means was needed to test the veracity of the parties to an alleged crime. In Europe, torture was employed wholesale. In England, this was not the case, generally due to the countrywide use of juries by 1240. However, the English legislators did create their own dilemma. In the initial period of jury use, defendants could elect to have the matter heard before the jury or accept banishment. Banishment was for life, but it had some advantages, principally, if you accepted banishment then you were not subject to forfeiture of your goods and property; they could be transferred to your family. The great advantage was that although you would no longer be with your family (you were dead) they would not be destitute. The applicable law of England at the time stated that if you elected to stand trial and lost, then the crown took all your belongings and your family would be turned out onto the streets. If you were never found guilty, the crown could not confiscate your chattels. Once this legal lacuna was recognized, the legislators decided to apply pressure upon defendants to accept trial. The pressure was a literal pressure; it was torture by pressing your body with weights until you either gave in and accepted a trial or you died under the weights placed upon your chest. This torture—as it clearly was torture—was known as *peine forte et dure,* a French term meaning pain, hard and long. Other pieces of French still influence our legal language today, just as does Latin. In England, William the Conqueror was French and so it became the fashion for French to be used at the royal court and then trial courts, alongside Latin and some Anglo-Saxon. If you enter a courtroom in England today, above the judge you will see the French words *Dieu et mon droit.* It is the motto of the British monarch,[39] and it is seen in all courts of law. This motto translates as "God and my right." 'Pressing' the accused involved stripping the defendant naked, starving him and then placing weights upon his chest, usually blocks of iron. The number of weights was then increased until such a time as the defendant elected to stand trial or the person responsible for conducting the pressing formed the opinion that the person must be innocent and released him. The third likely outcome was that the defendant died under the pressure or, if he was lucky, a few friends would bribe the gaoler and they would be allowed into the torture room and stand on the defendant's chest to help bring about an early death. Now at this point you may be questioning how it is possible to differentiate the application of torture across Europe with the isolated instance of the application of torture in England, particularly as the English would claim, vehemently, that they did not engage in the practice of torture. This is how the argument was put. England did not use torture. Pressing was used as a means to compel the accused to accept a rational form of trial. It was not used a means to secure evidence or a confession. The continental reason for using torture was to force an accused to admit guilt and in doing so eliminate the need for further evidential proof. These are very different positions to take and the English were convinced that pressing was not torture. You may wish to decide for yourselves whether or not a contemporary interpretation would be quite so flexible.

By 1100, English law started to look different from that of continental Europe. By the end of the 13th century and the reign of Edward I, it was truly a different system entirely. Edward made two significant contributions to history. He introduced the tradition of British monarchs being coronated on the Stone of Scone and he brought the Stone from Scotland to England. But, more importantly, Edward I took away the remaining vestiges of church involvement in the secular legal system and placed all trial matters in the hands of secular judges through the system of Inns of Court. Through his intervention, Edward initiated the formal training of lawyers, a practical seven-year apprenticeship based in courtrooms, and he paved the way for the creation of a Court of Chivalry, which dealt with matters of hereditary titles and paying off ransoms to foreign countries that held British hostages. The Court of Chivalry became what we today refer to as the Courts Martial. By 1361, England had a comprehensive system of trial courts that travelling judges on a circuit visited. Sheriffs were charged with holding suspects in a secure gaol before arrival of the judge and his court entourage. The travelling court would then set up in a local hostelry or meeting rooms and the sheriff would present the 12 local men he had selected for jury service. The jurors were responsible for ensuring they were familiar with the case, and so the court proceeded to try the defendant. If the accused refused to stand trial, he was encouraged to do so by a visit to the press. This ordinarily resulted in the defendant then returning to court the same day, and so the trial would proceed. Juries were active participants in the trial process, and they were expected to ask questions of the defendant and witnesses. The case was brought by the aggrieved party, who would be required to attend court alongside witnesses; failure to do so resulted in the aggrieved and witnesses being liable to a fine. The trial process was very quick by today's standards. Even murder trials only lasted minutes or perhaps an hour. All of the evidence for one trial was heard without recess and then the jury would proceed to hear other cases. It was rare for a jury to retire between cases, and ordinarily it would hear a number of cases in the morning, retire for lunch and come back in the afternoon to deliver verdicts. In capital cases, the defendant, who had no right of appeal, would be sentenced immediately and the death sentence would be carried out the following day unless it was a Sunday or a Holy Day. Hanging was the most common form of execution. Burning was used in cases of heresy, sometimes for traitors and also for women who committed petty treasons, such as killing their husbands. Sometimes a special punishment would be created if the offence was particularly unpleasant or if it caught the attention of the monarch. Attempts on the life of the king or his favorites normally attracted a gruesome death: beheading for aristocrats and hanging then quartering for commoners. Drowning was not a sentence except in cases of murder committed on board a royal vessel; the accused and the deceased victim were tied together and tossed overboard to a united watery grave. Also, women who committed murder in the royal dockyard city of Portsmouth were subjected to drowning; they were tied to a stake on the shoreline and drowned on the incoming tide.

Reference has already been made to the influence of the growing merchant classes and how they impacted the development of a body of commercial laws in England and Europe. This 'commercial revolution' influence should not be underestimated particularly with regard to the role that guilds took in ensuring their interests. Property and personal welfare were protected. This is still evident today in London where the financial center, the City of London, colloquially known as the 'square mile', still maintains its own police force, mayor and courts. Across Europe, cities expanded exponentially during the Middle Ages. This was followed by the concomitant problem, a rise in crime; in fact, property crime represented 50% of all the crime prosecuted in early modern Europe.[40] The growing disparity between rich and poor was acutely obvious in a geographical environment that had yet to separate the wealthy from the poor. The niceties of building in rich parts of the city and slums had yet to feature in the design of the medieval city, and consequently poor and starving citizens were rubbing shoulders alongside the rich on a daily basis; robbery and pick pocketing were rampant. The need for an effective police force was already apparent in the 13th century. Europe responded more quickly than England and had a measure of formal policing by the 17th century. England grappled with the problem for another 150 years, and the successes that finally came were largely as a result of the merchant classes, which paid for the establishment of a private police to protect their financial interests. It was such a success that the British government reluctantly followed by creating a small public police response. This history is the subject of a later discussion that will track how and why the police of the Civil

Law jurisdiction are similar yet different in nature and form from those of the Common Law countries.

A number of factors will always contribute to the changing nature of criminal law and why certain behavior becomes defined as criminal will fluctuate in response to natural and social impetus. During the Middle and Late Middle Ages, Europe underwent massive social changes as well as a number of natural disasters, such as the Black Death in 1348. Many of these events caused the criminal law to respond. This was also a time of expansion and changing frontiers with monarchs and the church vying for power and land. Territories changed hands and citizens were repeatedly subject to new leaders and new laws. War has always been the cause of significant domestic social change, and crime tends to increase locally at the cessation of war when thousands of displaced military return from periods of employment to vagrancy and petty crime. Despite the tragedy of war, it is an effective way to produce wealth and employment, and certainly England suffered enormously with the problem of millions of men returning from years of active service in Europe to long-term unemployment at home. Inevitably, many of these men resorted to crime as a source of income. A reverse problem can be seen when a localized natural disaster such as the plague decimates the workforce and pushes up the price of labor so that unskilled workers are left in a vacuum of unemployment and they too turn to crime as a source of income. Geographic mobility of the workforce in response to a lucrative employment market can cause local crime patterns to emerge in unexpected ways, and vagrancy laws that have been implemented too quickly have often caused the less fortunate and immobile workforce to be trapped in a spiral of petty crime and misconduct legislation that penalizes the already unfortunate segments of a society. Begging, vagrancy and prostitution have featured throughout history as a pattern of criminal behavior responses to legislation that has sought to control the movement of low wage workers. Terms such as rogue and vagabond are social constructs introduced into the lexicon by legislators to ensure a lack of mobility in times when the growing merchant classes needed a static and cheap source of labor. They learned this practice from feudal barons who wanted to keep the peasants static in the manorial farm place rather than encourage them to move about the countryside selling their labor skills to the highest bidder. Another factor in the story of criminality and its legal responses took place later in history, during the 17th century, when the low waged workforce across Europe was trapped in a life cycle of poverty due to reliance upon alcohol. The gin craze of London was so damaging to the working people that they would consume gin to the point of blindness and death to obliterate the reality of their destitution and miserable lifestyles.

For more than 500 years the collective response to crime was principally one of increasing the severity of punishment as a perceived deterrent. The use of the death penalty increased exponentially across Europe throughout the late Middle Ages and the early modern era. Prisons were rarely used other than for debtors with the irony that once sentenced to prison the unfortunate criminal was then required to pay for this room and lodging inside the prison, thereby exacerbating the very problem that caused him to be in prison in the first place. The first prison to open in England was located in Fleet Street, London. It is believed it was established during the 12th century.[41] Over time the distinction between those who could work and those who would not work divided the prison system into poor houses and houses of detainment. Regardless of the distinction, neither establishment was a pleasant experience for the inmates, as was made clear to women and children upon arrival at the Bridewell, London; they were whipped on arrival day to remind them that they had arrived at a correctional institution. In Europe, the concept of a dungeon was developing and the windowless pit in the ground or in the basement of a castle became synonymous with a secret and miserable place of confinement where many entered but few ever left alive. Eventually all of these factors combined. The establishment of defined countries, the nervousness of the Catholic Church (the Protestant Reformation was looming), the frequency of wars, local natural disasters, the growth of a merchant class and a massive growth in the overall population were leading all of the countries of Europe towards the need for a modern and effective criminal justice system with established and effective police, courts and corrections provisions. The monarchs and noble classes of Europe were rightly nervous; new crimes were occurring almost daily and social unrest was growing. The immediate solution was to increase the nature and scope of criminal offences, to use the death penalty more frequently and across a broader range of crimes. This would suffice for a brief period of time. What was really needed was a complete overhaul of the systems that had grown organically in two separate directions, the Civil and Common Law. If change was not to be introduced by the legislators, then the citizens of Europe would seize the responsibility themselves and force a new a legal order, one that reflected equality of treatment for all, regardless of rank or birth.

Henry VIII is viewed as one of the great characters of the British monarchy, in part due to his marrying so many times, but also because he was a strong and often rigid monarch who took his position as king to be an absolute endorsement of his ability to write and re-write the laws of England as he deemed necessary. Henry VIII was responsible for early editions of the codification of English law when he caused the writing of the Act of Supremacy in 1534. In creating a new religion for England, the Church of England, Henry sent shockwaves through the established Catholic Church and its local representatives, the bishops and lower orders of the clergy. How could it now be possible to employ the protections of Benefit of Clergy to those in holy orders and to the unfortunates who hid behind the protections but were not clerics, if the church itself was now an alternative creation? In effect, who were the clergy? Alongside this confusion was a distinct nervousness created by Henry that caused him to extend the reaches of the laws of treason, and for the first time we see the introduction of torture as a means of extracting a confession being used under the Common Law. It was, however, always deemed to be an extraordinary measure and required the personal signature of the king or his direct representative, the Privy Council. The religious confusion started by Henry plagued England for another 150 years, and his direct offspring, Edward, Mary and Elizabeth inflicted torture upon numerous citizens as they caused the country to fluctuate between Protestantism and Catholicism. The era of the Tudors was a truly dangerous time. This was evidenced by the instance of an unfortunate Jesuit priest who was found celebrating mass during Elizabeth I's Protestant reign; the man was tried and executed within three hours of committing his crime.[42]

The Stuarts succeeded the Tudors, and James I started his reign by repealing legislation that had provided the security of being able to plead the Benefit of Clergy for the offence of witchcraft. Under his reign numerous heresy trials were held and England embarked upon a mini-Inquisition type era with witches apparently appearing almost daily to create havoc and devilry across the nation; or at least that's how it seemed if the number of witches found operating were actually a reflection of anything other than a perverse male sexual repression or abject madness.[43] Guy Fawkes was also soon to make the king even more nervous with his attempt at blowing up the king and his parliament. Most importantly, it was the time that introduced the beginnings of constitutional government and direct involvement of the people in the affairs of the people. When attempting to trace the most influential events that shaped the development of the US and its legal system, we must consider this period in English history the most closely. Much of the distinctiveness of the Common Law can be tracked back directly to this time of political and actual civil war. Revolution seemed inevitable as the kings of England embarked upon increasingly negative and exclusory legislative provisions. Parliament was *de facto* excluded from attempting to influence the development of the legal system and the great divide between the 'haves and have-nots' of society was soon to be resolved on the battlefield. Since the time of Henry VIII, the crown of England had used the criminal law as a weapon to force conformity with the practices of the new Church of England. Any degradation of the sacrament of the host was punishable by death and any personal religious belief that did not conform to state doctrine was a crime. Never before had the English criminal law seen such a fusion of religion and criminal actions; even the courts had a level of overlapping jurisdiction. The strenuous efforts of William I and his immediate offspring to separate church and state had been undone over a period of a few years by Henry VIII. The people of England were both confused and frightened. James I was mistrusted and his interference in the criminal law confirmed that he was intent upon seizing regal power at the expense of meaningful legislation that would improve the lives of the citizenry. James even weakened the protections of the jury trial as more and more authority went to the king's courts of the Star Chamber and the Privy Council. And yet, despite these flaws and his questionable personal life, James was mourned when he died and left the crown to Charles I.

Like his predecessor, Charles believed in the Divine Right of Kings. He paid the ultimate price and was executed after a disastrous civil war forced him to be tried for treason. He was found guilty and beheaded on Tuesday 30 January 1649.[44] However, not all of Charles' reign was negative and he promulgated legal provisions that ensured citizens would not be subject to taxation without parliamentary approval and that there would be no imprisonment without cause. The demise of Charles I was followed by an unsuccessful interregnum period and then the British public invited Charles's son to assume the English throne. Charles II took the English crown on his 39th birthday, May 29, 1658, and so entered the period of the 'Merry Monarch', who undoubtedly had a penchant for the hedonistic life.[45] Charles II treated the interregnum period as though it had never happened, and after 1660 all legal documents were dated as though Charles II had immediately succeeded his father in 1649. During the interregnum period the custodian of the English republic was Oliver Cromwell. He was a dour and sober character, and soon after the regicide of Charles I legislation was enacted that made adultery and incest a capital offence. This pattern of sexual control legislation was a hallmark of the Cromwellian period and it is perhaps fortunate that Charles II abolished all of the interregnum legislative provisions as otherwise he would have been personally caught by many of them. During the Restoration, Charles II reintroduced theatre and plays to London as well as relaxing the laws relating to the consumption of alcohol and gaming; he also legalized brothels for England.

Restoration of the monarchy heralded a new social order and a retrenchment from Puritanism generally. It was also a time of renewal due to the destruction of London in the Great Fire of 1666. The flamboyant, boisterous and expensive lifestyle of Charles II was inevitably going to put him at odds with parliament, as he had incurred massive debts throughout his lifetime, and his detractors gained political mileage out of his failure to produce a legitimate heir even though he had fathered numerous bastards. The legal environment that Charles II inherited was severe and oppressive. Judges held their office at the pleasure of the crown, which had the adverse effect of making them far too likely to find in favor of the crown; and juries were equally hampered in their objectivity, as they were subject to personal fines if they failed to return a verdict directed to them by the presiding judge. What this amounted to was a situation where the crown or parliament could adversely influence the outcome of a trial. Given that during this time many of the most contentious actions appearing before the courts involved the right to free speech, spoken and written, the law was in retrenchment rather than development. Alongside this curtailment of freedom of speech, religious prosecutions were alive and well under Charles II and his successor James II. At the forefront of this religious suppression was 'Hanging Judge Jeffreys' who took a personal delight in characterizing defendants as worthless plagues upon society. This was rather rich given that Jeffreys himself often came into court drunk and fined people for swearing when he himself swore openly in the courtroom. During his most notorious trial, of the Monmouth Rebels believed to be attempting a monarchical coup, he informed the defendants that a "not guilty plea would mean the death sentence."[46] One wonders what sentence a guilty plea would result in.

The reign of James II was unsuccessful. Somehow he managed to annoy the British public to the extent that they were prepared to have a second overthrow of the monarchy in the space of less than one hundred years. His involvement in the legislative process was often petty and self-serving and his attempt to substitute Catholicism, yet again, for the Church of England was a step too far. The matter of the monarch being the head of the Church of England needed to be settled once and for all. William of Orange and his Protestant wife Mary were invited to take the English throne and James II imposed abdication upon himself by fleeing to France. William and Mary jointly held the throne from 1689. They both imposed conditions upon acceptance and had a number of conditions imposed upon them. The authority of parliament was enshrined in legislation and royal authority was restricted through the process of royal prerogative. A Bill of Rights[47] was enacted, which significantly improved the human rights and conditions of life for all British subjects. The Bill of Rights also established religious tolerance throughout the realm so that finally the jostling for religious supremacy started on the path to becoming a moment of history—well almost. The Bill did retain the provision that Roman Catholics were to be excluded from political life. Importantly, the Bill of Rights also prevented the monarch from holding a standing army and it guaranteed all Protestants the right to bear arms. Debates in parliament were now afforded exemptions so that freedom of political speech was no longer subject to criminal sanctions. Also under the criminal section it was now illegal to impose arbitrary and excessive fines or to make excessive demands for bail sureties. Cruel punishments were also prohibited and blanket immunity from prosecution for the king and queen was restricted so that they were, and would always be, answerable for certain criminal actions. Importantly, judges were to be appointed and remain in office on the basis of ability and good standing and not at the pleasure of the king. In treason cases, the defendants were now entitled to know the content of the indictment and they would be assigned legal counsel to assist them in the preparation of their defense and at trial. Evidentiary laws were also improved and two witnesses were required in all treason cases. This could be waived if a confession, without violence, was freely given by the accused. What is often considered a fundamental part of the Common Law, the right to silence—more accurately the right not to self-incriminate—was also now enshrined in the English legal system under the Bill of Rights.

Part of the period of sovereignty of William and Mary coincided with that of Louis XIV in France (1643–1715). He too was active in bringing about legislative reform and modernization of the criminal law. Assisted by his ministers Jean Baptiste Colbert and Guillame de Lamoigen, more than 150 pieces of legislation were drafted. An entire revision of the criminal law was codified under the 1670 Ordinance on Criminal Law and Ordinance on Criminal Procedure. Colbert was also charged by the king to establish a police force for Paris. For more than four centuries there had been a king's guard responsible for ensuring the safe passage of citizens between the rural villages and the market towns of France, but the capitol did not have a permanent police presence. On March 15, 1667, Louis authorized the appointment of the first Lieutenant of Police for Paris. To a student of the Common Law, this police force would not resemble contemporary policing, or at least only in part, as the sphere of responsibilities assigned to the Paris police was extensive and captured a number of activities normally associated with alternative occupations. In addition to arresting thieves and burglars, the Lieutenant was to manage a force required to: control begging; issue licenses for markets, wine shops and butchers; ensure adherence to the rules of no citizen eating meat on a Friday (France was a resolutely Catholic country); and have oversight of the public drainage system, sewers and the jails. It was also the responsibility of the police to light and extinguish the street lamps of Paris, a feature that was believed, rightly so, to deter crime. It took London another 150 years to recognize the importance of environmental crime prevention. It also took England another 150 years to establish a permanent police presence in its capital city, London.

The 16th and 17th centuries were periods of monumental legislative change in England and across Europe. They were also a time of global expansion and the establishment of permanent, often disputed, settlements around the world. In America, the British and French both sought to gain control and ownership of the new world, and for many years the burgeoning legal system was subject to influences from the old world as well as local interpretation and application. In the Southern colonies, a spirit of entrepreneurship pervaded. In the more religious communities of the north, biblical law was the mainstay of the new legal order. Perhaps obviously, the new world inhabitants brought with them practices and customs from the countries they were leaving behind. A complex fusion of contemporary European laws and rights and customs that resembled those from feudal England was put into use. Benefit of Clergy travelled with the colonists and came into use almost immediately. Why? Because the vast majority of permanent residents in the new world's Southern states had been transported to America as slaves to serve a minimum seven-year sentence in lieu of the death penalty. It was Benefit of Clergy that had spared them the hangman's noose, and so virtually all of the new workforce had some direct experience of the mitigatory plea and were comfortable subsuming it into the American legal culture. The adoption of the feudal protection system of 'Hue and Cry', and appointing local watchmen to secure the perimeter of the village at night, was also a practical solution to security in a land where individual and remote villages were commonplace and vulnerable. It followed that those who transgressed the village laws would be subject to feudal, village style, sanctions; in particular banishment from the village, which in the remote and dangerous new world, would effectively be a death sentence anyway. Over time, English criminal law became more useful to the colonies and it was subsumed in entirety in some states such as Virginia. This is apparent in the law pertaining to treason where in keeping with the English statute a convicted treasonist was stretched on a rack until his back was broken, then disemboweled while still alive, hanged until dead and then exhibited around the perimeter of the village to warn potential future transgressors. Eventually though, it was recognized that depleting the workforce of labor was not viable and many death sentences were commuted to extended periods of slavery. Public humiliation and denouncement by the community were also a carry-over from England and the stocks and pillory found full employment in northern and southern states. Women, in common with England and continental Europe, always received special treatment in law—treatment that invariably involved humiliation and had sexual connotations. If a wife was too liberal with her speech, she was placed in a device that literally held her tongue in pace, making conversation impossible. The device, a Bride's Scold, was a direct implant from England and Scotland where it had been favored as a humiliation tool for centuries. The 'ducking stool' was also reserved for women. Religious intolerance ran alongside sexual intolerance in the Northern states and homosexuality attracted the death penalty for centuries. It had been outlawed in England by specific statute in 1533 whereby it was a capital felony to "commit the detestable and abominable vice of buggery with mankind or beast," and this provision remained largely unchanged in English law until 1861. The new world colonies readily accepted these provisions intact. Europe was not slack in outlawing homosexuality either, but interestingly it also captured female lesbian acts, which the English law never did. Colonial Massachusetts seriously considered adoption of the Roman law provisions to 'prevent carnal fellowship of woman with woman', but this never made it to the statute book.[48] The Southern states adopted the English model of county courts where the majority of criminal cases were tried. Capital cases were tried before the superior, general courts.

The Northern states presented a sharp contrast to the 'business focused' South. Early settlers were attempting to escape religious suppression and the church featured in the lives of all citizens. The Quakers were absolutely opposed to the death penalty. Other English dissenters also incorporated religious orthodoxy into their legal frameworks so that religious compliance, regardless of the flavor of religion concerned, became the dominant feature in the application of the law. Leaving behind a history of religious confusion and multiple changes in required religious practice, the Northern new world colonists sought to achieve a level of equity alongside adherence to biblical principles. The New Worlders had a strong attachment to trial by jury and to ensuring that no citizen was subject to unreasonable searches or seizures. In keeping with the Mosaic principles of clarity, the colonists also wanted to draft legislation that was clear to all so that every citizen knew what was or was not a criminal action. A long list of felonies was eventually drawn up, and by the mid-1600s it was a capital offence to commit the following: idolatry, blasphemy, murder, witchcraft, sodomy, adultery, kidnapping, perjury and conspiracy. Reference to the Bible will show that all of these offences were also subject to a sentence of death in the Old Testament. They are almost a verbatim copy. Whereas Benefit of Clergy had survived passage to the Southern states of the New World, it was not permitted in the North. Clearly, it was the intention of the new settlers that all citizens would be treated equally before the law and the dexterity of the Catholic church to protect its own transgressors was not going to be replicated in the largely Protestant and Puritan north.

In time, particularly after the American Revolution, the Common Law was dressed into a modified English format to suit the social and political climate of the US It may seem curious that a new nation so intent upon breaking away from the restrictions and oppression of Europe would embrace with such vigor the familiar legal system of England, and yet the US had so integrated the customs of the English law before the Revolution that it was impossible for it to forge ahead without reliance upon the now established ways. Even those who may have wanted to reject the English law found it impossible to ignore the recent and applicable English legal system. Within 50 years of the Revolution, America produced its own version of Blackstone, Commentaries on American Law by James Kent. He quoted, "We live in the midst of the Common Law, we inhale it at every breath, imbibe it at every pore; we meet it when we wake, and when we lie down to sleep, when we travel and when we stay at home; it is interwoven with the very idiom that we speak; and we cannot learn another system of laws, without learning, at the same time, another language."[49] Amazingly, or at least so it appeared to users of the Civil Law, this system that the US was familiar with and embraced for its future was not written down; it was so common, so well known, so understood that it was not necessary for the English to ever write it down in a codified fashion and presumably it would also not be necessary for the US do so either. It was William Penn, an Englishman who came to the US, who famously challenged the familiarity of the Common Law and was rebuked for his audacity in doing so. In 1670, William Penn stood trial for illegally preaching in the streets of London. The jury ardently refused to find him guilty and they were held in contempt of court without food or water until they returned the verdict the judge requested. They refused twice and set a precedent for judges no longer to have the power to control juries. William Penn himself was confused about the actual charge he was answering to and asked the trial judge for clarity on what was the Common Law. An enraged judge retorted, "You are an impertinent fellow, will you teach the court what it is? It is lex non scripta that many have studied thirty or forty more years to know, and you would have me tell you what it is in a moment?" Penn replied "Certainly, if the Common Law be so hard to understand it is far from being common."

As the US firmly adopted the Common Law, France was undergoing a revision of its legal provision under the intense oversight of Napoleon Bonaparte. In 1800, Napoleon assigned four senior jurists to write a comprehensive legal code. The commission held 102 sessions and Napoleon himself attended 57 meetings. The *Code Civil des Français* was issued in 1804. It contained 2,281 articles. To the world, this work became known as the *Code Napoleon.* The blueprint for the new code had been the work of Justinian and his *Corpus Juris Civilis.* The Napoleonic Code has been replicated in varying degrees of mirror image throughout all the countries of the world that use the Civil Law. Revision of the criminal law soon followed so that by 1808 a new *Code Penal* was issued by Napoleon. Combined, the new codes totally revised the legal system and offences across France. However, like the predecessor code of 1791, the new criminal code did not interfere with religious crimes or same-sex conduct. Accompanying the new criminal code was a code of criminal procedure; this document set out the rules for arrest, interview, trial and sentencing. Bonaparte was personally concerned about the previous laws that made arbitrary arrest and long periods of detention prior to trial common in France. The new code strengthened personal freedoms and police and judicial accountability.

Article 294 of the code permitted criminal defendants to have representation by a lawyer, England followed this lead 26 years later. If the court failed to appoint a lawyer for the defendant, the proceedings were null and void. Remand remained the normal outcome for prisoners awaiting trial in murder and serious assault cases. In addition to revising the entire legal system and rewriting the criminal code, Napoleon also significantly strengthened the role of the police in France. As a military leader, he took particular interest in the civilian policing function of the military police, the *Gendarmerie.* He also strengthened and grew the second police force of France, the civilian police force of Paris, to provide a uniformed police presence in all the major cities of France. This force was the genesis of the modern-day *Police Nationale.*

Napoleon took over in France at a time of unrest and confusion. The dreams of the Revolution had become clouded by despotism and a reign of terror. Napoleon recognized the need for a strong police force for two primary reasons: The nation needed stability and he needed an efficient police force if much of his time was to be spent abroad conducting military campaigns. The result was a period of overkill and much criticism of Napoleon as his police forces were viewed domestically as a team of spies running a police state. It was the intense fear of a police state that caused the British to wait so long for a police force in London as, frankly, for the British parliament anything was better than what was happening in France. The delicate route to the establishment of a non-French police force for London is the subject of later discussion. At this point it is worth remembering though that with Britain at war with France, and the French suffering from internal unrest, criticism of the French police was easy from the comfort of an English armchair. In reality, the model of the French *Gendarmerie* was highly successful and was utilized extensively in colonial Common Law, as well as Civil Law, jurisdictions across the world. Louis Napoleon, Napoleon III, continued his uncle's legacy and extended the extraordinary powers of the civil police, the *Surete,* to the continuing chagrin of the French people. Although the detective limb of this force was undoubtedly highly successful and provided a model for the establishment of the Pinkerton private detectives in the US, dislike and mistrust of the French police was so strong in England that London's Metropolitan Police mimicked the *Surete* and then became their nemesis. The world remembers the famous Scotland Yard detectives, but for the English-speaking world the Surete have been relegated to musical hall songs and a few lines in a history of policing book.

The monumental impact of the commercial revolution of the 13th century was finally eclipsed by the revolution of thought, the Enlightenment. During the 18th century the modern world was overtaken by social reform and the advancement of knowledge. Not only were scientific discovery and social change promoted, intellectuality was too. The salons of Europe and the New World were alive with debate and the political order was about to be recast through the Declaration of Independence, the US Bill of Rights, and the Declaration of the Rights of Man and of the Citizen and the French Revolution. The buildup to these events started in the mid-1600s. Descartes's *Discourse on Methods* was published in 1637; Britain had had another bloodless revolution in 1688; and John Locke published *Concerning Human Understanding and the Second Treatise on Government* in 1690. By its conclusion, the Enlightenment had reshaped Europe and changed the relationship between the rulers and the ruled, forever. In due course, the Enlightenment led towards Romanticism as the philosophical thinkers of the modern world embraced former Athenian and Roman ideologies. Religion was relegated to a minor role in life and the last remains of a powerful church were either swept away or, more damagingly, totally ignored. Montesquieu's *The Spirit of the Laws* was placed on the list of banned books by the Catholic Church in 1751. The Age of Reason was most adamantly the age of man's reason not god's. Inevitably the movements across the modern world would result in significant changes to the way citizens were treated by the law. Napoleon was soon to undertake a total revision of the criminal law in France and the power of the French police courts was to be reined in also. Louis XVI had agreed to the concept of a presumption of innocence, but he signed the law into effect far too late to save himself. His 1788 proclamation in Versailles also banned the wearing of prison uniforms, even for those on death row, and the right of appeal was strengthened for criminal defendants. Many of the philosophical commentators of the time looked to England as a model, for after all there was no torture there. And the jury system appeared to protect the rights of innocent individuals, particularly when judges were banned from intimidating and coercing juries after the outrageous behavior of the trial judge in the William Penn case. What the voices of the day wanted were clear and unambiguous laws that would be applied equally to all citizens regardless of rank or status. Given the exchange between William Penn and his trial judge over the Common Law, it may seem incredible that England was heralded as an example. But what the *philosophes* were attempting to achieve was a sense of rightness and balance and, in the case of Beccaria particularly, a sense of legal certainty. Central to the list of objections was the use of torture, and there was general agreement, spearheaded by Voltaire, that torture could not, and would not, be tolerated in a civilized society. There was, therefore, some logical flow to the idea of looking at the Common Law as it could, allegedly, show that torture did not exist. If in the future punishment was to serve as a deterrent to crime then torture as part of the criminal process punished a person not for guilt but for simply having been accused. It was an inevitable concomitant of the Enlightenment movement that penology would emerge as the viable alternative to corporal and capital punishment. Europe was on the cusp of accepting this idea and had a mechanism in place—rewriting all the criminal codes—to accommodate these ideas. For England this would be decidedly problematic.

William Blackstone[50] undertook the task of attempting to make the Common Law appear as a cogent body of definable rules that could be written into a format that had some resemblance to a code. He published his findings as part of a series of lectures at Oxford University commencing in 1765. They were titled *Commentaries on the Laws of England.* They were, and remain, a resounding success and form the bedrock of all Common Law study. He is famous for the quote "Better that ten guilty persons escape than one innocent man be wrongly convicted." Blackstone was also responsible for finally bringing the study of law into English universities. He was the first person to hold the chair in law at Oxford. Adopted universally in Common Law jurisdictions, his work prevailed as well in the French-influenced state of Louisiana. "Even the French were to concede that the clarity of Blackstone's civil codes was unsurpassed."[51]

The period of the Enlightenment was the catalyst for a revision of all the criminal laws across the modern world. Parliaments responded with varying degrees of enthusiasm, and this period marked the beginning of the end for the wholesale use of capital punishment. The divisions between the Common Law and Civil Law were now firmly established and procedural developments began to take on increasingly diverse and complex rules that pertained exclusively to the two different legal systems. Policing was at various stages of development, and the urge to reject anything French was still in the mindset of Britain. Nevertheless, significant progress was being made and the citizens of Europe, regardless of their station in life, were about to receive a greater level of justice and clarity in the criminal law than they had ever experienced before.

But before we are overtaken by enthusiasm for the achievements of the philosophes, one question remains unanswered. Were they really the root cause of bringing about the downfall of torture under the Civil Law? One eminent American lawyer thinks not, and his argument is highly persuasive.

Yale Professor John Langbein is the author of *Torture and the Law of Proof: Europe and England in the Ancien Regime.*[52] In this fascinating work, he proposes that the contribution made by the Enlightenment era to the abolition of torture across Europe is much overstated. He argues that the end of torture was already in full swing and what has been sometimes claimed as a coup by the Age of Reason is in fact attributable to other factors that were less noisily taking place throughout the courtrooms of Europe. He posits that it was these procedural factors that would inevitably decimate the reliance upon torture as a means of legal proof. The argument goes something like this: Across continental Europe torture was part of ordinary criminal procedure, regularly used to investigate and prosecute crime before ecclesiastic and then secular courts. This can be termed *judicial torture,*[53] as officers of the state employed physical coercion for gathering evidence in state prosecutions. It was also later used to extract information not subject to trial, such as use after trial and before execution by French courts.[54] Torture had its own rules and procedures; there was a *jurisprudence of torture.* Much of the torture used across Europe originated in Italy with the start of the Romano-Canon law-based Inquisitions. It then spread until by the 15th century torture was commonly in use at both ecclesiastic and secular trial venues. It remained in widespread use until the last abolition of torture in the 19th century. The Law of Torture was devised to regulate how, where and when torture should be employed by the state. It is important to remember again that torture was a pre-trial measure; it was being used to obtain a confession or evidence. Torture used after trial is correctly called corporal punishment, and no matter how appalling this form of punishment may be, it is not accurate to call this type of activity torture. Torture, as we have established previously, was introduced by the Romans in lieu of two eyewitnesses or in instances where there was some circumstantial evidence but it was insufficient to convict on this alone. So the Romans had a scale: two eyewitnesses, convict; one eyewitness and torture, convict; circumstantial evidence and torture, convict. Torture could not be used exclusively to obtain a guilty plea; there had to be direct evidence supplied by the accused that only he would have knowledge of, so no innocent glory seeker who wanted a quick shot of fame could claim to be a serial killer. The official responsible was to bar asking leading questions while conducting the torture—well, in theory. Proceedings were recorded and officials designated to conduct criminal investigations were responsible for running the torture sessions also.

Convincing medieval man (and woman) that a secular judge was an acceptable substitute for the god meant creating, or replicating at least, a system of statutory proofs that a human judge could apply. Once the proofs had been obtained, there should be no question about the veracity of the judge or of the process, and so justice could be distributed. And just like the ordeal and Trial by Battle, none of the former legal redress options were available in matters of minor crime, i.e. misdemeanors. In many ways this becomes a crucial part of the entire torture discussion and one we will return to soon. Having achieved a system of infallible truths, the judge is a mere instrument of justice, and since no society wishes to tolerate serious criminal offending then the torture system might actually work. The church then starts the torture movement rolling and Pope Innocent IV issues a papal decree in 1252 authorizing the use of torture as part of canonical procedure. Just to remind you, it was Innocent III, 37 years previously, who banned clerical involvement in ordeals because clerics should not be involved in bloodletting. Langbein reminds us that the use of torture then became formalized in the secular law and was recorded by Gandius and later the Carolina Laws of Germany. By contemporary standards, we probably find torture unacceptable, perhaps with the exception of a little water boarding now and then. But to the Middle Age Civil Law jurists it was a thoroughly practical response to a legal dilemma. It was also a test of endurance though for the victim and many would admit anything to avert another session on the Wheel or with the Thumb Screws. So the gentle road of persuasion that we are led down is that numerous commentators, long before the Enlightenment thinkers, knew from personal experience that torture was thoroughly unreliable and that rather than use tortures at any and every opportunity the Romans were in fact selective about the use of torture, whereas the Inquisition was not. So at this point it is worth remembering what was taking place over in England. Torture was not routinely used. In fact, up until the time of Henry VIII there was really no evidence of torture being used—well, except for the matter of *peine fort et dure,* so England really wasn't hampered by the law of proof constraints that Europe was lumbering under until the idea of torture was offered on a spiritual plate. The premise of the general discussion is that torture ended due to the influence of the Enlightenment thinkers; and Langbein's position, one that I also support, is that this is not true. Europe formalized torture use, whereas England never did. Europe had no method of circumventing the evidential need for torture while England did; it had the jury. Europe insisted upon the use of torture in all capital cases; England did not. And exemptions from torture followed a typical path of hierarchy in Europe so that clerical members of the Catholic Church were exempt from torture, along with aristocrats (sometimes), the infirm, physicians, Doctors of Law and teachers; but virtually all of these exemptions disappeared by statute long before the new social order of revolution in Europe. And just to reinforce the solemnity and ecclesiastical nature of torture, whether during a church or a secular investigation, torture was never conducted on a Sunday or a Holy Day. Additionally, torture was applied in the sight of the investigating judge and a physician was always on hand to ensure that the defendant was not over tortured and might die before a confession was forthcoming. Mercifully, perhaps, a judicial threat was made before the application of torture. The defendant was shown the torture room and given the option of confessing before any torture was applied. Torture was viewed as a 'last resort' method. As we know, this was not always an option given the intestacy laws of the times. If a defendant did not confess, then he could be re-tortured. However, once a confession was obtained, there was a delay period before the defendant appeared in court in answer to the charge. One could surmise that this was related to ensuring that the defendant did not recant or to ensure that he appeared in a physical condition that made him capable of confessing, but either way, there was a pause for recuperation. If the confession was not freely given in open court, then the defendant was subjected to a new period of persuasion. Court confessions had to be made within a 'day and a night' of the torture chamber confession. The ludicrous idea of the public confession was that it would prevent confessions obtained by leading questions. If a person were capable of resisting torture for an unspecified period of time, the judicial official was the arbiter of this. Then the person was entitled to an acquittal unless further evidence was brought to the attention of the trial judge. Suffice to say, there were numerous instances where this latter rule was abused. We have noted that 'torture'—though not an accurate term for punishment—was applied after confession especially to those sentenced to death. The rationale was that they had nothing to lose by betraying their accomplices and in a time of severe monarchical insecurity *Torture Preable* was liberally applied.

So why did it change? Well, as the kings of Europe gained greater powers and became the dominant voices in the establishment of nations, so too they recognized the need to have able bodied men available for war and a system of laws that appeared equitable and fair to all the citizens. The kings of Europe needed to give their citizens something in return for the citizens' allegiance. The *quid pro quo* was protection, the King's Peace. One way to assert equity and peace was to have a system of rewards for the people; another was to grant pardons and allow an early return to citizens who had been banished. A highly effective method of garnering domestic citizen support was to have lots of crimes that attracted the death sentence and then pardon the convicted criminals before sentence was passed. Over time, all of these measures gained increasing levels of application. So too did the introduction of alternative punitive provisions. Rather than allowing the commoners to settle disputes by battle, which could have the adverse effect of killing or maiming future soldiers, kings started to introduce, or extend the use of, transportation, prison, hard labor, serving in the navy or serving time in a workhouse. Courts were increasingly encouraged to take mitigating circumstances into consideration and to apply sentences that 'fitted the crime'. As we have seen, this was a 'back door' option via the system of Benefit of Clergy, but what started to take place was a realization that depleting a family of its breadwinner was both costly to the standing of the king in the eyes of his subjects and costly to the family, which would now be dependent upon almsgiving and the charity of the local church. Over time it became the case that courts were encouraged to consider aggravating factors as well as mitigating. By the 17th century, judges' manuals started to include lengthy discourses on the circumstances under which mitigating circumstances were applicable. Sentence reduction or substitution started to become a regular feature of the courtroom and new punishments were being introduced regularly. Even in capital cases transportation to America or a life sentence of hard labor with no parole were seen as viable options. As Langbein comments, "Life and death now lay inside the courtroom, no longer the Ordeal or Wager by Battle.[55] In France, in cases where the death penalty was stipulated by law unless there was full proof of the crime, the sentence was to be reduced to reflect a lesser crime. The downside of this, of course, is that it meant a defendant could be convicted of a lesser crime on lesser evidence. This tended to obliterate the idea of innocent until proven guilty, but then that is not a standard feature of the Civil Law anyway. What it does do, however, is open the door to the option of reducing the severity of the crime and therefore reducing the level of evidence needed to prove the crime. If the standard of guilt were lowered, then the sentence could presumably also be lowered; and it would then follow that if the standard of proof were lowered sufficiently, then the need to apply torture would be reduced, as more people would admit to lesser crimes knowing they were not going to be sentenced to death for the crimes they were admitting. This starts to sound like a win-win situation for all the players. The courts get lots of convictions and the defendants plead guilty to the crimes that they have actually committed, and they do not plead to crimes simply to avoid torture. And if all of this were significantly underway before the Enlightenment philosophers arrived on the scene, then it is fairly hard to attribute the end of torture to Voltaire, Beccaria, Bentham and the many others.

What has been achieved with the relaxation of the standard of proof is that it was moved from being an objective standard to a subjective standard. Less serious penal sanctions were being applied to less rigorous standards of proof and crucially the courts did not have to invent a new standard of proof; they already had one ready and waiting, the standard of proof required in non-felony matters, the petty crimes. The harsher Romano-Canon law standards were now obsolete. If a trial court could sentence you to the Galley for life on insufficient evidence to hang you, and they could do this without resorting to torture, then it made abject sense to abolish torture altogether. With the new freedom to substitute the death sentence, France embarked upon a period of increased use of incarceration, especially against those suspected of treason. Alongside of this was the liberal use of early release and pardons, but with the caveat that, if you had been held without trial and were suspected of an offence but not subjected to a trial for that offence, then release was conditional. This was particularly useful to a nervous monarchy that wanted to prevent political dissenters from holding public office, so typically upon release the suspect was further 'sentenced' to a ban from holding public office or of making a will—the equivalent of a humiliation sentence or of naming and shaming for life. But it was a new era for Europe and judges finally had the level of judicial discretion their counterparts had in England. Over the course of the next 300 years, this would mature into parole, plea-bargaining, probation, community service, electronic tagging and the plethora of sentence options that are now at the disposal of the sentencing judge.

It is a persuasive argument that Langbein proffers. It is one that offers an alternative and satisfactory answer to the vexing question as to why the Civil Law was so keen to use torture and then so keen to stop using it. This position does not dismiss the importance of the great philosophical thinkers of the 17th and 18th centuries, but rather it more contextualizes their contribution and offers an alternative explanation for the series of events that led up to the birth of penology and to the alternative sanctions to the death penalty as a source of punishing those who commit the most serious level of crimes against society.

The following 200 years reinforced the rights of the individual around the planet as individual retribution and family-based legal customs gave way to government controlled criminal justice systems. What had once been a system of redress driven by the willingness of an individual party to pay for a trial process that might result in further personal loss, financially or bodily, had matured into a complex system of legal measures driven by the state on behalf of all the citizens of that country so that collective social values became available for scrutiny and testing. The protections and privileges once afforded by the church had been substituted for a different protective covering born out of the feudal monarchs of Europe, who in turn were themselves forced to give greater status and recognition to the common people due to the pressure and ability of the courts to modify and interpret legislative intention. What the courts achieved in a typically solemn and quasi-religious environment, the intellects of Europe professed from the written and oracular platform to collectively cause permanent changes to the legal culture, a legal culture that convincingly confirmed the establishment of two distinctly separate but workable legal families: the Common Law and the Civil Law. By the 20th century, the public face of retribution was already a large government machine constructed around policing, the courts and corrections, where the professionals employed within the three divisions each have separate levels of training, development and spheres of responsibility in assisting citizens to understand the parameters of acceptable behavior. We no longer rely on local citizens to provide nighttime security services, and we no longer are guaranteed that the members of the jury will know us personally and have a comprehensive knowledge of the case they are hearing. Under the Common Law, the role and function of the jury has changed forever; so too has that of the judge. Now relegated to a passive role, the jury and the judiciary sit back and have the facts told to them, the arguments manicured for them by lawyers and the investigation of witnesses conducted on their behalf. The judge, ever conscious of an appeal, is now a near silent umpire whose activity is limited to controlling the over-zealous lawyer and ensuring each warfaring party is adhering to the multitude of complex rules of play. Long gone are the days of jury questioning and judicial interruptions. What gains the jury and judge achieved to protect the innocent in the formative years of the Common Law have been traded out and handed over to the all-powerful lawyers. Today under the Common Law it is the lawyers who have real control of the proceedings. It is the lawyers who have an absolute right of audience when once they had none, and it is the lawyers who manipulate and test the law to bring about legal reform in lieu of the church and the knights of battle by wager. Without the lawyer our courtrooms may well not be so busy, for it is thanks to the lawyer that we have such an endless supply of litigants. But this path may not continue to be woven unabated, for the 21st century has already seen an increase in the nature and form of global crime—international drugs trafficking, terrorism and trafficking in humans, a return of piracy on the high seas and criminality never envisaged in the time of Blackstone: computer crime and software piracy. All of these new faces of crime are causing the criminal justice system to undergo significant changes again. Nation-bound criminal laws are no longer capable of making sense of terrorism, and the societal norms that domestic criminal justice efforts seek to protect and enforce are frequently irrelevant. Local law enforcement agencies are now being tasked with ensuring they have effective anti-terrorism measures in place, and yet these same agencies of the criminal justice system have little training or experience in international terrorism. It may be the case that the system that has been devised, piecemeal and with planning, over the past thousand years will itself now undergo another period of radical reform as the Common Law and Civil Law combine to provide an effective measure of redress for all citizens regardless of their legal culture.

As seen in this chapter, legal systems come and go and they are highly adaptable. The dominance of canon law has dissipated; Roman law is influential still but is no longer the primary legal system in the modern world; and although biblical law is no longer significant in the daily operation of the Civil or Common Law, religious based legal systems are still a major force in some parts of the world. These too may become a greater feature in a collective response to international criminality over the course of the next century. In the following chapters there will be discussion about these challenges. There will also be discussion about what is meant by certain actions that we define as criminal. For example, is murder the same offence regardless of jurisdiction and do we even deal with murders in the same way within a jurisdiction? Murder is a crime that attracts public attention and often pulls out the macabre in all of us. For the majority of people who will never kill another person there is a fascination with the idea of committing the ultimate crime; most of us cannot conceive of what it feels like to take another life. But fortunately murder is not the most commonly committed of crimes and whether a dispute ends in death rather than serious repairable injury is sometimes a matter of luck. Serious assaults, sexual, physical and mental, are far more commonplace in society, and these too are discussed in the following chapters. The repugnant nature of international crimes conducted by organized groups of criminals that form temporary or permanent affiliations are a burden upon all the people of the world; the vexing question becomes how we police these types of crime. Are contemporary policing responses equipped to deal with transnational crimes, let alone the myriad of new crimes that occur locally? How did the Common Law develop its policing response and why does it differ from the Civil Law, religious laws and the few examples of communist law that still operate? In order that we may effectively apply criminal justice systems we need effective police responses. How they are formed and why is a prelude discussion to how well they are now placed to provide a contemporary police presence. We can all learn much from the history of the criminal law and the actors that now operate with, in and around the systems. By knowing how we arrived at the current place of operation, it may be possible to prepare intelligent responses to where we are likely to go. The challenges of policing future crimes will conclude this book's discussion.

Before moving on to discuss homicide—what it is and how it is controlled—two legal systems have been mentioned above and in passing. They are intertwined and yet vastly different: canon law and religious law. Canon law is the body of law that has developed over the past two thousand years and is captured in the term ecclesiastical authority. It is the body of Christian religious laws that governs the behavior of members of Christian denominations. This body of law was highly influential across Europe between 500 and 1500 AD and to a lesser extent across Britain also. Canon law captures Catholic and Eastern Orthodox religious practices, as well as all other denominations of Christian following. A body of church leaders, often called a council, who hold authority to legislate—decree—for a particular denomination traditionally form canon law. Historically, due to the importance of the church in people's lives, canon law has featured as an integral part of a country's legal system. And even as the dominance of secular law took over throughout Europe, church law remained highly influential in matters relating to behavior and sexual and moral conduct for lay communities, as well as being the governing law for matters of misconduct committed by members of the church. Canon law has always been preeminent in matters relating to church property rights and the ownership of parishes. Canon law resembles Civil Law more closely than

Common Law even in those countries where the Common Law is the legal system in use. For example, in England the canon law courts operate in a manner that would be more familiar to a student of the Civil Law and yet they operate under the statutes of a Common Law country. Additionally, since the restructuring of the church in England by Henry VIII, students of canon law are now typically trained in Civil Law and hold a doctorate in Civil Law, DCL, rather than ecclesiastical degrees. Prior to the interventions of Henry VIII, medieval canon law was a mixture of laws drawn from Holy Scripture, the fathers of the church and the church's interpretations of Roman law. Until the Reformation, the church had absolute authority in all matters of marriage law and most cases of defamation and exclusive authority to hear 'clergyable' cases against clerics—those criminal offences for which it was possible for a defendant to claim the privilege of clergy and have the matter heard before the bishop's court rather than a secular court. The separation of the English church from Rome brought about by Henry VIII inevitably diluted the authority of the church in people's everyday lives. It was also during Henry VIII's reign that the Inns of Court started to assert authority over the training of lawyers in England and in doing so also caused a further reduction in the power of the church in secular matters. As with Common Law matters, canon law has itself undergone many changes and the entire body of catholic laws was codified in 1918. In 1983, Pope John Paul II promulgated 1,752 canons into law in a revised Code of Canon Law. Judicial vicars and judges that hear Catholic canon law cases are required to hold at least a licentiate in canon law and preferably a doctorate. In cases where there is a conflict between canon and secular law, secular law prevails. One exception to this was Malta where the canon law remained in full force until the introduction of a new Civil Code in 2007. Though rare, an example of conflict between canon and secular law has occurred in cases of ending marriages through the process of nullity. However, and despite Henry VIII's vigorous attempts to assert absolute control over all ecclesiastical matters, it was not until 1857 and the establishment of the Divorce Court in England that issues of divorce transferred totally to secular jurisdiction. Prior to this date a divorce was granted through the process of a private Act of Parliament that dissolved one individual marriage at a time.[56] As a legal reality, a marriage under the canon law of the Church of England, which is based significantly upon the previously applicable Catholic canon law, can only be valid or void; a voidable marriage is a legal fiction. In contemporary society these matters may not be of the magnitude of concern that they would have been in the

Middle Ages, as the distinction between a crime and a civil suit were not clear and matters pertaining to the death of a partner had serious implications with regard to liability, culpability and inheritance that could result in death by battle for a culprit and disinheritance for an entire family in an action brought by the relatives' deceased. In recent history, there have been numerous examples where a marriage has been forced upon a party and consequently has resulted in a void marriage or, in extreme cases, the murder of one party by the other due to the strains of forced living with another human. Recent developments in the criminal law of England relating to 'battered woman's syndrome' are directly related to cases of forced marriage and subsequent murders by wives who have been subjected to physical and emotional abuse.[57] The development of these laws is the exclusive preserve of the secular law today.

Sharia law is also a law based upon religious belief. The word is interpreted today to mean legislation. It is believed that the origins of the word are located in Arabic, meaning 'a pathway to be followed'. It is the applicable law for followers of Islam. Islamic law deals with all of the laws captured by public and private laws under alternative legal systems, such as the Common Law and the Civil Law. Additionally, sharia is a moral code of conduct and a body of religious law. Consequently, sharia law covers all crimes, moral behavior and contracts. There are two sources of sharia law, the Quran and Sunnah. For Muslims, the Quran is the word of god, Allah. The Sunnah contains the sayings and lifestyle examples of the prophet Muhammad. Across the world some nations apply sharia in secular countries, and in other countries it is applied as a religious law where the rulers of those countries are strictly limited in their ability to make legal changes. The criminal law of Islamic countries is therefore governed by the word of god and, as seen in biblical times, the range of actions deemed to be criminal is far greater than those viewed as criminal today under secular laws. To offend against sharia law is not only to commit a crime, it is also to offend against god. Criticism of sharia law would be viewed in the same way as criticism of the church in previous times. It is heresy. By Western standards, many of the punishments associated with sharia law appear to be extremely harsh, but it should be remembered that in recent history a child who refused to listen to his parents was liable to receive the death penalty in colonial America, though it was rarely applied. And when we view the imprisonment of a person for blasphemy as being extreme, it should also be remembered that this too was an available sentence in colonial America. Adultery too was a capital offence in many countries throughout the Middle Ages and the new world period. In fact, adultery is not a mandatory capital offence under sharia law, as the sentencing range is corporal punishment up to a death sentence of stoning. In keeping with other religious doctrine, the accuser is responsible for casting the first stone. Consuming alcohol is a serious offence under sharia law, and the offender is liable to receive corporal punishment, amputation or death, but again the context of the punishment needs to be considered. If it were the case that canon law had prevailed across Europe and Britain, then severe punishments for a range of social disorder offences would be normal in society. It is worth remembering that it was the Catholic Church that banned the writings of some Enlightenment thinkers because they dared to question the applicability and relevance of religion in the 18th century. And the Inquisition was still in full flood in Spain during this time, complete with burnings and alleged non-bloodletting torture. "The potential harshness of Islamic law is, however, modified by stringent evidentiary rules. The doctrines of the presumption of innocence and a prohibition against ex post facto charges protect the defendant. In the absence of a confession the prosecutor must produce two eyewitnesses (usually two male Muslims) with direct knowledge of the offense. The testimony of two women could be accepted in place of that of one man."[58]

Over the course of the last three thousand years, mankind has sought to define and record certain actions as so offensive, not just to the injured individual, but also to all of society that these actions should be subject to collective condemnation. The timeframes under which individual countries have delineated the action as public rather than private have varied hugely. However, in today's world those actions deemed as criminal are now prosecuted on behalf of the individual by the state. On occasion, the individual may not support a prosecution. On some occasions the victim is the offender and they most certainly do not support a prosecution. An example of this might be where a person consents to a level of physical harm that is so severe society deems that the individual cannot give consent even though he or she might wish to. Today crime is viewed as breaking a law that has been written by either god or the state. To commit a crime is to engage in some action for which a governing entity can impose a penalty. That penalty may be a fine, a reduction in liberty or the removal of life. No individual can impose these sanctions upon another individual, and it is the collectivity and ability of a group to impose a sanction that makes crime a unique feature of any body of laws. Due to the public nature of bringing a prosecution and imposing a sentence, criminal law is considered to be Public Law. Actions brought by an individual to seek redress for a harm or a wrong are viewed as Private Law. It is perfectly possible for a person to break a law and in doing so to commit an offence that is not part of the criminal law. This book is concerned with those actions that citizens commit that impact upon individuals and all of society as a whole, which in today's society we call a crime. The following chapters discuss the actions of individuals, starting with the most serious crime: killing another person. It is of course the case that when I kill you I not only inflict a criminal harm upon you but also a civil harm, the harm of tort. It is important not to confuse the two.

If we were to return to the early Middle Ages, there would be no discernible difference between an action in tort and an action in crime. A victim of a hurt could therefore pursue the wrong caused through an action in tort or in crime. Either way, the victim was responsible for collecting the evidence and paying for the matter to be brought to trial. Today the victim of crime has no choice in whether or not a prosecution is brought. That decision is made by the state. A victim of tort can still exercise choice; he may bring a prosecution or let the matter drop. But the differences are greater than this, as a crime may be an action that does not involve an individual harm. For instance, possession of pornographic material does not cause an individual harm but it is still illegal. And using illicit drugs may cause a direct harm to the user but nobody else; it is still an illegal criminal act. So from this discussion it is clear that a criminal act may be something that has not caused a harm but has the potential to, e.g. planting a bomb that does not explode. It may be engaging in activities that the community considers immoral or it may be criminal to inflict an injury upon myself when the community believes I need to be protected from myself, even though I disagree. And because the nature of all of these actions can have a serious impact upon individuals and the community as a whole, the sanctions are more serious than a private action. Tort law allows the individual redress of an offensive action that does not amount to a crime; the consequent remedies are therefore less and are also less clear. I might or might not win an action, and if I do the amount of damages will vary according to a number of factors. Across the US the sentence for murder is either the death penalty or life imprisonment. But perhaps the best known feature of criminal law when compared and contrasted with Civil Law is the standard of proof.

The classic interpretation of liability in criminal law is that there are two requisites, an action and a state of mind. The action may be doing an act or failing to do an act; the state of mind is the ability of the jury to open up the mind of the defendant and to see into his brain so that the jury can be convinced that it knows what it was the defendant was thinking at the time of the criminal act. Now this may sound like a piece of cerebral dexterity beyond the ability of the average jury member, as none of us can literally implant ourselves into the mind of another, and even if we could it would be the mind of the defendant today in court, not when the criminal act was done. What the state of mind, the *mens rea,* is attempting to achieve is the exculpation of defendants who did not mean to do what they did. In other words, it is trying to protect the innocent and convict the guilty. As Judge Oliver Wendell Holmes so eloquently put it, "Even a dog distinguishes between being stumbled over and being kicked."[59] The criminal law is seeking to establish that the defendant intended to do what happened: he kicked the dog. The private law of tort does not seek to achieve this to the same standard. It is reasonable to say that if the ultimate sanction for committing a crime is that the community imposes the death sentence, then the society imposing that sanction should be absolutely certain, or as certain as it can possibly be, that it is convicting the right person. Consequently, the standard of proof required to prove a person committed a crime is significantly higher than the standard we would expect for proving that a person did not deliver goods to my market stall or house as agreed. In the same vein, if a person hurts me but is negligent and not deliberate in actions, then it would be reasonable to hold that person liable for tortious harm but not for the more serious criminal harm. Consequently, the criminal law seeks to prove that the defendant was guilty of an inaction or inaction, *actus reus,* and guilty of intentionally causing the harm that resulted from the action, *mens rea.* As Professor Kenneth Simmons stated, "More fundamentally, criminal law targets conduct that is impermissible. Or, as economists might say, the optimal incidence of criminal conduct is zero."[60]

This chapter has established that certain actions are so offensive that all of a community suffers and, consequently, laws have been written, divinely or by man, to control the behavior of citizens. We call these actions and the law that controls them criminal. Regardless of when in history or where on Earth it has taken place, all societies punish those who transgress the criminal law. There always has been a lack of agreement though on the level of punishment that should be applied. This dilemma has not been resolved. Over time the leading civilizations of the Western world developed written bodies of law that had varying degrees of impact upon future generations. In Europe, the Roman laws played a significant role in shaping the ecclesiastical laws, canon law, as well as the secular laws that became known as the Civil Law. In England, the impact of the Romans was less and the influence of the Catholic Church was also less strong. Consequently, strong British monarchs, many of French origin, asserted their authority in place of canon law, so that over the course of five centuries the impact of canon law was minimal and England developed its own legal system known as the Common Law. Together the Civil Law and the Common Law form the two largest bodies of law in use in the world today. Canon Law and another religion-based law, sharia law, are also important and both impact the lives of many millions of people as well. The Common Law was for many centuries handed down through the decisions of judges, and it took many hundreds of years before users of this system recognized a need for any level of codification. By contrast, the French Civil Law was a fusion of custom and Roman and church law, and it became codified at an early stage in its history. Napoleon Bonaparte was instrumental in having the codes of France rewritten and modernized and his work is still considered a leading example of clarity and order. Alongside the development of legal families or systems of law, the developing nations of the world need to have state officials with the authority to implement the public parts of the law, especially the criminal actions of citizens. Taking the lead from the Roman example, the villages and towns of Europe started a vigilante and night watch system of protection. This grew into a county-wide system of protection that was under the direction of a royal appointee, the sheriff. Eventually the growth of the merchant classes and the desire to explore our world meant that trade, industry and the migration of people would need more sophisticated responses to control than local watchmen could provide. The communities of the new nations of Europe and America needed police, courts and corrections officers to service a complex society. The evolution of these authorities is discussed in greater detail later in this book.

By the 16th century the role of judges and the criminal law under the two legal families was clearly established. America not unsurprisingly followed Britain's lead and the Common Law with varying degrees of exactness depending upon the need for the laws, whether commercially based Southern needs or biblically based Northern. Throughout the journey, the legal systems so familiar to users of the criminal justice system today can be traced back time and again to the Greeks and Romans. Between them was instigated a comprehensive system of proofs, judges and juries, defined sentences, justifiable homicide, a written body of laws that would inform future generations and many more important influences that will feature throughout this book. In the following chapters we will look at a range of criminal offences that are viewed as serious. The first, murder, invariably attracts the greatest degree of media and social interest, and yet for all that the Romans did give to legal advancement, murder was not designated a specific crime.

Endnotes

1. R v Smith would indicate an action brought on behalf of the crown, Regina v Smith, or in the case of a King, Rex v Smith.
2. Some jurisdictions have struggled with the delineation of a fine as either a punitive action or a civil action that is outside of the scope of the criminal law, e.g. corporate liability.
3. See Jones, M. and Johnstone, P. *History of Criminal Justice.* 5th ed. New York: Elsevier; 2011, 5.
4. There are numerous examples to consider, particularly in the area of sexual conduct and offences governed by the church. Also consider that contemporary society has computer-based crimes that were not even thought of as potential crimes as recently as the 1970s.
5. There is some measure of disagreement over the actual date with opinion varying between around 2250 BC and 1750 BC.
6. Joseph Kelly. The fascinating code of Hammurabi: Wow! I didn't know that! *The History Teacher,* Vol. 28, No. 4, August 1995, pp. 555–563. Most probably the invader was the king of Elam who is believed to have removed five columns of the monument as a trophy. C. H. W. Jones, supra.
7. King Hammurabi ruled for 55 years sometime during the 23rd century BC.
8. Johns, C. H. W. The Code of Hammurabi, *The Expository Times,* March 1903; 14(6); 257–258.
9. Plebian is a term used to denote the common people or the working classes whereas a patrician is a nobleman or member of the aristocracy.
10. See further Kelly, supra.
11. See further Vincent, G. E. The Laws of Hammurabi, *American Journal of Sociology,* 6 May 1904; 9(6); 737–754.
12. See: Vincent, supra, who cites Pollock and Maitland at p. 748 and note 2.
13. See Vincent, supra, p. 749.
14. Talion meaning a punishment identical to the offense and taken from the law of talion. Although often viewed as a literal translation wherein the punishment is identical to the offense, contemporary understanding captures the concept of the punishment 'fitting' the crime.
15. Jones and Johnstone, supra, p. 18.
16. Jones and Johnstone, supra, p. 24
17. See "Halakhah" www.jewishvirtuallibrary.org

18. Capital of the Hittite empire located near modern Bogazkale, Turkey.
19. Intercourse with pigs, dogs and sheep was subject to the death penalty whereas intercourse with a horse or a mule was exempt from the death penalty. See further: Nestor's cup: Hellenic congeries. www.nestroscup.fr. For a detailed discussion see: Bryce, Trevor R. *Life and Society in the Hittite world.* Oxford: Oxford University Press; 1999.
20. Literally meaning to 'show a fig'. The fig sign denoted making an accusation in ancient Greece. Source www.thefreedictionary.com
21. E.g. the creation of the office of *praetor* who headed up the uniquely Roman invention of private law courts. Many aspects of the *praetor's* role are apparent today in the Prefect of France. Another important addition to legal history was the establishment of professional jurists. A public official who was not a judge or an advocate, the jurist held high social status in Rome and was available by appointment to members of the ruling classes, *nobilitas,* exclusively. As we shall see, infra, the exclusivity of appointment as a Justice of the Peace in England bears close resemblance to the Roman 'jurist'.
22. Although formally ended in America in the mid-19th century and soon after in England, the concept of a privileged status for priests remains and was seen in practice during the 1990s when the pope refused to allow Archbishop Paul Marcinkus to stand trial in Italy on charges of money laundering. Marcinkus was given diplomatic immunity by the pope under the protection of the papal city of the Vatican.
23. See Jones and Johnstone, supra, p. 23.
24. See Frank Wieacker. The importance of Roman law for Western civilization and Western legal thought, *Boston College International and Comparative Law Review.* 1981; 4(2); 257–281.
25. See Wieacker, supra, p. 259.
26. The term comes from the Roman law, *ius civile,* the law that all citizens, *cives,* were subject to.
27. For a discussion about the influence of Civil Law within the US see: The Common Law and Civil Law traditions, www.berkeley.edu
28. See Jones and Johnstone, supra, p. 44.
29. Battle was strictly controlled with a specific time and date set, as well as initially a field and then a marked arena being used for the event. The accuser brought an appeal of felony, *fello* (Latin), and combatants or their champions fought to the death, mutilation resulting in being unable to continue or until sunset. By a curious oversight of the English lawmakers, trial by battle remained an option under English law until 1819 when, embarrassingly, a man claimed his right and the legislators had to admit they had forgotten to remove it from legal options. See further: Jones and Johnstone, supra, p. 48.
30. Late O.E. scirgerefa "representative of royal authority in a shire," from scir (see shire) + gerefa "chief, official, reeve" (see reeve). In Anglo-Saxon England, the

representative of royal authority in a shire. As an American county official, attested from 1662; sheriff's sale first recorded 1798. http://www.etymonline.com/index.php?term=sheriff

31. We take the term from the 3rd century Roman firewatchers, Vigiles. The term has commonly come to mean legal, or extra-legal, citizen participation in law enforcement.
32. William also retained the services of a number of Englishmen sheriffs such as Marloswein, Freeman, Robert Fitz Wymarc, Round, Touid, Davis, Edric, Edwin and Elfwine. Source: Morris, supra, p. 26 note 52.
33. Johnstone, P. "The Real Influence of Robert Peel on 21st Century Policing." Forthcoming 2012.
34. "Have mercy on me, O God, according to your unfailing love, according to your great compassion blot out my transgression."
35.. Privilegium Fori was abolished in 1823.
36. Jones and Johnstone. Supra, p. 65.
37. They were known as the 'glossators of Bologna'. See: Apple, J., and Deyling, R. A primer on the Civil-Law system, Federal Judicial System. www.fjc.gov
38. Apple and Deyling, supra, p. 7.
39. Adopted by Henry V in the 15th century.
40. Jones and Johnstone. Supra, p. 73.
41. Fleet Prison at one time housed William Penn before his departure to America. It was known as the 'Largest brothel in England' as it housed male and female prisoners together and drunkenness and sexual debauchery were commonplace.
42. See further Jones and Johnstone. Supra, pp. 88–105.
43. The self-appointed 'Witch-finder General' Matthew Hopkins, who sold his services for payment to villages across the south of England, managed to find 200 witches over a two-year period. He eventually suffered the same fate as his victims and was drowned trying to prove his own innocence.
44. His son, Charles II, canonized his father for his preservation of apostolic succession. He is the only saint, Charles the Martyr, to be canonized by the Anglican Church.
45. Charles II acknowledged at least 12 illegitimate children from a number of mistresses.
46. Jones and Johnstone. Supra, p. 102.
47. This was also known as the Declaration of Rights and served as the blueprint for the US Bill of Rights.
48. See further Louis Crompton, *Homosexuals and the death penalty in colonial America.* University of Nevada-Lincoln, Faculty Publications. 1976; 1(3); 1–1. 76, 277–295.

49. James, K. *Commentaries on American Law.* New York: O. Halstead; 1826. Vol. 1. Lecture XVI. p. 322. Kent was himself quoting Du Ponceau *On Jurisdiction,* 19.
50. 1723–1780. A professor at Oxford University, a judge and a Member of Parliament, William Blackstone is revered as one of the great jurists of the Common Law.
51. Jones and Johnstone. Supra, p. 150.
52. Langbein JH. *Torture and the Law of Proof: Europe and England in the Ancien Regime,* Chicago, University of Chicago Press, 1977 (2006 Paperback edition). John Langbein is Sterling professor of Law and Legal History at Yale law school. He is author of more than 9 books and dozens of legal articles. He is an expert on, *inter alia,* legal history and his books are informative, thought provoking and thoroughly readable. I strongly suggest you try them.
53. Langbein, supra.
54. Infra
55. Langbein, supra.
56. The first recorded case of an Act of Parliament divorce was in England in 1666 when Lord Roos obtained a divorce. The couple was childless and Lord Roos obtained the divorce in order that he could re-marry and attempt to produce heirs. See: Scott, WL. Nullity of marriage in canon law and English law, *The University of Toronto Law Journal.* 1938; 2(2); 319–343. At p. 319
57. It is now widely accepted throughout most Common Law jurisdictions that sustained mental and physical abuse by a partner is a mitigating factor in some murder cases. Battered woman's syndrome is not a legal defense, per se, but it is permissible to raise the issue in the context of a defense or as a factor in provocation or diminished responsibility. The leading English authority is the case of R v Ahluwalia (1992).
58. Jones and Johnstone. Supra, p. 52. Drawn from Anderson, JND. *Islamic law in the modern world.* Westport, CT: Greenwood Press; 1975; and Lippman, SM and Yerushami, M, *Islamic criminal law and procedure: An introduction.* New York: Praeger; 1988.
59. Oliver Wendall Holmes Jr. *The Common Law.* Boston: Little Brown; 1881, 3 Available at www.gutenberg.org
60. Simmons, KW, Professor of Law, Boston University Law School, in The crime/tort distinction: Legal doctrine and normative perspectives, *Widener Law Journal.* 2008: 17(3); 719–733, p. 723.

HOMICIDE AND ASSAULTS

Chapter 1 discussed the history of how humans have come to agree upon certain actions being criminal and the manner in which societies have chosen to deal with the people who commit these criminal acts. This chapter introduces the most serious of all criminal acts, killing another human being. Killing a person has been considered the most serious crime that a person can commit since the first records of crimes were kept. It seems that we have always preserved the taking of another life to a special event—as a sacrifice, as a means of retribution to an individual who has suffered the loss of a partner or a wage earner or as a state imposed sanction against a person who has himself taken a life. Other than in the limited parameters of warfare, taking another person's life has always been subject to condemnation by the aggrieved party's family, the village

or local community and the society as a whole. The challenges therefore are not to determine the offensiveness of the crime of taking another life but the limitations to it. After all, we know that sometimes taking a life is excusable—to defend oneself, to protect another, to do one's duty, to apply an agreed sanction. So not all killing of a person is unlawful and nor is it always successful. Many culprits attempt to kill a victim and fail. Whereas sometimes it appears incredibly easy to take a life because we are frail and seem to die easily, at times humans are extremely hard to kill. In such a case, although an attempt to take a life has taken place the intended victim does not die but survives. These assaults, physical, mental and sexual, are also all relevant factors in the discussion about taking a life as they are frequently intrinsically linked. Also, and regrettably, many killers take the victim's life to attempt to avoid detection even though the crime that motivates the killing is not of itself the reason for the loss of life. And so killing another person is always complex. It arouses in us a curiosity, sometimes a morbid curiosity. Killing is a rare event and the vast majority of humans will never experience ending another person's existence. We are therefore fascinated by this crime. We are intrigued by it. Robbery, fraud, stealing and being a confidence trickster are criminal actions that many people can visualize themselves committing under certain circumstances, but ending a life seems beyond our comprehension, and the manner in which the crime is committed appears as varied and sometimes as inconceivable as the action itself. With every turn of humanity in every epoch it seems that we have the capacity to find even more inventive and unpleasant ways to inflict the ultimate crime upon each other. But in order to kill a human being, the victim must be human. Even this apparently simple aspect of the crime is complex. Just pause for a moment and consider: When is a life a life? When does it start and when does it end? Is a human life capable of being a murder victim at the point of conception? At the point of being capable of an independent existence? What about the person who cannot survive without constant medical support? The person is undoubtedly alive and many of these people make significant contributions to society from a machine or a complex life support mechanism. And what about when are we dead? Years ago it was when the hangman said we were. But he was no doctor. Are we dead when the heart stops—the mind? What bodily functions must cease in order that we can say a human is no longer? And what about those instances where life can continue with support and could do so indefinitely? When a life support machine is turned off, are we taking a life or allowing the patient to die naturally through starvation since the person cannot feed herself? Do we want to sanction starvation? Are there circumstances under which it is acceptable to participate in the cessation of another life? These are all very challenging problems that collectively society has to answer in order that we can make appropriate decisions about the actions of culprits when they take, or attempt to take, another person's life from them. It should not, therefore, be a surprise to learn that over time, victims, offenders, the courts and society have developed a complex language to describe killing.

Homicide means to kill another human. It derives from the Latin, *homo*, man and *caedere*, to kill. Not all homicides are criminal acts. Murder is one form of homicide and it is always a crime. To murder a person means to kill deliberately or to be so reckless in one's actions that the death was tantamount to acting intentionally. Homicides may, therefore, be criminal and they may not be. Killing another person when insane is definitely taking a life without authority or state approval, it is unjustified, but the person responsible may not be aware of the crime he is committing. Therefore, a homicide has taken place, but it is not a criminal homicide. In some countries, a homicide that occurs during the course of another criminal act, such as a robbery, may be treated as murder. The variety of classifications of homicide is clearly extremely diverse. Over the course of this chapter a number of these variations will be introduced. These include: homicide, criminal homicide, justifiable homicide, murder, serial murder, assassinations, child and baby killing (infanticide), manslaughter and voluntary manslaughter. Each of these terms can be broken down further depending upon the actual manner in which the offensive conduct was committed, as well as the degree of intention displayed by the offender towards his victim. In contemporary society we have become dependent upon exact interpretations of the law to provide us with clarity and understanding. The previous chapter demonstrated that this has not been the history of the law and the criminal justice system and until fairly recently homicides were rarely delineated in the way that we are familiar with today. According to the UNODC,[1] 468,000 humans were murdered across the world in 2010[2] of which 36% took place in Africa and 31% in the Americas.[3] Honduras and El Salvador have the highest recorded number of murders *per capita*, 82 per 100,000 in Honduras and 66 per 100,000 in El Salvador.[4] A recent study conducted by the Geneva Declaration on Armed Violence and Development concluded that a quarter of all violent deaths occur in 14 countries. El Salvador again features in this report, which shows that the murder rate in this country is now three times higher than in Mexico, and the total number of murders between 2004 and 2009 is even greater than in those countries that have been engaged in armed conflict, such as Iraq.[5] Current figures for El Salvador show an increase to 71 per 100,000; Honduras now has a figure of 87 per 100,000, and the Caribbean islands of St. Kitts and Nevis rank as the country with the world's third highest murder rates at 68 per 100,000 population.[6]

Current definitions for criminal homicide derive from three principal sources, legal families of law such as the Common Law, national legal codes or statutes such as the code penal in France, and statewide interpretations such as the Texas statute. In the US the primary sources are the Common Law, the Model Penal Code and state legislation. Under the Common Law any intentional killing was a homicide; consequently, assisting another person to commit suicide was a crime as the death was deliberate and intentional. Prosecuting those who assist in suicide is still a crime in many parts of the world, but it is generally regarded as an offence that is not prosecuted unless particular individual circumstances dictate otherwise.[7] Over time the Common Law developed the meaning of murder, or 'murther' as it was originally called, to become an offence of the unlawful killing of a human being by another human being, and not of unlawfully killing oneself. The contemporary view is that suicide is not homicide. Instances where the vehicle for a murder is not human, such as cases where an animal is used to kill a person, still amount to murder. It is not murder when an animal innocently kills a human and conversely it is not murder for a person to kill an animal.

Medical opinion has always played a large part in the criminal law and our ability to determine a cause of death is measurably better than it was during the Middle Ages when medical science was in its infancy. Consequently, there needed to be a practical way of establishing when a person was alive and when dead, as well as how long after an action the death could still be attributed to that action. For example, if a defendant struck a victim over the head and the person died one month later, could a tribunal determine that the actual cause of death was the blow to the head inflicted by the defendant on the alleged day. Today it would be possible with a considerable degree of accuracy to determine an exact cause of death. In the past, this was not the case and therefore the criminal law developed a number of practical workable solutions. One of these was the 'year and a day rule', which determined that if a victim survived an attack for more than one year and one day, the cause of death could not be attributed to the blow given by the defendant more than one year and one day previously. It was inevitable that with greater scientific knowledge this rule would disappear into legal history, and this has happened. It is no longer Common Law that one year and one day applies in murder cases. Establishing when a human is a human has also been a vexing question over time. When, for example, is a child within the womb actually a human being? Was it human at the time of conception, when in the womb or when once delivered and capable of independent breathing and independent existence? The Common Law established a rule that a fetus was not a human being. In practice, this meant that a pregnant woman who was assaulted and lost her child had been criminally assaulted but the unborn child was not the victim of murder. Many countries have now amended their laws to reflect greater medical understanding and social concern over killing a life and most statutes now have a provision to include a fetus under homicide, either through unlawfully killing a human being or killing a fetus or as a separate provision, thus creating a specific offense of feticide. The current legal dilemma has now shifted somewhat as it is often the case that the perpetrator of the homicide is not a third party but the mother. If feticide is a crime, then it follows that abortion is feticide as it is the deliberate killing of a fetus. To overcome this problem, many countries have now written laws that permit abortion up to a certain period of growth so that abortion is not a crime if conducted during the first trimester of pregnancy but will become a form of murder if conducted during the second or third trimester of pregnancy. Crucially, in all cases of murder, the law now requires that another human being conduct the killing or attempted killing. This has resolved the issue of suicide, but it still leaves open the potential for a prosecution in cases of assisted attempted suicide.

Having determined when a person is alive, the next issue is when are we dead? A Common Law death was when respiratory functions ceased. This is why the hangman could pronounce you dead even if you had only partially suffocated and could be revived later by family members. Rare though this occurrence was, there are recorded instances of people being hanged[8] and then sitting up in the surgeon's hall[9] or on route to the graveyard. By the mid-1800s, the 'long drop' method of execution had been introduced and death occurred by breaking the neck rather than through strangulation. With the development of medical knowledge, it is now possible to keep a person 'alive' for a far greater period of time and with far greater injuries than was possible previously. This has led to some need for modification in what it means to be dead for the purposes of the criminal law. Since we can now prolong respiratory functions indefinitely, this is clearly no longer an accurate way to determine when a person is dead. Contemporary determinations are that there must be a total failure of cardio respiratory systems and irreversible loss of all brain functions. What this means is that a person is dead in instances where she losses the ability to function independently and there is irreversible loss of brain functions. It does not mean that when a person is unconscious but can be kept alive on a cardiopulmonary system that she is necessarily dead for the purposes of the criminal law. In the US, all 50 states have adopted the Uniform Determination of Death Act provisions, which hold 'irreversible cessation of the entire brain' as the legal standard for death. When a person is dead is therefore a legal question and not a medical one. The role of the medical doctors in this discussion is to determine the applicable criteria for deciding whether or not brain death has occurred. Entire brain means all of the brain functions and does not mean only 'persistent vegetative state' as this may not include the entire brain functions. One question that this poses is whether or not the actions of a defendant causing severe brain damage are murder when the decision to remove life support is made by a family member. And what if it is the parents of a child that have caused the injuries resulting in the life support system being needed that are now determining whether or not life support should be withdrawn?[10] One of the most famous recent examples of the dilemma over when a person is dead or not occurred in Florida where a husband sought to have his wife's life support machine switched off and the woman's parents were opposed to this move. Terri Schiavo had been in a permanent vegetative state for 15 years. She was not 'dead' according to the law, as her brain was capable of some recordable functions that prevented a determination of the legal standard 'entire brain'. The law in Florida permitted her husband (or doctors) to remove her feeding tubes. This would lead to death by starvation. Terri Schiavo's parents were opposed to this and fought the action in court. The issue to be decided was who had authority to sanction removal of the feeding tubes and in what circumstances doctors were required by law to continue to keep a person alive who would die naturally if left to do so because, as seen above, the removal of feeding tubes can be construed as murder. After numerous appeals and counter-appeals, Michael Schiavo was permitted to authorize the removal of feeding tubes to his wife Terri. The tubes were removed on March 18, 2005 and she died on March 31, 2005.

The Model Penal Code is an attempt to codify the criminal law applicable to the US. Thomas Jefferson recognized the need for a single body of applicable laws and attempted a codification in 1776. It was not adopted and a series of revived and renewed attempts took place over the 19th century. Louisiana used a criminal code based strongly upon the Napoleonic code of France as early as 1826, and a New York Penal Code was passed into law in 1881.[11] In 1931, the American Law Institute started work on a criminal code for the entire country. The progress stalled over the period of the Second World War and was not started again until 1951. A final draft code was approved in 1962, and this formed the basis of what is now a six-volume set of codified penal laws that are available for adoption by all 50 states and the District of Colombia. The MPC is more than a code though as it provides laws pertaining to corrections and punishment in addition to substantive criminal law. As a result of the MPC, numerous states have now revised their own laws and set in motion, or have achieved, the codification of state criminal sanctions. Not only have the codes informed new state legislation, they also provide the basis for commentary in courts; and though not binding, *per se*, the MPC is frequently referred to in court decisions. The codes are divided up into "General" and Special." General principles cover issues such as imposing liability and principles of defense. Much of this part has not been adopted, as it is insufficiently specific for application in the specialized legal fori of federal and state criminal courts. Specific offenses are contained within the "Special" section. When looking at the MPC, it is clear that the originating basis for the law was the Common Law and not the Civil Law of Europe, as the text reads more like a series of guidelines than of specific rules that could be learned by wrote. Offenses are clustered together in groups so that there is a logical progression of types of offending that is often interrelated, such as; offenses against the person. Homicides, assaults and endangerment, kidnapping and sexual offenses are all organized together. One of the great achievements of the MPC has been to simplify some of the Common Law anomalies and dated language. For example, the Common Law notion of malice aforethought, which is linked to the idea of trying to prove that what a person did was his intention and that at the time of committing the act he intended the outcome, has now been reduced to a much more workable idea of did the defendant commit the act purposely and knowingly. The idea of a culprit acting recklessly is also tackled in the MPC and being reckless is substituted for the idea of doing something that the defendant knows will endanger life but still proceeds to do it. Ultimately the MPC has managed to reduce the entire array of criminal mental states to just four: purpose, knowledge, recklessness and negligence. An example of where the criminal law does not require proof of a mental state—in other words the crime committed is not dependent upon proving that the defendant intended to achieve the outcome—would be running a red light. The law does not care about the state of your mind and whether or not you justified the action to yourself; running a red light is an absolute or strict liability offence. Most crimes that fall into this category are really only regulatory offences and are at the lower end of the scale of seriousness. Under the MPC, all of this classification of offences is divided up to be either civil matters or violations that can only be punished by means of a fine or a civil style penalty. One exception to this was where at Common Law an offence is classified as being a felony murder. In this case a person who is committing a felony crime manages to kill another party while in the process of committing the offence. A classic example is bank robbery where in the course of the robbery a member of the public is shot and killed by the robbers. The question as to whether or not the robbers intended to kill the innocent victim is now not subject to legal debate. The unlawful killing occurred during the robbery and is now designated as a felony murder and proof of intention, the state of mind of the defendant normally required in murder, is not needed. The MPC altered slightly from this interpretation and provides for a rebuttable presumption. What this means is that the law will presume you meant the outcome of your actions, killing the innocent person during the bank robbery, unless you the defendant can show to the satisfaction of the jury that you did not intend that outcome.

If a defendant's intention or purpose cannot be established, then a charge of murder may be reduced to manslaughter. Manslaughter has its origins in the ancient Greek legal works written by Draco in the 7th century BC. Draco drew a distinction between a defendant who had a state of mind that was premeditated and that of a person who responded to a situation on impulse. Manslaughter is therefore a possible charge in instances where it cannot be proven that the defendant intended the death of the victim, but due to the defendant's actions a person has died. Manslaughter is classified into two categories, voluntary and involuntary. Voluntary manslaughter captures crimes that involve a diminished responsibility, provocation and infanticide. Involuntary manslaughter is where a person has been criminally negligent or committed manslaughter through vehicular intoxication or being drugged while driving. Involuntary manslaughter may also include assisted suicides depending upon the individual state's approach towards this issue.[12] One important distinction between these two types of manslaughter is that in the case of voluntary manslaughter the defendant may intend the death of the victim but there will be circumstances surrounding the killing that may make it excusable, such as provocation, self-defense or diminished capacity. In cases of involuntary manslaughter, the defendant does not mean to kill the victim. The defendant has committed an unlawful act and a death has occurred but the defendant did not intend the death or even foresee the death. In the US, this is considered criminally negligent manslaughter, whereas in England it is referred to as gross negligence manslaughter. A typical example would be where a defendant owes the victim a duty of care but has failed to deliver that duty of care and the victim has died. It is for the jury in the case to decide whether or not the behavior of the defendant amounts to gross negligence. Vehicular manslaughter caused by a drunk or drugged driver is typically regarded as a form of involuntary manslaughter as the drunk driver of the vehicle did not set out intending to take a life but did so due to the consumption of drink or drugs. Some states have refined this offence to a specific crime of intoxication manslaughter. A vehicle includes a boat, aircraft or other motorized craft, and in the state of Texas it even includes amusement rides if operated by a drunk or drugged defendant. Further classification of murder is often broken down by individual states to first or second-degree murder. The intention of the defendant (or total disregard for human life) is ordinarily the distinguishing feature of these divisions. In instances where a murder occurs during the course of a crime that is not a felony, a number of states have adopted a misdemeanor murder classification as well as a felony-murder classification. Felony-murder is treated as a first degree, premeditated murder and liable to the death sentence in those states where capital punishment applies. Misdemeanor-murder is treated alongside manslaughter in terms of severity.

Since the Middle Ages personal violence has been treated as a specific criminal matter that affects not only the victim and his family but society at large. In effect, murder moved from being a matter of personal redress to a state matter that potentially depleted the monarch of able-bodied men and families of their wage earners. During the reign of William the Conqueror, a village was responsible for the body of a murder victim unless a culprit was found. It was a legal presumption that the deceased was a Norman and therefore a greater fine was due to the king for the failure to catch the culprit than if the deceased were an Englishman.[13] In Europe, the prosecution was brought by the state but under the Common Law. Although the state was very interested in the outcome, and even claimed ownership of the body of the convicted murderer for medical dissections, prosecutions remained a private affair until the mid-18th century. Has that changed? Do we kill more often than in the past? Yes and no. It depends where you are looking. In medieval England, the average number of known murders per 100,000 population fluctuated between as few as 5 per 100,000 and as many as 42 per 100,000 between the 14th and 15th centuries.[14] In Florence during the same period, the murder rate was higher than in Honduras today, with a rate of 110 per 100,000 population.[15]

Under the law of England, murder was punishable by death. The manner of death depended largely upon one's rank or station in life; hanging was most commonly proscribed for the working classes and beheading preserved for the nobility and royalty. The charter granted to William Penn by Charles II in 1681 handed all of the applicable laws of England to Penn for application in the American colonies. ". . . as to felonies, shall be and continue the same as they shall bee for the time being, by the general course of the Law of our Kingdome of England, until the said Lawes shall be altered by the said William Penn . . .".[16] To which, if a person were to 'willfully or premeditatedly' kill another he shall suffer death. By the time of the reign of William and Mary, the requirement that the killing be either willful or premeditated had changed to being willful *and* premeditated. Following the design and form of the English Common Law would inevitably change after Independence, and so Frenchman Brissot de Warville commented that, "For the Americans indeed guard themselves against consulting the incoherent and barbarous laws of Europe—this Roman law, an eternal source of litigation and calamities; they guard themselves against believing in our prejudices, in our lawyers, but they listen to the philosophers; they follow a second time the profound Locke; they read and correct Montesquieu and Rousseau; they are especially careful against following England too closely."[17] During this time the death penalty was removed for buggery, sodomy, robbery and burglary, but it was staunchly retained for murder.

The MPC states that murder occurs when:

The defendant causes the death of another human being, and

a. It is committed purposely or knowingly or
b. It is committed recklessly under circumstances manifesting extreme indifference to the value of human life. Such recklessness is presumed if the defendant is an actor or an accomplice in the attempt or commission or flight after commission of the crimes of robbery, rape, deviate sexual intercourse by force or fear, arson, burglary, kidnapping or felonious escape.

It is rare if not impossible for any legislative body, regardless of the period in history, to anticipate the abhorrent depths that the human species will descend to in order that it can inflict pain and suffering upon others. The ability of humans to create new ways to impose harm and suffering upon each other appears inexhaustible. No century has been either immune or latent in constructing highly inventive methods of mental and/or physical torment upon other humans, and yet throughout the morbid and desperate history of murder one manifestation seems to be the most inexplicable regardless of geographical location or social conditions and that is serial murder. Of all the heinous crimes that we seem capable of projecting onto each other, serial murder appears to baffle our reasoning more than any other murder manifestation. What can possibly motivate another human to kill dozens if not hundreds of other people for what is sometimes an apparently motiveless reason? Is it hate, rejection, inability to embrace society, sexual repression or plain madness? Serial killing defies reason and logical explanation, and consequently it is often poorly articulated in the criminal law. Infrequently, serial killing may also be a manifestation of another closely related crime, mass murder. But they are different crimes and that distinction needs clarification. One example should help to start to bring understanding to a topic that is often confusing. Adolf Hitler was a mass murderer. He might be disguised as a serial killer, but once the definitions are articulated it is clear to see why he was a mass murderer. Hitler, a cruel dictator with apparently no regard for human life, used medical techniques, genocide, starvation, concentration camps and a range of degrading and demoralizing techniques to abuse and kill homosexuals, Jews, Slavs, Serbs, Germans, Czechs, Italians, Poles, French, Ukrainians and numerous indigenous groups. But what distinguishes Hitler from 'son of Sam' or Charles Manson? He killed his victims en masse in a single incident. The legal definition of mass murder is when a person kills four people or more at the same time (or over a relatively short period of time) with *no cooling off period* between the murders. Mass murder also typically occurs at a single location in which a number of individuals are killed together by one or more individuals. However, certain characteristics of mass murder resemble those of serial killing. For example, a notable reason for mass murder is revenge, which is also true of serial killers who are frequently taking revenge on women or homosexuals for the perceived injury they have received from that group, often in childhood. Mass murderers are also frequently motivated by a need for recognition, fame and glory. This can also be said of serial killers (and also terrorists who, like serial killers, often want to advertise their criminality). Most traditional killers want to obscure their crimes so that identification is impossible. Serial killers and mass murderers are not motivated in the same way and recognition of their criminality is often the pinnacle of success for them.

Serial killing differs from mass murder in that the motive for killing is different and the period of time over which the murders are committed also tends to vary. Serial killers often commit their crimes over months or years. They are frequently found wanting in terms of relationships, and once a killing is conducted they are often capable of living a 'normal' life until the desire to kill grows again within them to the point at which either months or years later they must strike again. Jack the Ripper is perhaps one of the world's best-known alleged serial killers. Whether he killed five, seven or more women will probably never be known. But he achieved notoriety in the east end of London at the close of the 19th century for killing a number of prostitutes over a short period of time and then apparently disappearing into folklore and history forever. Had 'Jack' been caught, he would probably never be as famous as he is today, but due to his cessation of crime he has now been immortalized in film and books and on the stage. The challenge that serial killers pose for law enforcement is the irrationality of their crimes. Often the perpetrators are travelers and therefore establishing a pattern of conduct is very difficult. Other killers have shown themselves location bound but live such 'ordinary' lives in between the killing sprees it is very hard for work friends, neighbors or the police to identify irrational behavior in a given area. Many serial killers have been found to have higher than average IQs, and this too possesses numerous problems for law enforcement, as the offenders are intelligent and adaptable, making detection even more difficult. And perhaps most worryingly of all, many serial killers believe that they have a divine mission. They are literally told by god to commit the killings to rid the world of some perceived plague manifest in a particular cohort of society: homosexuals, prostitutes, blond haired women or dark haired men; the motivating logic is illogical. Importantly for the purpose of distinguishing serial killers from mass murderers, serial killers take the lives of their victims one at a time. Mass murderers who engage in one off or multiple killing sprees are not serial killers and they are typically motivated by a completely different set of criteria of which sexual confusion is very rarely a factor. Repressed sexuality, hatred of women or homosexuals or the desire to change one's sexuality are common features among serial killers. To understand serial killing and mass murder requires an appreciation of the differences of each crime and an adjustment in the way we typically approach both topics. Serial killing has regrettably caught the attention of the media to a far greater extent than mass murder, and this translates into numerous books and films on the lives or fictional lives of serial killers as a saleable commercial commodity. Our interest in serial killers has grown greatly over the past 20 years, and the actual number of serial killings that takes place has also grown, and yet our morbid fascination with serial killers remains disproportionate to the actual number of serial killings that take place for we rarely seem to hold the same degree of interest in the victims. Perhaps it is the fact that a serial killer can be a neighbor or a work colleague for years before detection and yet whole societies soon know that they have a despotic madman as a country's dictator. Or perhaps it is the sense of local uncertainty that both frightens and yet also most thrills a population caught in the grip of a serial killer. The constant unknown—when will he (sometimes though rarely she) strike again and who is most vulnerable? Are the killings random or age, gender and ethnicity located? To be classified as a serial killing, there must be at least two killings, there must be no relationship between the victim and the killer, and the murders must be committed for a reason other than material gain. Certainly a number of serial killers in the US and the UK would meet these criteria: David Berkowitz, Charles Manson, Ted Bundy, Jeffrey Dahmer and, in the UK, Peter Dinsdale, Peter Sutcliffe, Dennis Nilsen and perhaps the man who has murdered more people singularly than any other, Dr. Harold Shipman. Contrast the manner of killing and these killers' motives with those of Amy Bishop or Adolf Hitler and they are clearly very different criminals. All of them appear to have some significant level of mental disorder that caused them to behave in the manner they did, but the nature of the delusional disorder would seem very different in the cases of the serial killers when contrasted with those of the mass murderers. A contemporary debate centers around whether in fact serial killers and mass murderers are disturbed with a psychiatric abnormality or a more socially located psychological abnormality. Defining a person as criminally 'mad' is quite a rare event. Defining a person as treatable through a sex offender program has gained considerable popularity over the past 40 years and being 'bad' rather than 'mad' seems to have gained traction in contemporary society. It might be that we can modify the behavior and the environment to make being bad less attractive, whereas outright insanity is far more difficult to explain and therefore to prepare against.[18] However, and regardless of the nature and form of the killing, whether singular over time or multiple at the same time, serial killing and mass murder[19] are murder and the basic definition of the crime will always apply regardless of the complexity of the killings.

Assassinating a person is simple murder. It is just when the victim holds a particular position in society, which they or society at large consider important, that the killing warrants a special classification. The history of civilization has shown numerous times that those who achieve positions of leadership often delude themselves into thinking that they are immortal and that their deaths should be treated differently than those of less famous people. The assassination of a person immediately invokes sentiments of nationalism and frequently associated horror. In a sense, the option that the people have to elect and remove an official has been taken from us by the action of the murderer and we are deprived of a say in the continuation of the elected official. But this is a contemporary manifestation of assassination. Its history has less democratic roots.

The origin of the word assassin is probably Arabic, and the word may have derived from the 'old man of the mountains' hasan-e sabbah (also recorded as al Hassan ibn-al-Sabbah), who gained notoriety and fear from maintaining a mountaintop stronghold against general travelers as well as against Christians and Muslims.[20] This is not, however, fully proven and the idea of a hashish smoking (as the word assassin is also associated with the word hashish) mountain man wreaking havoc across Persia may be a combination of fact and fiction. We do know that Alexander the Great engaged in assassinations and that there are numerous references to assassinating rivals in the Old Testament prior to his reign. Throughout history, emperors, popes and kings have been killed in secret and devious ways. These killings are most often termed assassinations, whereas the trial and execution of a king is given the specific name of regicide. In recent history, four US presidents were assassinated within the space of one hundred years.[21] The last of these, the killing of John F. Kennedy, resulted in changes to the law so that killing the US president became designated as a federal crime. Threats against the president are also captured in legislation as follows: "Whoever knowingly and willfully deposits for conveyance in the mail or for delivery from any post office or by any letter carrier any letter, paper, writing, print, missive, or document containing any threat to take the life of, to kidnap, or to inflict bodily harm upon the President of the United States, the President-elect, the Vice-President or other officer next in the order of succession to the office of President of the United States, or the Vice-President elect, or knowingly and willfully otherwise makes any such threat against the President, President-elect, Vice-President or other officer next in the order of succession to the office of President, or Vice-President, shall be fined under this title or imprisoned not more than five years, or both."[22] This legislation was most recently used in 2010 and 2011 when in two separate incidents threats were made against the life of President Barack Obama.

Methods of assassination have also changed over time; stabbing, strangulation and administering poison were popular until guns and bombs became more readily available. Guy Fawkes is credited with attempting to assassinate King Charles I and his parliament, the chosen method being bombing. He spectacularly failed and as a result the king declared that the British public should light fires to celebrate the continuation of the monarchy. This tradition is repeated on November 5 each year throughout Britain. Fires are lit as required by the king and fireworks are set off to pay some degree of recognition to Guy Fawkes also. The first known use of the word assassination appears in Shakespeare's play *Macbeth* when Macbeth considers killing King Duncan of Scotland. If only it were that simple he thinks . . . "If th' assassination could trammel up the consequence, and catch with his surcease, success."[23] Not only individuals but also nation states have employed assassinations throughout history. The US failed for almost 50 years in its attempts to have Fidel Castro assassinated. Some of the more fantastic schemes involved placing explosives inside shellfish so that when Castro pursued his passion for scuba diving a shellfish would explode and kill him. On another occasion, a former lover was contracted to kill Castro in bed. This failed when the poison pills that were secretly hidden in a jar of facial cream melted and the assassin decided against placing make-up in the Cuban leader's mouth while asleep as she feared he would wake with a mouthful of cream rather than die.[24]

To assassinate a leader means to unlawfully take the life of leader, most usually for a political purpose. Abstract killing of a leader such as the pope is an extraordinary event that has typically been motivated by the delusions of a lunatic rather than the planned actions of an individual or group of people who wish to overturn a political regime. The leading question for society as a whole is whether or not an assassination is justified; for example in the case of an extralegal killing of a despot. These are always uncomfortable questions to answer as they require individuals to attempt to justify murder or, more conveniently, killing, as the term murder is too evocative and incriminatory. So perhaps the question is, can we justify killing a leader? These distinctions are not unimportant as there was a time in the US when assassination was defined as the 'murder of a leader'. Today it is thought to mean the 'killing of a leader'. There is an important distinction as murder is always a criminal homicide, but killing is not. More importantly perhaps is whether or not assassination is at all restricted to the killing of a leader. What about instances of terrorist killings that slaughter citizens for political purposes. Could not, should not, these murders also be captured by the term assassination? It would be hard to deny that the killings in the US in 2001, Madrid in 2004 and London in 2005 were not politically motivated killings. And since the conversation is never a 'one way street', do the calculated killings of known terrorists not also amount to politically motivated killings even when conducted by 'legitimate' western governments? The eradication of Osama Bin Laden was never called an assassination, but the 'hot pursuit' of this man and his death were as close to an assassination as contemporary interpretation could possibly accommodate. The difficulty with assassinations is that they attract very high levels of media attention and they are often international in nature. As such, we have elected to classify these simple murders as a 'special case', perhaps in part to massage the egos of those in power and in part to explain a particular manifestation of the ultimate crime that helps explain why some murders are different from others and should be treated as such. Had the US been at war with a country represented by Osama Bin Laden, his killing would have been classified as a war crime.[25] Given that the events leading to the killing of Osama bin Laden were not a formal war event, then the justification for a killing of this nature rests with a liberal interpretation of the legal justification for a state sanctioned assassination. After all, the sanctioned but illegal killing of another citizen is murder. It's just that it is authorized and therefore hidden behind the cloak of legality that the action is politically and socially justified in the interests of the citizens of the country conducting the killing. Postmodern assassinations are indeed murky waters. How simple life was when Caesar was stabbed numerous times by other Romans on the basis that he had grown far too big for his proverbial sandals. Today even calling a killing a state authorized assassination is tantamount to an immediate change of White House leadership as the formal position is resolutely such that the US does not engage in assassinations and Executive Order 12333 confirms this to be the case.

But there was a simpler time when killing a leader was defined as assassination and the world knew it. For example, Abraham Lincoln was assassinated. Politically motivated rivals shot and killed him and his death was recorded as both a murder and an assassination. In fact, whenever a head of state is murdered, assassination is the term employed to describe the unlawful killing. William Wallace, Richard II, Henry VI, Mary Queen of Scots—all were assassinated despite the legal niceties of the terms employed to disguise their deaths. And the list is huge. Killing political, monarchic or presidential rivals is not new news, it is old news; and had it not been but for a simple twist of fate, many of those assassinated would themselves have been assassins of those who authorized their deaths. Europe has never been immune from such actions either, as the "revolution devoured its own children" and the leaders of the French Revolution were themselves subject to political death sentences and an appointment with 'Madame Guillotine'. Three hundred years later in the new world political assassinations were alive and well under President George Bush, who stated that "America has stood down enemies before, and we will do so this time."[26] It is easy to think of assassination as a crime that is unique to heads of state when deranged lone operators kill them. In reality, assassinations cover a far darker side of murder where historically the state has authorized killings political opponents for the protection of the incumbent head of state. Generally, assassinations are viewed as being an international crime, but there is no reason for them not to be prosecuted locally as murder. Also, and importantly, there may be circumstances under which an assassination is not criminal homicide but a state sanctioned killing that is legally justified and therefore not subject to the criminal law at all. Legal opinion on this point is divided.[27]

What causes a person to take the life of a political leader is often the belief that the actions of the leader have provoked the citizen to the point that an overthrow of the regime is the only perceived solution. Provocation is a powerful driver in many crimes and has attracted particular attention when women have killed male partners due to years of mental and physical abuse. Provocation is a possible defense to murder, which if successful may reduce the crime from first-degree murder to voluntary manslaughter. The elements of voluntary manslaughter are that the defendant must have acted intentionally, there must be adequate provocation for the defendant's actions and the defendant's actions must have caused the victims death. In plain language this means that the defendant must have been so provoked that a reasonable person would have responded by killing the victim. The challenge for the criminal law is to determine the level of provocation and whether the resultant action by the defendant was immediate. Because if the acts, the actus reus, of the killing is not immediate, it is impossible to argue that the provocation was a determining factor in causing the response, such as the defendant's violent outburst, which caused the person to kill the victim. In other words, there cannot be a 'cooling down' period where the defendant goes away after being provoked, thinks about what has happened and then returns later, even moments later, and takes revenge upon the victim and kills the person. The provocation must be immediately followed by the violent response that results in the death of the victim. The time factor for the response is crucial to the defense for, as we have established, the mental state of the defendant, his frame of mind or mens rea, at the time of the killings is all important because it establishes the guilty mind, the intention. If I respond to provocation without even thinking about the consequences—for example, if I walk into the bedroom and find my partner in bed with the neighbor and I shoot them both—this may be legitimate provocation and if at the time of shooting them my mind was so full of confusion and rushing emotions that I temporarily lost control of myself, then I may have an excuse in law. But if I see them in bed and go downstairs, get a gun and return to shoot them, this is clearly murder, as I have had time to consider what I am about to do and time to formulate the intention to kill them both. The legal challenge is to define what it means to say an event took place immediately. How soon after an event is immediate? Is it seconds, minutes? How long a timeframe might be permissible in law so that an abused victim could use the defense of provocation and have it still be valid without the law being open to abuse itself by allowing defendants to claim a defense that allowed them to escape a sentence for murder? Most states have utilized a two-pronged proof requirement; provocation must be adequate and the killing must be in the heat of passion. The Model Penal Code does not propose specific requirements, however, and under these provisions it reasoned that if a defendant were not so completely enraged by the circumstances, and responded as any reasonable person would, then the defense should not be available to that defendant. Under the MPC, this means that if the defendant were not under extreme emotional distress at the immediate time of the killing then 'cooling off' had happened and the defendant could not claim provocation. Most states have chosen to follow a different path by allowing the jury to decide what is a reasonable period of time between the event and the killing so that in theory at least there could be a minimal 'cooling off' period. The leading authority on 'cooling off' came from a battered wife case in the UK, which led to a separate defense in some Common Law countries, 'battered woman defense'.

Kiranjit Ahluwalia was subject to an arranged marriage and brought to Crawley in England to live. Her husband subjected her to years of physical and emotional abuse and restricted her access to society generally by making her mother-in-law and sister-in-law responsible for coordinating her activities. Among other restrictions, Mrs. Ahluwalia was not permitted to learn the English language and consequently was reliant upon her in-laws for basic needs. On the night of May 8–9, 1999, Mr. Ahluwalia threatened to beat his wife with a hot iron and demanded money from her. That evening, while he was asleep, Mrs. Ahluwalia threw a can of petrol (gasoline) on her husband and set fire to him. He died from the burns a few days later. When police arrived at the house, Mrs. Ahluwalia stood in the hall, greeted them and said she had given him a fire to wash away his sins. Mrs. Ahluwalia did not give evidence at her murder trial. Her defense was provocation. She was convicted of murder and appealed on the basis of diminished responsibility. There are a number of interesting issues to consider at this point: The actions of Mrs. Ahluwalia amounted to murder and she intentionally killed her husband, which is clear by her actions of getting gasoline, pouring it on him and then setting fire to him. However, if she was provoked, is the timeframe between the continual provocations such that her actions were tantamount to an immediate response to him? If not, then is it possible that Mrs. Ahluwalia's mind was so disturbed at the time that she killed him she was not responsible for her actions? if so, then she might have been legally mad, but that would mean an indeterminate period of time in a prison for the criminally insane. She did not appear insane at the time of trial, so perhaps she had a temporary insanity. Should the issue of the timeframe, the 'cooling down', be left to the jury and not, as happened in the murder trial, be subject to interpretation by the trial judge? Was there such a legal entity as a 'slow burn' scenario where the actions of the victim were such that over months or years the defendant grew in passionate hatred to the point of exploding, even though there was no event that caused the 'explosion' immediately before the killing? Was Mrs. Ahluwalia suffering from Diminished Responsibility as seen at the house by the police when she stated she had 'burned her husband to clean him of his sins'? But if this is an accurate interpretation of the law, then how can a reasonable person also be suffering from a mental condition? Her actions were either reasonable under the circumstances or she was temporarily insane. The Appeal Court decided to order a retrial on the basis of evidence being available about Mrs. Ahluwalia's state of mind that was not available to the original trial court. Battered women syndrome is now recognized as being applicable to both sexes and is commonly associated with physical or mental abuse of a partner over a sustained period of time that results in the victim of the abuse responding at a point in time that may not be related to an immediate provocation by the abuser. At her retrial, Mrs. Ahluwalia was found guilty of manslaughter due to diminished responsibility and was sentenced to three years and four months imprisonment (the exact period she had already served). She was released immediately. Subsequent to the Ahluwalia case, the law surrounding battered women has developed to the point at which it is now recognized as a mitigating circumstance that may reduce a charge of murder to manslaughter. There is currently no medical evidence to support battered person 'syndrome'. Although not bound by the Common Law of England, it is persuasive, and the Ahluwalia case prompted an investigation into the issue in the US, resulting in the Violence Against Women Act of 1984. States have elected not to adopt the MPC's suggested definition of manslaughter under MPC 210.31 where there is no classification of voluntary or involuntary manslaughter, simply an unlawful killing committed in a reckless manner or committed under the influence of extreme mental or emotional disturbance for which there is a reasonable explanation. It is important to understand that with the distinctions as applied across the states, voluntary manslaughter does require an intentional act, even if provoked, whereas involuntary manslaughter requires only that an act occurred resulting in death. Before looking at another specific classification of murder, when a mother kills her children, murder can be contrasted as follows: Murder is killing a human being and intending to do so and without justification or reasonable excuse. Voluntary manslaughter is killing a human being and meaning to do so but with a level of provocation such that society is prepared to a offer an excuse to the defendant and have the matter downgraded to a lower level of severity. Involuntary manslaughter is where a killing of a human being occurs but the defendant has been negligent. The culprit may still possess an intention to commit a criminal act, but he does not have the specific intention of bringing about the unlawful death of the person who dies. The exception to this rather broad allowance is that the unlawful act intended—the crime committed—cannot be a felony. If it is, then the charge will be felony murder. MPC 210.4 states that negligent manslaughter is when a criminal homicide is committed negligently. However, as previously stated, the majority of states and the federal criminal system have not adopted the MPC definitions with respect to manslaughter, as both systems appear to prefer the latitude that a jury has under voluntary and involuntary manslaughter.

Homicide is one of the oldest recorded crimes committed by human beings. In the ancient past little distinction was made between the types of killing unless it involved a slave or a member of the aristocracy. Women were not treated differently by the law insofar as the offence of murder went, but they were often treated differently in terms of punishment. Typically, if a wife killed her husband it was viewed as petty treason and she suffered death by strangulation and then burning. If a woman committed the offence of murder within a Royal Shipyard of the English crown, she was drowned on the incoming tide. During the 17th and 18th centuries when deportation, or transportation as it was popularly called, was liberally applied to London's criminals as an alternative to the death penalty, both men and women were exported wholesale to the US and later to Australia. Women were often then sold as wives or in some instances prostitutes to the male dominant, new world populations. Transportation ended in 1868. The death penalty for women arrived in the US at the same time as the earliest settlers. Perhaps the most tragic application of the law occurred in 1786 when a female child, Hannah Ocuish, was sentenced to death for the murder of another child in Connecticut. Her tender age and questionable mental capacity did not prevent the trial judge from passing a sentence of death. Hannah was hanged on December 20, 1786 in New London. She was 12 years and 9 months old on the day of her execution. In a number of countries today, women remain subject to the death penalty for the crime of murder, and according to *deathpenalty.info* more than 40 women have received the death sentence in the US over the past 100 years. There are 58 women on death row in America today.[28] The most recent execution of a woman in the US was of Teresa Lewis who was executed by lethal injection on 23 September 2010 in Virginia. She had contracted killers for the murder of her husband and stepson. Her motive was to receive the insurance money due upon their deaths. The contract killers were both sentenced to life imprisonment.[29] Overall, however, men are more likely to receive the death penalty for murder than women. It could be argued that this situation is fundamentally unconstitutional when applied in the US, as it does not mean that the law treats men and women equally.[30] Women are also not always treated equally by the law because the law seeks to recognize that there are circumstances surrounding being a mother that are unique. Infanticide is the crime of killing children. Men or women may commit this. It is most commonly committed by a mother, but not exclusively, and there are numerous instances throughout history where children have been killed by both parents due to the child having birth defects. In some societies, female infanticide was permitted as the community valued male offspring more highly than females. Abandonment resulting in death through exposure or starvation has also been a feature of all human groups and this practice continues in the world today. In ancient Rome, mothers threw unwanted children into the Tiber in daylight, as the practice was not considered criminal. The prevalence of mothers killing their children is so common when compared with fathers killing their children that the subject has been investigated and tested numerous times by the criminal law. It would seem that the effects of childbirth might cause some mothers to struggle with the arrival of a newborn child in such a way that they resort to murder of the infant. If this occurs after the first 24 hours of life, it is referred to as infanticide. If the killing occurs during the first 24 hours of life, the murder is called neonaticide. If the killing occurs prior to the birth of the child, it is referred to in some states as fetal homicide.

Under English Common Law, if a mother kills her child within 12 months of birth and at the time her mind is disturbed due to the effects of childbirth or the effects of lactation, she is considered to be suffering from postpartum psychosis and has a valid defense to murder. The jury may then return a verdict of infanticide in place of murder. This was recognized under English law by the passing of the Infanticide Act in 1922, as amended by the 1938 Act, which held that the felony of murder might be substituted for the offence of manslaughter of the child. To succeed with the defense, it must be shown that the mother was suffering from a mental illness at the time of the killing. It is believed by a number of medical doctors that women are more likely to experience severe depression, *postpartum depression,* after giving birth than at any other time in their lives.[31] The US tends to adopt a more strict view of mothers who kill their children than most other Common Law countries, and a number of women who have killed their children soon after birth have been prosecuted for murder and not postpartum depression. The recent case of Andrea Yates, a 36-year-old Texan mother, is a case in point. Andrea Yates waited for her husband to leave for work and then systematically drowned all five of her children. She then phoned her husband and told him what she had done. The question for the criminal law of Texas was whether she had been suffering from a mental disorder at the time of the killings or was acting with a criminal state of mind. The jury found her guilty of murder but did not recommend the death penalty and she was sentenced to life imprisonment. She will be eligible for parole at the age of 77, in 2041. However, her conviction was overturned on appeal and on July 26, 2006 a new jury found Andrea Yates not guilty by reason of insanity. The defense of infanticide was not an option, as it does not exist under Texas law, and even if it did, it would only have been applicable to some of the deaths due to the advanced ages of some of the children that she killed. Andrea Yates may not be a serial killer, but she is a mass murderer. Due to the lack of distinction available to mothers who kill their children due to the effects of a uniquely female medical status, Texas Representative Jessica Farrar proposed House Bill No. 3318 in 2009 that would change Texas state law and make the defense of postpartum psychosis available in instances where mothers killed their infant children. The proposed legislation would permit jurors to find a defendant guilty of infanticide rather than murder when the mother's judgment 'was impaired as a result of the effects of giving birth or the effects of lactation following the birth'. Specifically, the proposal states, "At the punishment stage of a trial in which a defendant has been found guilty of causing the death of a child to whom the defendant gave birth within the 12-month period preceding the child's death . . ." The recommended term of imprisonment would be two years. In April 2010, Texas lawmakers approved the bill to bring the Lone Star state in line with the 29 other nations that have infanticide defenses. Prior to, and since the Andrea Yates tragedy, a number of women have claimed they have suffered from postpartum psychosis. In 1995, Susan Smith alleged her children had been stolen and then changed her story to submit the defense of postpartum psychosis killing of her two sons. She was found guilty of murder and sentenced to a minimum of 30 years imprisonment. Marybeth Tinning is currently serving 20 years to a life term of imprisonment for the murder of one of her children and the suspected murder of all nine. At a recent parole board hearing, she told the hearing that she killed her 'because she was going through a bad time'. Her appeal was denied. It is the third time she has been denied parole since 2007. Two years after Smith, Susan Eubanks shot all of her four sons. She was convicted of first-degree murder and given the death sentence. On December 20, 2011 the California State Supreme Court upheld the death sentence for Susan Eubanks.

Twenty US presidents have been subjected to attempted murder. The action of trying to assassinate them was an assault, and like many assaults some result in death and become a murder investigation but many do not. To assault a person means to attempt to commit a battery, that is, to attempt to inflict a physical injury on another person or to put that person in fear of being subjected to a physical injury. It is possible to assault somebody criminally or tortuously. If criminal then the action, the actus reus, is to cause a victim to apprehend violence. If successful, and the assailant makes contact, then the assault is now complete with a battery, that is, there has been an application of force and an injury. Commonly, a battery accompanies an assault, and therefore both are charged together. The severity of the injury sustained determines the level of charge. Aggravated assaults are those that have resulted in serious injury or that accompany other serious factors, such as assault with intent to commit rape or assault with a dangerous weapon. The lower level assaults, common assault, can be as little as a threat to hit someone. The issue is really does the threat seem real, does the victim believe the threat. If so, and if it could be carried out and result in a battery, then an assault has taken place. We typically consent to many types of touching in everyday life. We allow a degree of contact with a shopping cart, rough play with friends or children and exchanging kisses that without consent are most definitely an assault. Professional boxing is permissible due to the enactment of rules to minimize injury, but still people regularly attempt to consent to injuries that are beyond reasonable and might result in serious harm. At this point, the law steps in to protect us from ourselves so that we cannot consent to self-mutilation in the name of art or severe physical injury in the name of sexual gratification. The general rule is, would the action be deemed reasonable to the everyday person. A hug or a kiss probably; sadomasochistic rituals resulting in permanent disfigurement of the sexual organs, probably not. Tattoos, well, that is hard to say. Body jewelry, well, that too depends. A battery is the unlawful, willful and offensive touching of the person of another.[32] Under the MPC, it is when a person recklessly causes bodily injury to another, negligently causes bodily injury to another with a deadly weapon or attempts by any physical menace to put another in fear of imminent serious bodily injury. You may at this point be wondering what happens when the injury is mental. That too will be subject to discussion in this section. Under the MPC, assaults are limited to physical injuries or threats of physical injury. Assaults are generally a misdemeanor. Most states have enacted legislation that makes assault by a peace officer or assault upon a peace officer a third degree felony.

Aggravated assault is far more serious and occurs when a person attempts to cause a serious bodily injury to another, or causes a serious bodily injury purposely, knowingly, or recklessly under circumstances manifesting extreme indifference to life, or attempts to cause or purposely or knowingly cause bodily injury to another with a deadly weapon. What amounts to a deadly weapon is for the court to decide depending upon the circumstances of the case before it. It has been held, however, that human hands cannot amount to a deadly weapon even when used against a child. Many other instruments that have an everyday use could become deadly weapons if the circumstances are such that they are used in the manner of a deadly weapon. For example, a car can become a deadly weapon when driven at a person with intent to cause that person serious bodily injury. So too can rings become a deadly weapon when used in the fashion of 'knuckledusters' to inflict greater injury upon a victim than bare fists would ordinarily achieve. But it is worth remembering that in order for there to be an aggravated assault, there must be an assault. So to commit an aggravated assault that is an attempt to cause a serious injury upon another there must be an offer of force directed towards another with an apparent ability for the assailant to carry out the force. Pointing a firearm at another is such a demonstration regardless of whether or not the weapon is loaded, as the victim does not know if the weapon is loaded and therefore is put in immediate fear of violence and physical harm. One issue that has come to the attention of the courts that was not anticipated when the MPC was drafted is HIV/AIDS. Johnson Aziga gained notoriety for being the first person to be convicted of murder for having infected two women with HIV. Johnson, a Canadian citizen, knew that he had AIDS and had consensual sex with a number of women. Under Canadian law a person cannot give consent to sex if not informed by the AIDS carrying partner of the disease. In Johnson's case, he did not inform his partners and two of them died. He was charged and convicted of first-degree murder. Prior to the landmark decision in Aziga's case, another Canadian citizen had been charged with the lesser offence of aggravated assault when he too transmitted AIDS to unknowing and therefore non-consenting partners. Aziga was sentenced to 25 years imprisonment with no parole. His sentence was subsequently extended to imprisonment indefinitely, as he is deemed by Canadian law to be a 'high-risk' offender. On June 7, 2012, the New York Court of Appeals dismissed an aggravated assault conviction based upon HIV/AIDS status and remitted the case back to the trial court for resentencing. In September 2006, police arrested David Plunkett, and during the course of his arrest he bit the ear of one of the police officers. Plunkett had HIV at the time and was charged with aggravated assault upon a police officer on the basis that his saliva was a dangerous instrument. The New York Court of Appeals ruled that saliva, like other body fluids, cannot be classed as a dangerous instrument for the purposes of aggravated assault and should not be used to enhance the gravity of the offence for which a defendant is charged. In Canada, a man was recently convicted of aggravated sexual assault when he poked holes into a condom he was wearing before having sex with his girlfriend. The consensual sex was ruled non-consensual in the same way that an HIV carrying defendant cannot obtain true consent if he does not disclose he is HIV positive. On May 17, 2010, a military court in the US released an army sergeant referred to as TD who had been falsely accused of being HIV positive. Sergeant TD had been arrested for having sex with four women whilst being HIV positive. The sergeant himself signed a confession, as he too thought he was HIV. After more than 200 days in military custody, it was revealed that the tests that showed TD to be positive were faulty and legally unreliable. To the relief of TD and the victims, he has been shown to be healthy and not infected. In 1996, the state of Maryland heard the case against Dwight Smallwood[33] who was charged and convicted of attempted murder for raping three victims without using a condom while knowing that he was HIV positive at the time. Smallwood appealed on the basis that the law in Maryland was an abrogation of his First Amendment rights. The appeal court held that unprotected sex when HIV positive was not sufficient to prove an intention to kill. The example given was that unlike firing a loaded gun at a person intending to kill, unprotected sex when HIV positive did not expose the victim to the same degree of likely death as the loaded gun. Therefore, unless a specific intent to kill by HIV was proven or death by HIV was a probable consequence of the defendant's action, having unprotected sex with the knowledge that one is HIV positive was not sufficient for the court to draw an inference of intent to kill. Smallwood had pled guilty to raping three women at gunpoint. On January 23, 2012, a former professional wrestler was sentenced to 32 years' imprisonment for having sex with women and not telling them he was HIV positive at the time. Andre Davis, known professionally as 'Gansta of Love' and 'Sweet Sexy Sensation', was not convinced that he actually had HIV. However, under Ohio law if a person tests HIV positive he is required to inform sex partners of that status regardless of whether or not they are HIV-positive. Davis had tested positive and not informed his partners; therefore, the offense was complete. He was sentenced on 14 counts of felonious assault.[34]

Not all sporting assaults are of a sexual nature. In fact, most are not. Many are never prosecuted at all due to the consent given by the victim to be assaulted during the course of the sport itself. Boxing is perhaps the clearest example of this, but football, soccer, rugby and numerous other 'contact' sports also contain an element of implied consent to be touched or struck. To ensure adherence to a reasonable standard of physical conduct, individual sports have developed a series of rules. Violation of the rules during a game can result in an array of sanctions, including prosecution for criminal assault. On June 28, 1997, in the MGM Grand Arena, Las Vegas former world heavyweight boxing champion Mike Tyson bit off a part of the right ear of his opponent, Evander Holyfield, during a world title boxing match. Tyson removed his gum shield between the second and third round. Holyfield noticed that his opponent was not wearing a gum shield and attempted to inform the referee. Before he could do so, Tyson bit a chunk out of Holyfield's ear. One inch of Holyfield's ear was removed in the outburst. Doctors subsequently reattached it. The world boxing board immediately suspended Tyson. He was not prosecuted for criminal assault albeit every element of the crime was apparent. As a general rule, players cannot be prosecuted for actions that do not violate the rules of the game. Players are liable to civil and criminal prosecution when they overstep that boundary. Gregg Williams, former New Orleans defensive coordinator, was suspended indefinitely and did not appeal for his part in knocking out opponents or leaving them so injured that they needed assistance in leaving the field of play. The NFL conducted an investigation into alleged systematic violence by New Orleans that found between 22 and 27 Saints defenders had been encouraged to accept improper cash bonuses for assaulting opposing team players. The saints were fined $500,000 for orchestrating the 'pay-for-pain' system that rewarded injuries caused to opposing players by Saints defenders.[35] The 'bounty' at the Saints is a clear example of where the boundary between consensual assaults implied during a football game is converted into an outright non-consensual criminal assault. There is no reason for the criminal law not to pursue charges against the defensive coordinator, the head coach and the complicit players for conspiracy and assault. The failure of the management of the team to intervene and prevent this activity is also a potential criminal negligence action.

Removal of a body part is undoubtedly a serious criminal assault if conducted without consent, such as by surgical operation. Under the English Common Law, if a person removed the limb of another that would be useful to that person in a fight, the offence committed was called mayhem. The idea at the time was that since protecting oneself and one's family was ordinarily conducted by physical action, to remove an arm, a leg or an eye was to seriously deprive a person of a fighting chance. Over time, the law was extended to include the dismemberment of any part of the body. The MPC does not include a specific offence of mayhem, but some states do, either as a specific intent crime or one that can be committed recklessly. Under the California Penal Code, 203 and 205, mayhem is referred to as maiming and the offense is aimed at dealing with severe physical assaults where body parts are removed or significantly disfigured and there is a likely permanence sustained to the injury. Under Nevada law, mayhem is "unlawfully depriving a human being of a member of his or her body, or disfiguring or rendering it useless."[36] Apparently Mike Tyson could have been prosecuted for mayhem under Nevada state law. Under New York law there is no specific crime of mayhem and yet the most famous case of body dismemberment that has ever taken place happened to a New Yorker, but at the time of the offence the victim was in Virginia. On the night of June 23, 1993, New Yorker John Bobbitt returned home to his wife Lorena. Allegedly he had been drinking alcohol and forced his wife to have sexual intercourse with him. (John Bobbitt was subsequently tried and acquitted of raping his wife.) After the alleged sexual assault, Lorena Bobbitt went to the kitchen and took a knife. She then returned to the bedroom and cut off a piece of her husband's penis while he was asleep. She then took the piece of penis, left the house and threw the penis into a nearby field. After a search, the piece of penis was recovered, placed in ice and reattached to John Bobbit during a nine and a half hour operation. Lorena Bobbitt was found not guilty of aggravated assault due to temporary insanity caused by an irresistible impulse to sexually wound her husband. Her defense lawyer, Lisa Kimler, described her client as the "classic battered woman." "What we have is Lorena Bobbitt's life juxtaposed against John Wayne Bobbitt's penis. It was his penis from which she could not escape and . . . I submit to you that at the end of this case you will come to one conclusion: that a life is more valuable than a penis."[37]

All of the criminal assaults discussed so far have been actions that result in a physical harm—death, loss of a limb, serious physical injury or non-consensual acts, sexual and physical resulting in a tangible physical harm. But assaults are not only restricted to a visual manifestation. People can be caused serious mental distress and temporary or permanent damage by the deliberate criminal actions of others. The use of electronic networks has increased this opportunity considerably and the drafters of the MPC were not aware of the vast potential for abuse that the Internet and other social networks have to inflict injury upon each other. Digital worlds such as Second Life started to appear in the late 1990s. These alternative environments are now an extension of many people's lives and the issue for the criminal law is whether or not there is the potential to be abused in the same way that electronic platforms can facilitate credit card fraud and trafficking in child pornography. If simulated violence is applied to the virtual life of a real person, can the application of the virtual offence have a criminal impact upon the real life?[38] Much of this discussion has been prompted by virtual environments such as *LambdaMOO*, and the fine line between a virtual world and reality is now gossamer thin for the criminal law. Is it possible to prove satisfactorily that the effects of a virtual attack upon a person can lead to a physical assault resulting in perhaps depression or post-traumatic stress disorder? The National Center for Victims of Crime (NCVC) is a leading resource for advocacy for victims of crime, and it holds the view that a person can be assaulted by a virtual as well as by a real experience as either medium is capable of causing the victim stress and emotional harm. Stalking has long been recorded as an actual assault since its infancy in the UK and the US. California was the first state to criminalize stalking in 1990 and now every state in the US has anti-stalking legislation in place. The NCVC has proposed that "virtually any unwanted contact between two people that directly or indirectly communicates a threat or places the victim in fear can be considered stalking." The topic of stalking gained some notoriety after students stalked an English university professor. As a result of this, the term became commonly accepted as a means to explain unwanted contact that could lead to emotional distress. The movie *Fatal Attraction* then added to our vocabulary so that now a female lover who pursues her male partner after the relationship has ended is sometimes referred to as a 'Bunny Boiler'. It is now recognized that it is possible to cause an assault without the application of physical force in the traditional sense of the word. The Internet is a vehicle through which numerous people have been harassed and stalked and the distinction between a real and virtual assault may soon become a figure of historical speech as more and more victims of assault are pursued by their attackers through the use of technology. Under Texas law, the Stalking by Electronic Communications Act 2001, use of the Internet to cause 'substantial emotional distress' is a criminal offence liable to up to 5 years of imprisonment. One of the supporters of the legislation, Senator Kay Bailey Hutchison, has herself been stalked for more than 15 years and has direct knowledge of the pain and suffering these unwanted and violent verbal attacks can be. Section 1, Chapter 33, states that "A person commits an offence if the person uses the name or persona of another person to create a web page on or to post one or more messages on a commercial social networking site: without obtaining the other person's consent; and with intent to harm, defraud, intimidate, or threaten any person." The offence is a felony in the third degree. Under Sec. 42.07, "A person commits an offense if, with intent to harass, annoy, alarm, abuse, torment, or embarrass another, he: initiates communication by telephone, in writing, or by electronic communication and in the course of the communication make a comment, request, suggestion, or proposal that is obscene; …" Silent phone calls are also captured by these provisions, as are blasting emails or any other form of communication whatsoever. This legislation is similar in spirit and form to the English Common Law that since 1994 has recognized that a psychiatric injury can be an assault for the purposes of the criminal law.[39]

Assaults are complex crimes that can vary enormously in terms of injury sustained. In general, violent assaults against women are more likely to be reported than those committed against men regardless of whether the offender is male or female. Simple assault is the most common form of assault committed, but even these are underreported. The total number of assaults reported across the US declined between 2008 and 2009, and the general trend is towards a convergence of violent crime rates with men and women now both being victimized at similar rates.[40] The age of victims of violent crime has decreased; those aged 12 to 15 are more likely to be victims of violent crime than persons aged 16 years and up. Women remain five times more likely to be victims of violent partner crime than men.[41] The law has matured over time to accommodate new forms of assault that were not envisaged when the MPC was written, so that today all states in the US have anti-stalking laws in place and many states have specific legislation to deal with physical and mental assaults that are caused through social networks and cyberspace. The tragic suicide of teenager Megan Meier in Missouri in 2006 is a clear reminder of the damage that can be caused through vicious and unwarranted emails and cyber bullying. There is hardly a day that goes by without a spousal, partner or child abuse case reported where the mental injury sustained by the victim has not had long term and life altering effects. The distinction between physical and mental assault is clearly narrowing. In part this is due to the propensity of offenders to utilize the Internet and other electronic devices to perpetrate their fear and intimidation. It is also an awakening of the criminal law to the fact that it is perfectly possible to cause an assault upon another person without saying a word, by using phone, email or chat room. Recognition of this delicate and growing area of criminal law has been reconfirmed recently in the Violence Against Women Reauthorization Act 2005 and the established cases at Common Law. However, it is important to have continuing recognition that the nexus between assault and spousal and partner abuse, or cyber bullying and abusive networking, is not limited to dominant males who abuse females, but that this is an area of criminality where males too are abused but are extremely reticent in reporting the matter.

We started this chapter discussing what it means to be a human and how we can criminally terminate the human existence. The ability of the human species to inflict grotesque pain and suffering upon each other that leads to an unnatural cessation of life appears, regrettably, to be endless. Our collective societal response has been to treat homicide as the most serious offence in the entire suite of crimes that a person can commit. Our array of punishments has at times been almost equal to the dexterity displayed by the murderers themselves, and public executions followed by mutilations have been commonplace throughout history and up to recent times. Whether the ultimate sanction of taking a life for a life should be applied is still open to debate, but over time we have attempted to modify the punishment for murder to reflect the sophistication and reasoning that a developed society is capable of displaying. Assaults that do not end in death are the next level of most serious crime an offender can commit. Serious assaults are most easily recognizable, as they result in the loss of limbs or in permanent long-term injury to the victim. For many years, the law was not capable of recognizing that, apart from physical injuries, the human being can sustain deep and devastating mental injuries that can impact the quality of the life of the victim as much as, if not more so, than a serious physical attack. This situation has now been rectified in most countries and mental anguish amounting to a measurable injury is now viewed as a criminal assault. Fortunately though, murder and serious assaults are a relative rarity, and it is the unwarranted minor assault that is most prevalent. Common assaults are a frequent occurrence across many societies and can be as minor as being the recipient of unwarranted affection or as extensive as a systematic and orchestrated method of securing professional sport victory by deliberately incapacitating the opposition. The advent of mass electronic communication has now brought a new dialog to the criminal justice table, and we are slowly making sense of what it may mean to be assaulted in a virtual world or emotionally assaulted by a cyber-stalker. Eventually, though, the taking of another person's life will always be deemed the most serious offence and consequently it will always attract the most lurid, morbid and uncomfortable interest.

Most hate to admit this but murder is fascinating so long as we are not the victim and the more grotesque and fantastic the killing the greater our contemptible interest appears to be. I will conclude this chapter by two graphic reminders. You may end your reading at this point and not engage in curious fascination with the bizarre. I very much doubt you will stop reading now though.

Edward Theodore Gein is perhaps the most famous gruesome serial killer of recent history. He was a murderer and a body snatcher who did all of the things that were subsequently made famous by Sir Anthony Hopkins in his role as Hannibal Lecter. Gein dug up bodies from the local graveyard and removed the flesh to make trophies and skin artifacts. He even fashioned human flesh so that he could assume the body of a woman. Although he probably killed just two women, Gein is the archetypal perverted killer who had every conceivable relationship with corpses that one can imagine and even not imagine. After his arrest in 1957, he was to become known as 'the Mad Butcher' and the 'Plainfield Ghoul'. The movies *Psycho, Leatherface, Texas Chainsaw Massacre* and *Silence of the Lambs* are all based in part upon Ed Gein. On November 16, 1957, he kidnapped and murdered a woman from Plainfield, Wisconsin. When his address was searched, the searchers found the deceased decapitated and hung upside down by the wrists. She had been severely mutilated after death. During his interviews with the police, Gein admitted stealing more than nine bodies from a local graveyard; he had then tanned the bodies to make a female body suit that he wore around the house. He denied having sex with the exhumed bodies due to the stench of the rotting corpses. Gein was found to be sane and therefore eligible to stand trial for the murders of three women. He was found guilty but legally insane and ordered detained for life in a mental institution. Gein died in prison in 1984 at the age of 77.[42]

Dennis Andrew Nilsen is a killer and necrophiliac who murdered 15 men in London over the course of 5 years between 1978 and 1983. Nilsen lured his victims to his house on the pretext of giving them food or drugs and financial assistance and then strangled or drowned them during the course of the evening. He then kept the bodies for varying periods of time to keep him company around the flat. Some were placed in the sitting position on a couch and others became his dead homosexual bed partners. Eventually he dissected the corpses and burned the body parts or flushed them down the lavatory. He was convicted of six counts of murder and two attempted murders at the Central Criminal Court, the Old Bailey, in November 1983. He pleaded diminished responsibility in an attempt to have the charges reduced to manslaughter. His plea was not accepted. He is currently serving life imprisonment[43] and recently wrote a complaining letter that his prison salary was insufficient for him to retire on.[44]

The following chapter will discuss the criminal offences of kidnapping and abduction. Many of the crimes discussed in this chapter are linked to kidnapping and abduction, particularly when the offender unfortunately murders the victim to avoid detection. In those instances where the victim is not murdered, there is a range of criminal assaults that typically take place during the course of the illegal moving of the victim. These range from simple assault to serious, as the offender violates the privacy of the victim, a very common trait among the broad classification of 'crimes against the person'.

Endnotes

1. United Nations Office on Drugs and Crime
2. See further Homicide rates: Murder most foul. *The Economist.* October 6, 2011. At www.economist.com
3. Ibid.
4. Ibid.
5. "Top murder rates in the world." www.worldnews.about.com
6. UNODC Global Study on Homicide
7. Suicide is still an offence at canon law as the ecclesiastical view is that assisting in taking a life is a crime against God.
8. On February 23, 1885, John Henry Lee survived the hangman's trap door three times on the same day. He was released and sentenced to life imprisonment.
9. William Duell 'woke up' on the surgeon's table after being hanged at Tyburn in 1740 and John Smith was hanged on December 24, 1705, at Tyburn. After 15 minutes he was cut down and later made a full recovery. In 1630 Anne Green was on the dissection table and the surgeons had commenced opening her up when she started to breathe. Anne went on to make a full recovery, married and had three children. It was not until the invention of the 'trap door' that the method of death was breaking the neck rather than strangulation. There are no recorded instances of a person surviving the fall from the trap door execution method. The 'Long Drop' method was introduced in 1865.
10. See further the case of John Jones, father of a 10-month-old child who was injured while in his care and then removed from life support. Jones was charged with murder on July 23, 2010, in Akron, Ohio. Jones was 17 years of age at the time of the alleged killing.
11. It was replaced in 1967 by the new New York Penal Law.

12. Voluntary manslaughter may also include suicide pacts and so too may involuntary manslaughter under the egis of assisted suicide.
13. One reason for this was due to the fact that the English were secretly assassinating a large number of Norman nobles and the implementation of heavy fines was viewed as one way to curb the practice.
14. Spierenburg, P. *A history of murder: Personal violence in Europe from the Middle Ages to the present.* Cambridge: Polity Press; 2008, 15.
15. Spierenburg. Supra, p. 16
16. Charter to William Penn and the Laws of the Province of Pennsylvania passed between the years 1682 and 1700, p. 84 (Commonwealth of Pennsylvania 1879) cited in Keedy, ER, History of the Pennsylvania statute creating degrees of murder, *University of Pennsylvania Law Review*, 97(6) (May, 1949) pp. 759–777 at p. 760
17. Selsam, *Brissot de Warville on the Pennsylvania Constitution of 1776*, 72 PA magazine of history and biography. 1948; 25,40 cited in Keedy, supra, at p. 767.
18. See further, Chris Grover and Keith Soothill, British serial killing: Towards a structural explanation. *The British Criminology Conferences: Selected Proceedings.* March 1999, Vol. 2.
19. Mass murder may, and often does, include the acts of Genocide and Crimes Against Humanity.
20. A Persian leader named al-Hassan did exist and lead a group known as the Ismallians around 1090, but the exact details are rather confusing as the first record of this man and his followers was recorded by Marco Polo some 150 years later.
21. Abraham Lincoln, James A. Garfield, William McKinley and John F. Kennedy
22. Class D felony. Enacted under Code Title 18, section 871, 1917. As amended. The prison sentence range has now been increased to be 5 to 10 years and the fine is now up to $250,000.
23. *Macbeth.* Act 1. Scene 7, 1–7
24. See further, Duncan Campbell, 638 ways to kill Castro, *The Guardian,* Thursday, August 3, 2006; at www.guardian.co.uk
25. See: Article 23 (b) Hague Convention IV, October 18, 1907.
26. President George Bush, September 11, 2001.
27. See further: Louis Rene Beres. Assassination and the law: A policy memorandum, *Studies in Conflict and Terrorism.* Vol. 18. 1995. pp. 299–315.
28. www.deathpenaltyinfo.org
29. Ibid.
30. Which would abrogate the provisions of the 14th Amendment
31. Marc Nesca and J. Thomas Dalby, Maternal neonaticide following traumatic childbirth: A case study. *International Journal of Offender Therapy and Comparative Criminology.* 2001; 55 (7), 1166–1178.

32. Harvey Wallace and Clifford Robertson, *Principles of criminal law.* 2nd ed. Needham Heights, MS: Allen & Bacon, 2001, p. 180.
33. Smallwood v State 680 A. 2d 512 (Md. 1996)
34. www.dailymail.co.uk
35. Mortensen, C. and Schefter, A. *NFL denies Saints appeals,* ESPN.com news services. www.espn.go.com/nfl/story
36. NRS 200.280. Examples include cutting or removing the tongue or eye, biting off a portion of the ear, nose or lip and cutting off or disabling any limb.
37. *The Los Angeles Times,* 11 January 1994. www.latimes.com
38. See further, Does virtual reality need a sheriff? Alan Sipress, *Washington Post,* Saturday, June 2, 2007. www.washingtonpost.com
39. R v Chan Fook. 1994.
40. Rand, M. and Truman, J. *National crime victimization survey; Criminal victimization,* 2009. US Department of Justice Office of Justice Programs Bureau of Justice Statistics Bulletin. www.bjs.ojp.usdoj.gov
41. Ibid.
42. See further www.biography.com
43. See further www.biography.com
44. www.dailyrecord.co.uk. "Serial killer Dennis Nilsen bleats: I won't be able to retire on £9.60 per week prison wages."

KIDNAPPING AND ABDUCTION

Kidnapping is a serious crime that involves an assault or a threat of violence, and it is carried out by the forcible removal of a person from one location to another or by preventing a person from moving from one location to another. There are invariably threats of violence as well as actual violence applied to the victim. The nature of the violence may be physical; in addition, it is undoubtedly mental for the entire duration of the ordeal for the victim. Kidnapping is frequently associated with sexual assault as well. In many instances the regrettable outcome is also murder, as their aggressors eventually murder a number of kidnapped victims in an attempt to prevent detection. So kidnapping is a very serious crime that captures numerous other offences against the person during the event. Perhaps surprisingly though, kidnapping was deemed a

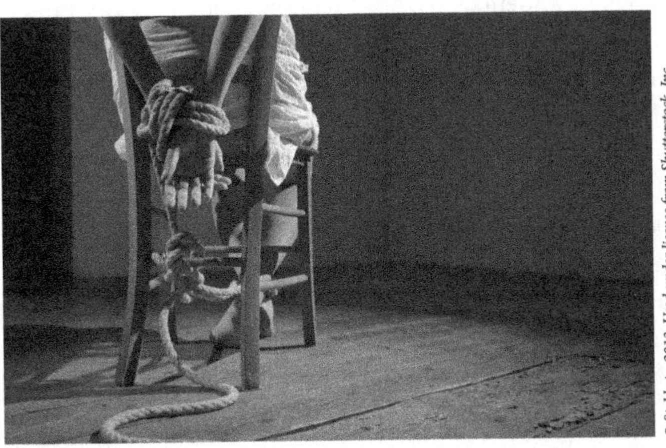

misdemeanor for centuries if it involved stealing women and children. The difference between kidnapping and abduction is the fraud committed by the aggressor, but in reality the words are frequently used interchangeably. In cases of kidnapping, the removal of the victim is completed by force. In cases of abduction, the victim willingly agrees to accompany the aggressor. In kidnapping cases, the victim is forcibly taken from one location to another or forcibly prevented from leaving a location. In both cases of kidnapping and abduction there may then be a demand for a cash payment in return for the victim—a ransom—or there may be forced or coerced sexual assaults inflicted upon the victim by the abductor/kidnapper. Kidnapping and abduction involve an invasion of the privacy of the victims as their liberty is taken away from them. The vast majority of abductions that take place are when a known aggressor fraudulently convinces the victim to accompany them. The number of stranger abductions or kidnappings per year is very few. For example, the rate of children abducted each year in the US is about 69,000 of which family members account for 82% of these illegal abductions. Of the remaining non-family abductions, 37% are by complete strangers.[1] The victim is returned home unharmed in 99.8% of child abduction cases. Of those that are not returned home, 76% are murdered within 3 hours of the abduction or kidnapping and the primary motive for the child stealing is sexual assault. In terms of kidnapping adults, it is very difficult to obtain accurate statistics as most kidnappings are recorded as missing persons until there is evidence of a crime. There are in the region of 2,300 recorded missing persons per day in the US.[2] According to *Business Horizons,* the US ranks sixth in the world in the number of adult 'for ransom' kidnappings that take place each year. A recent upsurge in kidnappings in Phoenix, Arizona has now made that city rank second in the world after Mexico City for the total number of abduction/kidnappings per annum.[3] The original concept of taking a woman or child against their will is no longer classified as such largely since the famous child stealing case involving the son of captain Charles Lindbergh in America during the 1930s. Since that time there are federal and state statutes that now treat most abduction and forced kidnapping as a serious criminal offence.

The origin of the word kidnap is probably located in the Common Law of England where 'kid' was a slang term for a 'child' and to 'nap' meant to steal or reduce. For example, one could 'nap' a coin to reduce the actual size of the coin and use the shavings to illegally manufacture new coins. According to a number of sources, the first recorded use of the term 'kidnap' was not in England but colonial America in 1678[4] when it was utilized to describe carrying off children or indentured servants by force to work in plantations.[5] The first recorded offence of kidnapping for ransom in the US occurred on July 1, 1874, when two boys were abducted from outside their home in Germantown, Pennsylvania. The kidnappers sent the parents of Charley and Walter Ross a ransom note two days after the forced abduction demanding $20,000. Walter was released but Charley never was, and the kidnappers murdered him despite Mr. Ross spending $60,000 searching for his son. The surviving brother, Walter, died in 1943.[6] Over time there has been a general use of the terms abduction and kidnapping to describe the taking of a person from one location to another against that person's will, or willingly but due to deceit or fraud. There are, however, distinctions for the purposes of the criminal law at the state, federal and international levels. At the federal level, an offender may commit simple kidnapping or aggravated kidnapping. Parental kidnapping is a separate offence. The California cases of People v Hyatt,[7] People v Moore[8] and Wilborn v Superior Court of Humboldt County[9] are all relevant to a discussion about parental kidnapping and why it has been deemed necessary to distinguish this specific offense in many states. Additionally, a number of states have defined specific types of kidnapping further in response to contemporary crimes, such as kidnapping during a carjacking or extortion by posing as a kidnapper. The California Parental Kidnapping Prevention Act became law in 1980. It was written to "prevent jurisdictional conflict and competition over child custody and, in particular, to deter parents from abducting children for the purpose of obtaining custody awards."[10] What this legislation achieves is jurisdiction of the issue for the state in which the victim lived for at least 6 months prior to the offence being committed. Even if a parent moves a child to a new state, the original state may still have jurisdiction or concurrent jurisdiction if in the best interests of the child. In common with California, many states have now sought to broaden the reach of kidnapping laws when the victim is a child and the aggressor a legal custodian.

18 USC. 1201 defines kidnapping as "whoever unlawfully seizes, confines, inveigles, decoys, kidnaps, abducts, or carries away and holds for ransom or reward or otherwise any person, except in the case of a minor by the parent thereof, when the person is willfully transported in interstate or foreign commerce, regardless of whether the person was alive when transported . . . shall be punished by imprisonment for any term or years or life and, if the death of any person results, shall be punished by death or life imprisonment." Special rules apply that provide the term of imprisonment

shall be not less than 20 years with regard to the kidnapping of children if the child is under 18 years of age and the person committing the illegal removal is not the parent, grandparent, brother, sister, aunt, uncle or a person with legal custody of the child. Under the MPC, kidnapping occurs when any person is unlawfully and non-consensually asported and held against their will. The meaning of 'asportation' is to move a person from one place to another under force or fraud; the amount of movement may be very slight, such as from one room to another. In the case of 'the red light bandit' Caryl Chessman, he forced his victims at gunpoint to move from their vehicle to his, a distance of a few feet, but this was still considered to be a kidnapping.

The period of Chessman's crimes was brief. Over a three-week period in January 1948 he committed a series of robberies, car thefts and kidnappings. The kidnappings involved Chessman approaching two women on separate occasions in a 'Lovers lane' area, forcing the women from their cars at gunpoint and then making then perform oral sex on him in his car that was parked nearby. On January 23, 1948, he led the police on a five-mile car chase. He was arrested and subsequently admitted the crimes. He was convicted of 17 felonies, including kidnapping the two women. He alleged that there had been no asportation, but the trial court ruled even the 20 feet that he forced them to take was sufficient to meet the law of kidnapping. He received the death sentence for the capital crime of kidnapping as it applied at the time. It can also amount to a kidnapping if a defendant prevents a person from moving, for example, where there is an unlawful detention of a person. In the case of children, a person can restrict a child's movements by preventing her from going home, without making any demands upon the child, and this can still amount to a kidnapping. Adult false imprisonments are rarely treated this severely, and a number of jurisdictions will treat these as a misdemeanor. Those instances where there is a demand for a ransom or there is a degree of physical assault will ordinarily amount to a charge of aggravated kidnapping. The condition for an asportation is not required in all states, and in some—for example, New York—it is the intention of the defendant that matters not whether or not there is a removal, to the slightest degree, of the victim. A challenge for a number of cases of kidnapping is double jeopardy. The 5th Amendment prohibits multiple punishments for the same crime and most kidnappings involve numerous other crimes, so the question becomes: Is it two crimes or one when a defendant forces a victim to move from one room to another to then sexually assault the person? Is there a crime of rape and a separate crime of kidnapping? There is no one answer to this, as some states have written their kidnapping laws to provide for a need to prove an asportation and others[11] have not and have stated distance is not a factor; it is the restraining of a person that makes the crime complete. The legal dilemma remains for some states though, as a strict interpretation of USC 18 1201 questions whether a person can be convicted for one offence of kidnapping as well as for a second, related offence of a separate crime of violence. If the second offence was incidental, then presumably only the kidnapping is charged. In a 2001 case, a man was charged with second-degree murder after he and a friend beat a 16-year-old female who refused to perform a sexual act on the defendant's friend after she had accompanied them willingly in their car. The victim was beaten unconscious and then driven in that state for some time before being dumped from the defendant's car. At the time she was thrown from the vehicle she was silent, but it was not known by the defendant if she was dead or not. The defendant was convicted of kidnapping and a second charge of second degree murder. He appealed his conviction on the basis that she initially entered the car willingly and then once unconscious she could not formulate a will about being taken for a drive until she was thrown from the vehicle; therefore, this period of time was not 'against her will'. In other words, her confinement prior to her death was a part of the death and not a separate offence. The US Tenth Circuit Appeal Court agreed. She was transported against her will as a murder victim who may or may not have been dead at the time of the movement and therefore this movement was an intrinsic part of the murder and not a separate offence.[12]

Apart from abductions and kidnapping associated with family members who steal children for custody or relationship revenge reasons, most other kidnappings are for sexual exploitation or ransom. In ransom cases, it is a federal crime to receive, possess or dispose of any money or other property, or any portion thereof, which has at any time been delivered as ransom or reward in connection with a violation of section 1201 of this title, knowing the same to be money or property which has been at any time delivered as such ransom or reward, shall be fined under this title or imprisoned not more than ten years, or both.[13] Any person who assists in transporting, transmitting or transferring such funds also commits an offense liable to a fine and/or 10 years of imprisonment. Taking people as a means of obtaining money has a long history and was prevalent throughout medieval Europe when opposing countries took soldiers and held them until a cash reward was paid for their safe return; the more important the captured person, the greater the ransom money that could be claimed. In some instances, kings and princes were held for years while teams of negotiators worked out the details of their return and the payment sums. In 858, a fortune was paid for the return of Abbot Louis of St. Dennis when his brother managed to amass 686 pounds of gold and 3,250 pounds of silver for the safe return of his brother.[14] The English court of chivalry was the forerunner to the contemporary courts martial and it had a specific role as the body that took responsibility for negotiating ransoms. King John II of France was unable to raise the ransom money requested for him by the English after the French defeat at Poitiers,[15] so he was allowed to return to France and make a personal plea. The country did not respond and, being a man of honor, he resubmitted himself to the custody of the English while alternative arrangements were made. He spent many years as a captive in the Tower of London, but as was appropriate to his status, he was allowed to hold his own court while prisoner and have a number of luxuries that most prisoners would not be permitted. His ransom sum was 4 million crowns, a fortune in 14th century Europe. King John's ransom was never paid and he remained in custody in England for the rest of his life. Alongside King John, Arnoul d'Audrehem, a marshal of the French army, and one of the military advisers to John II, was also taken captive at Poitiers. He too never paid the ransom but was released and went on to fight the English again, this time Edward, the Black Prince,[16] in 1367 at Navarette, Spain.

Abductions for the purpose of marriage have featured in numerous societies and are an integral part of many honor-based cultures. Under Roman law, the idea of taking away a female from her father, even with the female's consent, was *raptus,* and the person leading the girl away was viewed as an 'abductor' regardless of whether he used deceiving words or physical coercion to achieve the crime. By 1574, Venetian law included abduction as a crime alongside murder, rape, arson and various property offences. Also during this time, the Catholic Church investigated the position of canon law with regard to the potential validity of any subsequent marriage in instances where the abductee had been sexually violated. The staining of a woman's honor was a very serious matter in the Middle and Late Middle Ages, and in many cases, regardless of whether or not the abduction was consensual or not, a marriage quickly followed. Returning the victim to her family was not a viable option and the church would frequently take the role of mediator between the victim's family and the aggressors. If the matter were to make its way to a secular court, then charges of rape would most likely have been pursued, as the lesser crime of woman and child stealing was still rarely brought before the secular criminal tribunal.[17] Abduction of male and female children, as well as of adult females for sexual exploitation, was also not uncommon throughout the eastern European and Middle Eastern empires of the 15th and 16th centuries. Victims were often subsequently traded as a commodity, as their dishonored status made it virtually impossible for them to return to a previous family and exist in a manner similar to that before the violation. There are some extreme examples of the manner in which these offences were conducted and how the aggressors were dealt with in the Ottoman Empire. There the act of kidnapping for sexual exploitation was viewed as a crime against the sultan himself, as the victims taken were his property. For example, by 1540 the sentence for a person convicted of abduction and sexual exploitation was castration. Notwithstanding the possible sentence for aggressors, the ultimate humiliation that one leader could inflict upon another was the defilement of that conquered leader's wife and family. Under Bayezid II, "A person who abducts a girl or boy, or who enters a dwelling with subversive intent [to abduct], or who comes [on a raid] to abduct a woman or girl will have his penis cut off."[18] Between the 16th and 19th centuries, Muslim pirates (and some exiled Europeans) along the north African 'Barbary' Coast took numerous Europeans captive as kidnapping and the slave trade became a staple source of revenue for the loosely affiliated bands of renegades and privateers. One of the most spectacular and devastating mass kidnappings took place by a European Barbary pirate, Jan Janszoon van Haarlem, otherwise known as Murat (Murad, Morat) Reis the Younger, in Baltimore, Ireland in 1621. Murat Reis had himself been a captive of Barbary pirates and then joined them. On June 20, 1631, he stormed the west Irish coastal town of Baltimore and kidnapped 108 of its citizens. All but two of them died in slavery or forced prostitution. Although the majority of the victims from the 'Sack of Baltimore' were sold, two women, Joanne Broadbrook and Ellen Hawkins, were ransomed a number of years later and released. Murat also kidnapped a large number of people from Reykjavik, Iceland, in 1626, but this time 27 were released upon payment of a ransom 11 years later. Murat himself then became a victim of his own criminality and was captured in 1635 and held for ransom on the Mediterranean island of Malta. Some sources say he escaped while others say he paid an enormous ransom. Either way, he was free once again around 1640. The situation around the region of the world known as the Barbary Coast was troubled for centuries largely due to the lack of a single ruler, but rather more because of a series of despots.

Britain and France had a troubled relationship with many of the pirates in the region and this spilled over into war by 1801—not with Britain but with the US. Jefferson was inaugurated in January 1801 and was immediately met with a demand for the equivalent of $10 million ($225,000), as well as an annual payment of $25,000 from one of the rulers in the Barbary region, to ensure that American merchant ships received safe passage in the area. Jefferson refused and the Pasha of Tripoli, Yussif Karamanil, declared war. Although the US ultimately won the first of the Barbary Wars, during the conflict William Bainbridge and all the officers and crew of the *USS Philadelphia* were captured and held for ransom for the sum of $60,000.[19]

A more recent and far more spectacular ransom event took place in 1971 when a man kidnapped a plane and its passengers and demanded $200,000 in ransom. He was paid, escaped and remains on the FBI wanted list. Hostage taking and hijacking have become such regrettably familiar events that both are now subject to specific individual legislation to capture a difference between the taking of people against their will and the taking of a vehicle such as a plane. In hijacking cases, it is possible to steal a vehicle without people, whereas it is not possible to kidnap a boat or a plane. That said, most hijacking cases involve kidnapping also, as there are passengers and crew that are being prevented from doing what they want to do or are being diverted from a destination to another that is not of their choice. On November 24, 1971, a man who called himself Dan Cooper purchased a one-way airline ticket at Portland International Airport for a 30-minute Northwest Airlines flight to Seattle. Once in flight, he handed a stewardess a note that informed her he had a bomb in his briefcase. His direction was that the flight should land in Seattle and the crew should remain on board. His demand was for $200,000 to be delivered to the plane, and four parachutes. After a two hour delay while the FBI arranged for the money and parachutes the plane landed and the 36 passengers were released. Ten thousand unmarked $20 bills were placed on board as along with the parachutes. Mr. Cooper then ordered the pilot to head for Cuba. At 7.45 P.M. the plane took off with Cooper, two pilots, one stewardess and an engineer on board. All the crew was kept inside the cockpit. At 8.13 P.M. the crew experienced a significant uplift in the motion of the plane and it is believed that at this time Cooper opened the rear exit and departed. The plane landed at 10.15 P.M. with the rear exit still open. Cooper was not on board. A subsequent re-creation of the parachute jump was enacted by the same crew and the FBI to confirm that it was possible for Cooper to have departed the flight in the manner supposed. This trial was successful and the investigators are now sure that Cooper parachuted out of the plane at 8.13 P.M. Despite an extensive search of the landing area by the FBI and army personnel, no evidence of the landing has ever been found. Cooper has never been legally identified or located and he remains wanted today. The serial numbers of the $20 bills were circulated in 1972 and are still subject to an individual reward of $1,000 per bill if found. A portion of the ransom money was found by a young boy along the banks of the Columbia River in Washington in 1980. Over the course of 1972, fifteen copycat hijackings were attempted. On December 5, 2001, the *Daily Mail* reported that a woman named Maria Cooper had informed the press that her uncle Lynn Doyle Cooper had been seen the day after the 1971 hijacking incident and at the time he had serious bodily injuries. Mr. Cooper's niece never saw her uncle again after the Thanksgiving visit to her home, but she did tell reporters that he had died in 1999.[20] In 1973, the grandson of oil billionaire J. Paul Getty was held for 5 months. He was released upon payment of a $3.2 million ransom after the kidnappers famously removed a piece of the victim's ear. The original amount requested was $17 million for the safe return of 16-year-old John Paul Getty III. The victim was seriously affected by the event and took to abusing drugs soon after his release. He had a stroke in 1981, induced by drug abuse, and was left speechless, partially blind and semi-paralyzed. He died on February 5, 2011, aged 54. By the 1990s, kidnapping the children of wealthy business people was occurring across the world. In Taiwan, an unusual kidnapping and murder case occurred when the 17-year-old daughter of a Taiwanese television show host, Pai Ping-ping, was abducted after leaving her home for school on April 14, 1997. All kidnappings in Taiwan are subject to the death penalty, and this raises issues immediately with regard to whether or not there is ever any point in a criminal saving the life of a victim if the sentence will be the death penalty regardless. In the case of Pai Hsiao-yen, she was regrettably murdered soon after the kidnapping and her body was found weighted down in a drainage culvert 11 days after the abduction. She had been brutally murdered and tortured prior to death. Soon after Pai was taken, her kidnappers contacted her parents and demanded $5 million. They included a piece of Pai's finger along with the ransom note. After 11 days of intense negotiations, the police identified the kidnapper's location, but by this time the body of the victim had been recovered so a police raid would not jeopardize the victim's safety. During a dramatic raid one suspect was arrested but three others escaped after a gun battle with police. Some months later, the suspects were seen and a further gun battle took place. During the shootings one police officer was killed and one of the suspects, Lin Chun-sheng, committed suicide by shooting himself at the scene. The remaining two suspects then escaped, and in October 1997 they shot and killed a plastic surgeon and two nurses after forcing them to conduct plastic surgery on them to change their appearance. Shortly after this incident, police saw Chen Chin-seng and Kao Tien-min again, and Kao also committed suicide in front of them. Chen escaped, and on November 19, 1997, he forced entry into the home of the South African military attaché to Taiwan, E. G. 'Mac' Alexander, and held him, his wife and their two children hostage.[21] At one point, the police attempted to storm the house, and for more than one hour gunfire was exchanged. During this time Mr. Alexander and a daughter were injured. The kidnapper then made a series of announcements to the press, including a live broadcast in which he admitted committing the kidnapping and murder of Pai Hsiao-yen. The ordeal lasted for more than 20 hours. Due to their injuries, Mr. Alexander and his daughter were released first. Eventually Mrs. Alexander and the other child were also freed. The entire event was captured live on Taipei television. Chen Jhin-Hsing was arrested and convicted of numerous criminal offences, including the kidnapping and murder of Pai. He received three death sentences and was executed by firing squad at 9.30 P.M. on October 6, 1999.[22] Chen donated his body organs to patients in need.

Although the crime preceded the events of Chen by some 20 years, the kidnapping of Patricia Campbell Hearst in California is as strange and bizarre as the notorious Taiwanese kidnapping. About 9 P.M. on February 4, 1974, nineteen-year-old Patty Hearst answered the door to her apartment in Berkeley, California. Two men and one woman forced their way in and kidnapped Patty. The attackers were members of the Symbionese Liberation Army, SLA. The group leader was a man known as Donald Defreeze[23] who sought the overthrow of government and a more equal society. The kidnap victim was the granddaughter of the millionaire newspaper owner, Randolph Hearst. Very soon requests were made for food drops to be made to donation centers and various amounts of cash were demanded for Patty's release. The food donations were then manipulated by a number of criminal organizations and some food was stolen and then sold on the black market at inflated prices. Patty's father insisted on his daughter's safe return or otherwise the food drops would cease. Communication between the SLA and Patty's family ended. At this point an unusual turn of events occurred, and the SLA started to brainwash their victim to accept and then support their terrorist views—an overthrow of the US government. On

April 3, 1974, the SLA released a video of Patty Hearst in which she claimed to have joined the SLA and supported their aims. In the video, she was seen carrying a carbine rifle and she had changed her name to 'Tania' (after the name of Che Guevara's girlfriend). Soon after this, she was seen on CCTV participating in the armed robbery of a California bank. Ten thousand dollars were stolen and two bystanders were injured during the robbery. On May 16, 1974, two SLA members were followed to a safe house after having bungled an attempt to steal ammunition from a Los Angeles store. At the house, a lengthy shoot-out with police ensued and the safe house ended up catching on fire, killing the six SLA occupants. Patty Hearst was not inside the house at the time, but knowing of the events, she went on the run across California. On September 18, 1975, Patty Hearst was captured and charged with bank robbery. She claimed that she had been brainwashed. The trial jury did not accept this, and she was convicted and sentenced to seven years imprisonment. She served two years, as President Carter commuted her sentence. Subsequently she was pardoned. The remaining members of the SLA were also finally captured and the band was ineffective as of 2002.[24]

In California, the laws relating to kidnapping state that under Penal Code 207[25] it is an offence for a person to "move another person a substantial distance without that person's consent by using force or fear." It becomes an aggravated offence if the "victim is under 14 years of age, accompanying the kidnapping is a ransom demand, the victim suffers serious bodily harm or death, the offence is committed in the process of a carjacking." Aggravated kidnapping, Code 209, carries a life imprisonment term. Simple kidnapping is a felony and subject to 8 years of imprisonment in a California state prison. Under California Penal Code 210, there is an offence of "Posing as a Kidnapper." The offence is committed when a person pretends to be a kidnapper or pretends to have some ability to obtain the release of a kidnapped person for the purpose of extorting money or something else of value. In the state of California, parental kidnapping is known as a 'wobbler' crime because it can be charged either way, as a misdemeanor or a felony crime. Child abduction laws in California prohibit stealing a child. This occurs when a child is taken away from its parent or legal guardian. Child stealing is considered an offence against the rights of the parent. It is very closely linked to the general kidnapping laws within the state.

Under Texas state law, Title 5 deals with offenses against the person, and these include kidnappings, unlawful restraint of a person and smuggling of persons. Under Section 20.01, a restraint means to restrict a person's movements either by moving them from one place to another or to prevent them from moving. There is no requirement for there to be a specific distance moved or a time limit upon the restraint of the victim. If the victim is under 14 years of age, it is not material that a force, intimidation or deception occurred, as clearly a very young child may not even know if moved or restrained from movement. If the victim is between the ages of 14 and 17, then there is a specific offense if they are taken outside of the state and outside a 120-mile radius of the victim's home and the legal guardian has not authorized the movement. It is an affirmative defense if the victim is older than 14 but less than 17 years of age, no force, intimidation or deception is used and the actor is no more than 3 years older than the victim.[26] Under Texas law, the offense of Aggravated Kidnapping includes using a person as a shield. Sec. 20(4) states that a person commits an offense if he intentionally or knowingly abducts another person with intent to: hold him for ransom or reward, use him as a shield or hostage, facilitate the commission of a felony or the flight after the attempt or commission of a felony, inflict bodily injury on him or violate or abuse him sexually, terrorize him or a third person or interfere with the performance of any governmental or political function. These are extremely inclusive terms and extend the law of aggravated kidnapping into areas that some state, federal and international laws have determined to be individual though not mutually exclusive crimes. These crimes are a felony in the first degree but may be reduced to a second degree if the defendant voluntarily released the victim to a safe place.[27] Any person also commits a criminal offense that for financial gain transports an individual to conceal that person from enforcement authorities and in doing so creates a substantial risk of serious bodily injury or death to the victim.[28] If the victim of any of the offenses outlined above is sexually assaulted in any capacity, then the meaning of a 'child' is any person younger than 17 years of age and the specific proviso of being between the age of 14 and 17 years does not apply unless the defendant was not more than 3 years older than the victim at the time of the offense and the victim was not less than 14 years of age.

The state laws of Washington regarding kidnapping are similar in many respects to those of Texas other than it is kidnapping in the first degree to inflict any bodily injury on the victim. Under this state's code it is also kidnapping to "inflict extreme mental distress on him (the victim) or a third person."[29] It is the lower degree of seriousness, a felony in the second degree, to abduct a person, but at the time not to use or threaten to use deadly force and the purpose of the abduction to obtain custody by a relative. The offense reverts back to being a crime in the first degree if there is an intention to permanently remove the victim or the person is exposed to a serious risk of illness or physical injury. In addition to the simple and aggravated forms of abduction, there are also a number of custodial interference related offenses dealing with crimes that may be committed by parents and guardians.[30]

As we have seen above, the history of stealing people has reached far back in time and the classifications of the offence have been modified to capture societal changes that reflect equality between genders and ages. Today, taking a person of any age against their will or by some fraud is a serious crime. Parental and guardianship custody cases that involve adults who believe they have a right to remove a child from one parent or career have grown enormously over the past 20 years and today remain perplexing for many jurisdictions, especially when the victim is moved from one country to another. As yet, it is really only recent history that has stimulated the large number of laws pertaining to kidnapping and abduction, and as is so often the case in history it is a major act that captures large public attention that causes the law either to be written or changed. On Tuesday March 1, 1932, an intruder entered a house in Hopewell, New Jersey. What followed is one of the most recorded kidnapping events in history and led directly to the creation of the federal crime of kidnapping. Charles Lindbergh was a famous American aviator. He and his wife Anne had a 20-month-old son, Charles Jr. Sometime between 8 and 10 P.M. on March 1, a man broke into the Lindbergh home and stole Charles Jr. A $50,000 ransom note was left on the windowsill of Charles Jr.'s bedroom. Kidnapping at this time was not a federal crime and therefore the immediate policing response came from the New Jersey State Police. Due to Charles Lindbergh's fame, the news of the kidnapping was front page by the following morning and even President Herbert Hoover became involved. The other "Hoover"—John Edgar, head of the FBI—saw this as an opportunity to increase the profile and prestige of the FBI, and he took a strong interest in the case as well. On March 6, the Lindbergh family received a second ransom note, this time for $70,000. A third ransom note was then received, and a fourth to Dr. John Condon, a retired school principal who was named by the kidnapper as the appointed 'go-between'. Two further notes were exchanged and as a token of authenticity a baby's sleep suit was left at an agreed location. By March 29 the kidnapper was clearly getting very frustrated and a further note was received that raised the ransom to $100,000. This was followed by an item of Charles Jr.'s clothing left on the drive of the Lindbergh house. Later that evening the appointed go-between, John Condon, met a man and handed him $50,000 in exchange for a note giving the location of the kidnapped child. The location was false, and on May 12, 1932, the body of Charles Lindbergh Jr. was found in a shallow grave about four miles from the Lindbergh home. His cause of death was a single blow to the head. After a combined operation with the NYPD, the New Jersey State Police and the FBI, the ransom money notes and gold certificate serial numbers were circulated. More than two years later on September 19, 1934, Bruno Richard Hauptmann was arrested for the murder of Charles Lindbergh Jr. A search of his house revealed a number of notes and certificates from the ransom money. Hauptmann was indicted for the offences of extortion and murder. On February 13, 1935, Hauptmann was sentenced to death. He appealed for clemency. It was denied and Hauptmann was electrocuted on April 3, 1936. During the course of the investigation, various agencies experienced some difficulties as the existing law prevented them from conducting investigations across state lines. A federal crime of kidnapping was then created known as 'The Lindbergh Law', as it was as a direct result of this case that the federal crime law was established. This legislation provides that if a victim is not returned within 24 hours, there is a rebuttable presumption that the victim has been transported across state lines or foreign commerce (even though in the case of Charles Lindbergh Jr. it would seem that he never travelled across a state line, as he was murdered in New Jersey within 5 miles of the family home). Eight years prior to the Lindbergh tragedy, America had been stunned by a pointless murder that had also appeared to be a kidnapping, or at least that is how the murderers intended the crime to be viewed. On May 21, 1924, a 14-year-old boy, Bobby Franks, was abducted and murdered. The deceased boy was the son of a wealthy family from Kenwood, Chicago. One day after he went missing, his parents received a typewritten note stating that Bobby had been kidnapped. A ransom of $10,000 was demanded. The note was signed by George Johnson. However, before the ransom could be paid, the boy's body was found in a drain culvert near his home. He had died from a blow to the head with a sharp instrument. Due to the lack of a federal statute governing kidnapping, the state attorney general headed the investigation with assistance from state and local police. At the crime scene, a pair of horn-rimmed spectacles was found that proved crucial to the murder investigation. The glasses and ransom note were given to scientists, and it soon became clear that the writer of the ransom note was a well-educated person. Enquiries with local opticians found that only three pairs of the spectacles had been sold in the previous year. All of the customers were local to Chicago. Nathan Leopold and Richard Loeb were both sons of millionaires and moved about in the high society of Chicago. Leopold was the more intelligent of the two, and by the age of 18 he had graduated from the University of Chicago. He spoke at least nine languages. Loeb was the one who developed a passionate and morbid interest in crime and the challenge of committing the perfect murder. Together the homosexual lovers conspired to outwit the police and the world with an intricate and complex scenario that would start off appearing to be an abduction of a child from a rich family. In reality, money was never a motive and the victim was murdered a few hours after the abduction. During the course of the police investigation, wealthy, educated, Loeb even assisted the police with inquiries and evidence gathering. He was soon under suspicion, however, and combined with the very damaging evidence relating to the spectacles found at the crime scene (an identical pair had been sold to Nathan Leopold by the opticians in the previous year), Leopold and Loeb were arrested on suspicion of murder. Both men quickly confessed to the crime independently of each other and with sufficient knowledge of the facts that the police knew they had the right suspects. Much to the surprise of the nation, Nathan Leopold and Richard Loeb entered pleas of guilty to murder. It was a strategic plan that paid off. Had they pleaded not guilty and been convicted, they would very probably have been given the death sentence. By pleading guilty it was a chance, a slim chance, that the court would be minded to substitute death for life imprisonment. It did pay off, as after their lawyer, Charles Darrow, spent 14 hours arguing the case for the abolition of the death sentence,[31] Leopold and Loeb were sentenced to life imprisonment for the brutal and calculated murder of a 14-year-old boy selected at random for a test of skill by two intelligent and ruthless men who thought nothing of extinguishing a life for pleasure. The sentences were as follows: "In no 33,263, indictment for murder, the sentence of the court is that you, Nathan F. Leopold Jr., be confined in the penitentiary at Joliet for the term of your natural life. The court finds that your age is 19." "In no 33,624, indictment for murder, the sentence of the court is that you, Richard Loeb, be confined in the penitentiary at Joliet for the term of your natural life. The court finds that your age is 18." Both men were sentenced to 99 years each for the offence of kidnapping for ransom. Richard Loeb was murdered by an inmate in prison in 1936 (for allegedly making unwarranted homosexual advances towards the man). Nathan Leopold continued to use his 200 IQ in prison and went on to learn another 20 languages. He was released on parole in 1958, having served 34 years. Upon release, he moved to Puerto Rico and wrote his memoir, *Life Plus 99 years*. He died in 1971.

Instances of brutal murders associated with the kidnapping of children and the significant increase in parental kidnappings have all caught public attention over the past century. This has resulted in the passing of numerous legislative provisions: federal kidnapping as a result of the Lindbergh case and more recently the PROTECT[32] Act of 2003. This act was passed by Congress on April 10, 2003, and introduced to add further protections to children against sexual exploitation and child pornography, and also to authorize the use of wiretaps and other forms of communications monitoring in all cases related to child abuse and abductions, including parental. This law also abolishes any statute of limitation provisions for offenses of child abduction or child abuse. Previously the statute of limitations applied, mostly, when the victim turned 25 years of age. PROTECT also brought into law the 'Amber Alert' system. The amber alert system is named after Amber Hagerman a nine-year-old girl who was abducted and murdered in Arlington, Texas, in 1996. The system provides for amber colored alert messages to be broadcast across statewide and commercial communication systems when a child[33] has been abducted and is believed to be at risk of harm or death. Amber Hagerman was abducted and killed in January 1996, and her killer has never been found. During the four days between her abduction and her body being found, the family took extensive efforts to broadcast the kidnapping, and this method of early alert caught on, not just in Texas but also across the country. The PROTECT Act also strengthened other areas of law, such as procedures to facilitate the early return of children illegally removed abroad by a parent and the permitting of state and federal courts to hear cases brought under the International Child Abduction Remedies Act and the Parental Kidnapping Prevention Act. It also permits the Attorney General to collect and exchange information that would assist in the identification of unidentified deceased persons and the location of missing persons, including children. For the purposes of the 2003 act, a child is a person under the age of 18 years. Additionally, under the National Child Search Assistance Act of 1990, all agencies are required to furnish information about missing children (those under the age of 18 years) to the FBI for inclusion in the National Crime Information Center (NCIC) database. The subsequent Adam Walsh Child Protection and Safety Act (2006) amended the 1990 act to require that information to NCIC was supplied not more than two hours after receipt of a missing child report. The Adam Walsh Act also created a national child sex offender registry as a result of the abduction[34] and subsequent murder of Adam Walsh from a shopping mall in Florida. A convicted serial killer confessed to the brutal murder of Adam, who was decapitated, but then the killer later recanted. However, the police believe that killer Ottis Toole was responsible for the murder despite his retraction. As a result of the widespread public abhorrence for the crime against Adam Walsh, national support was gained for stiffening the laws relating to child abduction and the actions and reporting requirements placed upon the location of child sex offenders.

As Michael Agopian and Gretchen Anderson commented 30 years ago, "America is quickly learning that the family is no longer an oasis of serenity. Crime and violence between family members has become increasingly common and serious."[35] Thirty years ago there was one child theft for every 22 divorces.[36] By 2002, more than 800,000 children[37] were reported as missing each year and more than 200,000 of this number were abducted by a family member.[38] By 2009, the number of abductions had grown to about 260,000.[39] The figures released by the FBI's NCIC for 2010 show that a total of 692,944 missing person records were entered in that year of which 38,505 were under the age of 18 years and 10,248 were between 18 and 20 years of age.[40] Additionally, 703,316 reports were removed by the end of the year as the status of the missing person had changed. As of December 31, 2010, NCIC held a total of 85,820 active missing person reports of all ages.[41]

It is sometimes the case that in kidnapping ransoms the victims are never found. They are murdered and disposed of, but the bodies are either never recovered or are found many years later. This can present problems for a kidnapping trial, as there is no body or when a body is found it is so long after the event that a prosecution for kidnapping is statute barred. What this means is that generally there is a limit to the amount of time allowed between the offence occurring and bringing a prosecution. Murder is an exception to the general rule and is not statute barred. In a case brought against a man called James Ford Seale in 2007, it was alleged he kidnapped two people, Henry Dee and Charles Moore, 43 years previously in 1964. In his 2007 federal trial for kidnapping, he was convicted and sentenced to three life terms of imprisonment. Seale appealed on the basis of the matters being statute barred. On September 9, 2008, the 5th US Circuit Court of Appeals ruled that the statute of limitations applied and Seale's conviction was overturned. The prosecution appealed and on June 5, 2009 the *en banc*[42] panel of the 5th Circuit upheld the original conviction and Seale's sentence was re-instated. Seale appealed to the US Supreme Court. The Court declined to hear the case. James Ford Seale died in a federal prison facility in August 2011.

At some point in every abduction case, the victim is moved or restrained and a demand is then made of the victim or of another person. Taking a person for ransom has been, as we have seen, a common event throughout history, but in recent years hostages have been taken for means other than pecuniary gain, either as human shields or as tools for negotiation for the release of political prisoners or as a way to attempt to get a government to make concessions to a criminal or political group. Consequently some acts of hostage taking are now captured within laws relating specifically to terrorism and some remain within the area of kidnapping. Under USC. 18 sec. 1203 it provides that 'Except as provided in subsection (b) of this section, whoever, whether inside or outside the United states, seizes or detains and threatens to kill, to injure, or to continue to detain another person in order to compel a third person or a governmental organization to do or to abstain from doing any act as an explicit or implicit condition for the release of the person detained, or attempts or conspires to do so, shall be punished by imprisonment for any term of years or for life and, if the death of any person results, shall be punished by death or life imprisonment'. It is not an offence if all of the parties to the crime are US nationals and the detention occurred within the US unless the actions are designed to compel action by a governmental organization. So the bank robber using a person as a shield if in the US and everybody concerned is a US national is not captured by this particular legislation. In keeping with the International Convention Against the Taking of Hostages, hostage taking within the US will ordinarily be investigated by state and local law enforcement agencies unless the hostage is a federal official, international guest or a demand against the US is made or the perpetrators are international terrorists.

Many instances of abduction will not result in a ransom request but in the victim being forced into labor, sexual or manual. The stealing of persons for the sex industry is a worldwide enterprise with organized crime groups operating with total disregard for national boundaries in order to deliver human 'commodities' of all ages for the sex industry. Surprisingly, within the US there are more domestic citizens abducted and forced into the sex industry than illegal immigrants and domestic 'minor' sex trafficking is the unfortunate growth area of this illicit industry.[43] Under the Victims of Trafficking and Violence Protection Act 2000, any minor, including a US citizen, under the age of 18 years who is used in a commercial sex act is a *trafficking victim.* It is believed that there are in the region of 100,000 minors who are currently working in the illegal sex industry in the US,[44] and at least 70% of adult females now working in prostitution were brought into the industry before they were 18 years of age. Eighty-three percent of all human trafficking cases investigated in the US in 2009 were sex trafficking cases.[45]

On August 11, 2004, a local Texas weekly newspaper, the *Mineola Monitor,* ran a story titled "Sex in the City." Allegedly, a local club for 'swingers and swappers' called The Retreat had used children as young as six years of age to perform sexual acts on each other and upon adults. Operating a swingers club is not illegal in Texas provided that nobody is soliciting or paying for sex with adults, but on June, 22, 2005, Margie Cantrell informed the police that her six-year-old foster son and eight-year-old foster daughter had been forced to perform sex shows at The Retreat. The police were unable to find any witnesses or other complainants and the matter was dropped. A few months later, the reports of children performing live sex acts came to the notice of the Texas Rangers. After an 18-month long investigation, no witnesses could be located and no physical evidence was found. However, the Rangers arrested six people in July 2007, and in 2008 after a four-minute deliberation a jury found two of the defendants guilty and they were sentenced to life imprisonment. One of the defendants sentenced to life imprisonment was the biological life mother, Shauntel Mayo, of the eight and six-year-old victims that had made the original complaint. The difficulty, however, was that there was no corroborative evidence whatsoever to support the allegations against the defendants. By 2008, another defendant was given life imprisonment for his involvement in the child sex acts and the infamous events of Mineola, East Texas, were now national news and featured in *Newsweek.* Throughout the entire event there has been a series of allegations and counter-allegations that often centered on the foster mother of the victims, a person who had also been investigated for an alleged sex crime.[46] The author of the report about the Mineola incident, Michael Hall, followed up his initial investigation in April 2010. He found that the Smith County DA, Jim Wheeler, who did not take office until 2007, is deeply concerned about the case and the lack of evidence and the case has now been referred to the Texas Attorney General's office. In the meantime, the defendants appealed against their convictions to the 14th Court of Appeals. In June 2011, Michael Hall submitted his final report, "An absolute Honest-to-God Texas Frame-up."[47] "Why didn't they look closer at the kids' weird implausible stories? Why didn't they look closer at the foster mother of three of them, a woman named Margie Cantrell who moved to Mineola from California in 2004 and who has a history of manipulating her foster kids?" "Why didn't they give serious credence to the fact that not one of the seven defendants would testify against the others in exchange for a lesser sentence?" In June 2011, six of the seven defendants pled guilty to lesser crimes of 'child injury' and were released from prison. One of the defendants remains in prison. Child injury is still a serious offence[48] and a felony. The point of the Texas saga report is that kidnapping and child abduction for any purpose are always very serious crimes but they are also very difficult crimes to investigate, as children can be unreliable witnesses and can make up stories and expand upon the truth, and they can be manipulated by adults to make allegations that are unfounded. The nexus between kidnapping of all people, male and female and particularly children, and their supply to the illegal sex industry is very clear and it is growing due to the ease with which the Internet can be utilized as a tool to attract victims in the first instance. Causing a child to perform a sex act is a heinous crime and it will always involve an element of kidnapping, as the child cannot consent to the restraint placed upon it when held in a location for the purposes of the sexual conduct. Fortunately, legislators have preempted this by drafting kidnapping offences with children that make consent irrelevant.

False allegations made by children are disturbing and may have profound consequences, but they are rarely malicious. Falsely alleging that a child has been abducted to conceal murder of that child is another matter, as these issues present a level of challenge to investigators beyond the normally harrowing and time sensitive nature of a real abduction case. A study conducted by Kathleen Canning[49] at the National Center for the Analysis of Violent Crime found that false abduction allegations were 'extremely' challenging to agencies. This was because it was difficult to ascertain whether the investigation was an abduction or a murder enquiry from the outset, and the delay created by the offender was often planned well in advance, which in a number of cases never led to the discovery of the victim's body. Or if it did, the time lag was so great there was little forensic evidence useful to the prosecution. Additionally, it was not uncommon for the killers to make an elaborate trail of misleading clues designed to give the appearance of a genuine kidnapping/abduction. A further difficult element is that if the abduction is genuine, then it is a very delicate matter to imply to a distraught parent or caregiver that the person may in fact have killed his or her own child (known as filicide). Sixty-one false abduction claim cases that were adjudicated as murder were studied in Canning's study. The mean age of the victims was five, and they were murdered because they were viewed as either "unwanted or an obstacle to a desired goal, or they were victims of abuse or maltreatment that ended in fatality."[50] Of the 61 offenders, 51% were male, which is significantly different than in non-family member abductions where the offender's profile is 74% and the primary motive for the abduction is sexual assault. Also, the vast majority of offenders in the cases of filicide are biological family members, of which 39% are the biological mothers.[51] In 71% of the cases, the 'missing' child was reported by the offender; and in the overwhelming majority of cases, the victim was residing with the killer (93%). In addition to the factors above relating to motive, the home environment of the victim was frequently one of high stress and instability. The victims were often resource-deprived and maltreated, and in 58% of the cases there was a change in the family structure six months prior to the murder. "Staging is generally defined as the intentional manipulation of physical evidence, to redirect the investigation away from the offender, or mischaracterize the crime."[52] In the well-publicized—some might suggest totally over-publicized—Casey Anthony murder trial, the mother of the deceased was acquitted of murder even though at one point in the investigation she posted her child's mitten to herself. The death of two-year-old Caylee Anthony happened in 2008 when it is alleged the victim accidentally drowned in the family pool, but her mother was so sure that she would be accused of murder she took the body and illegally disposed of it. The victim's skeleton was found one mile away from the 'accident' site six months later. On July 17, 2011, Caylee's mother, Casey Anthony, was acquitted of murder. She left the Florida trial courtroom to shouts of "Baby Killer."[53] Casey had originally alleged that the babysitter had kidnapped her child. Jeff Ashton, a former prosecutor in the Anthony trial, believes that "Casey Anthony killed her daughter because she wanted a different, more carefree and single lifestyle, and she convinced herself she would be better off without her daughter."[54] It has recently been disclosed that Casey Anthony kept a diary throughout the ordeal and she now intends to write a book. "Make no mistake, Casey will absolutely be releasing a book, it's just a matter of time."[55] Casey Anthony was charged with providing police with misleading statements. Canning also cites examples of where staging has been used to mislead the police in carjacking abduction cases when vehicles have been removed to other locations before the alleged abductions are reported. In 52% of cases, the murder of the child is clearly intended from the outset, and in 18% of cases studied items were purchased prior to the killing for use in the disposal of the body.[56] The most common form of death was by blunt instrument. Eleven percent of victims were drowned and female offenders exclusively conducted these.[57] Body disposals were mostly out of doors (73%), of which 29% of these were dumped above ground. The next most popular method of body disposal was submersion in water (18% of cases). In 72% of these cases, female offenders chose water placement as a means of hiding the deceased. In 73% of the cases studied, the offender was familiar with the body disposal location prior to disposal of the remains, and in 36% of cases this was less than one mile from the victim's home.[58] Canning's comprehensive and informative report concludes that most false abduction victims are less than five years of age at the time of death and that cause of death is "primarily blunt force trauma and asphyxiation."[59] Regrettably, false allegation abductions are not an uncommon feature in society, and the very nature of the crime and the offender's relationship to the victim make investigation of these crimes particularly challenging. That is because what appears at first blush to be a tragic kidnapping may hide a devious and premeditated murder by a person best placed to mislead and obscure lines of investigation—the parent or primary caregiver.

False kidnapping claims are not unique to cases of filicide though and a recent increase in false 'virtual' kidnappings is now as mobile as the virtual platforms utilized for the crime. Many global companies are experiencing an upsurge in alleged kidnapping cases that are perpetrated through the virtual world. In countries where there traditionally has been a significant foreign employee workforce, individuals have been receiving text or phone calls reporting the kidnapping of a family member 'back home'. An immediate ransom is demanded for the release of the loved one. What has actually happened is that the 'kidnapped' person has been duped into not using her phone for an hour or so and while out of contact the virtual kidnappers call the overseas worker (family member) and make the demands. Frantic at the pre-recorded background screams, the innocent victim makes immediate payment and the kidnap victim is 'released' later. Once the victim calls home she finds out the truth, that there has never been a kidnapping. One recent scam involved the kidnap victim being called and told that the cell phone company needed to work on the line for an hour so he should turn his phone off. The overseas victim was then called during that hour and the entire crime was completed before the cell phone victim knew anything at all about what had occurred.[60] *InSight*[61] reported in December 2011 about a virtual kidnapping case where the victim was told he was speaking to Commander 25 of the Zetas. "In order for everyone to remain safe we are looking for a contribution," he was told.[62] According to the Mexican government, there have been 24,000 reported cases of virtual kidnapping in the past five years. "Private security analysts and non-governmental organizations monitoring Mexico's crime say that the real number of cases could be as much as 12 times higher."[63] On average, ransom demands are met in 34% of all Mexican hoax cases and more than $23 million has been paid out since 2006.[64] The private security consulting firm Steele[65] has reported on cases where children are lured into disclosing address and cell phone information in shopping malls when they participate in fictitious picture competitions. The information is subsequently used to call parents and conduct a virtual abduction.[66] The security consultancy company Stratfor writes about virtual kidnapping: "This new form of pseudo-abduction is based largely on psychological shock, scaring the victim's family into paying large ransom amounts without the victim ever having been in the possession of criminals."[67] Recent intelligence suggests that the growth of virtual kidnappings is rising and now impacting all countries across the world. China's embracement of new technology has sparked a growth in the virtual kidnapping area too, with numerous cases now being reported across the country.[68] The US has never been immune to innovative and contemporary methods of criminality and virtual kidnappings are now rife in this country as well. On Sunday, September 28, 2008, the late edition of the *New York Times* ran an article[69] explaining how illegal immigrants entering Arizona were now being subjected to virtual kidnappings. They are of course particularly vulnerable, as given their status within the US this particular group is highly unlikely to report the crime to the police. The criminals seem to conduct their crimes about four days after the new alien has entered the US. The new arrivals are often cut off from family members back in Central America and are therefore highly vulnerable to the scam, as they have little means of verifying the authenticity of the alleged abduction. In a recent case, one victim gave $7,000 to 'kidnappers'.[70] The success rate of the criminals is currently in the region of 10% in Phoenix, a city that at present has the highest number of reported cases. "In one case, a woman who was told that her former husband was kidnapped said she would not speak with them if she could not speak with him. The criminals then called the man's girlfriend."[71] *FocusPoint,* "Kidnap and Extortion Resolution Specialists,"[72] reports that its "Multi-disciplinary team have discreetly and successful (sic) managed over 430 (insured) kidnaps for ransom, 200+ (uninsured) kidnaps for ransom, 120+ "express" kidnappings, 50+ "virtual" kidnappings, 350+ extortions (both property and bodily injury) and 20+ product/recall contaminations. FocusPoint supports both insured and uninsured events'.[73] Part of the range of expert services offered includes a 24/7 Crises Center and event notification available in 150 languages. Consultants can be deployed anywhere in the world within 24 hours and consultants can interface with the kidnappers and local authorities and protect the victim's family during the negotiation process as well as advise on delivery of ransom and post incident recovery.[74] According to Castle Rock Global Insurance services, in 2005 the average amount paid out in kidnapping cases across the world was $62,071.83.[75] One of the largest amounts ever paid that is known—as many high profile kidnapping cases are never reported at all—was just under $77 million for the return of a property owner's son in Hong Kong. Ms. Kwong Siu-Hing, aged 79 years at the time, paid the vast sum over to a known criminal, Cheng Tze-Keng (Cheung Chi Keung)[76] after he kidnapped her son, Walter Kwok, in 1997. The return of the son, unharmed, followed soon after the money, in used thousand dollar bills, was handed over in a central Hong Kong location. Within a few months Cheng was arrested, made a full confession of all his crimes and was executed by firing squad on 16 December, 1998. He was 43 years of age. It is not known how much, if any, of the ransom money was recovered, as the matter was only disclosed to the press in July, 2008.[77] Also in Hong Kong, the same criminal, Cheng Tze-keng, kidnapped the son of another business magnate, Li Ka-shing, whose son Victor was kidnapped in 1996. It is reported that Li Ka-shing paid $100 million for his son's safe return. In the case of Ms. Kwong Sui-Hing she may have known what Li Ka-shing paid for his son Victor's return the previous year as she did not wait for a ransom note but made an offer of $77 million for her son. Cheng accepted the offer. A particularly disturbing element of kidnapping has recently surfaced in Mexico that will be an offence against international criminal laws, as well as US domestic laws, if the victims are US citizens. The new crime occurs when people are kidnapped by drug cartels and then forced to fight to the death in Roman gladiator style conflicts for the entertainment of the cartel leaders. According to a report in the *Mail Online* dated June 15, 2011, "Mexican drug lords are forcing kidnap victims to fight to the death." Forensic workers near Acapulco recently found the mass graves of mutilated kidnap victims who had died due to receiving blunt instrument blows to the head. A cartel member said the victims of the most recent event were bus passengers who had been stopped and abducted by the Zetas cartel and then forced to participate in fights to the death against each other. The eventual victor was then sent on a 'suicide' mission to kill an opposing cartel member.[78]

The stress that every kidnapping causes the victim and the family members remains forever in most cases. The traumatic experience of being abducted and not knowing whether you will live another day is almost unimaginable for those of us fortunate enough not to have suffered this level of privacy invasion. In some countries, kidnapping is a way of generating personal income or political leverage or, it has become, more recently, a form of grotesque sport. Victims are constantly subjected to mental, and often physical, abuse. In addition, some victims are also severely sexually abused. Research has shown that many victims experience immediate post-trauma stress disorder followed by long-term mental anxiety, hostility, depression, hypochondria and phobias years after release.[79] As reported in the *Los Angeles Times* on August 30, 2009, "For kidnap victims like Jaycee Lee Dugard,[80] recovery is rare. A full portion of her life—her entire teens and 20s—was poisoned by her abduction at age 11 and the 18 years of brutal captivity and deprivation that followed." [81] During her time in captivity she gave birth to two children as a result of the rapes she endured by her captor, Philip Craig Garrido. Since her release Jaycee Dugard has managed to write a book about her excruciating ordeal. Understandably the book title is *A Stolen Life.*[82]

Endnotes

1. www.kidsfightingchance.com taken from DOJ Office of Juvenile Justice and Delinquency Prevention
2. Source: www.nij.gov.org
3. www.project.org
4. Or 1666 or 1673 depending on where you look
5. www.thefreedictionary.com
6. www.ushistiry.org
7. People v Hyatt (1971) 18 Cal App. 3rd 618
8. People v Moore (1945) 67 Cal. App. 2d. 789
9. Wilborn v Superior court of Humboldt County (1959) 51 Cal. 2d 828
10. Cunningham v Cunningham 719 S.W. 2d 224, 226–227 (Tex. Civ. App 1986) cited by Frank Cracchiolo, Parental Kidnapping Prevention Act, *The Journal of Contemporary Legal Issues.* 2007; 16; 299–303, at 300.

11. For example, New York, Ohio, Florida and New Jersey
12. For an analysis of this case and an opposing view, see Christopher Villanti, A game of hold'em: Critiquing United States V Galbadon's "all-in" approach to federal kidnapping. *St. John's Law Review.* 2007; 81; 701–727.
13. USC. 18 Sec. 1202
14. Keen, MH. *A history of medieval warfare.* Oxford: Oxford University Press; 1999; at page 57.
15. 19 September 1356
16. Son of English King Edward III. The Black Prince, also named Edward, was the victor at Poitier also. On the night that John II was captured, the Black Prince laid on a feast for his royal captive and his son before departing the next day to resume battle in another region and leaving John II to be taken to England for ransom. See further www.archive.org
17. See further, Valentine Cesco, Female abductions, family honor, and women's agency in early modern Venetian Istria. *Journal of Early Modern History.* 2011; 15; 349–366.
18. Price, L. Abduction with (dis) honor: Sovereigns, brigands, and heroes in the Ottoman world. *Journal of Early Modern History.* 2011; 15; 311–329 at 316. Sultan Bayezid II lived from 1447–1512 and ruled the Ottoman empire from 1481 until his death in 1512.
19. See further, Gerard Gewalt, America and the Barbary pirates: An International battle against an unconventional Foe. The Library of Congress. Thomas Jefferson Papers. www.loc.gov
20. www.dailymail.co.uk
21. A brush with evil. *Taipei Times.* www.taipeitimes.com
22. www.taipeitimes.com
23. He called himself Field Marshall Cinque Mtume and modeled his terrorism on revolution similar to that espoused by Charles Manson.
24. www.fbi.gov
25. 207,208,209 and 209.5
26. Sec. 20.02 (e)
27. Sec. 20.04 (d)
28. Sec. 20.05
29. RCW 9A 40.020 (1)
30. See Sec. RCW 9A.40.060, 070 et seq.
31. See further www.law2.umkc.edu
32. The acronym stands for Prosecutorial remedies and other Tools to end the Exploitation of Children Today.
33. 17 years old or younger
34. Ottis Toole was convicted of serial killing murder, arson and necrophilia. He also confessed to cannibalism. Along with convicted killer Henry Lucas,

the pair confessed to more than 600 murders across the US. See further www.biography.com

35. Agopian, MW, Anderson, GL. Characteristics of parental child stealing. *Journal of Family Issues.* December 1981; 2(4); 471–483, at 471.
36. Ibid.
37. Many of these reports were of instances of 'overstaying' at friends and other family members' homes as well as custody visits.
38. www.missingkids.com
39. Child abduction statistics. July 8, 2009. www.WorldNews.com
40. www.fbi.gov/ncic
41. Ibid.
42. En banc is when a normally highly complex and difficult case is heard by the entire bench of judges rather than a panel of judges. Appellate courts in the US will sometimes agree to hear a matter en banc in matters of high public importance. The US Supreme Court will also sit en banc. The term derives from when French was the common language of Common Law courts. It means to all 'sit on the bench'.
43. Kotrla, K. Domestic minor sex trafficking in the United States. *Social Work.* April 2010; 55(2); 181–186
44. Kotrla, supra, p. 182
45. Ibid.
46. For complete coverage of this issue see Michael Hall, Across the line. *Texas Monthly;* April 2009.
47. Hall, M. An absolute honest-to-God Texas frame-up: The "Mineolta Swingers Club" cases come to a disgraceful end. *Texas Monthly.* June 2011.
48. Texas Penal Code Sec. 22.04. A felony crime
49. Canning, KE, Hilts, MA and Muirhead, YE. False allegation of child abduction. *Journal of Forensic Science.* May 2011; 56(3); 794–802.
50. Ibid.
51. Ibid.
52. Canning, supra, p. 797
53. Elizabeth Chuck. Casey Anthony breaks silence: "Obviously, I didn't kill my daughter." 13 June 2012. www.msnbc.msn.com
54. Kim Schmidt, Prosecutor. Pre-trial publicity helped acquit Casey Anthony. 25 May 2012. Kearney Hub. www.kearneyhub.com
55. Bruce Baker. Casey Anthony to turn journal into book about Caylee, life, and trial. 20 June 2012. www.examiner.com
56. Canning, supra, p. 798
57. Ibid.
58. Canning, supra, p. 800
59. Canning, supra, p. 801

60. www.ioma.com
61. www.insightcrime.org
62. Ibid.
63. Ibid.
64. www.ioma.com
65. www.steelefoundation.com. Kidnapping: A Big Business on the Rise in Mexico: Worse than you know.
66. See further Virtual kidnapping and Extortion: Combating a New Brand of Shock and Intimidation. Steele report, supra.
67. Stratfor staff, New Trend of "Virtual kidnapping" exploits personal information, fear. 12 April 2006. www.enterpriseinnovator.com
68. China-security memo: personal data, virtual kidnappings and credit card fraud. Stratfor staff writer. www.offnews.info
69. Fake kidnapping scheme hits illegal immigrants in Arizona. *New York Times.* 28 September 2008. www.nytimes.com
70. Ibid.
71. Ibid.
72. www.focuspointintl.com
73. Ibid.
74. Ibid.
75. www.castlerockinternational.com
76. Known as 'The Big Spender'
77. www.news.asiaone.com. 16 July 2008
78. www.dailymail.co.uk
79. Carmen Elvira Navia and Marcela Ossa. Family functioning, coping, and psychological adjustment in victims and their families following kidnapping. *Journal of Traumatic Stress.* February 2003; 16(1); 107–112.
80. Jacee Lee Dugard was abducted when aged 11 years and then held in a concealed dungeon in the home of Phillip Craig Garrido and his wife Nancy for the next 18 years. During this time she was deprived of all human contact except that of her abductors who subjected her to continual rape and sexual, mental and physical abuse.
81. For kidnap victims, recovery can be rare. *Los Angeles Times,* 30 August 2009. www.articles.latimes.com
82. Dugard, J. *A stolen life: A memoir.* New York: Simon and Schuster; 2011.

THEFT, BURGLARY AND ROBBERY

Historically at Common Law, what we call theft was referred to as a larceny. Protecting one's property was often very challenging during past centuries and the unlawful taking of somebody else's goods tended to involve violence, in which case it was a robbery or it was done with a degree of stealth, often at night, which was a larceny. Over time the complexity of the taking grew in accordance with the sophistication of society so that criminal taking in one century might involve very different goods than in another century. As paper money became the common method of business transaction, so too this introduced completely new levels of taking so that deception and fraud became prevalent and the criminal law had to respond with new legislation to reflect the changes in the meaning of property. Over time the law of larceny expanded and new crimes associated with larceny, such as criminal deception and blackmail, were created. The level of complexity became unwieldy in many cases though and there has been a trend towards synthesizing the various laws back into a single concept of theft under which there are specific methods of committing related crimes.

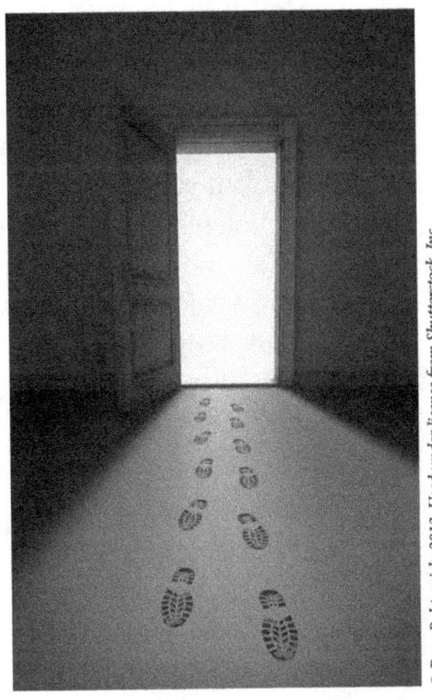

But to understand theft or larceny it is necessary to know what property is, so that it can be stolen. At Common Law, property meant the personal property that belonged to another person. It was any property other than land or buildings on land. Now you can see immediately that this would need a lot of alteration to fit into today's world of virtual ownership and space and also something as straightforward as transportation. Could you, for example, steal a horse, use it for a while and then return it to the stable before the owner was aware and still commit larceny? And if so, could you do this today with time on the Internet? Ownership of property means that the person with the title can do what he likes with the property, use it, throw it away, loan it out. It is his to do with as he choses (within the limitations of the law). But at Common Law the property needed to be tangible property to be covered by the larceny laws. In the 15th century, for example, many people lived as tenants of a landlord or of the church. So who owned the property that was inside a tenant's house? And could the lord of the manor arrive and take away property from inside the home in lieu of a debt? These would be very challenging issues and the key element would be ownership—actual, real, tangible ownership of personal property. Grand and petty larceny were both felonies, and grand larceny, which was ordinarily determined by the value of the goods stolen, was a capital offence. In those states that still use the term 'grand larceny' today, it is the value that determines the offence classification, and grand larceny is a felony whereas as petty larceny is a misdemeanor. Returning to the 15th century, the owner of property may give up possession, even temporarily, but still retain ownership. Just as in much the same way today when you might loan your car to a friend. The friend has a temporary possession of the car, but you retain the legal title to the vehicle to do with as you choose, including demanding the vehicle back. At Common Law it was possible for a landlord to steal property he owned. The reason for this is wrapped up in a deeper look at the entire offence at Common Law.

Larceny was considered the taking away by a trespassory action the personal property of another. At Common Law, my taking away, asportation, was a capturing of the property in a trespassory manner, and in taking it away, having an intention to permanently deprive the owner of the *tangible* property. If I manage to take the property away from you by committing a fraud so that you release it to me or consent to the removal, this is still larceny. The Model Penal Code (MPC), by comparison, defines property belonging to another to mean a person who has control over the property so that possession can be actual or constructive. In other words, physical control is actual but also constructive control, not physical at the time, but when a person has the ownership rights. Physical control of property does not imply ownership. I can be driving your car, but I certainly do not own it. Control of property may have many features, including temporary control, limited control or when property is obtained by fraud. At Common Law, I had to take the property away without consent and intend to permanently deprive the owner of the property. It follows then that when I enter a store intending to steal from the shelves and I place my hand on the goods and move them the slightest amount, at Common Law I have committed the offence of larceny. It is merely a practical evidential feature that the store waits until I leave without paying before arresting me, but the offence (though very hard to prove) was complete when I picked up the goods with the intention of stealing them. The MPC requires no asportation whatsoever. Importantly though, at Common Law it must be property; it cannot be, for example, land or buildings. Why? Because land was considered immovable and therefore could not be captured and moved, nor could buildings on land either. The MPC is wider in interpretation and 'property' is immoveable and moveable. Animals too created a dilemma at Common Law due to the significant number of wild animals in existence. Larceny could not be committed by taking wild animals. But once an animal had been captured into a person's possession then it was property and could be stolen. So a wild deer was not property, but once I killed it then it became my property and could be stolen in much the same way as farm animals, I have reduced them down into my possession and they may be stolen. Some domesticated animals were not considered property though; for example, a dog was not considered property but a horse, cow or sheep was. All domestic animals are now covered by theft laws.

Unlawfully taking away with intention to permanently keep the property meant at Common Law that it had to be shown I intended a permanent illegal use or ownership of the property. There had to be a 'specific intent' to steal the property. So if I could convince the jury that I removed the property on a temporary basis to return it to the owner later, then it was not theft. But if I acted recklessly with the property (and it is for the jury to decide if I have been reckless), then it will be construed as assuming a permanent deprivation of the property. So, what if I took your horse, alleging that I planned to return it later but then I rode the horse so hard it died; that is larceny of a horse. If you gave me permission to use your horse but I retained it for longer than you permitted, that too is larceny. But what if every year for the past 5 years you allowed me to take your horse in order to take my goods to market. Then you went away to visit friends on market day, so I assumed you would permit use of your horse as usual. You returned early and saw the horse had gone and now claimed I stole it. I have a lawful defense: I believed I had 'good faith' in that you would permit use of your property on the basis of the previous consent. A further potential complication is in cases where I believe that you have abandoned the property so I take it, or where I find the property but do nothing to establish the owner's identity even though it would have been reasonable of me to do so. For example, I take property I believe has been abandoned by the owner. Abandoned property is no longer in the possessory rights of anybody and I have a defense to a charge of larceny. This is not the same, however, as finding property and keeping it even though a reasonable person would make an attempt to find an owner. For example, what if on route back from the 15th century market, I find a gold goblet on the pathway. There is nobody around but I later learn that the bishop's carriage passed that way earlier in the day. At this point, an honest person would attempt to establish if the goblet belonged to the bishop. A dishonest person would say nothing and melt it down quickly. At the time I picked up the goblet with the intention of keeping it and treating it as my own, the offense of larceny was complete. At Common Law, unless property has been abandoned it is in the custody of somebody, even if that person does not have actual possession of the item at the time. This is still true of cases where a master gives property to a serf in his employ; the property is in constructive possession of the master even though it is in the literal possession of the serf. Consequently, the serf may steal the property from his master (as often happened). Over time, the use of checks and monetary instruments caused problems at Common Law, as they were not property. The paper the check is written on is property but has very little value. The check is a representation of an agreement to make a payment at some future time, but it is not property subject to the Common Law. Contemporary legislation overcomes this problem by treating the bond, promissory note, wire transfer and check as intangible personal property. Here is a further issue about property—what would be the status of stolen property at Common Law? Could a person commit larceny of stolen property? Yes. And could a person steal property that is itself illegal, such as drugs? Yes again. At Common Law you can steal stolen goods and you can steal illegal goods. At this point you might be considering how it is that the Common Law permitted unlawful, legal ownership, because it had to be lawfully 'owned by another' for me to illegally take it. Stealing electricity produces another contemporary Common Law conundrum as it's not really property. Well, creating legal fictions is not unique to the Common Law and sometimes the law needs a helping hand to make it work.

It is understandable that over time the law relating to the theft of property would expand to capture a wide variety of new devices in society, as well as the cunning of criminals who attempt to avert the law. The recordings of the Old Bailey, the City of London's and county of Middlesex's main criminal court since the end of the 16th century,[1] indicate that the most common offence tried before the justices was theft. Due to the large number of cases heard, the records have been broken down into categories—for example, grand larceny 1674–1827, petty larceny 1674–1827 and simple larceny 1827 onwards. Records are unavailable from the initial Tudor period and up to the rebuilding of Old Bailey due to the occurrence of the Great Fire of London in 1666. The new Old Bailey was opened in 1673[2] and the publication of proceedings started in 1674.[3] Grand larceny cases involved those where the value of the property stolen was greater than one shilling but where there were no aggravating circumstances associated with the theft. It was not uncommon for juries to find the value of the goods stolen to be less than one shilling to avoid having to impose a death sentence upon a poor or unfortunate defendant. Grand larceny was abolished under English Common Law in 1827 when the offence of simple larceny was introduced to abolish the distinction between grand and petty larceny. Petty larceny cases were the most common heard. They were those cases where the value of the property stolen was less than one shilling. It was never a crime punishable by the death sentence. Specific larceny offences were often brought into law to protect the ruling classes of England. For example, "Stealing from your master" was created in 1823 "for the further and more adequate punishment of servants convicted of robbing their masters."[4] The act was designed to protect all employers, not just traditional domestic servant relationships,[5] and the passing of this legislation was a clear indication of the concern parliament and property owners had about the impact of the industrial revolution and worker's rights. Theft from the post became a specific offence in 1767 and was a felony. Acts of 1741 and 1742 made the offence of stealing cattle or sheep a capital offence. Pickpocketing, so popular at public executions, was itself punishable with the death penalty, but it was classified as a private stealing from the person up until 1808. To commit the felony the value of the goods stolen needed to be greater than one shilling. Juries again applied discretion when it came to valuing the goods stolen, even to the point of reducing the value of money itself to below one shilling. In 1808, legislation was introduced that removed the death penalty and the 'private stealing' element of pick pocketing. Shoplifting became a problem crime with the increased wealth of the nation so that many more shops were opened and many more customers, not just from the aristocracy but also from the new merchant classes, had disposable income to spend 'shopping'. Similar to pick pocketing, this crime was also 'privately stealing' five shillings or more worth of goods. It too was a capital offence from 1699 until in 1823 when shoplifting ceased to be a death penalty offence. In 1968, all previous English Common Law offences relating to what had been larceny came together under the Theft Act for the purposes of the criminal offence of taking property belonging to another with the intention of permanently depriving the other of it.

Under the Model Penal Code (MPC), theft is contained within Article 223. Theft may be committed by the unlawful taking and disposal of property, by deception and by extortion. Four other specific offences of theft are also proposed under the MPC: theft of mislaid property, misdelivered property, receiving stolen property and unauthorized taking of automobiles and other vehicles. The intention of the MPC's drafters was to consolidate the various larceny and theft provisions. History had shown, and continues to show in those states that have not adopted the MPC, that theft is complex and has developed into a myriad of assorted provisions that provide defendants with numerous opportunities to avoid culpability.[6] A major development away from the Common Law is that the MPC opens up the meaning of 'to deprive' so that under section 223.0 (1) of the MPC, deprive is to "(a) Hold property of another permanently or for extended a period as to appropriate a major portion of its economic value, or with intent to restore only upon payment of reward or other compensation; or (b) to dispose of the property so as to make it unlikely that the owner will recover it." Under the MPC, theft is a felony in the third degree if the value of the property stolen exceeds $500 or if the property stolen is a firearm, automobile, airplane, motorcycle, motorboat or other motor-propelled vehicle, or in the case of receiving stolen property, if the receiver is in the business of receiving or selling stolen property.

On March 18, 1990, two men disguised as Boston police officers were granted entry into the Isabella Stewart Gardner Museum. Over the course of the following 81 minutes, they conducted the highest value theft that has ever been reported. Paintings and drawings by numerous world-renowned artists were stolen, and there remains today a $5 million reward for information leading to the recovery of the works. 'No questions asked' rewards are always subject to criticism, as they appear to support the illegality of the actions of criminals and, if anything, to promote the likelihood of further crimes. However, the current reward is offered on the basis that it is recovery of the works of art that is desired and not prosecutions.[7] The FBI estimates the value of the works stolen as high as $300 million. By May 2012, the value of the stolen works had grown to an estimated half a billion US dollars.[8] Perhaps one of the most intriguing aspects of the theft is that none of the pictures have turned up in the world's auction houses, suggesting that many of the 13 works were stolen to order from the outset. One single work, Vermeer's "The Concert" is valued at $200 million. Perhaps the most famous theft of all time has been that of the Mona Lisa when in 1911 Vincenzo Peruggia hid inside the Louvre until it closed and then stole the famous painting by taking it off the wall and hiding it under his smock coat as he walked past a guard during opening time. Perrugia hide the Mona Lisa for 2 years and then attempted to sell it to a dealer in Italy. The Da Vinci was too hot to handle and the receiver reported Perrugia to the police. At trial he alleged that he stole the work as an act of patriotism so that the work could be returned to Italy. He served 6 months' imprisonment for the theft and then returned home to Italy. He married and then came back to France where he opened a paint store until his death in 1925. Vying for 'most famous theft' is also that of the crown jewels from the Tower of London. The jewels were stolen by the definition of theft at Common Law; it's just that the thieves never managed to leave the Tower with them. On May 9, 1671, Colonel James Blood and three accomplices managed to gain entry to the jewel room at the Tower of London after befriending the Keeper, Talbot Edwards, for a number of months. On the day of the theft they bludgeoned Edwards and stole the crown, orb and scepter. Edwards, unfortunately for the thieves, regained consciousness and summoned help. Blood and his team were arrested. Blood had a colorful history and had served previously as a Justice of the Peace and fought for both the Royalists and Roundheads in the English Civil War. He was aware that the king had a penchant for adventurers—after all he was known as "The Merry Monarch"—so Blood informed his captors that he would only confess to the king himself. He was granted an audience and to the amazement of the British judiciary the king not only pardoned Blood, he even gave him a stipend of five hundred pounds per year.[9] The crown jewels have never been stolen since.

California is the only US state to have enacted a Theft Act similar to that under the UK (and a number of other English Common Law countries). The Theft Act of 1927 consolidated the theft laws across the state so that under the penal code petty theft is where property valued at $950 or less is stolen by larceny, by trick, by embezzlement or by false pretenses. The offence of theft occurs when "Every person who shall feloniously steal, take, carry, lead, or drive away the personal property of another, or shall fraudulently appropriate property which has been entrusted to him or her, or who shall knowingly and designedly, by any false or fraudulent representation or pretense, defraud any other person of money, labor or real or personal property . . ."[10] What the code achieves is a bringing together of a number of theft crimes so that simple theft, shoplifting or failing to return a household item valued at under $950 when the owner requests the return, are all theft. And to make the matters easier for the jury to understand, there does not have to be a specific distinction between the thefts. In the example of failing to return goods loaned to you, the clock ticks for 20 days after the request. Beyond that it is theft. The value tariff of $950 was raised from a previous amount of $400 in 2011. Many shopkeepers throughout the state opposed raising the monetary value as the majority of shoplifting cases involve sums below $950. The increased amount now means that theft of goods below $950 will be dealt with as a petty theft only. The maximum term of imprisonment for petty theft is three years and/or a fine up to $1,000. If the value of the goods stolen is lower than $50, the crime may be downgraded to an 'infraction', which has a maximum sentence of a $250 fine. Stealing property to the value of $950 and above is Grand Theft and an either way or 'wobbler' offence in that it may be charged as a misdemeanor or a felony.

Stealing from a motor vehicle, stealing a motor vehicle or stealing a motor vehicle to joyride (a temporary deprivation of the rights of the owner) is three different crimes. Auto burglary is a theft from a motor vehicle. Joyriding[11] is a temporary use of the car without an intention to 'permanently' deprive the owner of it and Grand Auto Theft[12] is stealing a car and keeping it or disposing of it as the owner. Normally under California law, the value of property stolen must exceed $950 to be considered a felony. Car theft is an exception and joyriding or theft of a motor vehicle is not subject to the monetary value factors. Monetary values in excess of $950 do not apply as well in cases of: "theft of citrus fruit or other deciduous fruits,[13] domestic fowl, avocados, olives, other fruits, vegetables, nuts, artichokes, or other farm crops exceeding a monetary value exceeding $250."[14] The $950 tariff is also lowered in cases of theft of a horse, mare, gelding, any bovine animal, any caprine[15] animal, mule, jack, jenny, sheep, lamb, hog, sow, boar, gilt, barrow or pig.[16] History always plays a significant part in the creation of laws, and this is clearly seen in the legislation relating to the fruit and wine industry of California. It is also a state where the largest number of car thefts occurs. According to the National Insurance Crime Bureau's figures for 2011, seven out of every ten cars thefts that occurred in the US happened in California.[17] The number one car theft 'hot spot' in the nation is Fresno, California.[18]

According to the California Department of Motor Vehicles, identity theft and identity fraud are two of the fastest growing areas of theft being committed in the state.[19] The California based Identity Theft Resource Center®[20] confirms that identity theft is one of the fastest growing areas of crime across the nation and is achieved when an "imposter obtains key pieces of information and uses them for personal gain." According to the State of California Department of Justice,[21] there were more than 8.1 million cases of identity theft across the US in 2010. In California, it is a felony crime to "use the personal identifying information of another person without the authorization of that person for any unlawful purpose including to obtain credit, goods, services, or medical information."[22] State law also prohibits the possession of scanning devices or a re-encoder for the purposes of obtaining or to record encoded information from the magnetic strip of a payment card with intent to defraud.[23] Using devices to remotely read card information, Phishing[24] or installing spyware knowing that it is to be used unlawfully are also state crimes.[25]

California is one of a number of states that implements a 'three strikes' law. It did so in 1994, twenty years after the first state to do so, Texas. 'Three strikes' means that a life imprisonment sentence is imposed upon offenders who have been convicted of three (or more) serious offenses. As a result of this, some unusual effects have been seen and many offenders were incarcerated for minor crimes until 60.8% of California voters, under Proposition 36, brought about drug treatment rather than 'Three strikes' for a range of drug offenders. This has not prevented some harsh applications of the law though, and there are instances of offenders receiving lengthy prison sentences for shoplifting due to their previous criminal records.[26] The 'Three strikes' provision is still operative in California (and a number of other states) even in cases where the crime that causes the life sentence to be implemented is not of itself a serious one. There have been successful appeals against the 'three strikes' provision, notably in 2002 by Richard Napoleon Brown and Earnest Bray Jr.[27] It was held that "This court recently held in Andrade v Attorney General of the State of California, 270

F. 3d. 743 (9th Cir. 2001) that a 50-year-to-life sentence for two petty theft convictions violated the Eighth Amendment's prohibition against cruel and unusual punishment, and that the California Court of appeal unreasonably applied clearly established Unites States supreme court law when it held otherwise. *Id.* At 747. Because these cases are indistinguishable from *Andrade* in any material respect, we similarly hold that the California Court of Appeal decisions upholding 25-year-to-life sentences for petty theft were contrary to and unreasonable applications of clearly established Supreme Court law. Like *Andrade,* "[o[ur decision does not invalidate California's Three strikes law generally."[28] In 2010, Jeremy Stewart broke into two unoccupied homes and committed a serious felony when he stole jewelry. He was at the time taking methamphetamine. Jeremy already had two strikes against him, one for burglary of a dwelling and one for stolen goods. In October 2010, he received a sentence of 25 years each for the two burglaries and 20 years for breach of probation contract. He will serve a minimum of four-fifths of the sentence as under 'three strikes' law convicts cannot be eligible for parole in the same way as with other sentences, that is, with 50 percent served. In Stewart's case, this means he will serve a minimum of 59.5 years in jail.[29]

Breaking into a person's home and stealing property has been viewed as a very serious offense throughout history and numerous countries have supported retribution by the homeowner or the courts. For example, Roman Law,[30] France,[31] Italy[32], and the Common Law[33] have all decreed at various times that a house owner may kill the intruder if found inside the home. Theft of musical instruments from a school is perhaps not quite as severe, and yet California has suffered a spate of tuba thefts. According to the education section of the *New York Times*[34] a number of high schools across southern California have been the victims of burglaries where brass instruments of high value have been targeted for theft. One school in Anaheim lost 20 instruments valued at more than $20,000 in a recent burglary. Some individual instruments are worth up to $7,000 each. The upsurge in popularity of Mexican Banda bands is believed to be the motive for the burglaries. "It is particularly popular in Los Angeles, where musicians gather in places like Mariachi Plaza to offer their services to parties, weddings, quinceaneras and other events."[35]

On September 28, 2011, *The Sonoma News* reported that two men had been arrested for theft of sheep. On September 8, a rancher had reported three sheep stolen; the victim noticed a black Mercedes in the area at the time and reported these facts to the police. On September 16, local police stopped a green pickup towing a trailer with 20 sheep inside. The officer was unable to ascertain whether the sheep were stolen or not, and the driver, Luis Ortiz Orea, was released after the officer took photographic and identifying evidence of the sheep. Later in the day sheriffs responded to a report of the theft of 20 sheep from a ranch on Watmaugh Road. As a result, detectives from the sheriffs' Rural Crimes Task Force placed Luis Orea under surveillance. Soon after this commenced, his property was searched and a number of the stolen sheep were found and positively identified.[36] Orea has been charged with grand theft of livestock.[37]

Theft of livestock is by no means restricted to California, and dozens of instances of sheep theft and cattle and horse stealing are reported each year. Texas is one state where cattle theft is commonplace and a lucrative illegal industry. The Texas and Southwestern Cattle Raisers Association (TSCRA) reported in February 2012 that cattle stealing (rustling) is on the rise generally. In 2010, thieves stole 7,500 head of cattle across the state. Cows will sell for around $1,000 per head and bulls $1,500.[38] In 2011, Texan Carl Wade Curry received a 99-year term of imprisonment for cattle rustling.[39] He was convicted of stealing 400 head of cattle worth more than $200,000. During the trial it came out that Curry had stolen more than 2,000 head of cattle, valued at almost $1 million, since 2007.[40] Under the Texas penal code a person is guilty of theft if he unlawfully appropriates property with intent to deprive the owner of the property.[41] Like most states, Texas has a monetary value associated with different levels of seriousness. It is a Class C misdemeanor if the value is less than $50 (or $20 if a passed check) and a Class B misdemeanor if the value of the goods is more than $50 but less than $500. A felony is committed once the value exceeds $1,500 but is less than $20,000 or is less than 10 head of sheep, swine, or goats valued at less than $20,000.[42] It is a felony in the third degree to steal property to the value of more than $20,000 but less than $100,000, or any cattle, horse, exotic livestock or exotic fowl having an aggregate value of less than $100,000 or 10 or more head sheep, swine, or goats stolen during a single transaction with an aggregate value of less than $100,000. A felony of the first degree is committed when the value of the property stolen is $200,000 or more. Other thefts can become first degree under specific circumstances, such as if the criminal actor was a public servant at the time of the offense and the property appropriated came into the actor's custody, possession or control by virtue of his status as a public servant.[43] Such theft offenses in Texas are now consolidated under the single Title 7, Offenses Against Property, so that it is a crime not only to steal property but also to take property that you know another person has stolen.

In September 2011, local CBS news reported that a major retail theft ring had been broken.[44] Operation No Return resulted in the arrest of 14 people suspected of running an elaborate retail theft ring involving gift cards and stolen clothing. The offenders are alleged to have taken bags of their own clothes into stores and then removed the devices from the security tags of new clothes and replaced their clothes with these and left the stores. The stolen clothes were then returned to the store without receipts and gift cards were accepted as refunds. The gift cards were then sold for cash on ebay®, craigslist® and Facebook®. It is believed that the gang had stolen "hundreds of thousands of dollars in merchandise, before they were caught."[45] Under the Texas penal code it is an offence to possess, manufacture or distribute certain instruments to commit retail theft.[46] Under the section, a retail theft detector is listed as one such device and means, "an electrical, mechanical, electronic, or magnetic device used to prevent or detect shoplifting, it also includes a 'Shielding or deactivation instrument','"[47] meaning any item or tool designed, made or adapted for the purpose of preventing the detection of stolen merchandise by a retail theft detector. The term includes a metal-lined or foil shopping bag and any item used to remove a security tag affixed to retail merchandise. Manufacturing such devices is also a criminal offense. On 3 April 2012, the *Huffington Post*[48] reported that a huge shoplifting operation in Austin, Texas, had been busted. What the case shows so clearly is that even the continual theft of small priced items builds up into a massive and profitable illicit industry. In this case, the ringleader encouraged other women to steal low value household cleaning items from a range of retail stores. The goods were sold at flea markets and netted more than $50,000 in one year for the thieves. Police found $35,000 worth of goods at the home of the alleged ringleader, Maria Villegas, when they raided her home. Six accomplices were also arrested. According to a National Retail Federation survey conducted in June 2011,[49] shoplifting rings had targeted 94.5 percent of retailers in the past year. One of the major problems associated with this type of crime is that it appears to be just another case of small scale theft by an individual and therefore often not subject to investigation by the police if the value of the goods stolen is less than $50. The Chief of the Dallas Police Department, David Brown, was questioned about his force's policy not to respond to shoplifting complaints of lower than $50 value. "That's a very simple way to describe a very complex change we made," Brown said. He said that

$50-and-under offenses are Class C misdemeanors and typically have around a 4 per cent conviction rate. Over $50, and the crime's bumped up to a Class B, and Brown said the conviction rate there jumps to around 30 per cent. By focusing more intently on higher-dollar crimes, he said, "we create greater consequences."[50] One crime that has been traditionally strictly enforced in Texas is identity theft. In 2008, the retail pharmacy group CVS was fined $315,000 in the state for exposing customers to identity theft by improperly disposing documents that contained sensitive customer information.[51] In 2008, a Dallas woman received a 38 year jail sentence for stealing thousands of dollars through customer credit cards when she worked at restaurants. Furnioes Giddings Parker pleaded guilty to stealing tens of thousands of dollars when working at Braum's, Whataburger and Luby's restaurants. She stole 78 restaurant customer identities and also stole the identities of 14 elderly people when working in a retirement community center.[52] Prior to 2008, identity theft was a state jail felony in the second degree. The new laws implemented in 2008 were applied against Parker and she was charged and convicted of first degree felony. According to the Texas Attorney General, "we have one of the toughest ID theft laws in the nation."[53] And yet over 4.7 million Texans are believed to have been subjects of identity theft between 2001 and 2007, and it was the fourth worst state in the nation for the rate of identity theft *per capita* during the same period with a 16 percent increase *per capita* every year since 2003.[54] The 2012 figures show a slight reduction, and Texas is now ranked fifth in the nation for the number of identity thefts that occur in a 12-month period.[55] By using electronic skimmers to retrieve personal data from credit cards, personal ID is stolen from numerous retail outlets. There are instances reported of car dealerships that have had their own staff 'mining' credit applications from customers to then sell the details to criminals.[56] Even fake drivers licenses have holograms and appear perfect in every way until subjected to laboratory forensic testing. As attorney general Abbott said, "We know we can't prosecute our way out of this. We have to educate people about how to protect themselves."[57] The Texas Attorney General's Office provides a free service to the public to assist victims of identity theft.[58] The Identity Theft Enforcement and Protection Act defines what personal information and identity theft are and that it is the legal responsibility of businesses to ensure that customer information is protected and disposed of appropriately. Property illicitly obtained as a result of an identity theft would be subject to the provisions of the penal code.[59] The crime of identity theft is a felony. Prior to the new increased severity with regard to identity theft, it was still possible to receive a significant jail sentence under Texas's three strikes law. In 1980, in the case of Rummel v Estelle,[60] the US Supreme Court held that the defendant who had received a mandatory life sentence after being convicted for fraudulent use of a credit card to obtain $80 and passing a forged check in the sum of $28.36, was convicted of a third felony, obtaining $120.75 by false pretenses. The petitioner appealed his life sentence conviction on the basis that it was cruel and unusual punishment and abrogated his Eighth and Fourteenth Amendment rights. The Supreme Court justices found that, "The mandatory life sentence imposed upon petitioner does not constitute cruel and unusual punishment under the Eighth and Fourteenth Amendments"[61] and that "Texas is entitled to make its own judgment as to the line dividing felony theft from petty larceny, subject only to those strictures of the Eighth Amendment that can be informed by objective factors. Moreover, given petitioner's record, Texas was not required to treat him in the same manner as it might treat him were this his first 'petty property offense.'"[62]

The term larceny is used to describe theft offenses in Wyoming. In this state, a person who steals, takes and carries, leads or drives away property of another with intent to deprive the owner or lawful possessor is guilty of larceny. It is a felony punishable by imprisonment for not more than 10 years and/or a fine of not more than $10,000 if the value of the property is $500 or more. It is a misdemeanor if the value of the property stolen is less than $500.[63] Unlike California, which has increased the financial bands to make more cases of theft misdemeanors, Wyoming took an opposite stance and since 2004 has lowered the value of property stolen. Prior to this amendment, the value of property stolen was one thousand dollars. A person who steals any horse, mule sheep, cattle, buffalo[64] or swine is guilty of livestock rustling, which is a felony. The law does not specify the value or head of animals that need to be stolen, as all rustling is a felony. The adoption of the criminal code of Wyoming formally ended any legal use of the Common Law, but it does not prevent the court from regarding the Common Law as being persuasive or used as an interpretive aid. 'Property' means anything of value whether tangible or intangible, real or personal, public or private.[65] The intention of the penal code is to bring together a range of related theft type offences. That said, it has not always worked in the way designed, which happened in the case of a woman charged with larceny from her employers. She was not guilty on appeal due to the fact that the money she obtained had never been reduced into the possession of the people she 'stole' it from. The key issue was the interpretation of the statute with regard to 'taking' as opposed to 'conversion'. Francis Xavier Guerrero[66] appealed his conviction for larceny on the basis that the trial court had erroneously instructed the jury on the elements of larceny. He also contended that the evidence presented at trial was insufficient to support his conviction. The court concluded the evidence was insufficient to sustain conviction and reversed. Guerrero was previously employed at the Tortilla Factory restaurant in Cheyenne, Wyoming. The restaurant operated a system of electronic cashiering and all employees entered a two digit identifying code to enter sales details. Management had a four digit code that could be utilized to override errors, permit discounts and void items sold. Guerrero was seen entering a four digit code and a check on his activities showed a significant number of errors logged during the times he was at work. The duty managers on those occasions had no recollection of making the entries. Subsequently, Guerrero was charged under Title 6 with larceny in that he "took and carried, led or drove away property of another with intent to deprive . . ." At trial, the state alleged that the defendant had been voiding and discounting customer orders without the customers' knowledge and retaining the difference between the full prices paid by the customers and the discounted prices entered in the register. In total, the amount estimated that he obtained throughout 2008 was $7,223.38. At the conclusion of the state's case, the defendant argued that he should have been charged with larceny by bailee and not with larceny. The offence of larceny by bailee is when "A bailee, a public servant as defined by W.S. 6-5-10 (a) (vi) or any person entrusted with the control, care or custody of any money or other property who, with intent to steal or to deprive the owner of the property, converts the property to his own or another's use is guilty of larceny." Guerrero was convicted of larceny under 6-3-402 (a) and not as a bailee under 6-3-402 (b). The appeal court then considered it necessary to review the meaning of a "caption, carrying away or asportation" as "established under Common Law" (note the use of the Common Law as persuasive) and Wyoming precedent. The crucial part of this discussion lies in the fact that larceny requires a trespass in the taking, meaning that if you have possession of another person's property lawfully and then convert it to your own use with the intention of permanently depriving the owner of it, there is no trespass in the taking under larceny. There is in many subsequent revised theft acts but not under larceny at Common Law or under the Wyoming penal code. In an attempt to prevent this, Wyoming legislators drafted the larceny offences under one definition but separated out larceny by bailee (and embezzlement). As the

Wyoming appeal court noted, "Unfortunately, as one well-respected treatise on criminal law had recognized, the legislative solution has had unintended consequences: [T]he fact . . . that the borderlines between the three crimes [of larceny, embezzlement, and false pretenses] are thin and often difficult to draw, gave rise to a favorite indoor sport played for high stakes in our appellate courts: A defendant, convicted of one of the three crimes, claimed on appeal that, although he is guilty of a crime, his crime is one of the other two. Sometimes this pleasant game was carried to extremes: A defendant, charged with larceny, is acquitted by the trial court (generally on the defendant's motion for a directed verdict of acquittal) on the ground that the evidence shows him guilty of embezzlement. Subsequently tried for embezzlement, he is convicted; but he appeals on the ground that the evidence proves larceny rather than embezzlement. The appellate court agrees and reverses the conviction."[67] The court went on to note that "The distinction between stealing and conversion turns on how possession is obtained. One gains possession of property by wrongfully taking it from another steals it. Morissette [v United States], 343 US [246] [271] 72 S.Ct. 240,254, 96 L.Ed. 288 (1952). One who comes into possession of property by lawful means, but afterwards wrongfully exercises dominion over that property against the rights of the true owner, commits conversion . . . There is no way in which both offenses can be committed by the same person involving the same property at the same time for the simple reason that one cannot wrongfully take property and still come into possession of it in a lawful manner."[68]

Shoplifting appears to be a problem everywhere there are shops. In Wyoming, the law states that "if a person willfully conceals or takes possession of property offered for sale by a wholesale or retail store without knowledge or consent of the owner and with intent to convert the property to his own use without paying the purchase price is guilty of a felony if the value of the property is one thousand dollars or more";[69] and "a person who alters, defaces, changes or removes a price tag or marker on or about property offered for sale by a wholesale or retail store with intent to obtain the property at less than the marked or list price is also guilty of a felony."[70] On January 26, 2012, a number of papers reported that Zach O'Dell, a college student, had agreed to pay a fine of $200 and $10 court costs, as well as 79 cents, for the theft of a donut. The student was accused of eating the donut without paying for it in November at Blair's Market in Powell, Wyoming. The student is a major in criminal justice.[71] In case you are now trying to work out the additional cost of his donut, he paid 380 times what it would have been if he had simply purchased the donut. There is no doubt that in the donut case the defendant concealed the stolen property by consuming it. In the appeal against conviction by Glen Eddie Garcia, the issue was that he was charged with concealing stolen property, a car, and yet he was driving it around in a city center and then involved in a chase with the police. The defendant appealed his conviction on the basis that he most definitely did not 'conceal' the stolen goods. The Supreme Court of Wyoming heard the matter in 1989.[72] On November 1, 1987, a blue Toyota Celica was stolen in Laramie. Later that evening, the vehicle was seen being driven by the defendant and stopped by the police in Cheyenne. Garcia was identified as the driver and he then drove off at high speed and a police chase followed. When finally stopped (and after he had driven at a number of police vehicles causing them to take evasive action that resulted in injuries to some officers), Garcia was arrested and charged with aggravated assault on three police officers and concealing stolen property of a value greater than $500. He was convicted and sentenced to four and one half to six years state imprisonment. The elements of the charge of concealing property are contained within W.S. 6-3-403 and state that "A person who conceals property of which he knows, believes or has reasonable cause to believe was obtained in violation of the law is guilty of a felony." The state's case was built in part on the fact that by Garcia using the vehicle he had placed it out of the owner's sight and therefore 'concealed' it. Garcia had admitted to the police that he had stolen the vehicle on November 1 in Laramie. The Supreme Court held that "The district court correctly denied appellant's motion to acquit with respect to the charge of concealing stolen property." Justice Urbikit filed an opinion concurring in part and dissenting in part. He agreed with the convictions for assault on the police officers brought about by the driving of Garcia. However, he dissented: "For Garcia, the act conceptualized into a concealing stolen property offense for trial in Laramie County, Wyoming is substituted for the actual offense of felony larceny or misdemeanor joyriding committed in Albany County. In that process, we create what is not so as to be something by a mirage of language. Garcia did everything but conceal that dark-blue, 1984 Wyoming license plate Toyota Celica and, in concurring with the appropriate conviction of the offenses for what he did do, I would not convict him of what he obviously did not do . . ."[73] Citing the English Common Law authorities of Regina v Coggins,[74] Regina v Perkins[75] and Rex v Owen,[76] Justice Walter Urbikit argued that it is well established law that a thief cannot handle the goods he has stolen and therefore it is not possible to create secondary charges of theft of goods if the receiving had been charged, although he noted with alarm that the courts had not been consistent in observing this legal position. "However, the ingenuity of effort of the courts to affirm convictions and ease venue choice problems in conviction came to recognize that there could be a theory of a separate event as a second crime by either concealment or property disposition."[77] He concluded his dissent with, "It is my reasoned conclusion by following the general concept of law, that Garcia's activities did not provide sufficient evidence to justify his conviction for a post-theft offense of the felony of concealment under W.S. 6-3-403. He did not conceal and should not be convicted of what he did not do . . ."[78]

At the beginning of this chapter 1 introduced the idea that theft is a basic crime that often leads into more serious offenses. It has always been the case that when a defendant has used force the law has responded by treating the matter more seriously. Also, when a person has broken into a home or committed a crime at night, society has responded by recognizing the potential for serious injury to the victim and has always treated home invasion as a very serious matter. Under the Common Law, burglary was defined as "The breaking and entering the house of another in the nighttime, with intent to commit a felony therein, whether the felony be committed or not."[79] It was punishable with the death sentence. However, it is not, and has not been, the case that people breaking into homes at nighttime have always sought to steal property; sometimes the motive is assault of the inhabitants. Therefore, to reflect the general seriousness of the potential crimes that can occur when a dwelling is broken into, whether occupied at the time or not, the English law considers home invasion to be burglary. Burglary is committed when a person enters a building or part of a building as a trespasser with intent to steal, to commit serious bodily injury on any person in the building or to commit any unlawful damage to the building. Also, a person commits burglary if having entered a building or part of a building as a trespasser he steals or inflicts or attempts to inflict any serious injury on any person in the building.[80] What this amounts to is that a person can commit burglary by entering a building with an intention even if he does not go ahead and complete that intention. The mere fact that he is a trespasser in a building or part of a building with a specific intent is sufficient to commit the offence. If the building entered is a dwelling, the term of imprisonment shall not exceed 14 years; in any other cases, 10 years. The offence becomes 'aggravated' if at the time of committing a burglary the defendant has a weapon. The use of a weapon is broken down to mean a firearm or an imitation firearm, a weapon of offense or any explosive. A weapon of offense is perhaps the most challenging to contextualize, as it is the case that it would be possible for a person to enter a dwelling with intent to steal and have with him scotch tape to bind the mouths of victims. The scotch tape would become a 'weapon of offence' and the charge would be aggravated burglary. Aggravated burglary is subject to life imprisonment.[81] It was the case that entering a building intending to rape a woman was part of the crime of burglary. This has been repealed and rape now includes rape of any person and burglary with intent to rape is now an offence of trespassing with intent to commit a sexual offence contrary to section 63 of the Sexual Offences Act 2003.

In the US, burglary is mostly contained within state legislation. In California, under Penal Code 459, "Every person who enters any house, room, apartment, tenement, shop, warehouse, store, mill, barn, stable, outhouse or other building, tent, vessel, . . . with intent to commit grand or petit larceny or any felony is guilty of burglary." This is a far broader application than the burglary law in England that restricts the meaning of a building to be a structure with a degree of permanence, whereas under the California statute a tent could be burglarized. It is also possible under the California penal code to commit burglary of a cargo container or a railroad car or an aircraft. The difference is that inhabited premises are a felony in the first degree and the others are a felony in the second degree. Inhabited buildings do not have to be occupied at the time of the invasion if they are buildings designed to be inhabited. In February 2012, a defendant admitted burglary of a number of motor vehicles after he was arrested for punching a car driver in the face to obtain cash. Dominic Jacobs also admitted burglary of seven other vehicles that were unoccupied at the time. He entered locked vehicles by smashing the glass with a brick and then stole whatever contents of value he found.[82] Importantly for understanding burglary is that the historical notion of the offence having to be committed at nighttime has been abolished. So too has the term 'breaking and entry' as there is no need for the attacked property to be forcibly entered. In California, burglary can be a 'wobbler' offence and may be treated as a felony or a misdemeanor. The distinction now rests with the premises attacked; residential premises will result in a charge of felony burglary whereas commercial premise burglaries may result in a misdemeanor charge or a felony.

Of course it is possible to argue that every case of shoplifting is a burglary, if the 'intention' of the defendant can be proven. As a practicality, shoplifting is charged under theft, as it is far easier to prove the theft than it would be to prove a burglary. The nighttime requirement for burglary was abolished in 1982. There have been a number of cases over the years that have challenged parts of burglary legislation, for example, when have you entered a building? Is it when all of your body is inside or would an arm suffice? Is it burglary if I use an instrument to enter the building and steal, for example, an extension piece that would allow me to remove a cell phone from a hallway without my having to personally enter the building? Would it be burglary if I got a young child to enter on my behalf and steal, a child so young that the law would not prosecute him, as such are deemed incapable of committing crime, *doli incapax*. Would this theft be an 'entry'? What if I have a key to the premises and enter? Is this still a burglary or is it a simple theft? The answer to all these examples is that they are all burglary. However, auto burglary happens when you 'break' into a car. It does not occur under California law when there is a non-forcible entry into the vehicle. That offence is theft.

One of the most famous recent series of burglaries occurred throughout wealthy areas of Los Angeles when over the course of three years $10 million worth of cash and valuables were stolen from 150 homes. These crimes were reported as being part of the 'Hillside Burglars' for which Troy Cosby Thomas received 17 years' imprisonment in a plea deal. Thomas is believed to be the person who organized and orchestrated the burglaries, but the actual invasions were conducted by teenagers.[83] The term 'cat burglar' has been used for centuries to epitomize nighttime burglars who use skill and physical agility to commit housebreaking. The term is now in use again to describe a burglar who appears to be making the Hillside burglaries seem inconsequential in terms of the value of items stolen. In 16 months, Ignacio Pena del Rio has conducted more than a thousand burglaries and netted goods valuing more than $16 million—and some estimates are that it is closer to $40 million. Del Rio had a simple *modus operandi.* He knocked at the door of a wealthy house and if there was no reply he went around the back and opened a window or levered a sliding door. He then kept his valuables in a lock up storage facility. In 2005, the owner of the storage center mistakenly opened del Rio's unit and found so many high value items he contacted the police. The police recovered 26 Swiss gold bars, 572 rings, 546 necklaces, $150,000 in gold coins and a fake Degas painting. The police estimated the haul to be worth $10.5 million. Also in the lock-up facility was a USB with Photoshopped IDs. Before the police were able to mount a surveillance operation, a burglar in Encino was disturbed and the police attending the scene arrested Del Rio.

He had mistakenly thought the house was empty when in fact the maid was asleep inside and he disturbed her. Over the course of the next few months in custody, Del Rio attempted suicide three times. He then struck a plea deal and is now serving time at R.J. Donovan Correctional Facility. He will be deported back to his native Spain on release in 2013. He had 6 months reduced from his sentence for agreeing to help the LAPD make a video about burglary methods. He was eventually convicted of stealing $16 million worth of property.[84]

On April 9, 2012, the US District Court Northern District of California San Jose heard the appeal of Ali Foroutan. The petitioner sought a writ of *habeas corpus* on the basis that his indeterminate life sentence with a minimum of 25 years for possession of 0.03 grams of methamphetamine was grossly disproportionate to his crime and in violation of the Eighth Amendment. Foroutan received his sentence under the California 'Three Strikes' law. The appeal court concluded that "Although this is a close case, the Court is unable to conclude that petitioner's sentence is the 'exceedingly rare', 'extreme', and 'extraordinary case' for which '[t]he gross disproportionality principle reserves a constitutional violation'." Accordingly, the Petition for Writ of Habeas Corpus is denied."[85]

Chapter 28 of the Texas Penal Code (TPC) deals with offenses against property including burglary and criminal trespass. The offence of burglary is committed when a person, without consent of the owner, enters a habitation, or building not then open to the public, with intent to commit a felony, theft or assault or remains concealed on premises with intent to commit a felony, theft or assault or enters a building or habitation and commits or attempts to commit a felony, theft or assault.[86] Texas, therefore, no longer utilizes the Common Law offence of burglary, so under the state code there are three basic ways in which a burglary may be committed: entering with intent, remaining on premises with intent or having entered attempting or committing a felony, theft or assault. If the burglary occurs in a 'habitation', then it is a felony in the first degree. There are also two specific burglary offenses in the state: burglary of coin-operated machines[87] and burglary of vehicles.[88] In the case of Richardson v State,[89] the issue at stake was whether stealing from the back of an open pick-up truck was burglary of a vehicle. The Appeal Court held that, "Although it may be open to the elements the bed of a pickup is clearly an interior portion of the truck itself. There is no need for the bed to be enclosed by a tarpaulin or camper shell or some other structure for it to be protected under section. 30.04."[90] Burglary of a coin-operated machine was charged against Aaron

Lee Niles and Dale Bruce Niles, son and father, after they were found breaking into coin-operated washing machines in an apartment complex. Dale Niles was a resident of the apartment block.[91] For the purposes of this type of burglary, 'entry' includes every type of entry except one made with the effective consent of the owner.[92] The offence of criminal trespass occurs when a person enters or remains on or in property, including an aircraft or other vehicle, of another without effective consent or enters or remains in a building of another without effective consent and he had notice that entry was forbidden or received notice to depart and failed to do so.[93] This is not an offence of burglary and there is no need to have an intention of committing a crime. When contrasting the offences of burglary in California and Texas, it can be seen that in California it would be possible to burglarize your own home with an intention of committing a minor theft. In Texas, this would not be possible, as each of the three elements requires that the building or premises belong to another. The issue of 'entry' in terms of amount of body intrusion is defined as "Any part of the body" or "Any physical object connected with the body."[94] This is not the case with the offence of criminal trespass, as under Sec. 30.05 (b) (1) "Entry" means the intrusion of the entire body. Perhaps not surprisingly, the two most populated states in the US—California and Texas—are also the two most burglarized states in the nation. In 2011, there were 228,857 burglaries in California and 228,597 in Texas. In Wyoming, there were 2,461 burglaries recorded in the same year.[95] According to the Texas Department of Public Safety, of all reported burglaries in 2008, "69 percent occurred at residence. Forcible entry accounted for 66 percent of all burglaries, while 30 percent were unlawful entries without force . . . Of the offenses for which the time of the occurrences was known, 58 percent were during the day . . ."[96]

Texas is a 'castle doctrine' state. This term is used to describe the right at Common Law that a person had to protect their own property, family and their own life against intruders. It was originally used to capture the idea that "An Englishman's home is his castle."[97] 'Make my day'[98] or 'Stand your ground' laws are used nowadays to apply to those states that have a defense of habitation law that will permit the use of deadly force, if necessary, against an intruder. In some states, this is restricted to a dwelling; in others, such as Texas, it is broader in concept and applies to many other places that are occupied, such as the workplace or when in your own car. On Tuesday, March 22, 2007, Texas Governor Rick Perry signed into law Senate Bill 378,[99] which extended an individual's 'habitation' to a vehicle and the workplace as well as to the home, which was already covered under previous law. Bill 378 "Extends a person's right to stand their ground beyond their home to vehicles and workplaces, allowing the reasonable use of deadly force when an intruder is: Committing certain violent crimes, such as murder or sexual assault, or is attempting to commit such crimes; is unlawfully trying to enter a protected place; or unlawfully trying to remove a person from a protected place."[100]

On November 14, 2007, Joe Horn, a 61-year-old resident of Pasadena, Texas, shot and killed two men he believed were burglarizing his neighbor's home. Horn called 911, and during the conversation with the dispatcher he stated, "Well, here it goes buddy, you hear the shotgun clicking and I'm going." Shortly after this on the 911 tapes, Horn is heard saying "Boom! You're dead!" This is followed by the sound of a gun being cocked and fired. It is then heard being fired a second time.[101] Police identified two dead males at the crime scene: Hernando Riascos Torres and Diego Ortiz. They were found in possession of a bag of jewelry stolen from the neighbor's home. The shooting part of the incident was witnessed by a plain clothed police officer that had arrived at the scene and remained in his car. Horn was not arrested. The local police conducted an investigation and submitted a report of their findings to the District Attorney's Office for consideration of criminal charges against Horn. On June 30, 2008, Horn was cleared by a Harris County Grand Jury, which concluded that his actions were a justifiable use of deadly force and not murder.[102]

There is, as seen above, a difference between 'Make my day' and 'Stand your ground' laws. 'Stand your ground' laws are those that do not require a person to retreat if in their dwelling. 'Make my day' laws are far broader in application, as seen in Texas. Wyoming is a 'Stand Your ground' state. Under Title 6-1-204 of the Wyoming Criminal Code, "a person who uses force as reasonably necessary in defense of his person, property or abode or to prevent injury to another is immune from civil action for the use of force."[103] House Bill 0167 enacted on July 1, 2011, modified the existing law to delete the term 'occupied structure' to become 'home or habitation'. Habitation means: any occupied structure which is designed or adapted for overnight accommodation, including buildings, modular units, trailers, campers and tents and 'home' means any occupied residential dwelling place.[104] There is no implied intention of the Wyoming legislators to extend the Castle doctrine to the workplace or motor vehicles.

Burglary is an offence under Wyoming Criminal Code 6-3-301 and occurs when a person, without authority, enters or remains in a building, occupied structure, or vehicle, or separately secured or occupied portion thereof, with intent to commit larceny or a felony therein. It is a felony punishable with a term of imprisonment of not more than 10 years and/or a fine not exceeding $10,000. As a result of the case of Smith v State,[105] a semitrailer from which the wheels have been removed and is used for storage is a building for the purposes of burglary. The offence is 'aggravated' when at the time of committing a burglary a person armed with or using a deadly weapon or a simulated deadly weapon, knowingly or recklessly inflicts bodily injury on anyone or attempts to inflict bodily injury on anyone. Aggravated burglary is subject to a minimum 5 years sentence and not more than 25 years and/or a fine of $50,000.[106] Breaking, opening or entering a coin machine with intent to commit larceny is a misdemeanor.[107]

Colton Harris-Moore was arrested in the Bahamas on July 11, 2010, after more than two years of evading the police for conducting burglaries over at least six states, including Wyoming. Harris-Moore stole cars, boats and planes as he moved across the states committing an assortment of burglaries to provide cash to support his lifestyle. Like many 'cult' heroes, however, accounts of his escapades vary and even the circumstances surrounding his capture are reported differently. For example, one source states that at the time of his arrest he was attempting a high-speed getaway in a stolen boat. An alternative version is that he crashed a small plane he had stolen from Indiana, and another is that he was arrested in 2006 after he was found living on the islands and that at the time of his arrest he was eating pizza.[108] At 20 years of age, he has already gained a level of notoriety and according to France24.com there is a Hollywood producer thinking of making a film about him. He has added to his 'legend' by acquiring the name 'Barefoot Bandit' after his footprints were found at numerous crime scenes. On December 6, 2011, Harris-Moore was sentenced to six and one-half years imprisonment in Seattle and told the judge "It would be no stretch of the imagination to say I am lucky to be alive." Known to have a very flippant attitude towards law enforcement, 'Colt' Harris-Moore sometimes called out to the police as they attempted, and failed, to capture him; and on one occasion he even left a message in chalk at a crime scene. It read 'C'yal'.[109] On another occasion, police found a handwritten note and a $100 bill at a veterinary clinic in Raymond, Washington. It read, "Drove by, had some extra cash. Please use this money for the care of animals. Colton Harris-Moore (AKA 'The Barefoot bandit')."[110] Harris-Moore has a sizeable following on Facebook with 22,000 members—or that could be 50,000.[111]

On September 9, 1983, James Schuller had his appeal against sentence heard before the Supreme Court of Wyoming.[112] He had been sentenced to four to eight years for burglary and this was enhanced to life imprisonment under the Wyoming habitual-criminal statute. The appellant raised the issue as to why the trial judge had not considered probation for his third felony crime and in doing so would not have held him as a habitual criminal likely to receive a life sentence. The Supreme Court held, "Defendant was found guilty of burglary, under S.6-7-201, WS 1977. Because of the habitual-criminal statute, S.6-1-110, supra, the burglary sentence was enhanced to life. When a crime carries a mandatory life sentence, as does the appellant's enhanced conviction of burglary, the trial judge has no discretion to consider probation . . . We adhere to the principle that habitual criminality is not a crime, but a status . . . the defendant is not thereby sentenced to life imprisonment for the 'crime' of being an habitual criminal. Rather because he is an habitual criminal, he is sentenced to life imprisonment for his fourth felony."[113] The Court affirmed the judgment and imposition of a single, enhanced life sentence for burglary.

Many of the most famous crimes throughout history have been called 'great robberies' whether they were actually robberies or not according to the law. Robbery evokes fear and interest. It is a crime of violence and theft combined. Many of the largest value robberies have involved the theft of cash or diamonds; some have been of artworks. Whatever property was stolen when a multi-million dollar robbery was pulled off and nobody was hurt, there is always a sense of implicit admiration from the press. Robbery goes to the very heart of the "Robin Hood" syndrome. We don't know whether there really was a Robin Hood, and we also do not know if he really gave his takings to the poor, but the number of contemporary Robin Hoods who give their illicit takings to the poor is small if not zero in number. As a reminder to start our discussion, four armed men stole $108 million from a jewelers in Paris in December 2008;[114] $100 million from the Antwerp diamond Exchange in 2003; $118 million in diamonds from Amsterdam's Schiphol Airport in 2005; $300 million in artwork from the Isabelle Stewart Gardner Museum, Boston, in 1990; £292 million in London in May 1990 when bearer bonds were stolen by a single thief carrying a knife; and—one of the best known robberies—The Great Train Robbery of 1963 when £2.3 million was stolen from a mail train. The gang, including Ronnie Biggs and Buster Edwards, did not carry guns to complete the crime. And for sheer luck, there was the Brinks Mat warehouse robbery of 1983 when thieves broke into the Heathrow airport storage area thinking they were going to steal 3 million in cash and to their great surprise found 10 tons of gold bullion.

Robberies are often grouped together in terms of severity classification along with other related violent crimes, such as kidnapping, extortion and rape. The MPC does not, however; it is a totally separate offence defined as: "A person is guilty of robbery if, in the course of committing theft, he: (a) inflicts serious bodily injury upon another; or (b) threatens another with or purposely puts him in fear of immediate serious bodily injury; or (c) commits or threatens immediately to commit any felony of the first or second degree."[115] According to the FBI crime statistics for 2010, occurrences of robbery have declined, the largest drop of all violent crimes, by 10 percent in 2010 compared with the previous year. The arrest rate for robbery is low, however, 6.5 per 100,000 inhabitants.[116] The FBI Uniform Crime Reporting (UCR) defines robbery as "the taking or attempting to take anything of value from the care, custody, or control of a person or persons by force or threat of force or violence and/or putting the victim in fear." In 2010, there were 367,832 robberies reported. There is a robbery rate of 119.1 per 100,000 inhabitants with the average dollar value amount stolen being $1,239. Firearms were used in 41.4 percent of the cases.[117] In 43.2 percent of the cases, the robberies occurred in the street. There were 17.3 percent at residential locations, 2.2 percent at banks and 5.2 percent at convenience stores.[118] Fewer street robberies occur in the South than in any other region of the country, with 36.1 percent of all robberies in the South happening in the street.[119]

Robbery has three distinct elements: a theft of property, taking the property from another person and using force or fear of force at the time of the robbery. At Common Law, 'Highway Robbery' involved the offence taking place out of doors, the assailant being either on horseback or on foot. Those on foot were called 'Footpads'. Today we call highway robbery 'mugging'. Under the statutory law of England that has now replaced the Common Law definition of robbery, the violence or threat of violence must be "immediately before or at the time." So a robber demanding money from you at the ATM is robbing you if he sticks a finger in your back and you believe it is a gun and hand over your cash. He may not be committing robbery if, having taken your cash, you chased him and as he got in a car he produced a knife. Many years ago pick pocketing was a common crime. Was this robbery? No, because there was no knowledge of force or fear of violence. But mugging involves an element of force or the fear of force and therefore mugging is robbery. Interestingly, under the MPC it is possible to commit robbery without obtaining any property, as the requirement is that "in the course of committing a theft" the MPC does not require that there is a theft. This was not possible at Common Law, where robbery was defined as "Felonious and violent taking of money or goods from the person of another, putting him in fear." The standard language of the value being greater than one shilling was not required to prove this offence[120] and any money value could be charged. Also, it is not possible to rob without obtaining any property under the UK's Theft Act.[121] The MPC also proposes to criminalize as robbery the circumstances where a person has obtained property lawfully and then uses force or fear to retain the property. The vast majority of states have adopted the MPC or drafted versions of law very similar so that robbery now has a broader interpretation than at Common Law.

In California, robbery is defined as the "felonious taking of personal property in the possession of another, from his person or immediate presence, and against his will, accomplished by means of force or fear."[122] The fear of injury may be by the person being robbed or by a relative or a person in the company of the person being robbed. So the bank teller can be in fear of injury for his co-worker. Under section 212.5, it is robbery in the first degree to commit a robbery on a person operating a vehicle as employment. This applies to drivers of streetcars, cable cars, buses, trains, taxis or any vehicle for hire. This also includes any passenger on any vehicle, such as train passengers, i.e. 'Robbing a passenger train'. It is also robbery in the first degree to commit a robbery at an ATM machine, including *immediately after* the victim has used the machine. All other robberies in California are robberies in the second degree. 'Carjacking' is a separate property crime and involves the felonious taking of a motor vehicle in the possession of another from his or her person or immediate presence. This can also be achieved by taking the vehicle forcibly from a passenger, for example, when the driver is away from the vehicle but the vehicle is still occupied, with intent to temporarily or permanently deprive the person in charge of the vehicle of that vehicle, and the offence is achieved through force or fear. A person charged with this offence may also be charged with robbery. Carjacking is punishable with three, five or nine years of state imprisonment.[123] Without thieves, there would be no receivers, but no all receivers are thieves, whereas all thieves may be receivers. 'Fencing' stolen goods has become much easier thanks to ebay and Craigslist, and the thieves themselves now offer many proceeds of theft, burglary and robbery for sale in this manner. In California, the legislators have attempted to overcome selling stolen goods with Section 496, which contains the provision that it is a crime to buy, sell, receive, conceal or withhold property you know to be stolen. The purchaser of the goods may of course be an innocent purchaser, but the person selling the goods who knows them to be stolen completes this offence.[124] However, if you purchase innocently and then become aware of the fact that the items you purchased are stolen, you must disclose this immediately, as otherwise you are then concealing/withholding per Section 496, which is a 'wobbler' offence.

Overnight on Sunday 16 April 2003, a team of criminals cut a hole from an adjacent restaurant building into the Lang Antique & Estate Jewelry premises in Union Square, San Francisco. In the morning, when staff arrived for work, the thieves tied up victims and took 1,297 pieces of jewelry valued at $4.5 million. From the outset there was a question about inside assistance, as safes that should have blocked the entrance the robbers made had been moved, the camera surveillance system had run out of tape and the restaurant's exterior door had been jammed to allow entry. "Once inside the jewelry store, the intruders briefly set off a motion detector alarm in the safe room, but when the alarm company called the store owner, he took no action."[125] Over the course of the next three years, an investigation resulted in the prosecution of Troy Devin Smith, Dino Smith and George Turner. All three were convicted of robbery and received substantial terms of imprisonment. The robbery was the largest ever in the history of San Francisco in terms of monetary value. Troy Smith appealed against his conviction[126] on the basis that it was an inside job set up by the jewelry store owner, Mark Zimmerman. Zimmerman has always denied any involvement in the crime. He did receive $4 million in insurance payment for the loss.[127] "At appellant's robbery trial, the prosecution's theory of the case was that the robbery was an 'inside job', set up by the store's owner in order to collect on the insurance. Based on this theory, appellant contends that if indeed the store owner conspired with the robbers and gave them his permission to rob the jewelry store, the elements of the crime of robbery have not been established. In a case of first impression in this state, we reject appellant's claim, holding that even if the owner of a retail store consents to the taking of the store's property by third persons, those persons still commit robbery if they take store property, by means of force or fear, from the custody of store employees who are unaware of the consent given to the robbers by their employer."[128] The justices concluded, "If the property that is taken was in the possession of the owner's innocent employees or agents, that is sufficient to make the taking felonious, even if the owner himself is secretly in league with the perpetrators."[129]

Penal Code Title 7, Chapter 29, defines robbery in the state of Texas. It occurs when "In the course of committing theft as defined in Chapter 31 and with intent to obtain or maintain control of the property, he intentionally, knowingly, or recklessly causes bodily injury to another or intentionally or knowingly threatens or places another in fear of imminent bodily injury or death." Robbery is an offence in the second degree. Property means all tangible and intangible property. The offence becomes aggravated when a person commits robbery and causes serious bodily injury to another or uses or exhibits a deadly weapon or causes bodily injury to another person or threatens or places another person in fear of imminent bodily injury or death, if the other person is 65 years or older or a disabled person.[130] Aggravated robbery is a felony in the first degree. In June 2012, Ruben Rincon was sentenced to life imprisonment for aggravated robbery of 71-year-old David Thomason when, with another, Rincon robbed his home and assaulted him with a deadly weapon. The intruders then drove over Thomson's leg as they attempted to flee. They left the victim for dead. Thomason survived the attacks though and gave evidence against Rincon. Rincon received a second life sentence for the shooting of Thomason, which occurred after the robbery was complete.[131]

I started this section on robbery by suggesting that legitimate society has a fascination with robbery that differs from many other crimes in that if the robber displays a sense of the 'Robin Hood' he can be almost admired or revered in history. But it is history that makes these thieves, who steal and then additionally inflict violence and fear upon people, which offers the kindest memory. For the victims, there is nothing pleasant or courageous about being terrorized or being held hostage and not knowing whether they will survive. Somehow we often forget the tragic and remember the escapade, the daring escape or the dramatic shootout or the quasi-hero disappearing forever so that the events can be magnified along with glorification. The truth is rarely so glamorous.

The Santa Claus Robbery began on December 23, 1927, in Cisco, Texas, when Marshall Ratliff, Henry Helms, Robert Hill and Louis Davis robbed the First National Bank around noon. This was a period in history when up to four banks a day in Texas were being robbed, so bank staff and police were very nervous of strangers and groups of men coming into a bank together. It was also a time when banks were offering $5,000 rewards for the shooting of bank robbers, which although an incentive for some citizens was also an incentive to some robbers to use extreme violence to avoid being shot. Ratliff was the 'brains' behind the robbery and he planned to commit the crime with his brother, but he was arrested before this event so he called on friends he knew to help out. On the day of the robbery, the team stole a car in Wichita Falls and headed for Cisco. Ratliff was concerned though that he was now fairly well known as a criminal and he might be recognized in the small town so he decided to wear a Santa Claus outfit during the crime. When the group entered the bank many customers were happy to see Santa Claus and greeted him and initially not all the customers or staff realized a robbery was taking place. During the holdup a customer and her daughter entered the bank and immediately saw what was happening and ran out and alerted the police. There then followed a massive exchange of gunfire not just by the police but numerous local citizens joined in to try to protect their friends and neighbors and their local bank. During the shootings, two police officers died. Two young girls were taken as hostages and used as body shields by the robbers as they left the bank in an attempt to reach their getaway car. Two of the robbers, Ratliff and Davis, were also wounded during the exchange of gunfire, but they still managed to leave the scene and attempt to hijack a car. When this failed, they further used the two small girl hostages as shields and held up another car to make off. Davis was too injured to join them and he was left at the scene to die later that night. The three then took the driver of the second hijacked car, Carl Wylie as their hostage and made off towards South Bend. As the three attempted to cross the Brazos River, sheriffs and a Texas Ranger ambushed them. Even though there was an extensive exchange of gunfire, the three managed to escape again. After what was the largest manhunt in Texas history to date, the three were captured alive and held pending trial. Hill pleaded guilty to armed robbery and received a 99-year sentence; he was released on parole after 20 years, changed his name and settled down to a quieter life in Texas. Helms was identified as the one responsible for killing the police officers and he was given the death sentence. He was electrocuted on September 6, 1929, after failing to convince a jury that he was insane. On January 29, 1928, Ratliff was convicted of armed robbery and he too was sentenced to 99 years imprisonment. On March 30, 1928, he was sentenced to death for his part in the murder of the two police officers. Ratliff also tried an insanity plea and his case was stronger than Helms'. The townsfolk of Eastland County were apparently infuriated that he might get off death row. In the meantime, Ratliff was being held in the Eastland County jail awaiting his murder trial when on

November 18, 1928 he murdered one of his jailers in an escape attempt. By the following day, a thousand local citizens were demanding immediate justice. They rushed into the jail, dragged out the robber and tied him up. A rope was thrown over a nearby power pole and they attempted to lynch him. The first attempt failed and the rope broke. The second attempt was successful and he was pronounced dead at 9.55 P.M. that evening. No one was ever tried for the lynching. Ratliff's family was permitted to have the body, and he was taken and buried in Olivet cemetery in Fort Worth.[132]

Wyoming has had its fair share of bank robbers. The most famous—Robert LeRoy Parker, better known as Butch Cassidy—may or may not have died in a shootout in Bolivia in 1908 (or retired to Casper, Wyoming) after Cassidy and his 'Wild Bunch' committed a series of bank and train robberies across Wyoming, Utah, Montana and Idaho. At one point, Cassidy even secured a chance of amnesty from the governor of Wyoming in return for not carrying out any more crimes within the state. He never kept his promise and robbed a train near Tipton in August 1900. Robbery is an offence contrary to Wyoming Criminal Code 6-2-401.[133] A person is guilty of robbery if in the course of committing a crime defined by W.S.6-3-402 (larceny, livestock rustling, theft by a bailee), he or she inflicts bodily injury upon another; or threatens another with or intentionally puts him in feat of immediate bodily injury. Robbery is a felony punishable with not more than 10 years imprisonment unless it is aggravated. Aggravated Robbery[134] occurs when a person intentionally inflicts or attempts to inflict serious bodily injury on another or uses or exhibits a deadly weapon or a simulated deadly weapon. The sentence is imprisonment for not less than 5 years and not more than 25 years.

In the case of Charles Edward Jones v The State of Wyoming,[135] the appellant who had been charged with aggravated robbery and murder received a life sentence without parole at trial. He appealed, *inter alia*, on the basis that the trial judge had erred in omitting the intent element from the jury in defining robbery. The District Court had defined robbery as "The stealing, taking away **or** carrying away of property belonging to another with infliction of bodily injury upon the person of another" (emphasis added by the Supreme Court). The Court found that there was no question that Jones shot Whitehead to death with a deadly weapon, and it was not disputed that Jones took and carried away money from the crime. However, Jones argued that the money he took was *his money* and therefore he did not take and carry away property belonging to another. The justices held that Jones did not contest the 'taking and carrying away' element at trial, and Jones himself had testified that after he shot Whitehead he grabbed the money and fled. Therefore, the insertion of **taking or carrying away** rather than **taking and carrying away** did not materially prejudice Jones. The justices also found that it was undisputed that Jones intended to take the money; it was whether or not the money 'belonged to another'. The justices found that "In reaching its verdict, the jury necessarily[136] resolved the factual dispute against Jones. Jones has failed to establish he was prejudiced by the error." The Supreme Court of Wyoming concluded that "After our review, we conclude that there was no prejudice to Jones from the jury instructions, that the evidence at trial was sufficient to sustain a conviction of robbery, and that Jones was not denied his right to a fair trial due to the cumulative effect of any alleged prosecutorial misconduct that may have occurred. Affirmed."[137]

Most crimes that are committed are investigated and prosecuted locally or by the state in which they occur. Some crimes transcend state boundaries and a national response is needed. This happens in many countries that have a large landmass like the US that experience criminals who operate across state lines and where local agencies are potentially hampered by the lack of jurisdiction they have to pursue criminals into states where similar but different criminal legislation may be applicable. As seen in the previous chapters of this book, sometimes federal responses are authorized after a crime in recognition of the problems encountered—for instance, the Lindbergh kidnapping—or when the recognition that a crime is of such magnitude and will stretch local enforcement forces to such a point that a federal agency needs to take control of the investigation—such as organized crime or killing the President. Less frequently but equally challenging are instances of child theft and abduction, where the FBI has seen its powers extended again since Lindbergh. For instance, in 1956 as a result of the Weinberger case[138] the waiting period in kidnapping cases was reduced from 7 days to 24 hours, and again under the Protection of Children from Sexual Predators Act in 1996.[139] Many thefts that would be prosecuted under state laws are also federal crimes due to the specific nature of the thefts—what was stolen or who the property was stolen from or of, course, what was stolen is then transported across state lines. Robbery too may be a federal crime. Robbing banks is always a federal crime though such robberies may be prosecuted in either a state or federal court. Theft of livestock too becomes a federal crime under certain circumstances, as well as theft of artwork and mail fraud. Many Controlled Substances Act[140] drug crimes are federal offences too.

Crimes that are clearly and always identifiable as federal crimes are those that occur on federal or Indian reservation land. Most but not all of the crimes that are deemed federal offences are contained within US 18. Tax evasion, the crime that famously managed to get Al Capone jail time, is a federal offence under US Title 26, and many federal white collar and economic crimes are penalized under the Crime Control Act of 1984. Burglary is not automatically a federal crime, but it can become a federal offence if the building or property stolen is federal, in instances such as burglary from a bank or burglary from a firearms store.

In the case of livestock theft under US 18 sec.667, "Whoever obtains or uses the property of another which has a value of $10,000 or more in connection with the marketing of livestock in interstate or foreign commerce with intent to deprive the other of a right in the property or a benefit of the property or to appropriate the property to his own use or the use of another shall be fined or imprisoned not more than five years."[141] On January 24, 2012, Allen John Foos pleaded guilty to federal theft when he admitted to transporting stolen livestock across state lines. The case was prosecuted by a US Attorney in federal court, the Western District of Missouri. The investigation into the crimes was conducted by the FBI, the US Department of Agriculture-Packers and Stockyards Administration and the Missouri State Highway Patrol.[142] Illegally disposing of government property, no matter how slight in value, is a federal crime. So that embezzling, stealing, purloining[143] or knowingly converting any record, voucher, money or thing of value of the United States or any other department or agency thereof or if a person conceals or retains the same with intent to convert to his own use . . . shall be fined or imprisoned not more than ten years or both. If the total value of goods purloined does not exceed $1,000 the jail term is not more than one year.[144] In the case of US v Manning, Private Bradley Manning was arrested for communicating national defense information. He has been charged with 22 offenses so far, which include theft of government property and espionage. Manning is due to stand trial in September 2012. He has gained international fame for his alleged crimes, as he is at the center of the WikiLeaks saga involving the disclosure of more than 400,000 classified army reports to the web site. One of the charges, aiding the enemy, is a capital offence. Prosecutors have stated that they are not seeking the death penalty though.[145] The only American government official to date that has been convicted of espionage and theft of government property is Samuel Loring Morison.[146] President Bill Clinton subsequently pardoned him in 2001 on his last day in office.[147] Both Morison and Manning have been allegedly involved in what are commonly called "Leaks" and criminally called federal theft.

Robbery and Burglary are both listed under Chapter 103 of US 18. So that under Section 2113 bank robbery can also be bank burglary. If a person uses force or fear or fraud to commit a bank robbery, then it is robbery; also, if a person enters a bank, and bank includes credit unions, savings and loans institutions, with intent to commit any felony or larceny, and there is no requirement for a force fear or fraud so this could be entering at nighttime, either form of the offence is liable to not more than 20 years of imprisonment. If during the course of committing any felony or larceny as described above, a person assaults any person or puts any person in jeopardy of life with a dangerous weapon, the term of imprisonment is not more than 25 years. If any person is killed or taken as hostage and death results, then the offence is a capital crime. Robbery of a person having control of US mail is liable to a 10-year jail sentence; but again, if a weapon is used at the time and a person is wounded or his life is put in jeopardy, the term of imprisonment is not more than 25 years.[148] Burglary of a post office, gaining entry or attempting to with intent to commit larceny is punishable with not more than 5 years of imprisonment.[149] Whoever by violence enters a post-office car, or any part of any car, steamboat or vessel, assigned to the use of the mail service, or willfully or maliciously assaults or interferes with any postal clerk in discharge of his duties in connection with such car, steamboat, vessel or apartment thereof, shall be fined or imprisoned not more than 3 years, or both.[150] The old Common Law concept of 'breaking and entering' appears in the section that deals with carrier facilities where section 2117 states that any person who breaks the seal or lock of any railroad car, vessel, aircraft, motortruck, wagon or other vehicle or of any pipeline system, containing interstate or foreign shipments of freight . . . with intent to commit larceny shall be imprisoned for not more than 10 years.[151]

Theft, burglary and robbery may all be committed as a federal crime. All the crimes are also governed by state legislation and the degree of seriousness will determine the sentence. However, federal crimes take precedence over state crimes, and since federal crimes tend to attract more significant jail sentences and are viewed as more serious due to the impact the crimes may have upon the entire nation, federal crimes will typically be prosecuted first. In many instances, if the crime is committed against a federal building or an employee the offender is liable to stiffer sentencing than if the same crime was committed against a non-federal building or a regular citizen. When a federal crime is committed, it does not matter in which state the offence took place, whereas state theft, burglary and robbery committed within that particular state are liable to interpretation and statutory provisions for that offence within that state.

On November 14, 2000, the BBC reported that the London Metropolitan Police had foiled what would have been the largest robbery in history.[152] Unknown to the gang of thieves, the real jewelry on display in the Millennium Dome had been replaced with worthless fakes. The intention was that 12 diamonds, including the 203-carat De Beers 'Millennium Star', together valued at £350 million, would be taken in the heist. The criminals used a JCB digger to smash through a perimeter fence to the Millennium Dome before they were arrested by numerous plain clothes police officers posing as builders and cleaners. Three robbers were arrested as they used sledgehammers and nail guns in an attempt to gain entry into the jewelry display cases; police arrested two men as they attempted entry to the 'Money Zone'; and a they arrested a third from inside the JCB. A fourth was arrested as he waited in a high-powered speedboat getaway vehicle on the River Thames nearby. A fifth man was arrested downstream in what was believed to be the transfer vehicle from the boat to land transport. A number of the men were found in possession of automatic weapons, as well as tools necessary to affect the break in. The operation involved more than 200 police officers and started due to a 'tip off'. On Monday 18 February 2002 at the Old Bailey, the five suspects were convicted of conspiracy to commit robbery.[153] Robert Adams, driver of the JCB digger, said, "I was 12 inches from pay day . . . it would have been a blinding Christmas." After capture, another member of the gang said, "We would have got away with it but for the fact there were 140 police waiting for us."[154]

Endnotes

1. For a history of the Old Bailey and its proceedings see www.oldbaileyonline.org
2. Part of the structure was three and not four sided to allow 'fresh air' to pass through the building, as apparently in the previous building the stench was unbearable and justices were given nosegays to sniff whilst hearing cases. The building was fully enclosed in 1774, but soon after typhus broke out due to the insanitary conditions and the use of nosegays was re-introduced.
3. By 1729, the publication of proceedings became more organized and formal with a level of detail often not included in earlier publications. By 1907, legislation was passed that required taking shorthand notes of all public trials; and by 1913. the 'Proceedings' were no longer required. The April 1913 issue

simply stated "The publication of the C.C.C. Sessions papers is now discontinued.' Source: www.oldbaileyonline.org

4. Ibid. www.oldbaileyonline.org
5. Legislation in 1713 made it a capital offence to steal from a dwelling house any goods valued at more than 40 shillings.
6. For an interesting discussion about the problems of defining theft, see Richard W. Ireland, Law in action, law in books: The practicality of medieval theft law. *Continuity and Change*, 2002; 17(3); 309–323.
7. Details of the reward are available at www.gardnermuseum.org
8. Source: www.dailymail.co.uk
9. See further: www.historic-uk.com
10. Penal Code Sec. 484-502.9
11. Vehicle Code 10851
12. Penal code 487 (d) (1)
13. Penal code 487 (1) (a)
14. Ibid.
15. Any ruminant related to sheep but with straight horns and a beard. This certainly means goats.
16. Ibid.
17. Source: www.thecarconnection.com
18. Ibid.
19. See: www.dmv.ca.gov
20. www.idtheftcenter.org. California was ranked 2nd in the US for the total number of reported cases per annum (2007).
21. www.ca.gov
22. Penal Code Sec. 530.5
23. Penal code. Sec. 502.9
24. Posing as a legitimate company or agency in an email, on a webpage or through the Internet to obtain information
25. See: www.leginfo.ca.gov
26. For example, Leandro Andrade who received a 25 year sentence in California for shoplifting in 1995 and Gregory Taylor who was sentenced to 25 years to life for breaking into a soup kitchen. See further www.scholarship.law.duke.edu
27. Richard Napoleon Brown v Att. Gen of California and Earnest Bray Jr. v Att Gen of California 283 F.3d.1019, February 7, 2002, United States Court of Appeals, Ninth Circuit.
28. Ibid.
29. Walshe, S. Why California's three strikes law is out of order. Wednesday, 25 January 2012. www.guardian.co.uk
30. See Laws of Justinian. Law IV.
31. Code Penal Arts. 322, 329

32. Codice Penale Art 376
33. Henry VIII Chap 5.
34. Lovett, I. Tuba raids' plague schools in California. 9 February 2012. *New York Times*. www.nytimes.com
35. 'Banda black market suspected as California tubas vanish'. 9 March 2012. www.usatoday.com
36. www.sonomanews.com
37. Penal Code. Sec. 487 (d) (1)
38. Cattle rustling on the rise in Texas. 21 February 2012. www.nbcfw.com
39. For a discussion on the history of the term 'rustling' and its practice in Texas, see: Texas State Historical Association. www.tshaonline.org
40. Texas man gets 99 years for cattle rustling. 25 August 2011. www.huffington post.com
41. Texas penal code. Sec. 31.03
42. Texas penal code. Sec. 31.03 (4) (A)
43. Supra, 7. (f) (2)
44. 'Dallas officials bust sophisticated retail theft ring'. 9 September 2011. www.dfw.cbslocal.com
45. Ibid.
46. Texas penal code Sec. 31.15
47. Ibid 31.15 (2)
48. www.huffingtonpost.com
49. Ibid.
50. Mike Hashimoto, 'New Dallas police policy: It's OK to steal, just not too much?' 30 December 2011. www.dallasnews.com
51. See Identity 'Theft in Texas: White Paper'. May 2008. By Identity Theft 911. LLC. p. 2. www.idt911.com
52. 'Texas woman gets 38 years in ID theft case'. 1 July 2008. Nations Restaurant News. www.nrn.com. Also at: www.dallasnews.com
53. Ibid.
54. Ibid.
55. 'Texas ranks 5th in the Nation for reported cases of ID Theft'. 17 April 2012 Better Business Bureau. www.austin.bbb.org
56. Supra. Identity Theft 911, p. 20
57. Supra. Identity Theft 911, p. 23
58. www.oag.state.tx.us
59. Texas Penal Code. Title 7. Chapter 32. Sec. 32.51
60. US Supreme Court. Rummel v Estelle, Corrections Director. Certiorari to the United States Court of Appeals for the Fifth Circuit. No. 78-6386
61. Supra. Rummel v Estelle, p. 268
62. Supra. Rummel v Estelle, p. 284

63. The Wyoming Criminal Code. Title 6. Chap 3. Art. 4. 6-3-402
64. Buffalo and bison are used as interchangeable terms in the US, whereas the buffalo and the bison are not the same animal. Buffalo are only found in Africa and Asia. Bison are found in North America and is the correct name for a large bovine mammal of the family ungulates.
65. Title 6. III (viii)
66. Francis Xavier Guerrero v The State of Wyoming, 2012, WY 77 S-10-0263. Decided 05/31/2012.
67. Ibid. at page 8 [16]. The court cites LaFave 19.8 at 141. Wayne, R. LaFave, *Criminal law.* 5th ed. St. Paul, Minn. WestLaw, 2010.
68. Ibid.
69. Wyoming Criminal Code 6-3-404
70. Wyoming Criminal Code 6-3-404 (b)
71. www.huffingtonpost.com, www.2.nbc4i.com
72. Glen Eddie Garcia v The State of Wyoming No. 88-205. July 13, 1989.
73. Ibid. page 1098. Urbikit. J.
74. Regina v Coggins. 12 Cox C.C. 517
75. Regina v Perkins. 2 Den C.C. 458, 169 Eng. Rep 582
76. Rex v Owen, 1 Moody C.C. 96, 168 Eng. Rep. 1200
77. Supra. Justice Urbikit at p. 1100.
78. Ibid. 1105
79. As defined by Sir Matthew Hale. Commentaries on the Laws of England.
80. Theft Act 1968 Burglary
81. Theft Act 1968 (As amended) section 10
82. www.nola.cime
83. Defendant in 'hillside burglaries' sentenced to 17 years in prison. 30 September 2010. www.latimes.com
84. Blankstein, A. Cat burglar rats out his techniques for police. 13 August 2008. www.latimes.com and www.lapdonline.org
85. Ali Foroutan v Domingo Uribe, Jr. Case No: 5:10-cv-02411-LHK. United States District Court Northern Division of California San Jose Division. Dated: April 9, 2012
86. TPC 30.02
87. TPC 30.03
88. TPC 30.04
89. Richardson v State 888 S.W. 2d. 822 Tex.Crim.App. 1994
90. Ibid.
91. www.sanangelopolice.org
92. TPC 30.03 (b)
93. TPC 30.05
94. TPC 30.02 (b)

95. Source: Bureau of Justice Statistics. www.bjs.gov and FBI annual crime statistics, www.fbi.gov
96. www.txdps.state.tx.us. Index Crime Analysis. 2008. P. 11
97. See further: Sir Edward Coke. *The institutes of the laws of England.*
98. Used by actor Clint Eastwood in his portrayal of detective Harry Callaghan in the movie "Sudden Impact" (fourth in the Dirty Harry series) where Callaghan says, "Go ahead, make my day."
99. www.capitol.state.tx.us
100. Gov. Perry signs law allowing Texans to protect themselves. Tuesday 27 March 2007. www.capitol.state.tx.us
101. www.cbsnews.com
102. Ellick, A. Grand jury clears Texan in the killing of 2 burglars. *New York Times.* www.nytimes.com
103. Ibid.
104. Ibid.
105. Smith v State 902 P.2d 712, 1995 Wyo. LEXIS 173 (Wyo 1995)
106. W.C.C. 6-3-301
107. W.C.C. 6-3-305
108. See for example the report on Wikipedia and compare with the report "Barefoot bandit" pleads guilty to crime spree charges, www.reuters.com and that in the *Guardian* newspaper, www.guardian.co.uk and the single line entry of "pizza eating" at www.xtimeline.com
109. www.dailymail.co.uk. 28 January 2012
110. Spillius, A. "Barefoot bandit" caught. 11 July 2010. *The Telegraph.* www.telegraph.co.uk
111. Ibid. for 20,000 and 50,000? That depends on which fan site you look at.
112. James Schuller v The State of Wyoming. No. 83-33 Supreme Court of Wyoming, 9 September 1983, 668 P.2d 1333
113. Ibid., p. 1341.
114. Harry Winston Jewelers, Paris. December 5, 2008.
115. MPC. Sec. 222.1
116. www.fbi.gov. 2010 Crime Statistics.
117. US DOJ. FBI Crime in the United States' robbery 2010. www.fbi.gov
118. Ibid.
119. Ibid.
120. Sir Matthew Hale, supra.
121. Theft Act 1968 Section 8
122. California Penal Code Section 211
123. California Penal Code Section 215
124. C.P.C. Sec. 496
125. People v Smith infra

126. People v Smith, No. A118208, September 29, 2009. Court of Appeal, First District, Division 4, California.
127. Mills, SM. CA upholds convictions in S.F. jewelry store robbery. Thursday 1 October 2009. *Metropolitan News.* www.metnews.com
128. People v Smith. supra, 1. Introduction
129. Reported at www.caselaw.findlaw.com
130. TPC Sec 29.03
131. Full details in *Jacksonville Daily Progress.* Harper, F. Man receives 2 life sentences for shooting. 23 June 2012. www.jacksonvilleprogress.com
132. See further Texas State Historical Association. www.tshaonline.org
133. W.C.C. Title 6, Chapter 2, Article 4 (2011)
134. W.C.C. 6-2-401 (c) (i) (ii)
135. Supreme Court of Wyoming, June 14, 2012. S-11-0073
136. Ibid. at margin note 23.
137. Ibid. at margin note 38.
138. July 4, 1956, the kidnapping and murder of one-month old Peter Weinberger. After which President Eisenhower signed legislation to reduce the time period for FBI involvement from 7 days down to 24 hours.
139. Title VII: Murder and Kidnapping Investigations—Amends the Federal Judicial Code to authorize the Attorney General and the Director of the Federal Bureau of Investigation (FBI) to investigate serial killings when requested by the head of a state or local law enforcement agency.

     (Sec. 702) Amends the Federal Criminal Code to specify that: (1) the kidnapping offense applies regardless of whether the person was alive when transported across a state boundary if the person was alive when the transportation began; and (2) the fact that a presumption that a person has been transported in interstate or foreign commerce has not yet taken effect because 24 hours haven't passed since the abduction does not preclude a federal investigation of a possible kidnapping before the 24-hour period has ended.
140. Signed into law by President Richard Nixon October 27, 1970.
141. US Title 18. Part 1. Chapter 31. Sec. 667
142. See further Nebraska man pleads guilty to cattle theft. US Attorney's Office. 24 January 2012. Western District of Missouri. www.fbi.gov
143. Meaning to appropriate wrongfully and often by breach of trust. Source: Merriam-Webster. www.merriam-webster.com
144. US 18 sec. 641
145. See further: www.guardian.co.uk
146. For main entry see: www.wikipedia.com. Also see: Stephen Engelbert "Spy photo's sale leads to arrest. 3 October 1984. *The New York Times.* www.nytimes.com

147. Apparently the CIA was not comfortable with this decision. For a discussion about the Clinton pardons see Anthony Lewis, "Abroad at home: The pardons in perspective." 3 March 2001. *The New York Times*. www.nytimes.com
148. US 18. Sec. 2114
149. US 18. Sec. 2115
150. US 18. Sec. 2116
151. US 18. Sec. 2117
152. "Great Dome robbery foiled. Tuesday, 14 November 2000. BBC News. www.news.bbc.co.uk
153. See "Operation Magician." www.met.police.uk
154. Gysin, C. and Wright, S. Downfall of the Dome raiders. Mail Online. www.dailymail.co.uk

DRUG TRAFFICKING

The term 'Drug Trafficking' evokes visions of groups of Latin Americans, usually from Mexico, who are responsible for the mass killing of their own countrymen on the borders of Mexico and the US as they attempt to gain domination of supply routes for the distribution of illicit drugs into the US. But this is a simplistic view of an activity that engages thousands of criminals throughout the world who participate in the growing, manufacturing and supply of a range of substances that are currently deemed illegal. In reality, drug trafficking is a trade that has been in existence for thousands of years and has occupied individuals, groups and nation states;[1] and the substances that we loosely refer to as 'drugs' have themselves moved in and out of being legal and illegal over time. Therefore, it is important to bear in mind that historical, social and legal pressures may impact any discussion about drug trafficking and stimulate a highly fluid conversation that frequently changes due to a wide range of stimuli. What is illegal or illicit today may not have been in the past and may not be in the future. The commodities that today are 'trafficked' may themselves be illegal in some countries and legal in another, or they may be legal substances but the manner in which

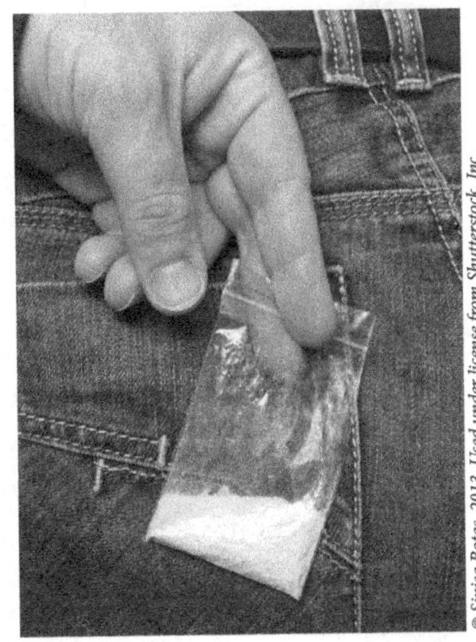

they are sold and distributed is illegal. Opium is a contemporary example. In some parts of the world the substance opium, which derives from the poppy plant, is a legal commodity. It is from opium that we create a number of other substances, such as morphine and heroin. Of these, morphine has been used extensively in the treatment of pain. When heroin was first synthesized, it was used as a substitute for morphine, as we mistakenly believed that heroin could prevent morphine addiction. Opium is not a banned substance in many countries and those nations have a long history of opium use. Conversely, a number of countries consider opium a dangerous addictive substance and they criminalize its possession; therefore, to supply opium to the citizens of those countries is invariably a serious criminal offence. Tobacco is a substance that is a drug and legal. However, to manufacture tobacco products without a license and to distribute those as the genuine article is a criminal offence. Some countries would describe that activity as trafficking; other countries would use the term smuggling. The commodity tobacco is ordinarily legal to possess, but dealing in stolen or fake cigarettes are both crimes. Therefore, the distinction between whether or not the tobacco is being smuggled or trafficked may be a point of legality, but to the general population the distinction may not impact upon understanding that the actions are illegal.

Typically, if a group of people is engaged in the supply and distribution of the illegal substance, for example opium, we refer to this group as an organized crime group, or since the 1970s a drug cartel.

Interestingly, although criminal offences are ordinarily a matter for an individual nation state to design and prosecute, we deem some crimes so offensive to all of humanity that we assign them the status of being a crime against humanity—meaning that any country may proceed to bring a prosecution against the offender. Drug trafficking, as well as war crimes, human trafficking and terrorism, are assigned as crimes prosecutable by any nation state.

Throughout this chapter the term Drug Trafficking Organization (DTO) is used to mean a drug trafficking group, a drugs cartel and an organized crime group comprising a group of people engaged in the growing, manufacturing or supplying of an illegal drug or drugs. Whether or not individual nation states decide to call such groups cartels or drug trafficking organizations or Organized Crime Groups (OCGs) may be pertinent to the laws of those individual states, but for the purposes of the general discussion about the nature and form of trafficking that occurs, the diverse array of terminology does not impact the criminal actions.[2]

The United Nations Office on Drugs and Crime (UNODC) views a drug as follows: "This is a term of varied usage. In medicine, it refers to any substance with the potential to prevent or cure disease or enhance physical or mental welfare. In pharmacology, it means any chemical agent that alters the biochemical or physiological processes of tissues or organisms. In the context of international drug control, 'drug' means any of the substances listed in Schedule I and II of the 1961 Single Convention on Narcotic Drugs, whether natural or synthetic."[3] This means that caffeine, tobacco and alcohol, as well as heroin, cocaine, amphetamines and cannabis are all drugs. The difference is that some are legal to possess and others are not depending upon where on earth you are located at the time of the possession. The 1961 Single Convention on Narcotic Drugs states: "This Convention aims to combat drug abuse by coordinated international action. There are two forms of intervention and control that work together. First, it seeks to limit the possession, use, trade in, distribution, import, export, manufacture and production of drugs exclusively to medical and scientific purposes. Second, it combats drug trafficking through international cooperation to deter and discourage drug traffickers."[4] But even this can be misleading as the convention title uses the term 'Narcotic', but a narcotic is strictly speaking a substance that derives from an opiate, the poppy plant; morphine and heroin are opiates, whereas cocaine and methamphetamine are not and nor is cannabis. Yet we have law enforcement personnel throughout the world that operate as narcotics agents, which are in fact drug agents, as they disrupt and arrest actors engaged in the illicit supply of many more substances than narcotics. According to the 1961 Convention, "Drug trafficking is a global illicit trade involving the cultivation, manufacture, distribution and sale of substances which are subject to drug prohibition laws."[5] Therefore, any individual or group of individuals engaged in any of the above specified activities is drug trafficking, and any country that is a growing or transit country for illicit drugs is a drug trade country. In real terms, it would be hard to find any country that is not a 'drug trade country' as most nations have citizens engaged in the illegal growing of cannabis. This narrow interpretation though does not capture the spirit of the term in its common usage and the label drug trade country is most probably meant to imply a nation state that has large scale illicit manufacturing and supply operations taking place.

International responses to both drug trafficking and drug trade countries vary. In the US, there are specific legislative provisions to deal with members of DTOs, as well as the leaders of DTOs, and the President[6] may designate an individual a "Drug Kingpin."[7] Enactment of these provisions will have the effect of blocking all US property interests of the designated person and companies or individuals that trade with the designated person are also subject to criminal sanctions.[8] A small number of countries are also believed to be actively involved in drug production and supply and these countries are frequently referred to as 'narco-states'. In some instances, the fragility of the regime within a country makes it susceptible to being overtaken by DTOs, and in other instances there is positive action by the leaders of a country to generate income and retain power by alignment with DTOs. In still other instances, a country may have a history of producing and using a drug base product, such as the coca leaf that is the base for cocaine, and the official position of that country is that production of the coca leaf is not criminal *per se* and therefore the country is not of a mind to criminalize the production of a leaf that its citizens have used for thousands of years when the criminal offence of using cocaine is happening thousands of miles away by citizens in another country. Given the wide range of issues that surround the growing and manufacturing of drug substances, it is easy to understand why drug trafficking is a highly complex and multi-faceted problem that impacts citizens[9] across the entire planet and that one single response is neither desirable nor possible. It is also understandable why the US places such a high priority on the interdiction of drug trafficking, as North America is the world's largest illicit drug market.[10] Currently, the most widely abused substance is marijuana. The consumption of cocaine may have plateaued,[11] and amphetamine type substances (ATS) (including methamphetamine) are likely to become the number one choice of abused substance over the next decade. Currently over the entire planet, cannabis[12] represents 70% of all illicit substances seized *per annum.*[13]

The response of individual countries to the 'drug problem' varies according to a range of drivers that include economic stability and wealth, social attitudes, historical influences, the position taken by the leader or leaders of the nation, religion and customs. Consequently, many nations do not agree with or understand the apparent acceptance or rejection of drug use in other countries. This is so much so that despite attempts to have a uniform and united approach to the drug issue it is not 'an issue' for some countries. Somewhere within this complex conversation, the UNODC is "mandated to assist Member States in their struggle against illicit drugs, crime and terrorism. In the Millennium Declaration, Member States also resolved to intensify efforts to fight transnational crime in all its dimensions, to redouble the efforts to implement the commitment to counter the world drug problem and to take concerted action against international terrorism."[14] Bringing informed discussion to a mixed audience of nation states is a laudable objective as it is only through understanding why a nation takes a particular stance that we can hope to achieve consensus over the way forward in a united approach towards reducing the consumption of substances that have significant detrimental health implications for millions of humans.

Over the past 20 years, Mexico has become the world's leading transit country for numerous illegal substances. It is also rapidly becoming the major manufacturing nation for a number of substances. Marijuana has been grown and shipped from Mexico into the US for dozens of years, but the changes that have occurred in the last two decades are the primary reason for the massive amounts of narco-terrorism now seen in northern provinces of the country for Mexico has shifted from a transport country into a manufacturer not only of marijuana but also of cocaine, heroin and ATS's. What was once a lucrative transportation enterprise that provided the means for Colombian cocaine cartels to ship into the US markets is now a colossal DTO that is 'farm to arm' for a broad range of illegal substances grown, manufactured and shipped directly from within Mexico. Accordingly, the illicit financial returns are no longer a transportation charge of millions of dollars; there is now a complete full service drug enterprise worth billions of dollars. The concomitant battles between rival DTOs, the Los Zetas and the Gulf cartel or the Sinaloa and Juarez factions were always inevitable. The prize was, and remains, far too great. Domination of a multi-billion dollar illegal industry was always going to result in the death of thousands of innocent (and guilty) people.

Smuggling is a term that implies the movement of an illicit substance or a legal substance that is supplied to avoid payment of fees or taxes. Illegal booze was 'smuggled' across state lines during Prohibition. Trafficking is generally used to capture a broader range of criminal activities, such as manufacturing and supplying illicit goods and services so that a person who transports illegal goods may be smuggling and a person who makes or manufactures those goods and supplies them is trafficking. Smuggling implies a complicity on behalf of the person doing the transportation, whereas trafficking may or may not involve willing complicity so that a drug mule may be forced to traffick drugs into the US and a drugs smuggler may willingly transport illicit drugs for a fee. And although these are elastic terms, it can be said that prior to the 1980s there were very few DTOs in Mexico but there were many drug smugglers.

As the magnitude of illicit drug trade grows in any country, there comes a point in time when complicity in the illegal enterprise by the government becomes a possibility—and in some countries a reality. It is the case that for some illicit drug operations to be successful the local or national government must at least 'turn a blind eye' to the activities of the DTO. A number of countries around the globe are now at this tipping point. In the case of Mexico, there is no direct evidence to support an assertion that previous or current governments have been directly involved in facilitating drug trafficking, but the ability of its government to prevent a narco-state is weakened every year that the DTOs gain further wealth and influence. The danger for citizens of Mexico and the southern border states of the US is that unless there is an effective cessation of the growth of the DTOs, then Mexico could drift into a general state of lawlessness that could seep not only northwards but also into neighboring Central American states. In fact, this may already have occurred.

Since the early 1980s, a number of groups have fought to achieve the dominance of previous smuggling routes in the north of Mexico. From the original relationship with Colombian DTOs where the Colombians supplied cocaine and the Mexicans transported it into the US, the Mexicans agreed to split the cocaine 50/50 rather than accepting a cash payment for transportation services. This new deal meant that the burgeoning Mexican DTOs were themselves about to move into the supply and distribution business—a far more lucrative venture. Within a short period of time, groups of smugglers banded together to form crime groups, and the regions of their operations frequently informed the groups' names so that those from the Sinaloa region became the Sinaloa Cartel and similarly those form Juarez became the Juarez Cartel. Infighting and inter-group rivalry were inevitable and the picture of control fluctuated greatly over the first 10 years of operations. In an effort to curb the influence and criminality of the new DTOs, the Mexican government sought assistance and expert training from the US. This led to the formation of a Special Forces unit known as the *Mexican Grupo Aeromovil de Fuertas Especiales* (GAFES). In 1997, 31 members of the GAFES deserted from the Mexican army and formed their own mercenary unit available for hire to the DTOs. Given that these ex-soldiers were trained by US Special Forces, they had exactly the skills needed to supply specialist security to drug kingpins and the lower level smugglers. The group of ex-military named themselves Los Zetas, as they had previously carried the assignment call sign code of 'Z' when working for the Federal City Police. By the early part of the 21st century, the

Los Zetas had branched out into becoming their own DTO, which now operated independently of the other drug enterprises. Due to their specific skills and ability to carry out extreme levels of violence against other DTO members, the Zetas have rapidly become one of the most powerful and largest DTOs operating across Mexico, Central America and, recently, the globe. Attempts to curb the expansion of the Zetas have resulted in many of the large scale and graphic killings of rival DTO members as well as of local citizens. Additionally, and like many DTOs, the Zetas are expanding their portfolio of criminality to capture human trafficking and an assortment of criminal allegiances that straddle the drugs-terrorism nexus. In August 2010 in the San Fernando region of northern Tamaulipas state, 200 bodies were found in a single grave.[15] According to one survivor, the Zetas had slaughtered the group for refusing to carry drugs across the border into the US. The ability of the Zetas to inflict extreme violence upon other cartel members resulted in a number of the DTOs forming alliances with each other for mutual protection. Few of these temporary arrangements have been sustained and the current situation reflects varying degrees of loosely affiliated DTOs with members who move in and out, as well as across, what were firmly established DTOs, such as La Familia Michoacana (LFM), the Gulf cartel, the Sinaloa and most recently smaller groups of young criminals who mimic the Zetas and others, such as the 'new Zetas' and the *Caballeros Templarios*, the Knights Templars.

The strength of the Mexican DTOs is now so well established that there really are no other DTOs in existence throughout the entire Central American region. Those that do exist are traditional local crime families that have inevitably succumbed to the strength and influence of the DTOs, such as the Zetas, so that they remain in operation largely due to support from the DTOs, or at least by their tacit permission. Due to low employment prospects, poor infrastructure, poverty and poor educational opportunities, many of the impoverished Central American nation states are highly vulnerable to being overtaken by the Mexican DTOs. If it is true that the US market for cocaine is saturated, cannabis is being grown more and more at the local level and Canada remains the dominant supply line for ATS's, then the DTOs of Mexico will look further afield for new illicit drug markets. There is already evidence that Honduras, Guatemala and Costa Rica are deeply impacted by the Sinaloa, Gulf and Zeta DTOs,[16] and Nicaragua, Belize and El Salvador are likely to be impacted soon. Already Honduras has overtaken Mexico since 2010, in the number of murders *per capita,* and it is currently the world leader with 82.1 murders per 100,000 people.[17] Until the mid-1990s, the Honduran government relied heavily upon the military to maintain law and order across the country. More recently, the civilian regime has been hard pushed to provide the funds needed to effectively prevent the encroachment of the DTOs, and the US government now views Honduras as a 'major drug trafficking country'. In 2011, the country made the top 20 drug trafficking countries list for the first time. One clear indication of the presence of the Mexican DTOs is that the press is no longer reporting atrocities within the country. This silencing of the press has become an established and regrettable feature of life in Mexico and is now being repeated across much of the Central American region. The government of Honduras is now receiving military training from US Special Forces to create an elite unit of personnel who can take on the DTOs. Recent history in Mexico suggests that extreme caution should be taken when equipping government forces with Special Forces skills and training, as those that have learnt how to combat DTOs may themselves become a DTO in the future. (In July 2009, ten members of the Honduran operation group were arrested for transporting 142 kilos of heroin.)[18] On January 14, 2012, Honduran police uncovered a shallow grave of 25 people. The police believe that the local gang *Barrio 18* was contracted by the Zetas to conduct the killings as reprisal for police killings of 7 DTO members in La Lima. Perhaps a new branch of Los Zetas in Honduras is no longer a discussion point; it appears they have arrived.

Guatemala is also highly susceptible to becoming a narco-state, as it too has high poverty levels (42 in 1,000 children die before age 5),[19] low educational achievement (1 in 4 adults cannot read),[20] lenient gun laws (every 16 in 100 of the population own a gun),[21] and an increasing number of desertions from the National Police.[22] It is also a country that has an ideal climate for growing a range of drugs (including the poppy for heroin production) and governmental instability after years of being run by a military dictatorship. When all of these factors are combined with the extreme wealth brought into the region by drugs (and the associated crimes of prostitution, money laundering and human trafficking), it is difficult to see how Guatemala can resist a DTO takeover. The current government is making strenuous efforts, however, and in spite of budget shortfalls, to stem the influx of DTO influence and the surge in brutal drug related killings.[23] As the International Crisis Group has reported, "Geography has made Guatemala an important conduit for narcotics heading into North America. Add to that institutional weakness and endemic poverty, and you have conditions for a perfect storm of violence and corruption."[24] Over the past 5 years within Guatemala, there have been numerous examples of the formation of allegiances between existing domestic crime groups[25] and the Sinaloa, the Zetas and the Gulf DTOs. The initial flush of allegiances has now broken up into a series of temporary pacts, such as the 'Pacto de Petan'; but, as seen further north, these are typically short-lived relationships that ultimately result in bloodshed that spills over into the local populations. One Guatemalan crime family, the Mendozas, appears to have packed up and moved over into neighboring Belize, as it can no longer operate with impunity in its native country due to the power and influence of the Zetas.[26] As seen recently in Honduras, the Zetas are not averse to extreme violence to ensure compliance with their wishes. On May 15, 2011, 27 farm laborers including a 13-year-old child were found decapitated. The gang responsible was comprised of 200 members and they left a message for the authorities written in the blood of the murder victims. The message informed the police that the Zetas had ordered the killings in response to a local drug dealer who had stolen from them. In the same month, an assistant public attorney was kidnapped and beheaded. His corpse had a note that said "Zeta 200." Guatemala's new President Molina took office in January 2012 on a platform of fighting the DTOs with an 'iron fist'. History will disclose whether or not he can be successful against the new Guatemalan/Mexican DTOs.

The situation in Bolivia is rather different in that the country is a main producer of the coca plant and native Bolivians have ingested the coca leaf for centuries. Eva Morales, the president, is a former representative of the coca growers union and he strongly supports the right of Bolivia to grow the coca leaf. He does not support the manufacturing of cocaine and has taken a strong stance[27] against those found dealing in cocaine within the country. However, the country has withdrawn from the 1961 Convention Narcotic Drugs as the UN has determined that the coca leaf should be defined as an illegal substance. Bolivia has indicated that if the classification of the coca plant is reversed it will rejoin.

The destination for Bolivian coca leaves has historically been Colombia. The very word cartel is invariably associated with Colombia and the Medellin or Cali cartels. The world's first multi-millionaire drug lord was Colombian Pablo Emilio Escobar Gaviria and much of the history of trafficking cocaine originates from within Colombia. Escobar was a smalltime crook who managed to gain notoriety and fear by moving into the cocaine world and immediately being prepared to use levels of violence unseen previously. Within a short period of time, he managed to assert himself into the position of leader of the drug operations in the city of Medellin, and through his 'silver or lead' policy with local and national officials he soon dominated the entire criminal drug industry not only in Colombia but throughout South, Central and North America. In spite of his attempts to cultivate a 'Robin Hood' image with locals, Escobar sank into a deep and violent war with the government of Colombia during which time he blew up a commercial airline,[28] kidnapped government officials and even used a tank to blow up the Supreme Court building whilst in session, in the nation's capital of Bogota.[29] The global market for cocaine was so vast in the 1980s and 1990s that Colombia could support other cartels in addition to Escobar's Medellin, and soon two educated and wealthy brothers, Gilberto and Miguel Rodrigeuz-Orejuela, formed a new DTO in Cali. Internal factions and a strong effort by the government of Colombia eventually led to the killing of Escobar and the destruction of all the major cartels within the country. Another and highly relevant factor was that the Mexican DTOs had also moved into the supply and distribution of cocaine instead of being transporters for the Colombians. This too was a major factor in bringing about the end of the domination asserted by the Colombian DTOs in the world of cocaine. Colombia is no longer the world's largest producer of cocaine, and this dubious accolade rests with neighboring Peru. Where the balance of power in terms of criminal drug operations will rest across all of Central and South America remains unclear. For many years, leftist and right wing paramilitary groups have been a feature of the drug discussion in numerous countries throughout the region. Recently, the Colombian group FARC and the Peruvian Shining Path both announced a cessation of violence. A short time ago in the tri-border region (TBA) zone of northern Brazil a number of DTOs established moneylaundering operations for themselves and for other criminal organizations.[30] There has been a significant increase in the number of banks in the area and the remote and quiet region now has all of the appearances of being a haven for laundering drug money. Worryingly, a number of terrorist groups are also known to be operating in the area and the drugs-terrorist nexus[31] is no longer a potential threat—it is a reality. Neither DTOs nor terrorist groups have any compunction about who they work with to achieve criminal domination and absolute wealth. It is simply, and dangerously, just a case of what will the billions of drug dollars be spent on—the vulgar display of criminal wealth so vast that it can never be totally consumed or the funding of blowing up humans in an attempt to topple democratic regimes.

DTOs are not a feature exclusive to the Americas. Many of the world's better known DTOs have evolved into drug trafficking and are better known for more traditional organized crime activities, such as prostitution and gambling. Soon into a discussion about organized crime one will hear the names Yakuza, Triads and Mafia. Many of these historically better known groups have operated across the globe for centuries and have modified their suite of criminal enterprises to suit changing opportunities, so that today the Yakuza, the Triads and the Mafias will all engage in drug trafficking alongside and often in association with the cartels to form loose and sometimes temporary allegiances of DTOs to effect a mutual though temporary criminal advantage. Australia is among the world's highest *per capita* consumer nations of illicit substances; generally across Oceania[32] drug abuse is high.[33] Large quantities of cannabis are produced locally. Some ATS's are produced by small scale illegal domestic laboratories and the remainder of illicit substances are imported into the countries mostly by established crime groups that have now taken up drug trafficking.[34] The ubiquitous Mexican DTOs are also now present. Historically, Australia has many links to Europe, and the Italian Mafia has had a presence in the country for many years. DTOs from Thailand, Malaysia and Myanmar are becoming prominent producers and suppliers of ATS's to the region. Also, the Zetas and Sinaloa DTOs are beginning to establish relationships with the domestic Australian mafia of whom the Calabrian Ndrangheta are believed by internal law enforcement agencies to be dominant. The world's largest seizure of MDMA to date occurred in 2007 when Australian customs officers seized 15 million pills during Operation Inca.[35]

Further north into Asia there is a long history of drug use for medicinal and recreational purposes and the influence of organized crime groups in the manufacturing and supply of these substances. Legend suggests that Chinese triads originated in the 17th century when a group of rebel monks formed a secret organization. Today there are numerous triads as DTOs across the world. Within Hong Kong the better known groups include Sun Yee On, and in Mainland China the Big Circle Boys are one of the larger DTOs. In Japan, the publically advertised Yakuza[36] are a well-organized and commercial criminal organization that has a vast portfolio of services, including drug trafficking. In considering Asia as a whole, opium remains the largest illicit product produced. However, this is rapidly being overtaken by ATS manufacturing and supply within and outside of Asia itself. Overall global production of opium has declined though and the combined efforts of Afghanistan and Myanmar have dropped to 87% of world production from a high point of 98% a few years ago. The changes are due to the ability of Mexican DTOs to grow opium inside Mexico now and to convert this to heroin.

The entire Golden Triangle region of Myanmar, Northern Thailand and Laos is becoming a center point for small laboratories to produce ATS's on the banks of the Mekong River and have immediate and easy access to major shipping routes further south. Combined with traditional and well-established land routes through Thailand and Malaysia to Singapore, the Golden Triangle remains a major source of drug manufacturing and supply for the world. All that has changed is the commodity being produced and illegally exported as the wealthy youth of the world use more and more synthetically produced substances for recreational drug abuse than traditional opiates and cannabis products. DTOs consequently flourish in an area of jungle and difficult terrain, political instability, poverty and few educational opportunities. Additionally, China and Afghanistan have joined in the highly lucrative ATS global market of which China itself is a major market with a burgeoning middle class that seeks to emulate the legal and illegal consumer activities of the West. A recent addition to this list is Iran, which too is now a producer of ATS, and especially methamphetamine.[37]

Methamphetamine is known locally as 'Shabu' in the Philippines, and this country is also experiencing a large growth in the number of manufacturers and suppliers of the drug. Manila has a significant sea and airport and is an ideal distribution location for a number of global markets. Internally, the country is made up of numerous small islands that are variously interconnected by a complex series of roads and air and shipping ports. It is extremely difficult for authorities to police the country given the geography, and the diversity of the country makes it very suitable for establishing small size ATS labs. These factors have not escaped the Mexican DTOs, which are now believed to be operating directly and in association with a number of domestic crime groups across the country. Evidence of the growth of criminal activity is clear, for in 2010 police and customs seized 222 kilograms of methamphetamine, 17 million cannabis plants and 2,000 kilograms of marijuana, as well as arresting 6,435 individuals for drug offences.[38] The Regional Centre for East Asia and the Pacific of the UNODC reported in 2011 that methamphetamine production has increased fourfold between 2008 and 2010 from 32 million pills to 133 million *per annum.*[39]

India is located between the Golden Triangle and the Golden Crescent of Afghanistan, Iran and Pakistan. It is another country situated at a global crossroad and it has numerous transportation outlets. The country is traditionally poor but is quickly becoming wealthier and establishing a middle class of young drug users. Seventy percent of the entire population is below 35 years of age. India is one of the only two countries[40] permitted to legally produce opium for pharmaceutical purposes. It is a nation that has a large chemical industry and dozens of large scale laboratories. India is the world's largest producer of pseudoephedrine. ATS production is increasing and is of major concern nationally and internationally. Cannabis as hashish has been consumed by Indians for centuries. Like many of the countries discussed that are easily infiltrated by DTOs, India suffers from high levels of systemic corruption. It has a long history of DTOs due to its prevalence in using and supplying cannabis products. Alliances between domestic DTOs and external groups are now increasing due to the global nature of the drug market and the changing pattern of illicit drug use and abuse. Evidence of Mexican DTOs operating across India is sparse, but it is anticipated that these groups will become prominent over the course of the next few years as established Western drug markets become saturated and the Asian and African markets begin to open up further.

It is predictable that as the African drug market grows, India will become a major manufacturing and supply source of ATS to the continent. Latin American DTOs have already formed allegiances with west coast nation states and domestic DTOs in the Cote D'Ivoire, Guinea Bissau, Nigeria and Senegal. The transit routes up through Mali and into Algeria, Tunisia and Morocco are already well established as former trade routes that have now become cocaine trade routes. On the east coast, trading patterns with India by Somalia, Tanzania and Mozambique have existed for centuries. As is so very often the case, language and historical partnerships will frame future drug allegiances and route patterns, and India is set to become a supply partner to Africa on the east coast as the desire to obtain ATS's across Africa expands. Generally across Africa, the level of illicit drug consumption is increasing. Cocaine use has increased particularly in those countries that are transporting for the Latin American DTOs from arrival points in Africa towards European delivery markets. Heroin use is also up; the highest reported increases are in Kenya and Mauritius. Barbiturate abuse, known locally in South Africa as 'Smarties', has surged recently; and throughout all countries that report drug use cannabis consumption has increased across all income levels and urban and rural localities. Evidence of the arrival of Latin American DTOs is clear now throughout a number of West African countries.

The most affected country so far is Guinea-Bissau, a tiny nation state of 14,000 square miles and a population of 1.6 million people. Today the capital city of Bissau sports massive mansions and top end luxury cars. Beer is now selling at the equivalent of two days' wages for a local and a bottle of scotch costs a month's salary. Locals offer residents and tourists cocaine by the kilogram. Three years ago cocaine was unheard of; today it has a local tag, 'Pedra'. Drugs are shipped mostly by sea and travel from South and Central America by night to avoid detection by spotter planes. The journey takes on an average five days and once within the extensive small island coastline of Guinea-Bissau detection is almost impossible. Small aircraft also make deliveries into the nation state, either landing at sea or into small makeshift landing strips prepared by locals. The former head of the country's navy, Jose Americo Bubo Na Tchuto, and its air force, Ibraima Papa Camarra, were both recently named as 'Drug Kingpins' by the US. It is estimated that the illicit drug trade through Guinea-Bissau is now worth $1 billion per year.[41] What makes this entire relationship even more of a concern than any other allegiance between DTOs is that as the illicit product moves further north its handlers are known terrorists and the drug-terrorist nexus becomes a fact rather than speculation. After departing the African gold coast countries, cocaine heads north through the Maghreb region of Africa. The Maghreb comprises Morocco, Algeria, Libya, Tunisia and Mauritania. In 2003, three members of Al Qaeda in the Maghreb, AQIM, were charged in the US for drug trafficking.[42] This confirmed for authorities the long held suspicion that Al Qaeda had a relationship with Latin American DTOs. It is also now known that drug money provided the revenue needed to conduct the terrorist train bombing in Madrid that occurred on 11 March 2004, resulting in 191 deaths and 1,800 injuries, and the London bombings of 7 July 2005 when 48 people were killed and 700 were injured. Hezbollah (also written as Hizballah) is a Lebanese militant group that was formed in 1982. Links between this organization and Latin American DTOs have been established in the Tri-Border region of South America as well as further north in Mexico and California. Prosecutions against members of Hezbollah within the US have confirmed that funds created from smuggling operations conducted within the US have been used to support terrorist campaigns. The array of crimes that many terrorist organizations are prepared to conduct conforms to the diversity typically seen within any DTO: drug trafficking, extortion, human trafficking, intellectual property theft and even diamond smuggling.[43] Diversification of criminal enterprise is a common feature among all DTOs and organized crime groups generally, and globalization is as attractive to these illegal entities as it is to legal conglomerates such as McDonalds®. There are also always ample favorable local circumstances for crime, which is certainly the case for a number of groups in the Middle East where the production of hashish and opium has a long history. Hezbollah, Hamas, Al Qaeda and the Taliban all have links to the illicit hashish and opium trade within their own countries, and many of these groups have an established pattern of taxing, *ushr,* domestic producers of both drugs as a means of generating funding. The changes that are being witnessed most recently show that drug trafficking is now a major source of funding rather than what was once a subsidiary income source, as the opportunity for state support from sympathizers such as the Soviet Union or Cuba have ended. The symbiotic relationship between terrorist groups and DTOs is now well established and is expected to grow. In fact, to term the activities of a number of terrorist organizations as anything other than organized crime would be difficult given the propensity of contemporary groups to engage in all manner of crime manifestations and to form allegiances with other crime organizations that have no objective other than to amass illegal cash.

Europe and North America have been primary targets for all manifestations of organized criminal enterprises for many years and both regions have spawned numerous domestic DTOs. One of the best known is the Mafia. The origins of these groups are disputed. A general consensus dates the Sicilian group back to the 19th century and then the following larger mainland Italian groups comprised of the Naples based Camorra, the Calabrian Ndrangheta and a number of smaller families or associations such as the most recent Rome based Lazio. The word 'mafia' is also disputed. It may be a derivation of the Sicilian word *mafusi,* whereas Cosa Nostra (*Our Thing*) is a uniquely American creation. Popular myth has periodically implied that the mafia was not involved in drug trafficking. This was not, and is not, the case, and the suspected links to drug trafficking by mafias were firmly proven in cases such as the 'Pizza Connection'. There is no longer any doubt that contemporary mafias are dealing in the entire range of illicit drugs. For example, the Camorra are known to have relationships with Nigerian DTOs where the Nigerians receive cocaine from the Mexican DTOs and transport it north to Europe when the Italian groups then take over for distribution.[44] *Operation Crimine3* conclusively showed that Ndrangheta have links with the Zetas and the Albanian mafia for the distribution of cocaine across Europe.[45] Further north and east, the Russian mafia (also commonly referred to as *mafiya*) has operated across the country for years. It is since the end of the communist regime though that these groups have been able to flourish and grow with impunity. The fame of these groups caught the attention of the American public when it was found that the Russian mafiya had infiltrated North American ice hockey and players were throwing matches due to threats or for cash. Following this, a number of Russian DTO leaders have been prosecuted in Russia and the US for drug trafficking and these groups too have now found new criminal partners with the Mexican DTOs. It is not clear how many Russian DTOs are operating within the US at this time. The FBI has identified 27 major groups. For a country that was once a superpower, Russia's slide into chaos and lawlessness has been rapid. The fragility of the infrastructure of the soviet bloc has been exposed, and clearly internal criminal operators knew this beforehand, as the ease with which it has been possible for DTOs to take over has not been seen in any other nation in recent history. The laundering of dirty crime money is now a major enterprise within Russia, and it has been possible for any customer to avoid the nuisance of bank disclosure regulations as virtually anybody with enough cash could buy their own bank. Complicity by the world's banks in facilitating global money laundering by DTOs has been admitted by a number of respected and established banks, including most recently the HSBC.[46] There is no question that legitimate banks and financial service providers have been complicit in money laundering; the challenge is how to prevent an escalation of the addiction that this industry has for dirty money.

In North America drug trafficking has been located within geographical areas. The southern US has received drugs from Mexico and Central and South America, while historically Europe or Asia supplied the northern states and Canada. The eastern seaboard typically had heroin deliveries from Europe and the West Coast deliveries came from Asian gangs that traded with the local Asian communities. Mafia families that arrived many generations ago from Italy have dominated eastern Canada.[47] This situation has now morphed into a supply chain that involves the mafia and Mexican DTOs. Over on the West Coast, Asian gangs, prevalent in China as well as in Canada, have had a stronghold on the drugs industry for many years, and Big Circle Ten, Sun Yee On and 14k are operating across the region. These groups also have a presence in Toronto and Quebec, but less so than the MexMafia. As the Mexican DTOs expand, there is fresh evidence of alliances with the Chinese and Taiwanese (the United Bamboo

Gang) and Vietnamese DTOs in Vancouver and throughout the western regions. In the far north, the drug scene is more local and many law enforcement operations have resulted in seizures of marijuana that is being grown locally by locals.[48] Canada has been a significant producer of Ecstasy (MDMA) for a number of years and it remains a sizeable supplier of this drug to the US. Supply services appear to be from both individual operators and illegal commercial systems.

The ability of DTOs to flourish within the US is due to a number of complex factors. The US has sought to prevent the use and abuse of harmful substances, legal and illegal, for many years. Prohibition was itself an experiment that some view as the genesis of organized crime in the nation. This is probably over simplistic as many crime families had already arrived and were operating in the country before the 1920s. What Prohibition did achieve though was an environment that allowed organized crime to grow, as millions of ordinary law abiding citizens were prepared to break the law so that they could have a beer or liquor. Since that time, successive governments have dipped in and out of legislating against the use and possession of a range of substances, and the American population has responded by increasing the range and volume of substances it wishes to use. To say that the human species is addicted to mind altering opportunities is clearly true, as there is evidence of mankind making and taking a variety of drugs as far back as 10,000 years ago. Today the US has every DTO discussed present inside the country. These groups exist in every state and have concentrations in those cities and towns where immigrant populations have traditionally settled so that, for example, the Italian mafia are most noticeable on the East Coast in cities like New York, Boston and Philadelphia (as well as in Chicago); and the Russian mafiya are most sizeable in Brighton Beach, New jersey, as this was an area where many Russian immigrants grouped when they first arrived in the US. On the West Coast, there is a sizeable Asian origin population and so the greatest number of DTOs are the Chinese, Vietnamese and Taiwanese, as well as some Korean, Cambodian and Thai. Those states with closest proximity to Mexico have large Latino populations and are represented by the Zetas, the Sinaloa, the Gulf, the Tijuana and every other DTO known at present. Alongside these groups are gangs that have provided supply services, such as the Hells Angels to whom some attribute the street slang name for Angel Dust (PCP). Over the course of the last 20 years, the Mexican DTOs have become the most dominant group by far, and although there are numerous examples of collusion between many of the above DTOs, the current greatest threat to the US comes from Mexican groups.

Now that we have an overview of the reach of DTOs across the planet, the question is how to deal with them. Should responses remain local so that national agencies and laws are brought to bear? Or is the magnitude of the problem so great that a concerted global response is the only solution? At present we have a bit of both. There are UN treaties and a plethora of domestic statutes in every country of the world. We have multi-lateral and bi-lateral agreements and we have local, national and international enforcement agencies charged with the prevention and detection of drug trafficking. The lead agency from a global perspective is the UNODC. Established in 1997 as a merger between the UN Drug Control Programme and the Centre for International Drug Prevention, UNODC is mandated to assist nation states fight drug trafficking. It is not of itself an enforcement agency. The legislative framework for global drug prevention is through the UN Single Convention on Narcotic Drugs 1961 (as amended 1972), the Convention on Psychotropic Substances 1971 and the UN Convention Against Illicit Trafficking in Narcotic Drugs and Psychotropic Substances 1988. The aim of these treaties is to encourage and facilitate nation states to standardize drug terminology and to limit or ban outright the production and/or supply of narcotic and psychotropic substances. Once a treaty is in existence, there are normally a number of following protocols that act as amendments to the original. Expert advice, trends and new drug information are supplied to signatory countries through a range of UN bodies, such as the International Narcotics Control Board, which, *inter alia*, supplies a list of substances in English, French and Spanish.

Trafficking in drugs can be committed within one nation state or more typically across international borders. The United Nations Convention Against Illicit Traffic in Narcotic Drugs and Psychotropic Substances (1988) states that:

Article 3: OFFENCES AND SANCTIONS*

1. Each Party shall adopt such measures as may be necessary to establish as criminal offences under its domestic law, when committed intentionally:
   (a) (i) The production, manufacture, extraction, preparation, offering, offering for sale, distribution, sale, delivery on

any terms whatsoever, brokerage, dispatch, dispatch in transit, transport, importation or exportation of any narcotic drug or any psychotropic substance contrary to the provisions of the 1961 Convention, the 1961 Convention as amended or the 1971 Convention;

(ii) The cultivation of opium poppy, coca bush or cannabis plant for the purpose of the production of narcotic drugs contrary to the provisions of the 1961 Convention and the 1961 Convention as amended;

(iii) The possession or purchase of any narcotic drug or psychotropic substance for the purpose of any of the activities enumerated in (i) above;

(iv) The manufacture, transport or distribution of equipment, materials or of substances listed in Table I and Table II, knowing that they are to be used in or for the illicit cultivation, production or manufacture of narcotic drugs or psychotropic substances;

(v) The organization, management or financing of any of the offences enumerated in (i), (ii), (iii) or (iv) above;

(b) (i) The conversion or transfer of property, knowing that such property is derived from any offence or offences established in accordance with subparagraph (a) of this paragraph, or from an act of participation in such offence or offences, for the purpose of concealing or disguising the illicit origin of the property or of assisting any person who is involved in the commission of such an offence or offences to evade the legal consequences of his actions;

(ii) The concealment or disguise of the true nature, source, location, disposition, movement, rights with respect to, or ownership of property, knowing that such property is derived from an offence or offences established in accordance with subparagraph (a) of this paragraph or from an act of participation in such an offence or offences;

The Convention encourages nation states to enact domestic criminal laws that will permit the prosecution of drug traffickers under a commonality of terms that every signatory state agrees to, so that, for example, trafficking in the US is similar to trafficking in drugs in France. This does not mean that the sentences will be identical, and this is not the intention.

The purpose is to have a unified approach towards prosecuting global drug traffickers so that there is no safe haven for them. For example:

Article 4: JURISDICTION*

1. Each Party:
   (a) Shall take such measures as may be necessary to establish its jurisdiction over the offences it has established in accordance with article 3, paragraph 1, when:
      (i) The offence is committed in its territory;
      (ii) The offence is committed on board a vessel flying its flag or an aircraft which is registered under its laws at the time the offence is committed;
   (b) May take such measures as may be necessary to establish its jurisdiction over the offences it has established in accordance with article 3, paragraph 1, when:
      (i) The offence is committed by one of its nationals or by a person who has his habitual residence in its territory;
      (ii) The offence is committed on board a vessel concerning which that Party has been authorized to take appropriate action pursuant to article 17, provided that such jurisdiction shall be exercised only on the basis of agreements or arrangements referred to in paragraphs 4 and 9 of that article;
      (iii) The offence is one of those established in accordance with article 3, paragraph 1, subparagraph (c)(iv), and is committed outside its territory with a view to the commission, within its territory, of an offence established in accordance with article 3, paragraph 1.

2. Each Party:
   (a) Shall also take such measures as may be necessary to establish its jurisdiction over the offences it has established in accordance with article 3, paragraph 1, when the alleged offender is present in its territory and it does not extradite him to another Party on the ground:
      (i) That the offence has been committed in its territory or on board a vessel flying its flag or an aircraft which was registered under its law at the time the offence was committed; or

(ii) That the offence has been committed by one of its nationals;

(b) May also take such measures as may be necessary to establish its jurisdiction over the offences it has established in accordance with article 3, paragraph 1, when the alleged offender is present in its territory and it does not extradite him to another Party.

3. This Convention does not exclude the exercise of any criminal jurisdiction established by a Party in accordance with its domestic law.

Therefore, within the US there is nationally applicable legislation under the Controlled Substances Act of 1970 that defines what offence it is to manufacture, supply or possess controlled drugs within the US. Under the UN Convention, as incorporated into US law, the jurisdiction of the US includes any territory, vessel or aircraft flying that country's flag; and it is also an offence to commit the crime of manufacturing, supplying or possessing outside of US territory, vessels or aircraft if the intention of the actor is to bring those items within the US territory, ship or aircraft. It is therefore a crime to manufacture cocaine in Mexico intending to supply that illegal substance to the US even if the drugs never reach the US and if the person responsible is not a citizen or national of the US. When the country in which the manufacturing occurs has an extradition agreement with the US, that person may be extradited to the US and be indicted to appear before a US federal court. The 1988 UN Convention is the mechanism for the legal application of the 1961 Single Convention on Narcotic Drugs; and in the case of the US, the CSA 1970 (as amended) is the legislative vehicle through which the UN provisions are brought into the criminal law.[49] But the 1988 UN Convention seeks to do more than encourage the criminalization of manufacturing, possessing and supplying illicit drugs, it also wants countries to work together to prevent and detect money laundering and to have measures in place to confiscate the proceeds of drug trafficking:

Article 5: CONFISCATION*

1. Each Party shall adopt such measures as may be necessary to enable confiscation of:

   (a) Proceeds derived from offences established in accordance with article 3, paragraph 1, or property the value of which corresponds to that of such proceeds;

(b) Narcotic drugs and psychotropic substances, materials and equipment or other instrumentalities used in or intended for use in any manner in offences established in accordance with article 3, paragraph 1.

2. Each Party shall also adopt such measures as may be necessary to enable its competent authorities to identify, trace, and freeze or seize proceeds, property, instrumentalities or any other things referred to in paragraph 1 of this article, for the purpose of eventual confiscation.

3. In order to carry out the measures referred to in this article, each Party shall empower its courts or/other competent authorities to order that bank, financial or commercial records be made available or be/seized. A Party shall not decline to act under the provisions of this paragraph on the ground of bank secrecy.

For the US, the money laundering and forfeiture requirements have been enacted (principally) within two pieces of legislation: RICO, the Racketeer Influenced and Corrupt Organizations Act 1970, and more recently The Money Laundering Control Act of 1986. These provisions are of federal application under US Title 18 section 1956 and have been supplemented since enactment by further legislation.[50] Federally applicable penalties for knowingly or intentionally manufacturing, possessing or distributing a controlled substance are defined under USC 21 Section 841. These are reiterated in DEA literature in a simplified manner so that it is possible to look quickly at standard ranges of imprisonment for amounts of substances, such as up to 5 kg cocaine possession with intent to supply for a first time offender.[51] The great disparity that existed between the amount of 'crack cocaine' considered to be for personal possession and cocaine have been visited and addressed to some extent in the Fair Sentencing Act 2010, so that some of the discrepancies that made minor possession of 'crack' as serious as possession of considerably more actual cocaine have now been rectified. [52] A drug trafficking crime under federal law means: "any felony punishable under the Controlled Substances Act (21 USC. 801 et seq.), the Controlled Substances Import and Export Act (21 USC. 951 et seq.) or chapter 705 of title 46.[53] As stated by the Supreme Court of the United States, "A plain reading of this definition identifies two elements: First, the offense must be a felony; second, the offense must be capable of punishment under the Controlled Substances Act (CSA)."[54] It is important to recognize that common use of the term 'drug trafficking' may not, therefore, be legally accurate as it is possible to traffic in drugs without crossing a state, national or international border and, although often a crime committed by DTOs, there are many convictions each year for trafficking in controlled substances that occur entirely within a state border by individual or small numbers of operators.[55] Even larger scale operations that involve dozens of criminals who are prosecuted under federal statutes are by no means the exclusive purview of groups classified as DTOs, as a number of DEA press releases show:

News Release

FOR IMMEDIATE RELEASE
Date: July 13, 2012
Contact: DEA Public Affairs

Forty Individuals Charged With Drug Trafficking, Identity Theft, and Firearms Possession in Oakland

July 13 (Oakland, CA)—A federal grand jury in Oakland recently returned indictments against 40 members and associates of the Burn Out Family Mafia gang for drug trafficking, identity theft, and firearms possession charges, United States Attorney Melinda Haag announced. Over several months, 27 of the charged individuals have been arrested by law enforcement, including 15 who were arrested two weeks ago during sweeps conducted by the Drug Enforcement Administration, United States Secret Service, Oakland Police Department, Bureau of Alcohol Tobacco Firearms, and Explosives, United States Marshals Service, Alameda County Narcotics Task Force, Alameda County Probation Department, California Highway Patrol, Contra Costa County Sheriff's Office, Brentwood Police Department, and Stockton Police Department.

"Illegal open-air drug markets operating on our street corners in East Oakland beget violence and other criminal activity. By shutting down the open-air drug markets run by the Burn Out Family Mafia—particularly the three markets targeted by this investigation, which operated within feet of Oakland schools—we hope to contribute to the reduction of violence in East Oakland," stated United States Attorney Haag.

According to one indictment, 31 defendants are alleged to have engaged in the daily sales of heroin and cocaine on three corners in East Oakland, which are controlled by the Burn Out Family Mafia gang. A second indictment charges four defendants with various identity-theft related crimes. Five other defendants have been charged with firearms possession in separate indictments.

> "These indictments demonstrate that criminal street gangs are branching out beyond traditional drug-trafficking operations to other illegal enterprises such as identity theft. They further demonstrate the importance of cooperative law enforcement efforts, such as the instant investigation led by the Drug Enforcement Administration, United States Secret Service, and Oakland Police Department," added United States Attorney Haag.
>
> The maximum statutory penalty for violation of Title 21, United States Code, Sections, 846, 841(a)(1), and 841(b)(1)(B) (conspiracy to distribute heroin) is 40 years in prison, with a mandatory minimum of five years in prison, and a fine of $8 million. The maximum statutory penalty for violation of Title 18, United States Code, Section 1029(b) (2) (conspiracy to commit identity theft) is seven and one-half years in prison and a fine of $250,000. The maximum statutory penalty for violation of Title 18, United States Code, Section 922(g) (1) is ten years in prison and a $250,000 fine. However, any sentence following conviction would be imposed by the court after consideration of the US Sentencing Guidelines and the federal statute governing the imposition of a sentence, 18 USC. § 3553.
>
> The indictments and arrests in this case stem from a year and a half long investigation conducted by the Drug Enforcement Administration, United States Secret Service, and Oakland Police Department

However, there are many instances of major DTO leaders being convicted of trafficking, money laundering and sometimes racketeering, as witnessed by the sentencing of Benjamin Arellano-Felix in April 2012. Arellano-Felix is one of the two brothers that headed up the Mexican Tijuana drug cartel. He was sentenced to 25 years imprisonment and forfeited $100 million of criminal profits after he pleaded guilty to two charges before a US federal judge in San Diego on April 2, 2012—not for drug smuggling though, but money laundering and racketeering. His brother, Francisco-Javier, is already serving a life sentenced imposed upon him by the same judge in 2007. Once Benjamin has served his US sentence, he will be returned to Mexico to answer drug trafficking charges. Benjamin managed to escape a life sentence under a plea bargaining agreement. However, Judge Larry Burns informed Arellano-Felix that he would have imposed a longer sentence had it been possible.[56] As can be seen from these glimpses into drug trafficking offences and offenders, a person may be convicted of trafficking in drugs at the federal level or the state level. Regardless of which forum, the basic ingredients of the crime are the possession of a narcotic of other illegal drug or the possession of a legal drug that is being supplied illegally. Possession should be given its ordinary meaning, which is a right to exercise control over the drug with either constructive possession or actual possession of sufficient amount that it is usable. To be considered supplying then, the amount is going to be more than would ordinarily be considered for personal consumption. Some states have a rebuttable presumption that the drugs are for sale if the amount exceeds a certain specific amount, e.g. more than 5 grams of pure methamphetamine or more than 10 grams of PCP. Since the nature and form of the illicit drug discussion is constantly moving, legislators need to respond quickly to new trends and trafficking developments, as well as to new use patterns by consumers. For example, the Combat Methamphetamine Epidemic Act 2005 was passed in response to growing concern over the apparent increase in the abuse of 'crystal meth'.

In addition to the CSA, the Uniform Controlled Substances Act 1970 (UCS) was created and then enacted to provide states with a blueprint for uniformity in drug crimes and scheduling. In 1990 and 1994, the Act was supplanted by newer versions: "This Uniform Act was drafted to maintain uniformity between the laws of the several States and those of the federal government. It has been designed to complement the federal law and provide an interlocking trellis of federal and state law to enable government at all levels to control more effectively the drug abuse problem."[57] From these proposed guidelines and examples, states are then invited to draft local laws to prevent and prosecute drug manufacturing, supply and use. The UCS should be viewed in the same way as the Model Penal Code. It is not binding upon any state but represents a series of proposed laws that are available for adoption if they appear to suit the needs of an individual state. A particular example is marijuana which, if strictly interpreted, is a schedule 1 CSA drug for federal law purposes but that may be considered a misdemeanor or even permissible in a state. What this makes clear is that there are obvious differences between federal and state criminal laws, and although federal law may 'trump' state law in theory it may not in practice, as the Supreme Court has, on a number of occasions, confirmed the right of the individual state to create legislation and additionally may acknowledge that the state legislation is legally operative.[58] A tacit acceptance of the glaring disparity between the federal position on marijuana and some states was recognized when in 2009 the US Attorney General informed the press that federal agencies would no longer conduct raids upon medical marijuana dispensaries. "Graham Boyd, the director of the American Civil Liberties Union drug law project, said Mr. Holder's remarks created a reasonable balance between conflicting state and federal laws and 'seem to finally end the policy war over medical marijuana.' He said officials in California and the 12 other states that have authorized the use of medical marijuana had hesitated to adopt regulations to carry out their laws because of uncertainty created by the Bush administration."[59] There are currently 14 states that have medical marijuana laws in place. None of these state laws protect or support the trafficking of marijuana.

Texas is a state that is viewed as one that has generally severe criminal laws. It is a death penalty state and is regarded as being 'tough on crime'. In terms of drug trafficking, Texas defines 'delivering' as to transfer, actually or constructively, from one person to another, and this includes offering to sell to another person. If the delivery or supply of a controlled substance is conducted by a member of a street gang then the severity of the classification and punishment for the offence increases significantly. Possession with intent to supply, a felony drug offense, is assumed if the quantity exceeds 400 grams or more of a narcotic drug[60] and the punishment range is 10 to 99 years or life in prison and a $250,000 maximum fine. Conversely, possession of less than one gram of a schedule one drug is liable to 180 days to 2 years of state jail and/or a fine of not more than $10,000. Any drug possession conviction will result in a 6 month driver's license suspension under Texas laws. Due to the location of the state and its border with Mexico—there are 23 international vehicular bridges/ports and 1,254 miles of border—Texas has become a major transit state for marijuana, cocaine, heroin and methamphetamine arriving from Mexico. The ease with which access to the rest of the US can be achieved through the extensive interconnections of interstate highways around Dallas has made Dallas an attractive venue for drug deliveries and cash deposits before laundering and transportation out of the US. There are four designated HIDTAs (high Intensity drug trafficking areas) in Texas: Houston, North Texas, South West Border West Texas and South West Border South Texas. An area designated as an HIDTA is given additional support and resources by the federal government to tackle the drug problems in those areas. 'The North Texas region is a national distribution center for illicit drugs due to its transportation and financial infrastructures and its proximity to Mexico. Ice methamphetamine is the principal drug threat. Mexican DTOs are the primary suppliers of wholesale quantities of methamphetamine, powder cocaine, commercial grade marijuana, and black tar heroin in the area. The DTOs use "cell heads" in Dallas to manage the wholesale narcotic distribution within individual markets'. [61] The Texas Health and Safety Code is the primary source of classification of drugs and criminal possession offences. Substances are divided into six categories with Group One containing the most dangerous substances, such as cocaine, heroin and methamphetamine. Trafficking in marijuana is a Class B misdemeanor if the amount delivered is less than one-fourth ounce, whereas it is a felony in the first-degree to deliver more than 50 pounds but less than 2,000 pounds.

On May 18, 2012, as a result of 'Operation Dirty Dozen', the US Attorney's office of the Southern District of Texas reported that "Lauro Arturo Treviño Sr. and Roberto Lee Coronado were sentenced to federal prison for their roles in a large scale drug trafficking organization operating out of Starr County, Texas. Treviño pleaded guilty to possession with the intent to distribute approximately 818 kilograms of marijuana and was sentenced to 65 months imprisonment to be followed by a three-term of supervised release. Coronado, 33, of Edinburg, Texas, pleaded guilty to possession with intent to distribute approximately 285 kilograms of marijuana and received a 52-month-term of imprisonment to be followed by three years of supervised release. The convictions are the result of a Nov. 1, 2011, indictment charging more than 20 men with conspiracy to possess with intent to distribute more than 1,000 kilograms of marijuana as well as substantive counts of drug trafficking and money laundering. In June 2009, federal agents began investigating the organization which revealed that large loads of marijuana were being importing from Miguel Aleman, Tamaulipas, Mexico. Once the marijuana was in the United States, the organization stored it in various stash houses in Roma, Mission and Edinburg before transporting it to Houston. During the course of the investigation, agents seized 11 loads of marijuana weighing approximately 4,700 kilograms (five tons) and seized approximately $120,000 in drug proceeds."[62]

On April 13, 2012, US Immigration and Customs Enforcement (ICE), the principal investigative arm of the Department of Homeland Security, reported on a resolved case that involved the supply of drugs to Louisiana through the Texas corridor:

> **Louisiana ring leader sentenced to 19 years in prison for drug trafficking**
>
> **LAFAYETTE, La.**—A Louisiana man was sentenced Friday to 19 years in federal prison and five years supervised release for his leadership role in a large-scale cocaine and marijuana drug trafficking organization. The investigation was initiated in 2004 by US Immigration and Customs Enforcement's (ICE) Homeland Security Investigations (HSI) as an Organized Crime and Drug Enforcement Task Force (OCDETF) investigation code named "Operation Lion's Pride."

Eric Joseph Alexander, 35, of Lafayette was sentenced by US District Judge Rebecca F. Doherty as a result of Alexander's guilty plea in December 2008 to conspiracy to possess with intent to distribute cocaine, cocaine base and marijuana; possession of a firearm by a convicted felon; and, conspiracy to commit money laundering.

The investigation revealed that Alexander received hundreds of pounds of marijuana and five to 40 kilograms of cocaine per month from his sources of supply in Mexico and the Rio Grande Valley of Texas for distribution into the Acadiana region of Louisiana. A large portion of the cocaine received was converted into "crack" and distributed in the Lafayette-New Iberia area. Alexander's drug trafficking organization used a variety of couriers to receive and transport the controlled substances to end-line distributors in Acadiana. In order to conceal the narcotics, Alexander used a local after-market automobile store, B&M Auto Sound and 4×4 (B&M), to construct secret compartments in vehicles used by his organization when transporting the drugs.

Alexander's money laundering conviction was related to financial transactions that he engaged in with B&M. Specifically, Barry Neveu, a co-owner of B&M, asked Alexander for loans of cash to help with B&M's financial difficulties. It was agreed that Alexander would provide drug proceeds to B&M and Alexander would then be repaid through a scheme where B&M would issue false payroll checks to Alexander. The repayment arrangement was designed to create the illusion that Alexander was an actual employee of B&M with a legitimate source of income. Neveu instructed his staff at B&M to create false invoices to disguise the source of the currency received from Alexander.

On February 16, Alexander's co-conspirator Antonio Luna Valdez Jr., of Weslaco, Texas, was convicted of drug trafficking at the conclusion of a nine-day jury trial in Lafayette, La. Valdez is incarcerated pending his sentencing. The sentencing date has not been set. Due to his two previous drug related convictions, Valdez faces a mandatory life sentence.

The investigation initially focused on co-conspirators Rusty Honore and Peyton Knatt, two occupants of an apartment in Lafayette, La. Interception of the garbage at the apartment occupied by Honore and Knatt produced numerous kilogram-size wrappings with cocaine residue and empty boxes of baking soda, indicative of the manufacture of large quantities of cocaine base. As a result of court authorized audio and video monitoring equipment installed in the apartment, special agents identified Alexander as the source of narcotics for Honore and Knatt. On May 6, 2005, a search warrant was executed at the apartment, resulting in the seizure of $146,000.00, cocaine, cocaine base, marijuana, firearms and an electronic money counter. Honore was Alexander's primary customer for cocaine. Honore and Knatt were converting the cocaine into cocaine base, or "crack," and distributing it in Acadiana.

Thereafter, the OCDETF investigation established that Maria Aide Delgado, along with her mother, Sabina Valdez, and two brothers, Victor Valdez and Antonio Luna Valdez Jr., all residing in the Rio Grande Valley area of Texas, utilizing SUVs and 18-wheelers, were transporting large quantities

> of controlled substances to various locations around the United States, including to Alexander in the Western District of Louisiana.
>
> In June of 2005, HSI special agents implemented court ordered wiretaps of cellular telephones being used by Alexander confirming that members of the Valdez family were regularly transporting controlled substances from south Texas to Alexander, and that Alexander was using couriers to deliver controlled substances to various "stash" houses and apartments used by Alexander'.[63]

Legislation with regard to trafficking in drugs in the state of Virginia is based upon drug classification that mirrors the federal CSA. For example, trafficking a Schedule 1 substance such as heroin, methamphetamine, MDMA, LSD or GHB is liable to 5 to 40 years imprisonment and fines up to $500,000. However, marijuana is not considered a class 1 substance and has less severe penalties so that possession of amounts between half an ounce and 5 pounds is a felony liable to up to 10 years of state imprisonment. Virginia has a long history of growing one strain of cannabis, hemp, and has continued a fairly liberal attitude towards marijuana possession for many years. Cultivation, regardless of the amount, for personal use has historically been considered to be a relatively minor offense and it remains the case that possession of even a large amount of cannabis is not proof of intent to supply. This contrasts starkly with Florida where the law requires no proof of an intention to supply to be convicted of trafficking. Virginia cannabis possession laws were extended further under the Code of Virginia section 18.2-251 that permits the use of cannabis for the treatment of cancer and glaucoma. Virginia is, therefore, a medical marijuana state. What the law states is that: A. No person shall be prosecuted under S 18. 2-250 for the possession of cannabis or tetrahydrocannabinol when that possession occurs pursuant to a valid prescription issued by a medical doctor in the course of his professional practice for the treatment of cancer or glaucoma. The law also states that no medical doctor shall be subject to prosecution for making such a prescription and that no pharmacist shall be prosecuted for dispensing. Attempts to repeal these provisions have been tried and defeated. Possession of marijuana without a prescription is an unclassified misdemeanor punishable with up to 30 days imprisonment and/or a $500 for first time offenders; the legal provisions extend to the use of synthetic cannabinoids also. Trafficking in marijuana by bringing the substance into the state is considered a serious crime and transporting 5 pounds or more into Virginia is a felony punishable with a minimum mandatory sentence of 5 years, maximum 40 years and a fine not exceeding $1,000,000.

In 2004, Dr. William Hurwitz of Mclean, Virginia was convicted on 50 counts of supplying narcotics to his patients. He received a total sentence of 25 years imprisonment. The 4th Circuit Court of Appeals subsequently ruled that the trial jury were improperly prevented from considering whether he acted in good faith. The prosecution had alleged that Hurwitz overprescribed drugs such as OxyContin, in one instance giving a single patient more than half a million pills over a 40-month period. The prosecution also alleged that Hurwitz's patients had been selling their drugs illegally and that he must have suspected this due to the number of repeat prescriptions given within such a short time period. On April 27, 2007, the jury in his new trial found Hurwitz guilty on 16 charges of drug trafficking. He was acquitted of 17 other trafficking counts and the trial judge dismissed 12 of the charges.[64] On July 13, 2007, Hurwitz was sentenced to four years and nine months imprisonment.

In Florida, trafficking in drugs carries mandatory imprisonment sentences. In the case of cannabis (a), "Any person who knowingly sells, purchases, manufacturers, delivers, or brings onto this state, or who is knowingly in actual or constructive possession of, in excess of 25 pounds of cannabis, or 300 or more cannabis plants, commits a felony of the first degree, which felony shall be known as 'trafficking in cannabis.'"[65] For the purposes of the law, 'plant' includes a seeding, cutting, a root formation and it does not matter whether the 'plant' is alive or not. Similar provisions apply with regard to possession of cocaine so that any person in possession of more than 28 grams is assumed to be "trafficking in cocaine."[66] The offence of "Trafficking in illegal drugs" applies to those other substances not covered by trafficking in cannabis or cocaine so that, for example, possession of 4 grams or more of opium, morphine, heroin, or oxycodone is a felony defined as "Trafficking in illegal drugs." All of the above crimes carry mandatory prison sentences. Bringing drug precursors into the state is also a felony and subject to mandatory terms of imprisonment.

Florida law 893.101 deals with the issue of knowing that the substance possessed is illegal. It was the case according to two Florida cases: Scott v State, Slip opinion No. SC 94701 (Fla. 2002) and Chicone v State, 684So. 2d 736 (Fla. 1996) in which the state had to prove the defendants knew the substances in their possession were illicit. Under this provision, 893.101, it is stated that these case decisions were contrary to 'legislative intent' and that proving the defendant knew the drugs were illegal is not an element of the crime under this section. In other words, it is a presumption of Florida law that the defendant knew the drugs were illegal. The law as it now stands came about in 2002 and was challenged by defendants on the basis that it was unconstitutional. The most recent challenge started in July 2011 when Judge Mary Scrivens ruled in Shelton v Department of Corrections that it was unconstitutional[67] for prosecutors not to have to prove that the defendants knew the drugs they were carrying were illicit. What the judge believed is that the law failed to differentiate between a person who intends to traffic in drugs and a defendant who accidentally or unknowingly possess an illegal drug. This decision resulted in a number of convicted prisoners appealing their convictions. Following this ruling, Circuit Judge Milton Hirsch applied the findings to a number of drug trafficking cases resulting in numerous cases being withdrawn. The Third District Court of Appeals ruled on June 27, 2012 that Judge Hirsch was incorrect (the same court had already ruled that Judge Scrivens was wrong back in November 2011). State Appeal Court Judge Leslie Rothenberg said that Hirsch incorrectly relied on federal rulings and that he had incorrectly ignored previous Florida Supreme Court rulings on the issue. The matter is likely now to go forward to the Florida Supreme Court.

This chapter has discussed the issue of drugs and drug trafficking. It is a problem with numerous manifestations: large scale illicit drug manufacturing resulting in the supply of substances deemed illegal internationally and nationally for a number of countries; local small scale laboratories producing dangerous and illegal substances to friends and neighbors; Drug Trafficking Organizations that have grown enormously over the past 30 years and whose nature and form have changed and adapted to suit changing market trends like many conglomerates. Whereas once the Colombian cartels were the most expansive and feared of all DTOs, today they are largely local and controlled and most trafficking of cocaine from Colombia is within the country. The groups that were once transporters for Colombia have followed the Medellin and Cali cartels, but they are now fully-fledged criminal enterprises. An example is the Los Zetas, the former Mexican military turned traffickers. The grip on drug trafficking that Mexican DTOs have established throughout Central America is now a major problem to nation states that lack the resources, or sometimes the will, to prevent a narco-state. Due to the world's apparently insatiable appetite for mind-altering substances, the DTOs have always worked in every country and region. In recent history that has altered, and we now see alliances between criminal groups that previously worked largely independently of each other. Additionally, terrorist groups are increasingly aware of the huge amounts of finances that can be created by the sale of illicit drugs and many terrorist organizations have now formed working ties to DTOs to increase the flow of funds into their criminal activities.

Murder, assaults, kidnapping and abductions, theft, burglary and robbery and drug trafficking—all of these crimes can be completed by individuals or by groups. All of these crimes are frequently within the portfolio of criminality expressed by criminal groups that can be collectively named DTOs. It has become the case that singular crimes are a rarity for DTOs, as they seek to expand the reaches of their operations across national and international borders. Less dramatically, though no less disturbing for victims, are the actions of lone operators who kill, assault, abduct and steal from us. They too have a major impact upon our feelings of safety and in most instances more so than a DTO that we read about but rarely see in everyday life. The nexus between drug trafficking groups and terrorist organizations has existed for years, but the magnitude of the operations and the scope of the enterprises is reaching such proportions that it is challenging to see how legitimate society can form effective barriers to prevent even more criminal alliances in the future. The vulnerability of small states, weak infrastructures, high levels of poverty, corruption and low educational achievement make many countries the ideal arenas for the establishment of narco-states. But perhaps that should not be a dominant concern, as unlike terrorists DTOs appear to have no interest in taking the reins of government; they simply want to control the legitimate government by 'silver or lead'.

The sheer diversity of criminality is bewildering and increases every year due to new technology. Many crimes today were not even conceived of as little as 5 years ago. The greater use of electronic devices will undoubtedly feature in kidnappings (we can now kidnap virtually), thefts and drug trafficking; it has become easier and easier to facilitate cash transfers between unknown purchasers via the Internet. The ability to transform a phone into a credit card receiving device is now commonplace and this technology will improve our legitimate world alongside the illegitimate world of paying for drugs; we will swipe a card rather than pay cash for 'scoring' in the future. Electronic funds transfer will pay kidnap ransoms just as large-scale bank thefts are now completed via computer without the criminals ever leaving their own jurisdiction or physically entering any bank premises. Crime is an international trade. It is and always has been a commodity. The more local, the greater the effect policing has had. The more international, the less effective we become; it is inevitable. Criminals do not respect national borders and legitimate society does; crimes are committed across borders but defined locally, within the state or the country. We want to control our own version of what it means to steal and kidnap and have drug traffic. We want to be able to influence the legal system and its outcomes in relation to our own customs and social framework. No nation state totally embraces the idea of international crimes; the designation of drug trafficking or war crimes as crimes against all of society is a laudable objective, but they will always be hampered in application by the vagaries and attitudes that one nation state holds for another. There is unlikely ever to be a time when every country of the world freely exchanges its drug trafficker to another country for trial. We all hold some degree of suspicion about alternative legal systems that may not fully embrace our concept of justice. And all of this is and will remain to the advantage of the criminal.

Now that we have explored some of the more common crimes that individuals and groups commit in every country of the world, it is time to look at the responses. How do we train police and law enforcement agencies to prevent and detect crimes that can be local, national or international, separately or together? Will the increased globalization of crime lead to more international police responses? The existing legitimacy of police outside of our own borders is based upon international treaties, and bi-lateral and multi-lateral agreements. Are these sufficient for the future or will a new conduit of legal co-operation need to be established? So what does it mean to 'police crime', especially when what appears to be a regular local criminal event can hide a complex international criminal enterprise that has inadvertently spilled over into a small town or village event? Recent international banking scandals have clearly demonstrated that the relationship between legitimate and illegitimate enterprises is far closer than we suspected. Greater public vigilance, transparent legal borders and a sophisticated policing response is the *sine qua non* for policing crime in the 21st century. Has it arrived or is it still under construction?

Endnotes

1. For example, Great Britain and the 'Opium Wars' with China during the 19th century.
2. For a more detailed discussion about nomenclature, see Johnstone, P. *Drugs and drug trafficking.* Iowa: Kendal Hunt; 2012.
3. www.unodc.org/informationabout. The UNODC also clarifies the terms for illicit drugs and how drugs are classified as follows: **Licit/illicit drugs:** "The United Nations drug control conventions do not recognize a distinction between licit and illicit drugs; they describe only use to be licit or illicit. Here,

the term illicit drugs is used to describe drugs which are under international control (and which may or may not have licit medical purposes) but which are produced, trafficked and/or consumed illicitly." Drug types. "**Drug types** are described in various ways, depending on origin and effect. They can either be *naturally occurring, semi synthetic* (chemical manipulations of substances extracted from natural materials) or *synthetic* (created entirely by laboratory manipulation). The main categories are Narcotics, Stimulants, Depressants, Hallucinogens, Steroid and Inhalants." C.F. Johnstone. Op. cit.

4. www.unodc.org
5. Ibid.
6. In consultation with *inter alia,* the Director of the FBI, DEA, CIA, Secretary of Defense and Secretary of State
7. Under the Foreign Narcotics Kingpin Designation Act. 21 USC. (1999)
8. Corporate transgressions can lead to fines up to $10 million and individuals may be fined up to $5 million and receive terms of imprisonment up to 30 years.
9. The UNODC estimates in its 2011 *World Drug Report* that 210 million humans consume illegal drugs every year and 200,000 die from this use. UNODC World Report 2011. Page 8 cited in Johnstone, supra.
10. Ibid.
11. However, it still represents one third of all cocaine consumption in the world. Johnstone, supra, p. 58
12. Cannabis is a generic term that captures all three products of the plants cannabis sativa and cannabis indica: marijuana, hash and hash oil.
13. UNODC Report, supra, p. 49
14. www.undoc.org
15. Johnstone, op. cit., p. 122
16. Ibid., p. 132
17. UNODC World Report. Op. cit.
18. Johnstone, op. cit., p. 136
19. *International Crisis Group* Latin America Report Number 39. October 2011. Page 1. At www.crisisgroup.org
20. Ibid.
21. Ibid.
22. 64 in 2010 and rising to 110 in 2011. 2012 figures are not available.
23. There were 6187 assassination style killings in 2011.
24. Op cit. International Crisis Group Report, p. 20.
25. The main local groups are family based; Lorenzanas, Mendozas and Leones.
26. Johnstone, op. cit., p. 138
27. C.f. Law 100 and Diego Giacomen, "Drug Policy and the Prison Situation in Bolivia" at www.reformdrugpolicy.com
28. Avianca Airlines 1989. 110 passengers and crew were killed.
29. 6 November 1985

30. C.f. Johnstone, op. cit., p. 177
31. The term 'narco-terrorsim' was first used to describe the criminal activities of the Peruvian group *Sendero Luminoso,* Shining Path. The word is attributed to President Belaunde Terry of Peru.
32. Oceania comprises a number of southern Pacific islands, Australia and New Zealand.
33. E.g. New Zealand reports some of the highest per capita use of ATS's in the world. Johnstone, op. cit., p. 97.
34. E.g. 'China White' is the most popular and prevalent heroin in Australia. It accounts for 80% of all the heroin in circulation within the country. Source: The Australian *Illicit Drug Reporting System* and UNODC Report 2011, op. cit., p. 43.
35. For details see the Australian federal police website at www.afp.gov.au
36. Also known as the *Boryokudan.* In the term Ya Ku Za, Ya represents the number 8, Ku is 9 and Ya is 3. A combined total of 20, the losing hand in hanafuda. The desired 'Robin Hood' image of the Yakuza is therefore 'justified' on the basis that they have been dealt life's losing hand. It is estimated there are in the region of 80,000 members worldwide.
37. In 2011, 56% of all global heroin seizures were made in Asia, 99% of ketamine seizures, 24% of cannabis resin, 74% of ATS and 53% of Methamphetamine. Johnstone, op. cit., p. 99. Detailed breakdown available at UNODC *World Report* 2011. Op. cit.
38. UNODC 2011. Op. cit.
39. www.unodc.org/eastasiaandpacific/en/2011/09/global-ats-assessment-2011/story.html
40. The other is Turkey.
41. Johnstone, op. cit., p. 181.
42. See *LA Times* article at www.latimes.com/2009/dec/19/.../la-na-al-qaeda cocaine19-2009de
43. C.f. www.ncrjs.gov
44. C.f. www.wfad.se/wfad2010-presentations/253-mafia-and-drugs-organized-crime-and-drug-trafficking-in-italy
45. C.f. www.Robert-friedman-red-mafiya_8539.html
46. "HSBC's nightmare on money laundering" July 18, 2012 by Shahien Nasiripour in Washington at www.ft.com
47. For example the Dubois family, Rizzuto and Cortini's
48. A sizeable seizure of cannabis being grown hydroponically was made in Manitoba in 2010 when a commercial illegal enterprise was cultivating 15,000 plants in a warehouse. C.f. www.policechiefmagazine.org
49. For an evaluation of the success of the provisions after the first ten years see: Jimmy Gurule, The 1988 U.N. convention against illicit traffic in narcotic drugs and psychotropic substances—A ten year perspective: is international

cooperation merely illusory? *Fordham International Law Journal.* 1998; 22(1); Article 2.

50. Sometimes controversially such as under the Patriot Act under which some commentators have expressed concern that there is a potential threat to civil liberties with the wide ranging powers provided to combat terrorism that can be used to also investigate alleged money laundering by DTO's.
51. Not less than 5 years and not more than 40 years. If death or serious injury, not less than 20 years or more than life. Fine of not more than $5 million if an individual and $25 million if not an individual. (As revised by the Fair Sentencing Act 2010.) www.justice.gov/dea/agency/penalties
52. For a discussion and explanation of the current position, see: Yeh, BT. 'Federal cocaine sentencing disparity: Sentencing guidelines, jurisprudence and legislation'. Congressional Research Service. 5 August 2010. www.crs.gov
53. USC Title 18 Sec. 924.
54. Lopez v Gonzales (No 05-547), December 5, 2006, 417F. 3d. 934. Reversed and remanded.
55. For example, the recent trend in the illegal supply of OxyContin to school children, the so called "Big 80s" issue because the drugs supplied contain 80mgs of OxyContin per pill. The vast number of cases coming to trial involves loosely organized groups of local suppliers.
56. Watson, J. Benjamin Arellano-Felix, Mexican drug kingpin, to be sentenced in San Diego. 2 April 2012. www.huffingtonpost.com
57. Uniform Controlled Substances Act 1994 Prefatory note, p. 9.
58. For example, with regard to 'medical marijuana' where a number of states permit the prescribing of marijuana for medical purposes contrary to the CSA per US v Oakland Cannabis Buyers Cooperative. 532 US 483 (2001).
59. Johnson, D. and Lewis, NA. Obama administration to stop raids on medical marijuana dispensers. 18 March 2009. *The New York Times.* www.nytimes.com
60. For the purposes of the Texas Penal Code, a narcotic drug includes cocaine. Chart 17-C. HSC definitions 57. Sec. 481.002(29).
61. Texas Drug Control Update, p. 6 ONDCP at www.whitehouse.gov
62. Two area men sentenced for money laundering and drug trafficking. 18 May 2012. www.justice.gov/usao/txs/1News/Releases/2012%20May/120518%20Trevino%20and%20Coronado.html
63. http://www.ice.gov/news/releases/1204/120413lafayette.htm
64. Tierney, T. Dr. Hurwitz convicted on 16 counts of drug trafficking. *The New York Times.* 27 April 2007. www.nytimes.com
65. Florida drug trafficking statutes appear as: 2005 Florida Code. Crimes Drug Abuse Prevention and Control Chapter 893.135 applies to the specific offense of trafficking in cannabis.
66. Ibid. at (b).
67. On the basis that it violated the Due Process clause of the 14th Amendment

CHAPTER 6

POLICING

Providing or requiring a body of citizens to take responsibility for protecting each other and their property is recorded in the earliest records of human activities. That is not to say or suggest that in history there were police forces as we understand them today. In most instances, policing was fragmentary and comprised of local men often unwillingly conscripted into a role that they performed under duress. Those in power often created the position of bodyguard to make sure they were personally protected. Today we usually consider this a paid position, but it was certainly not the case for those providing protection to ancient kings, pharaohs and Caesars. Additionally, many males were employed or forced into door keeping roles to protect valuables, not just the leader or temples

but also food and supplies for the citizenry. Night watchmen and guards were also either military personnel or, in remote rural communities, men and boys from the village who took turns watching the perimeters of the village to ensure that others in the community could sleep safely at night. There are records from ancient Egypt of an organized force of men providing security to tombs and living souls, and these men appeared to receive a salary for their work from the pharaoh's treasury. Exactly when in history this transformed into 'policing' is not clear. The word itself has origins in the Greek 'politia', but this had a far broader application than we now apply to many of the law enforcement responses in countries such as the UK and the US. As we shall see soon, in many continental European countries the police undertake a considerably larger number of civic activities than seen in the Common Law countries, such as Canada, the US, the UK, India and Australia. And in many respects, the original *politia* with its connotations of civic administration is one model of policing still applied today; and a different model, the non-military with more limited responsibilities is a different model used in those countries that are not following their roots back to Greece so closely. The word 'police' first appeared in use in France, probably as a derivation of policy, and the UK during the 16th century, although Chaucer alluded to a *policie* in his *Canterbury Tales.*

It is not my intention to cover the extensive history of policing from Hammurabi through Greece and Rome. That said, it is important to recognize that many of the police forces of the world today owe their origins to either the Greek and Romano based Civil Law policing systems or the Common Law derivation. They are fundamentally different. Those nations that adhere to Civil Law principles tend towards a military or quasi-military form of policing with armed officers who look and feel like military personnel. These police are normally highly centralized and may answer to a Ministry of the Interior or a Ministry of Defense. Frequently the officers live in barracks and have a rigid, hierarchical rank structure. Police officers under the Common Law model tend to be local and de-centralized; they may or may not carry a weapon and they are answerable to a combination of local interest and a minister. They rarely if ever live in barracks, and the value of this model is believed to be that the people serving are part of the community they serve. It is important to recognize these differences from the outset as there is no one model of policing and what it means to be a police officer can and does vary greatly in different jurisdictions.

In this chapter, I am going to talk about the origins of the police under the Common Law. These are the sheriffs and helpers and night watchmen and beadles, the Bow Street Runners and eventually full-time uniformed police officers providing a local service to the citizens of cities and towns. In Chapter 7, I will introduce a number of other police forces that operate under alternative legal systems, but for now let us look at the history of policing in England and how this informed policing in a number of other countries, including the US.

There is a widely held view that is authored in a number of US criminal justice textbooks that the overwhelmingly major influences upon policing in America have been Robert Peel and the Metropolitan Police Act of 1829. In this chapter, I will explore this position and suggest that the influence of Peel is important but represents only one part of a far more complex policing history for the US that draws in part from 17th century Paris and evolved in England around 1720 with adoption of the word 'police', more by accident than by choice. Over the course of the following 100 years, and frequently to the chagrin of the British political elite, England subsumed a number of European policing models alongside the work of uniquely English marine insurance detectives. Thus, by the end of the 18th century the Fieldings, Colquhoun and eventually Peel all recognized that elements of the French policing model were advantageous and applicable to England and eventually to the US. The product of these modern developments, alongside the public and private law enforcement responses of greater antiquity, was transported in stages and absorbed into the policing landscape of the US. In effect, 21st century policing in America is the result of a complex and multi-faceted policing history influenced by an English metropolitan police, a French gendarmerie, a Roman vigilante, a contemporary 12th century Norman tax collector (who acted as a part-time peace officer) and private detectives from French prisons.

Influences upon policing in the US are as diverse[1] as the pattern of policing within the country. It was perhaps inevitable that given the swaying power of Britain upon the early development of the USA there would be an adoption of established criminal justice practices from Britain, especially those from England and the Common Law. Consequently, the English criminal justice lexicon—sheriff, constable, 'Hue and Cry', magistrates, justices of the peace, circuit judges and a concept of what it means to 'police'—are all largely, but not exclusively, informed by England. However, a closer inspection of the informing factors reveals that much of what occurred in policing in England throughout the Middle Ages and into the 18th century was not exclusively a domestic creation. Subsequently, what transferred to the US as an English system was in fact a concomitant of

Anglo-Saxon[2] and Nordic customs with influence from France in the 11th century and then again, significantly, in the 18th century.

"The office of sheriff is the one secular dignity generally known in English-speaking lands which for more than nine centuries has maintained a continuous existence and preserved its distinguishing features."[3] Variously known as the shire-reeve, sheriff or *scirgerefa*,[4] and eventually elevated to the title of vice-count or viscount[5] in some instances, the sheriff[6] is a well-known feature of the Common Law criminal justice landscape that has a history that can be traced back to at least the reign of Ine[7] as a royal appointee with local administrative functions.[8] Over time the responsibilities of the shire-reeve increased and his role developed into, *inter alia*, those of tax collector, jailer and court administrator.[9] The task of securing felons and then holding them until the arrival of a court was a responsibility assigned to the sheriff from the period of Alfred the Great.[10] "Moreover he was a royal steward and was associated with the king's *tun* by the fact that he fed the king's prisoners there."[11] Securing the attendance of suspects before a trial court remains a primary function of the office of sheriff today. In his role as the chief law officer for a shire the sheriff held authority to demand assistance from local village people. Over time various appointments were made to provide a level of local rudimentary protective services that from modest beginnings as watchmen and vigilantes[12] would eventually form the basis of a professional police force for England. In London, we have specific references to the official powers of the sheriff in the laws of King Athelstan.[13] "For this district the reeve has apparently been holding a folkmote, within it he takes pledges for the observance of the peace, and in London region its men are to be led by him in pursuit of the thief."[14]

William the Bastard,[15] Conqueror and first Norman king of England, significantly increased the responsibilities of the sheriff. Within the first few years of his reign he appointed numerous fellow countrymen to the county shire-reeves position to ensure that there was a close watch upon the fiscal as well as local feudal responsibilities.[16] Importantly though, local and new French sheriffs did not lose any of the previous responsibilities of the office. "Among these may be named his powers connected with peace and with police."[17] Whereas in the pre-Norman period the sheriff had authority to preside over a hundred court hearings, to uphold the king's peace and to apprehend suspected criminals, under William these functions were formalized and positively encouraged.

The office of constable also existed prior to the arrival of the conqueror. At the time of the invasion, sheriffs were ordered by Harold of England to ". . . appoint constables in the hundreds, townships and neighbourhoods." All were to obey the head constable of the shire in matters 'ad defensionem regni et pacis conservacionem contra alienigenas, vel contra quoscunque alios pacis perturbatores'.[18] Aside from his famous dispute with Thomas Beckett, Henry II was responsible for many legal innovations. The Assize of Clarendon, 1166, has frequent references to the sheriff[19] in their policing and custodial roles: "And when a robber or murderer or thief, or harbourers of them, shall be taken on the aforesaid oath, if the Justices shall not be about to come quickly enough into that county where they have been taken, the sheriffs shall send word to the nearest justice through some intelligent man, that they have taken such men; and the Justices shall send back word to the sheriffs where they wish those men to be brought before them: and the sheriffs shall bring them before the Justices."[20] King John reluctantly signed the Magna Carta in 1215, one year before his death. This famous document contains 63 clauses, 27 of which relate to the role and functions of the sheriff. Clause 47 states that "We will not make men justices, constables, sheriffs, or bailiffs, unless they are such as know the law of the realm, and are minded to observe it rightly."[21]

By the time of Henry III,[22] roving felons were a significant problem and constables were regularly assisting sheriffs in providing patrols within villages and across the countryside to ensure safe passage between villages and to market towns.[23] Henry III also increased the remit of his peace officers to take responsibility for patrolling the English coastline and vulnerable fortifications.[24] Towards the end of Henry's reign, the sheriffs and their assistants, the constable, had accumulated significant powers, including the provision of protection to inland castles. To counteract this encroachment upon their 'bailiwick',[25] the barons collaborated and managed to reaffirm themselves as the primary custodians of the shire. This marked the end of shrieval dominance in county peacekeeping, albeit a number of the newly appointed shire and region keepers were themselves former sheriffs.[26] Under the new system sheriffs were still responsible for apprehending and securing the attendance of felons, and in real terms the new shire keepers often served under the sheriff when he exercised policing powers and functions. It was not the case, however, that the shire keepers would answer to the constable, who remained a lower level 'peace keeper' answerable to the authority of the sheriff. By the close of this century, the 'shire keepers' role had developed into a regional responsibility,[27] which in some respects had the effect of restoring the primary policing function within the bailiwick back with the sheriffs[28] and constables. The elevated office of shire keeper remained and gained in stature to become the primary administrative functionary of a county. It still exists in England today as the, largely ceremonial, Lord Lieutenant[29] who is served by his assistant the High Sheriff.[30] As Professor Raymond Moley of Columbia University once stated, "Today in England the sheriff is a dignified and gentlemanly non-entity who guarantees for one year the proper performance of work in which he plays no part. An under-sheriff performs legal routine chiefly in relation to civil proceedings such as the summoning of jurors, the execution of civil judgments, and the returns of the results of parliamentary elections."[31] The first person to hold the office of sheriff in America was William Stone in 1634 in the County of Accomack, Virginia.[32] One visible policing aspect of being sheriff was the ability to require that local citizens assist in the apprehension of offenders. This right to demand help existed in medieval England as well as in colonial America. The formation of a posse[33] gained greater actual, as well as fictional, notoriety during westward expansion in the US. It has also been attributed to the development of vigilantism and private policing during the 18th and 19th centuries.[34] In terms of policing models, the sheriff is one of the only examples of centralized policing ever to occur in England. Its transposition to the US alongside decentralized city forces gives the US uniqueness lost to England centuries ago.

In England, the night watchmen, beadle and constable limped through protecting citizens and apprehending criminals for the next 500 years. In France, the king had created a policing presence, the *Maréchaussée,* as far back as the early 1100s. This was followed by a larger military police response from 1337[35] onwards. Between 1536 and 1544, King Francis I implemented a range of measures to formalize policing across the nation. The 'Sun King' Louis XIV reigned in France from 1643 to 1715. He was renowned for his work on legal reform largely instituted and executed by his minister Jean Baptiste Colbert.[36] In October 1666, Louis ordered Colbert to design a plan for a Paris police force. By March of the following year, Louis authorized the creation of the office of Prefect of Police for Paris,[37] followed in 1699 by a royal decree that authorized the establishment of Prefecture of Police for each major city in France.[38] The range of policing responsibilities was very broad and went extensively beyond the activities associated with contemporary policing in the US.[39] Over the period of the next 150 years, the role and function of the city police of France expanded. This occurred particularly with the Prefecture of Police and his officers, who assumed judicial responsibilities unfamiliar to sheriffs and constables in England. In one instance, the 'police court' at *Le Châtelet,* Paris, heard 200 cases in a three-hour period. Forty-five women and 16 men were sentenced that day, May 25, 1759.[40] The sentencing powers of the police court were also extensive. Benjamin Dechauflour was tried for sodomy on May 24, 1726. He was convicted the same day and sentenced to death by burning. The punishment was carried out the following morning.[41] As the pending revolution gained momentum in France, so too did the anxiety of the monarchy, and Paris slid into a period of sinister policing where spying became the main thrust of police work within the capital. Often quoted but never verified, Gabriel de Sartines, Lieutenant-General of Police from 1759 to 1774, reportedly told the king that wherever three persons speak to one another on the street, one of them would be one of his police spies.[42] Undoubtedly, the pre-Revolution Paris police[43] represent a well-organized body of law enforcement personnel that had specialist skills and responsibilities far beyond those represented in England during the same period. The cities of France had a formal civilian police presence and the smaller towns and villages had the protections provided by a military police. By 1788, there was one police officer for every 193 residents of Paris.[44]

After the tumultuous events of the revolution, the *Maréchaussée* managed to remain in form but were renamed the *Gendarmerie Nationale.*[45] "The accession of Napoléon Bonaparte as first consul in 1799 reinvigorated the trend towards the centralization of the police."[46] The Napoleonic Codes brought order to the legislation of previous regimes and provided a comprehensive body of all applicable law to all citizens. Application of the new codes rested with the existing civilian police forces and a re-designed and higher profile military police force to be called the *Gendarmerie Nationale.* Drawn from the ranks of serving military personnel, the *Gendarmerie Nationale* consisted of well trained, well resourced, well paid military men who lived in barracks[47] and provide police services to the citizens and the highways of rural France. As 'the man who would restore order to a society plagued by crime, violence and uncertainty',[48] Napoléon created a military police force that was copied throughout continental Europe. His less famous civilian police continued to employ dubious spying methods under the directorship of Joseph Fouché;[49] but combined, the military country police and the civilian city police provided a comprehensive and effective policing response for France that was superior to every other nation state in the world at the time. All that remained was to ensure effective supervision within those towns of smaller populations and this was achieved through the creation of the *Commissaire de Police.* The commissaire reported to the Prefect of the Département but with the ability to circumvent this line of authority if needed. "This made the *commissaire* a very powerful and influential figure locally. Thanks to his 'direct-line' to powerful figures like Fouché and Savary,[50] he was often able to outflank not only the prefects[51] and mayors of his department, but even the judiciary and the gendarmerie, when it came to identifying common criminals, political subversives or wayward, allegedly corrupt local officials." In 1829, the same year that Robert Peel finally managed to convince the British parliament to authorize a police force for London,[52] France re-established the *sergent de ville.* A uniformed civilian appointment that had been present in a variety of forms across Europe for more than 200 years,[53] the Renaissance version was charged with providing a police presence in the smaller towns of France that would supplement the work of the *Commissaire de Police.*[54] Much like Dickens' ridicule of the beadle and watchman of London,[55] the *sergent de ville* did not escape the critical tones of Victor Hugo in the role of Javert[56] in *Les Misérables.* The comedy of policing the combination of a military gendarmerie and a civilian police force across all of France positioned the country to be at the forefront of policing in the later years of the 18th and the early years of the 19th centuries. "Perhaps the highest compliment ever paid to the Napoleonic Gendarmerie came from Britain, the arch-enemy of Napoleonic France, when in the 1820s, the secretary for Ireland, Sir Robert Peel, chose it as his model for the new Royal Irish Constabulary. Even Napoléon's bitterest enemies came quickly to acknowledge the usefulness of this particular institution."[57]

In 18th century England, the word police was virtually unknown.[58] When the word was introduced ". . . it was regarded with the utmost suspicion as a portent of the sinister force which held France in its grip."[59] As Edward Burt wrote in 1720, ". . . Soon after his arrival in London, he had observed a good deal of Dirt and disorder in the Streets, and asking about the *Police,* but finding none that understood the Term, he cried out, Good lord! How can one expect Order among these people, who have not such heard a Word as Police in their Language."[60] London was reeling under a crime wave and the local watch and beadle system was woefully incapable of dealing with the organized serial felon. The constable system was still a reflection of medieval England and the night watchmen were old, inept and frequently asleep or drunk on duty.[61] In 1792, the Middlesex Justices Act created the establishment of a police office within London. In reality, much had been achieved before passage of this legislation and a recognizable police force had been in existence in a number of manifestations for the City of Westminster and the River Thames for many years. "In fact, there were a number of police offices, all rather similar to the Bow Street police office which had been functioning for 30 years."[62] In the early years of the 18th century, Thomas de Veil was appointed as magistrate to the City of Westminster. Over the course of the next 17 years he established his Bow Street office as one of the most efficient within the metropolis. In 1748, the novelist Henry Fielding and his half-brother John Fielding succeeded De Veil.[63] Henry soon authored *An Enquiry into the Cause of the Late Increase of Robbers* and, to the surprise of some of his contemporaries, Fielding immersed himself into writing about[64] and working towards the establishment of a police force for the City of Westminster and Middlesex County from the Bow Street residence. Over time, the mixed bag of assistants that Fielding managed to employ proved themselves to be reliable thief catchers with an in-depth knowledge of the criminals within the immediate vicinity of Bow Street.[65] His associates were soon nicknamed the Bow Street Runners,[66] and their official title was Principal Officer of Bow Street.[67] The Bow Street Police Office was far from an ideal solution to the London crime problem. What it represented was a practical move towards a permanent police force for the metropolis. Regency England was still plagued with reward systems and general mistrust of a permanent force that might in any way appear to represent a standing army. Sir Leon Radzinowicz described the Bow Street Office as "The headquarters of a closely knit caste of speculators in the detection of crime, self-seeking and unscrupulous, but also daring and efficient when daring and efficiency coincided with their private interest."[68]

The combined efforts of De Veil, the Fieldings and Patrick Colquhoun all amount to a significant influence upon policing London. Armed officers patrolled the main streets of London during the nighttime;[69] the highways into and out of the metropolis were 'policed' by 68 patrols;[70] and on the eve of the 1829 Act, uniformed officers patrolled the central streets during daylight hours.[71] In 1792, a Scottish born merchant who had spent a number of years in Virginia was one of the first appointees under the new legislation that created stipendiary magistrates.[72] Patrick Colquhoun[73] immediately took up the issue of providing London with a regular, paid, full-time police force. He anonymously published *A Treatise on the Police of the Metropolis* in 1795 in which he estimated that the indigent population of London was so great that there was in existence a class of habitual criminals, 50,000 in number, who had no alternative but to engage in crime.[74] He even suggested that the French police[75] were a suitable model[76] for adoption in England.[77] Needless to say, these views won him no friends in the British parliament and his strenuous attempts to bring about the adoption of legislation that would establish a London police force were repeatedly defeated.[78] Undaunted by the intransigence of the British ruling elite, Colquhoun persisted. and he can certainly be credited with playing a significant role in the establishment of a full time police force for the River Thames.[79]

By the late 18th century, more than 13,500 vessels were competing daily for space on the River Thames.[80] Crime was rampant and the merchants of London united in supporting the establishment of a permanent protection force.[81] In June 1798, the merchants of London established a Marine Police Establishment[82] with a permanent staff of 80[83] and a reserve of more than one thousand. By the end of the year, *The Times* reported that, "It is astonishing the effects the institution has already achieved in the preventing of piracies and robberies. . . ."[84] In 1800, the British government endorsed the private policing enterprise and a Police Bill[85] was passed to formalize and make public policing of the River Thames. The main proponents of the bill[86] were John Harriot,[87] Patrick Colquhoun[88] and Jeremy Bentham.[89] There can be no doubt that London now had a permanent, uniformed police force that operated as a "public institution, regulated by statute and designed to safeguard commercial and other property on the river."[90]

Views about the impact of the Fieldings and Colquhoun are varied. Emsley refers to them as a "veritable holy trinity" in the eyes of Whig historians,[91] whereas Critchley considered their achievements meager.[92] In a sense, both opinions are correct. The Fieldings undoubtedly moved the policing agenda forward to the point at which, small though it was, London had a group of paid, permanent 'police' officers. Colquhoun, although personally frustrated by the lack of recognition he received for his attempts to change the hearts and minds of the British parliament, also raised the level of awareness and the volume of discussion, as well as achieving the personal satisfaction of ensuring that a marine police force was established that still exists within the Metropolitan Police today. If we attribute the introduction of the word 'police' to the Fieldings, then it is to Colquhoun that we owe thanks for its absorption into the English lexicon. What the "holy trinity" did not achieve was to convince the British public that a permanent police force would be anything other than a foreign invasion. This sleight of hand was left to a politician, Robert Peel, and another round of crime waves in the early 1800s.[93] However, one of the great achievements of this trio, whether by design or default, was that they managed to change the negative perception of foreign policing to a uniquely English entity that focused exclusively upon maintenance of the peace and the prevention and detection of crime.[94]

Opposition against a fulltime land force for London was still strong in the early years of the 19th century. Britain was at war with France and the populous, the press and the parliament repeatedly rejected anything that had the slightest resemblance to a *Gendarmerie.*[95] "The necessities of time, emphasized by the crime wave and frequent riots, created the stage for London police reform; however, little could have been accomplished without the political skills of Sir Robert Peel."[96] Peel[97] was promoted to Chief Secretary for Ireland in September 1812. His responsibilities included the maintenance of law and order in the country, and to this effect he was responsible for the Peace Preservation Act 1814,[98] which established the Irish Peace Preservation Force,[99] a forerunner to the Royal Irish Constabulary of 1822.[100] Public disturbances had become a regular feature of life throughout Ireland and the government frequently faced the task of quelling public disorder. "Peel's arrival coincided with a lull in banditti activity, but it was his job to muster the forces of authority in anticipation of the inevitable trouble to come."[101] Peel was much impressed by Napoléon's *Gendarmerie;* he approved of the military rigor and the utilization of a barrack system to house members of the force. And whereas he might not have been as enamored as Colquhoun, who had referred to the French police as having "The greatest degree of professionalism,"[102] he certainly recognized the value of having a countrywide paramilitary policing response that was answerable to a central authority. Peel was pleased with his creation and wrote somewhat prematurely, "Although the police bill has been but a few weeks in operation, the effect is already such as to justify the most sanguine expectation of its ultimate success."[103] Peel retired from his post as Chief Secretary for Ireland in 1817 and returned to England. His departure from Ireland was lamented in many quarters,[104] and it has been said, perhaps generously, that he may have intentionally created the Peace Preservation Force to help alleviate the "pitiable condition of Ireland"[105] by providing a source of employment. Peel left Ireland with the blueprint for a Common Law Gendarmerie that was to be exported around the globe to almost every former British colony. Some considered it as, "Being without parallel in its semi-military organisation, with exception, perhaps, of the French gendarmerie. . . ."[106] In 1822, Peel was elevated to the position of

Home Secretary where he would now have the opportunity to grapple with the police issue back in England.[107]

"Coloring the entire discussion was the example of an efficient and repressive system of police in France, where extensive intelligence networks caught ordinary criminals as well as those who spoke and acted in ways that undermined the stability of the regime. . . ."[108] Peel had become an astute and cautious politician. He recognized that to move forward he would need to advocate a moderate approach that emphasized preventative measures and crime detection provided for by a uniformed but distinctly civilian force.[109] A compromise was inevitable. One significant factor for Peel was the strong opposition voiced by the financial 'City of London'.[110] He decided not to attempt to bring the 'Square Mile' into his new plans,[111] and on Tuesday September 29, 1829,[112] the first uniformed officers of the London Metropolitan Police commenced evening patrol across the metropolis, save the City.[113] Their uniforms were carefully chosen to reflect civilian fashion of the day, top hat and blue tunic tails,[114] and they carried no more than a truncheon to protect themselves against the criminal underworld of the metropolis. Within eight months the initial intake of one thousand men[115] had risen to more than three thousand.[116] Two commissioners led the new police force, both of Irish descent, one a lawyer, Richard Mayne,[117] and the other a former military officer, Lt. Colonel Charles Rowan.[118] Despite initial criticism of Peel and his influential supporter the Duke of Wellington, London's 'Raw Lobsters'[119] slowly turned the hearts and minds of its skeptics and the more endearing terms 'Peelers' and 'Bobby'[120] began to enter the 'new policing' language. As one commentator noted, "And yet a couple of years later these same vestries agreed the unfavourable impression and jealousy formerly existing against the new police is rapidly diminishing . . . and it has fully answered the purpose for which it was formed. . . ."[121] Every recruit to the new London Metropolitan Police was issued with a handbook of *General Instructions* compiled by Sir Robert Peel. It stated: "It should be understood at the outset that the object to be attained is the prevention of crime . . . The absence of crime will be considered the best proof of the complete efficiency of the police."[122] These words have endured and are still viewed as the fundamental basis for policing in many parts of the world today. By 1856, the County and Borough Police Act required every county and borough in England and Wales to establish a police force.[123] The following year similar legislation was passed in Scotland.

One of the dilemmas Peel faced was whether to establish a uniformed or a plain clothed police force. Either way he was likely to be criticized.[124] If uniformed, they would be a *Gendarmerie,* and if plain clothed, they would be Paris police 'spies'.[125] As we know, he opted for uniforms. A detective unit was not established in London until 1842. During the interim period, Principal Officers[126] from the disbanded Bow Street Police Office served as a detective agency available for hire to individuals as well as to the Metropolitan Police. In France, a significant detective police department, much maligned by the English as 'sinister', had been operational for more than one hundred years. Then under Fouche, this unit gained greater notoriety and the name *brigade de sûreté.* But it was not until the arrival of a former criminal, Eugène Vidocq, in 1812 that the *Sûreté* became synonymous with sleuths and undercover work associated with contemporary police detection.[127] Vidocq was variously described as, "A lower type of man, yet still a great name in the history of French police . . . who began his career as a thief"[128] and "From unpromising origins as a two-bit thief, army deserter, grafter and convict, he rose in fame to become the celebrated chief of the Paris Sûreté police and an internationally renowned private detective."[129] The 'poacher turned gamekeeper',[130] Vidocq was apparently a larger-than-life character who captured the friendship and imagination of Dumas and Balzac. He was "Known to embellish his tales, and historians have difficulty separating fact from fiction in his accounts."[131] Regardless of the criticism and colorful nature of his character, Vidocq was a pioneer in detective techniques. Not only did he utilize handwriting, paper, and ink analyses to solve cases, but he also foresaw the day when fingerprints would be used to identify suspects'.[132] After his departure, the *Sûreté* continued to rise in stature as the preeminent detective police agency until the arrival of 'Scotland Yard'. Notwithstanding the rise of the 'Yard', Vidocq's impact traversed the Atlantic and he is credited with inspiring Allan Pinkerton[133] and J. Edgar Hoover.[134] The quality and effectiveness of the *Sûreté* did not go unnoticed in London either and a number of years after Vidocq's[135] resignation, a London Metropolitan Police officer implemented a version of his model. There are two dates associated with the introduction of plain clothed detectives in London, 1842 and then 1878.[136] The first attempts to run an effective detective unit were plagued by allegations of corruption and scandal[137] culminating in the "Trial of the Detectives" in 1877.[138] The following year Charles Howard Vincent,[139] a lawyer, police officer and politician, was given the opportunity to re-organize the detective branch and form the modern C.I.D. Over time, Scotland Yard detectives became synonymous with criminal investigation excellence[140] and surpassed the *Sûreté* in stature.

Between 1605 and 1905 policing in America was influenced by a multitude of European forces. There is a collective agreement among a number of authors[141] that early policing methods were drawn from the established roles of the sheriffs, constables,[142] Hue and Cry, night watchmen, vigilantes and 'watch and ward', along with the wide and varied assortment of criminal justice law enforcement officials that had developed over the previous sixteen hundred years, mostly from England.[143] Attractive as this simplistic and often very brief approach may be, these accounts rarely, if ever, pay any attention to the role of France and the influences made upon English policing by the French. In reality, much of the old world systems were either irrelevant or rejected by the new settlers and the utilization of an established system of policing was adopted due to familiarity until a better system was created that would be uniquely American. For the time that colonies were forced to operate under the English crown, adoption of English law, and its policing style, was inevitable. But once the opportunity arose to forge a new body of policing and laws the colonists moved forward swiftly, modifying the familiar and substituting the irrelevant.[144]

Although few formal policing systems were in place in 17th century America,[145] informal ancient and familiar vestiges of a manorial system were prevalent, especially in the Northern states. In England, bringing a prosecution for a criminal matter was still an individual affair. The private citizen bore the entire cost of the prosecution until legislation partially relieved this burden in 1752. In an effort to encourage the participation of the public in curbing the 18th century crime wave, the crown offered increasingly large rewards[146] to those who gave evidence against felons.[147] Due to the high cost of taking a case before the courts, it became common practice for merchants, farmers and civic groups to form associations to help defray the cost of bringing a criminal prosecution.[148] A version of the English associations manifest as a more forceful 'crime-control vigilantism'[149] was the preferred adoption in America, where a relationship between the sheriff and the posse, of which a number grew into vigilantes, was not an uncommon feature of the American frontier.[150] A crucial distinction should be drawn, however. The English societies never operated outside of the law whereas the American development into vigilante groups[151] frequently did.[152] Nevertheless, the similarities are clear; both developments were in response to inadequacies in established policing provision and failures of the criminal justice system to protect the interests of the individual. The similarities between the extra-legal methods employed by the American frontier vigilantes and the emergence of private policing groups that used strong arm tactics on behalf of railroad and mining companies should not be understated.[153]

By the close of the 18th century, much of England was struggling to make sense of its own crime problems, especially those in the capitol. America too needed to apply a diversity[154] of police responses to the wide variety of challenges facing Southern business entrepreneurs, Northern biblical refugees and Westward bound migrants. Critics of this view may seek to take refuge in terminology and explain the history of individual entities such as sheriffs as being distinctly different from those of the police. Yet we have seen that the term police was unfamiliar in England during much of the colonial years and, once adopted, had a broad and varied application. Narrowing the parameters of the word to Peel's application may indeed have been for the English a way of circumventing something overtly French, but the early role of the police constable in America carried a very broad portfolio of responsibilities far more closely resembling a *sergeant de ville* than a 'Bobby'. As Inciardi reminds us, "But while the powers of the English sheriff diminished over time, those of the American sheriff expanded to include not only the apprehension of criminals, but also the conducting of elections, the collection of taxes, and the custody of public funds."[155]

Alongside appointed local and municipal law enforcement officials, America also adopted private policing.[156] This was due in part to the slow development of city and statewide policing responses, as well to the expansion of railroads, industry and commerce that sought to protect its own interests often in the face of worker unrest and labor disputes. Familiar names like Wells Fargo,[157] Brinks,[158] The Pinkerton Agency[159] and The Burns Detective Agency[160] identified a lacuna in the protection of goods and property that public entities were unable to fill. At the same time, population growth, industrialization and the development of cities drew much of American society closer to contemporary European standards. Consequently, the policing needs of the burgeoning East Coast cities were very different from the needs of the rural communities and the pioneers. Social unrest, unemployment and vagrancy needed a policing response in accordance with contemporary European models. Pioneers attempting to conquer 'the Elephant'[161] made do with self-help, vigilantes, posses and the sheriff.[162] There is mixed evidence with regard to the proactive nature of these 'self-help' organizations, but it is clear that these groups were ". . . appendages to the institutionalized legal system with intention to circumvent it."[163]

By the end of the 19th century, Alan Pinkerton, "The Vidocq of the West,"[164] and other private police agencies found it opportune to transition from personal protection to property protection. By the close of the 19th century, unemployment was at 20 percent in America's declining employment market, 600 banks had closed and unions had become a significant force in US employment,[165] which meant that American industry increasingly needed to have a body of 'Cossacks'[166] or hoodlums to break strikes.[167] In 1902, the Great Anthracite Coal Strike devastated Pennsylvania. Coal prices soared[168] and the national and state governments were at a loss how to deal with the private labor dispute. Municipal police officers were either incapable or unprepared to arrest striking miners, and the private police responses provided by the Coal and Iron Police[169] under the supervision of Pinkerton's Detective Agency were heavy handed and frequently accused of brutality by the miners.[170] It was clear to many observers that these groups ". . . owed a duty to no one but their employers, and these in turn hired for their private police force the most irresponsible toughs and rough-necks obtainable."[171]

In 1905, the Pennsylvania state governor, Samuel Pennypacker, signed Senate Bill 278 into law. This legislation created the first statewide police agency in America, The Pennsylvania State Constabulary. Captain John Groome,[172] formerly of the Philadelphia City Cavalry, was tasked with creating and supervising a working statewide police force. During a subsequent Congressional investigation[173] into alleged reprisals against striking miners by the new force, Major Groome stated, "Of course there were no rules, no regulations, and nothing to go by; and these men were divided into four troops.[174] They were sent to barracks. I designed the uniforms, decided how they should be armed, and decided that it would be necessary for each man to be mounted; and purchased the horses and drilled men and gave them as much instruction."[175] When questioned about the inspiration for the force, he replied, ". . . I got the Italians, the Germans and Royal Northwestern police, and the Irish police; and from going over their reports I came to the conclusion that the conditions in Ireland were more similar to those in Pennsylvania, so far as the industrial and agricultural conditions and the character of the population were concerned."[176] Major Groome then reported to the Committee that he had paid a three week visit to the R.I.C. to fully investigate its organization and operations.[177]

Advocates and opponents of the Pennsylvania State Police[178] are agreed; the statewide force copied the Royal Irish Constabulary.[179]

By 1845, New York had abandoned its previous system of watchmen and adopted a London-style municipal police force. It was the first outside of the British Empire.[180] The new force appeared very different from the London model. Officers did not wear a uniform,[181] simply a copper badge, and very soon they exchanged truncheons for firearms.[182] But it was not the external appearance of the officers that denoted fundamental differences; it was the exercise of power.[183] The London force had been created to be politically neutral and institutionally controlled.[184] The New York officer's authority was limited by the ballot box.[185] Interestingly, in New York there was a general concern that the London 'Bobby' was too centralized and accountable to the government, and yet the London force was considered de-centralized and independent within England. By 1857,[186] the municipal force was abolished and a metropolitan force was created that would be commanded by state-appointed commissioners.[187] The New York police,[188] although allegedly modeled on the English police, were soon undertaking a range of tasks far closer in practice to the Paris police than to their London brothers. For example, New York officers provided babysitting services at the police station, helped people find employment, fought fires, fed the homeless and provided basic medical care.[189] They ". . . returned lost children by the thousands, shot stray dogs, enforced sanitation laws, inspected boilers, took annual censuses, and performed myriad other small tasks."[190] "Arrests were of little importance, the primary mission of the police was to provide services to citizens and garner votes for politicians."[191] In Paris, the police were tasked with controlling begging, issuing licenses to wine shops and food stores, firefighting and flood control, as well as providing care for abandoned children and pursuing unfaithful wives, inspecting the jails and having oversight of the public drainage system and sewers.[192] The London Bobby was maintaining the peace and preventing and detecting crime. Not only was there a remarkably different political and social setting for policing New York, there was a remarkably different job specification.[193] In reality, adapting the London police model to New York meant discarding political neutrality and increasing individual discretion.[194] This looks very much like a different force altogether, one that more closely resembles the French police who, like America, were born out of political instability resulting in a broad palate of responsibilities. As Monkkonen noted, "At best, one could say that the creation of the police force reflected a growing intolerance for riots and disorder, rather than a response to an increase in crime."[195] It was not until after the impact of initial formation settled that the city forces of America became practitioners of the narrow term police[196] and "urban reformers took over the welfare functions of the police."[197]

Sheriffs from Anglo-Saxon England whose powers were enhanced by a Frenchman, Hue and Cry vigilantes[198] in "rural areas and small towns across the nation,"[199] uniformed officers patrolling Paris in the 17th century and military police, policing civilians in rural France and Ireland,[200] a convict turned sleuth who inspired the establishment of private policing in America and city police officers responsible for political policing and the provision of welfare services—all were part of the development of American policing. We have credited Robert Peel with being the 'father' of American policing. But perhaps it is time to adopt a contemporary view and consider him more of a 'Significant Other' than the exclusive patriarch.

In the following chapter, I am going to discuss a number of contemporary police forces that have origins other than Common Law. Once we have established that there are a variety of ways to effectively police a country, the book will move into a discussion of how we police the specific crimes covered in the first five chapters, from a national and an international point of view.[201]

Endnotes

1. It is believed that there are in the region of 20,000 assorted law enforcement agencies in the US. Many of these are very small in size and comprise of as few as five or six sworn officers. For the purposes of this paper, my discussion will focus upon the development of state and local forces. Each of the large number of federal agencies in the US has produced a version of its history that can be viewed on the agency website. Also c.f. the following article that discusses the history of the reorganization of federal agencies: Grafton, C. The reorganization of federal agencies administration & society. February 1979; 10: 437–464, doi:10.1177/009539977901000403
2. Comprehensive coverage of the entire period is contained within the influential works of, *inter alia,* William Maitland's *History of the English law,* William Holdsworth's *History of English law* and, more recently, Leon Radzinowicz's *A history of the English criminal law.* These works are voluminous and remarkable reading.
3. Morris, W. The office of sheriff in the Anglo-Saxon period. *The English Historical Review.* Jan. 1916; 31(121); 20–40 at 20
4. Late O. E. scirgerefa "representative of royal authority in a shire," from scir (see shire) + gerefa "chief, official, reeve" (see reeve). In Anglo-Saxon England,

the representative of royal authority in a shire. As an American county official, attested from 1662; sheriff's sale first recorded 1798. http://www.etymonline.com/index.php?term=sheriff

5. First recorded usage is in the 12th century to denote the deputy count or holder of a shire. Shire having replaced the Anglo-Saxon term scir. C.f. http://www.etymonline.com/index.php?search=count&searchmode=none
6. For a thorough discussion, see: Irene Gladwin, *The sheriff: The man and his office.* London: McCartney; 1984.
7. King of Wessx 688 to 726. Known for formulation of legal codes, Ines laws, 694 and later subsumed into the legal code of Alfred the Great. Ine abdicated in 726 to pilgrimage to Rome.
8. Supra, Morris, p. 20.
9. During the later part of the Anglo-Saxon period, the alderman was the chief judicial officer within the shire and the sheriff served as the second.
10. Alfred the Great reigned from 849–899. He was responsible for the division of lands into boroughs and a number of boroughs together were designated as a shire. Consequently, many cities in Britain are named as boroughs, such as Edinburgh, Peterborough and Wellingborough and numerous counties are shires, e.g. Cambridgeshire, Worcestershire, Leicestershire. In the late 880s or perhaps the early 890s, Alfred issued his legal codes known as the *domboc.*
11. Supra, Morris, p. 21 and footnote 5
12. We take the term from the 3rd century Roman firewatchers, Vigiles. The term has commonly come to mean legal, or extra-legal, citizen participation in law enforcement.
13. The first king of England. Ruled from 924–939.
14. Supra, Morris, pp. 21–22 citing 5. Athelstan, 1.5 and 6 Athelstan, 10.
15. His mother never married his father, hence he was referred to as 'William the Bastard'. He invaded and conquered England in 1066. He already held the title William of Normandy from 1035.
16. William also retained the services of a number of English sheriffs, such as Marloswein, Freeman, Robert fitz Wymarc, Round, Touid, Davis, Edric, Edwin and Elfwine. Source: Morris, supra, p. 26, note 52
17. Supra, Morris, p. 30.
18. Harding, A. The origins and early history of the keeper of the peace. Transaction of the Royal Historical Society (Fifth Series). 1960: 10: 85–109 at 87. ". . . for the preservation of the peace of the kingdom and against foreign invaders or against others acting against the peace of the realm."
19. Clause 1. Referring to the harboring of robbers, murderers and thieves, "And the Justices shall make this inquest by themselves, and the sheriffs by themselves." Cited in Ernest Henderson, Select historical documents of the Middle Ages. London: George Bell and Sons; 1896, 16 (Taken from Stubbs, Charters. P. 142).

20. Ibid., p. 17.
21. Op. cit., Henderson, p. 147.
22. Henry III of England 1207–1272.
23. Harding, supra, cites an example form the Public Record Office J. I. 1/734 where in Shropshire 1256 "there were . . . 186 cases of homicide presented, but only 19 felons executed . . . Crime after crime was presented as committed by *malefactores ignoti* [persons unknown]. The system was incapable of dealing with the hardened criminal who wandered from shire to shire." At p. 86
24. Harding, supra, p. 89.
25. Bailiwick is an interesting term that is a combination of French and English, *balli* a French administrative official and *wick* an Anglo-Saxon village. The Oxford English Dictionary Second Edition apparently implies that the term originates from the 15th century. Harding, supra, p. 92 has sourced this term to the 13th century with his specific reference p. 92 note 5 to C.P.R. 1258–66 at p. 283. C.f. http://www.wordorigins.org/index.php/bailiwick/
26. E.g. Fitzpeter, Clifford, Lestrange, Nevill, Gesemuth, Montalt and Eustace de Balliol. Source: Harding, supra, note 6, p. 92.
27. Perhaps an early example of auxiliary policing, to support the local police in cases of civil disobedience, is found within the Harding, supra, p. 99 where "Edmund of Cornwall was appointed general 'keeper of the peace' in the English counties with power to appoint deputies to deal with improper assemblies beyond the sheriffs' control" citing Calendar of Chancery Rolls, various, pp. 271–218. Footnote 5.
28. E.g. In 1236 we see the sheriff continuing to have responsibility for forming a jury. C.P.R. 1232–47, p. 65 cited in Harding, supra, p. 103 at note 9. This function remained with the sheriff until 1857. (In 1856 all policing functions were transferred to local police constabularies, and all prison functions were transferred, in 1857, to the prison service.) The other previous primary role, tax collection, had already been handed to the Exchequer under Henry I. For further discussion see: Carpenter, D. A. The decline of the curial sheriff in England 1194–1258. *The English Historical Review.* Jan. 1976: 91(358); 1–32.
29. The Lord Lieutenant is the monarch's personal representative in a county.
30. The High Sheriff is the sovereign's judicial representative in a county.
31. Moley, R. The sheriff and the constable. *The Annals of the American Academy of Political and Social Science.* 1929: (146); 27–33 at 27.
32. See: Harry C. Buffardi. The History of the Office of Sheriff, Schenedachy County Sheriff, 1998. Not paginated. The appointment was soon followed by numerous other counties and states across colonial America and the sheriff became the *de facto* ranking police officer and chief tax collector for many counties. In 1679, the sheriff of Middlesex County appointed a jailer to run the county prison. Ibid. Accomac [sic] County Records 1640–1645, p. 150

in Karracker, CH. *The seventeenth century sheriff.* Chapel Hill: University of North Carolina Press; 1930.

33. *Posse comitatus,* meaning "the power of the county," was the legal basis for sheriffs to recruit assistance from any male over the age of 15 years to assist in the pursuit and capture of felons.
34. infra
35. This *connetablie,* or military unit, was directed by a Constable of France.
36. In association with his legal colleague Guillame de Lamoigen, Colbert drafted more than 150 pieces of legislation, including the 1670 Ordinance on Criminal Law and Criminal Procedure.
37. The office was first held by Nicholas Gabriel de la Reynie.
38. Jones, M. and Johnstone, P. *History of criminal justice.* 5th ed. Boston: Anderson; 2011; 220–221.
39. E.g. supervising markets, repairing municipal drains, inspecting food and wine, surveillance of foreigners, arresting sorcerers and directing firefighting. C.f. Jones, supra, p. 219.
40. Jones, supra, p. 220.
41. Ibid.
42. Ibid.
43. By 1716, the police wore a blue uniform, walked a defined beta and were the only citizens of Paris permitted to carry a firearm. Jones, supra, p. 221.
44. Ibid.
45. Germinal 28, Year VI of the French Revolution. April 17, 1798.
46. Jones, supra, p. 222.
47. Typically in brigades of six to ten men. Preference was for single men but married men were permitted to serve. It was intentional that the officers were recruited from an area different from where they would be policing. However, the Gendarmerie was eventually close to the people and held in higher regard than the despised Administrative Police of Fouche. Notwithstanding this, the period between 1789 and 1799 placed France under enormous internal conflict and upheaval and the Gendarmerie was often interpreted as a pro-revolutionary faction that was caught between supporters of the old regime and those who were forging a new. C.f. Broers, supra, p. 28.
48. Broers, M. The Napoleonic police and their legacy. *History Today.* 1999; 49(5); 27–33 at 27.
49. Minister of Police 1799–1810 and 1815–1816
50. General Anne Jean Marie Rene Savary. *Aid-de-camp* to Napoléon and then succeeded Joeseph Fouche as Minister of Police until Napoléon's abdication.
51. Broers, supra, p. 29.
52. infra
53. For a comprehensive discussion see: Catherine Denys, The development of police forces in urban Europe in the 18th century. *Journal of Urban History.* 2010; 36(3); 332–344.

54. The *sergents* were designated specific beats or areas of a town to patrol rather than to replicate the previous model of walking around without specific purpose. The result rarely led to arrest and supplied ample material for ridicule.
55. E.g. Little Dorrit, Oliver Twist, The Old Curiosity Shop, The Detective Police.
56. Believed to be based upon the real life criminal-turned police detective Eugene Francois Vidocq. infra
57. Broers, supra, p. 33.
58. Emsley, CFC. *The great British bobby: A history of British policing from the 18th century to the present century.* London: Quercus, 2009. Radzinowicz refers to the influence of Henry Fielding in bringing the term 'policing' into popular use. He cites Maitland's definition as "such part of social organisation as is concerned immediately with the maintenance of good order, or the prevention or detection of offences." Radzinowicz, supra, p. 4 and footnote 18.
59. Radzinowicz, L. *A history of the English criminal law.* London: Stevens; 1956. Vol. 3.; p. 1.
60. Cited by Radzinowicz, supra, p. 1.
61. Jones, supra, Chapter 10.
62. Supra, p. 227
63. Blinded at the age of 19 years Sir John Fielding could recognize criminals by their voices. It is reputed he knew 3,000 London criminals by their voices alone.
64. Henry Fielding was well known for his work of fiction *A History of Tom Jones.* He also authored 15 plays and a novel based upon the life of London criminal Jonathan Wild. He also wrote the weekly law digest the *Covent Garden Journal* as well as the *Police Gazette* (which remains in publication today as a source of information for serving police officers).
65. Contrary to some incorrect reports (a 'Google' search of this term shows five incorrect entries on the first page), this group did not wear uniforms and were never referred to as "Robin Redbreasts." They did, however, carry a truncheon as a weapon and this instrument frequently bore a crown or other insignia denoting authority. Dodsworth, F. Civic police and the condition of liberty: The rationality of governance in eighteenth century England. *Social History.* May 2004; 29(2); 199–216 at 212.
66. For a full account of the establishment of the Bow Street Runners, see: David Cox, *A certain share of low cunning: An analysis of the work of Bow Street Principal Officers 1792–1839.* London: Whillan; 2010. The somewhat disparaging term "Runners" may have been first used during a criminal trial at The Old Bailey in 1755. Cited by Emsley, supra, in Cox at pp. 2–3.
67. Six were initially appointed. This grew to eight by the early 19th century. All were 'sworn constables' of the City of Westminster.
68. Radzinowicz, supra, p. 263 cited in Jones, supra, p. 229.
69. In 1792, policing for London was divided into seven districts.

70. Emsley, supra, p. 22.
71. This later group wore blue trousers and red waistcoats. They were soon dubbed the "Robin Redbreasts." C.f. "The Police of London," *London Quarterly Review.* July 1870; 129; 50.
72. The Middlesex Justices Act 1972.
73. He established himself at Worship Street and then moved to Queen Square where he remained until 1818. Source: Radzinowicz, supra, p. 212.
74. Jones, supra, p. 229.
75. "In his opinion the French police were worthy of careful and impartial consideration." Radzinowicz, supra, p. 249.
76. For further discussion about the impact of Colquhoun, see: David Barrie, Patrick Colquhoun. The Scottish enlightenment and police reform in Glasgow in the late eighteenth century. *Crime History and Society.* 2008; 12(2); 57–79.
77. His *Treatise* appeared in French in 1807. Radzinowicz, supra, p. 221, note 3.
78. He was alone in attempting to introduce legislation. William Pitt introduced a Police Bill in 1785 and four Police Bills were introduced in 1799. All were defeated.
79. Colquhoun was closely associated with the Thames Marine Police and at one time held an official position with the office as its Receiver.
80. Patterson, D. *The Thames Police history.* Article compiled by PC 128A Richard Paterson 1974–2001. Thames Division available at Thames River Police Museum, Wapping, London. pp. 1–8 at p. 2. For a comprehensive discussion see: Leon Radzinowicz, *A history of the English criminal law and its administration from 1750.* London: Macmillan; 1957. Vol. 2. Part IV. New Departures, Chapters 12 and 13.
81. By the end of the 18th century, nearly four-fifths of all imports into England came through the Port of London. Source: Radzinowicz, supra, Vol. 2, p. 350.
82. Located at No. 259, Wapping New Stairs. Source: Radzinowicz, supra, Vol. 2, p. 363; and Patterson, supra, p. 4.
83. The force had written "General Instructions" pertaining to roles, responsibilities, conduct, rates of pay and the entire range of standing orders that are associated with a police force. Radzinowicz, supra, Vol. 2, p. 365. In addition to the 80 permanent staff, a further 1,120 were available and utilized as needed on a part-time basis. Radzinowicz, supra, Vol. 2, p. 372.
84. Quoted in Patterson, supra, p. 5.
85. It was also in 1800 that Colquhoun authored *Treatise on the commerce and police of the River Thames London, Baldwin, 1800,* a work that included specific costs associated with the level of crime being committed on the river estimated by Colquhoun to be at least £232,000 in 1798.
86. The final version was significantly different from the previous draft supplied by Colquhoun and Bentham. The bill passed into law on 28 July 1800. 39&40 Geo 3. C. 87

87. Master mariner and friend of Colquhoun's who later served with Colquhoun in the Wapping Police Office. John Harriot was himself a justice of the peace and is credited with being the author of the first written plan for the river police. "I have lost no time in transmitting your very sensible paper to Mr. Dundas, which contains a very excellent plan for the protection of shipping in the River Thames . . ." cited in Radzinowicz, supra, Vol. 2, p. 373 and note 65. Reprinted in Harriot's memoirs *Struggles through life, Exemplified in the various travels and adventures in Europe, Asia and America, etc.* (3rd ed. 1815) 3 vols. Vol. 3, pp. 112–113. Radzinowicz also supplies evidence of Harriot having first submitted his plan to the Duke of Portland in 1797 in Radzinowicz, supra, Vol. 2, p. 373 and at footnote 66.
88. By this time Colquhoun was already deeply involved with the Marine Police Establishment as noted in the *Lloyd's Evening Post and British Chronicle* June 27–29, 1978, A new office sitting at Wapping New Stairs, to be under the direction of Patrick Colquhoun, Esq. cited in Radzinowicz, supra, Vol. 2, pp. 371–372
89. In an earlier version of the attempts to gain support for the establishment of a government funded river police, Colquhoun, May 1, 1799, refers to assistance from ". . . a friend of great legal knowledge." This legal friend was Jeremy Bentham. Radzinowicz, supra, p. 385 and note 19. Bentham later reports on this involvement in his own memoirs and works, "Memoirs . . . including autobiographical conversations and correspondence" (Bowring's ed. 1843) Vol. 10, pp. 330–333. Ibid.
90. Radzinowicz, supra, Vol. 2, p. 389
91. Emsley, C. The English police; a unique development? in *Ideology, Crime and Criminal Justice: A Symposium in Honour of Sir Leon Radzinowicz.* Bottoms, A. and Tonry, M., editors. Cullompton, UK: Whillan; 2002. Chapter 4, p. 75.
92. Critchley, TA. *A history of the police in England and Wales 900–1966.* London: Constable; 1967 cited by Mark Neocleous, "Policing and pin making: Adam Smith, police and the state of prosperity." *Policing and Society.* 1998; 8; 425–449 at 426.
93. Jones, supra, p. 231 and also, in particular, the Ratcliffe murders of 1811. Reported variously e.g. Radzinowicz, supra, p. 315.
94. The new 'Police science'. Neocleous, supra, p. 440.
95. For example, the MacDonald Bill had failed in 1785 for these reasons and little had changed as the fervor of war and jingoism increased at the end of this century. See: Neocleous, supra, p. 209.
96. Jones, supra, p. 230
97. Robert Peel served as British Prime Minister from 10 December 1834 to 8 April 1835 and again 30 August 1841 to 29 June 1846. He went to Harrow boys school and then read classics, physics and mathematics at Christ's College Oxford where he took a double first. He trained as a lawyer, Lincoln's

Inn, and then entered politics in 1809. He made his maiden speech in the Commons in January 1810. Throughout his career Peel was supported by the Duke of Wellington.

98. Act, 54 George III, c. 131, July 25, 1814. "To provide for the better execution of the Laws in Ireland, by appointing Superintending magistrates and additional Constables in Counties in certain cases," Herlihy, infra, p. 29. This act created a permanent police force for rural Ireland. It did not include policing for the city of Dublin that had established a city force under the Dublin Police Act 1786 comprising 10 officers, a chief constable and a night watch. The force wore a uniform dress and carried muskets. Herlihy, J. *The Royal Irish Constabulary: A short history and genealogical guide.* Dublin: Four Courts Press; 1997. P. 27. The force was short-lived. It was abolished in 1795. Dublin maintained a separate force until merger in 1836 when one combined constabulary was established for all of Ireland.
99. John Brewer, Max Weber and the Royal Irish Constabulary: A Note on Class and Status. *The British Journal of Sociology.* Mar. 1989: 40(1); 82–96 at p. 82.
100. Bestowal of the title 'Royal' upon a police force was unique at the time. ". . . a circumstance unparalleled and unprecedented in any police force in the world." Brophy, M. *Sketches of the Royal Irish Constabulary.* London: Burns and Oates; 1886. P. 17.
101. Broeker, G. Robert Peel and the Peace Preservation Force. *The Journal of Modern History.* Dec. 1961; XXXIII(4); 363–373 at 363.
102. Barrie, supra, p. 5 citing Critchley, TA. *A history of police in England and Wales 900–1966.* London: Constable; 1967.
103. Herlihy, supra, p. 31. Shortly after this statement there were intense disturbances in Ireland and the army was called in to assist the new force in establishing order.
104. Fifty-seven Irish Protestants in the House of Commons signed a petition requesting he not leave.
105. Brophy, supra, p. 3. "One could almost believe that Sir Robert Peel, inspired by Mr. Drummond, seeing the pitiable condition of Ireland, and feeling that the powerful sister-country had a hand in bringing that condition about, determined on making some small restitution by creating employment of some useful kind, one branch of which assumed the shape of a police force twelve thousand strong." Ibid. There is some degree of support for this if consideration is given to the number of Irish aristocracy who joined the R.I.C. "Serving in the ranks are to be found the sons and heirs of the embarrassed or utterly ruined landed gentry." Ibid.
106. Brophy, supra, p. 14.
107. For comprehensive discussion see: Elaine Reynolds, *Before the bobbies: The night watch and police reform in metropolitan London 1720–1830.* London: Macmillan; 1998.

108. Jones, supra, p. 231
109. The Royal Irish Constabulary required all officers to wear a uniform but to have available a suit of civilian clothing to perform duties that required a civilian presence. Brophy, supra, p. 18. This was likely to be interpreted as far too similar to the Paris police 'spies' in London, and therefore the metropolis did not have a detective plain clothes presence until 1842. Jones, supra, p. 232. Initial detective work was provided for by the Bow Street Principal Officers. Cox, supra.
110. "Even had the City authorities been anxious to co-operate with the metropolitan force, either in action or in the exchange of information, their very multiplicity would have made it impracticable." Radzinowicz, supra, Vol. 4, p. 171
111. The 'Square Mile' established its own police force under the City of London Police Act 1839. Daniel Whittle Harvey was the first Commissioner of a force of 500 men. The City of London Police continue to operate today across the "Square Mile." There are currently 850 officers and 450 support staff of London Police that were formed. For further comprehensive discussion see: Andrew Harris, *Policing the city: Crime and legal authority in London, 1780–1840.* Columbus. OH: The Ohio State University Press; 1968.
112. Ten years later, the 1839 Metropolitan Police Act extended the initial ten-mile zone from Charing Cross to 15 miles. This Act also increased the force size to 4,300 officers.
113. Officers were required to walk a beat at a regular and steady pace. Initially set at three miles per hour this was soon reduced to two and a half miles per hour. Infra, Emsley.
114. For those opposed to a full-time police presence even the uniform was criticized as "The chief offence of the new police in the eyes of these patriots was the similarity of their dress to that of French gendarmes. Any coats would have been forgiven but blue coats." Hayden, BR. *Correspondence and table-talk.* London: Chatto and Windus; 1897. 2 Volumes. Vol. 2, p. 340.
115. Eight Superintendents, 20 Inspectors, 88 Sergeants and nearly 900 constables. Radzinowicz, L. *A history of the English criminal law. Grappling for control.* London: Stevens; 1968. Vol. 4, p. 161.
116. Emsley, C. *The great British bobby: A History of British Policing from the 18th Century to the Present.* London: Quercus; 2009. P. 39
117. Mayne was born in Dublin and after attending Trinity College was called to the bar at Lincoln's Inn. He served as the first joint commissioner and then second joint commissioner after the retirement of Colonel Rowan. Mayne finally became sole the first sole Commissioner of the force in 1855. And remained in this post until his death in 1868. He served a total of 39 years with the London Metropolitan Police and remains the longest serving commissioner to date.

118. One source of criticism even suggested that, "The appointment of a military officer, Colonel Rowan, of the Irish Constabulary, betrayed the intention of creating a 'veritable gendarmerie'." Major Arthur Griffiths, *Mysteries of police and crime: A general survey of wrongdoing and its pursuit.* London: Casell and Co; 1899. Vol. 1, p. 85. Charles Rowan served in the British army and then as a magistrate in Ireland, his country of birth, before accepting the position as Commissioner of the London Metropolitan Police in 1829. Rowan was not Peel's first choice, which was Col. James Shaw, but he refused and Rowan was offered the position.
119. Ibid.
120. Numerous sources trace the introduction of the term 'Peeler' to describe a 'new' police officer. It is specifically mentioned in the press: "The 'Peelers' withstand riots in London." *The Guardian.* Friday, 12 November 1830.
121. Griffiths, supra, p. 87
122. Reith, Charles. 1948. *A short history of the British police.* London: Oxford University Press. P. 62 also cited by Radzinowicz, supra, Vol. 4, p. 163. There are a number of variations upon the actual number of "Principles" that Peel developed. Some sources cite 9, others 12. E.g. Reith, ibid. and Jones, supra.
123. This Act established the system of HM Inspectors of Constabulary who conducted inspections of each force annually. Every force needs to achieve an 'efficient' grade if they were to receive one quarter of their budget from the Treasury.
124. Radzinowicz makes numerous references to the obstacles facing Peel especially, supra, Vol. 3. His treatment of the subject is discussed by Emsley in *Ideology, crime and criminal justice,* supra. There is also discussion of these matters in Philip Stead, *The Police of Britain.* New York: Macmillan; 1985, and Eric Monkkonen, *Police in urban America, 1860–1920.* New York: Cambridge University Press; 1981. An overview of these contributions is available in Wilbur R. Miller, Police and the state: A comparative perspective (review essay). *American Bar Foundation Research Journal.* Spring, 1986; 11(2); 339–348 at 343.
125. A discussion about the concern over police spies and the Popay affair, infra, is found in Emsley, supra, *The great British bobby,* pp. 56–64.
126. The Principal Officer was disbanded in 1839 after 90 years of service. It was replaced by the Metropolitan Police Detective Branch in 1842. Jones, supra, pp. 232–233.
127. For a colorful description of policing from the eyes of an early 20th century magazine, see: Richard Kemp, The evolution of the Police. *Munseys Magazine.* April 1910 to September 1910 at July 1910; XLIII(4); pp. 439–450.
128. Kemp, supra, p. 446
129. Walz, R. Vidocq, rogue cop. In: Francois Eugene Vidocq *Memoirs of Vidocq: Master of crime.* London: AK Press; 2003: xi.

130. Emsley, supra, p. 89
131. Jones, supra, p. 223
132. Ibid.
133. See also: Morris and Vila, supra, pp. 40–42
134. Vidocq memoirs, supra, p. ix
135. 1829. He opened a paper mill, lost all his assets and returned to working for the police, but after a scandal involving theft he was dismissed. Francois Eugene Vidocq died in Brussels in 1857. As was stated about him, "He has two valid claims for inclusion in the rolls of fame—as the Legendary Detective and as The Father of the Detective Story." Translator's notes form the 1935 original edition of Vidocq, supra, 1935 Edition translated by Edwin Gile Rich, p. 367.
136. Another plausible reason for the delay in establishing the detective unit is that Richard Mayne 'distrusted' the existing detective police and therefore was not motivated to increase the size or sphere of its responsibility. Miller, supra, p. 92
137. The Sergeant Popay affair of 1833, the Mazzini mail scandal of 1844, both cited by Emsley, supra, p. 90
138. Also known as the Turf Fraud Scandal, it was prosecuted at The Central Criminal Court (The Old Bailey), 22 October 1877. R v Clarke and Others. The case involved a horse racing fraud perpetrated by a number of senior Metropolitan Police detectives. Inspector Meiklejohn, and Chief Inspectors Clarke, Druscovich and Palmer, all stood trial for corruption. D.C.I. Clarke was acquitted; the other three were convicted and given two year terms of imprisonment.
139. He was placed in an unusual situation in this role in that he reported not to the Commissioner of the Metropolitan Police but directly to the Home Secretary. His rank was equivalent to assistant Commissioner, but he never held the formal title. His familiarity with the French *Surete* came about during his time studying law at the *Faculte de Droit,* Paris (now Pantheon-Assas II). He resigned from the force to enter politics in 1884. His title in the police was Director of the Criminal Investigation Department, C.I.D.
140. "The detective branch of the (French) civil police, aided by broad powers in investigation and evidence gathering arising from the state's concern for security developed a reputation for being the best in the world during the nineteenth century." Miller, supra, p. 344
141. E.g. John Fuller, *Criminal justice: Mainstream and crosscurrents.* Upper Saddle River, NJ: Pearson; 2006; 146–152; Robert Bohm and Keith Haley, *Introduction to criminal justice.* 5th ed. Boston: McGrawHill; 2008; 139–142; James Inciardi, *Criminal justice.* 5th ed. New York: Harcourt Brace; 1996; 163–167; Roy Roberg et al, *Police & society.* 5th ed. New York: Oxford University Press; 2012; 30–36; Gene Scaramella et al. *Introduction to policing.*

Los Angeles: Sage; 2011; 6–7; Kenneth Peak, *Policing America: Challenges and best practices.* 7th ed. Boston: Prentice Hall; 2012; 4–18.

142. Also referred to as 'Schouts' in the Dutch settlements. See: Brian Vila and Cynthia Morris *The Role of police in American society: A documentary history.* Westport, CT: Greenwood Press; 1999; 8.
143. E.g. Fuller, Bohm and Haley, etc., supra. "Every cunstable . . . hath, by virtue of his office, full powr to make, signe, & put forth pursuits, or hues and cries, after murthrers, manslayrs, peace breaks . . ." Taken from Massachusetts statute 1646 reprinted in Inciardi, supra, p. 167.
144. Jones, supra, pp. 112–132.
145. Boston introduced paid night watchmen in 1648 and the Dutch copied this model for New York in 1663, but the expense of running these systems proved too great and both were disbanded due to cost. Jones, supra, p. 233. See also *The Boston night watch.* Vila and Morris, supra, pp. 6–8.
146. Of course the reward concept has never left either the UK or the US where it operates nationally and internationally today. One manifestation of the 'reward' that is enshrined in legendary views is that of the reward for the capture of a frontier outlaw. See further: "One feature of the early police system in England that was generally accepted and profoundly affected American law enforcement practices in the eighteenth and nineteenth century was the offer of a reward for the return of stolen property and the arrest and conviction of criminals." Traub, SH. Bounty hunting, and criminal justice in the West: 1865–1900. *The Western Historical Quarterly;* 19(3); August, 1988; 287–301 at 288.
147. E.g. 5 Anne, c. 31 (1706) that created a reward of £40 for prosecuting burglars. For a comprehensive discussion, see; J. M. Beattie, *Policing and punishment in London 1660–1750.* Oxford: Oxford University Press; 2004; and also Frank McLynn, *Crime and punishment in eighteenth century England.* London: Routledge; 1989.
148. "Emerging evidence suggest that 'associations' found in this region (Halifax, Yorkshire) are very similar to the numerous others that spread throughout the rest of the country during this period," Little, CB and Sheffield, C. Frontiers and criminal justice: English private prosecution societies and American vigilantism in the eighteenth and nineteenth centuries. *American Sociological Review.* Dec., 1983; 48(6); 796–808 at 798. At least 450 associations were formed between 1744 and 1846. Ibid.
149. Ibid.
150. As Little and Sheffield comment though, "It would be wrong to infer that vigilantism arose on the American frontier solely in response to a tidal wave of lawlessness. To the contrary, in many cases the *lack* (original emphasis) of crime posed no need of a regular, full-time system of law enforcement . . ."; supra, p. 804. Note 18.

151. See further: C.C. Rister, Outlaws and vigilantes of the southern plains, 1865–1885. *The Mississippi Valley Historical Review.* March, 1933; 9(4); 537–554; J.W. Smurr, Afterthoughts on the vigilantes. *The Magazine of Western History.* Spring 1958; 8(2); 8–20. Published by the Montana Historical Society.
152. A limited number of English style societies did exist in America, in particular, anti-horse theft societies, some of which were incorporated into state law and achieved constabulary powers. Ibid.
153. "The big 'establishment' security companies, Pinkerton and Burns, abandoned labor espionage and union-busting services completely by the 1930's in favor of the burgeoning areas of industrial espionage and counterespionage, corporate embezzlement and fraud, and residential and commercial security policing." Weiss, RP. From cowboy detectives to soldiers of fortune: Private security contracting and its contradictions on the new frontiers of ccapitalist expansion. *Social Justice.* 2007–2008; 34(3–4); 1–19 at 6.
154. Boston had a 'warden' as early as 1749 and day watches were prevalent in most major cities by the middle of the century: Philadelphia, 1833; Boston, 1838; New York, 1844; San Francisco, 1850; and Los Angeles, 1851. By the end of the decade these cities had combined the day Constables with the Night Watch to provide comprehensive municipal police cover.
155. Inciardi, supra, p. 168. In some states the sheriff had authority to direct and control the police and in some cases order the call out of the state constabulary. Milton, C. Legislative notes and reviews. Edited by W. F. Wood. *The American Political Science Review.* Feb. 1921; 15(1); 82–93.
156. England was very familiar with private policing as this had been the model within the City of London for 700 years. The Bow Street Runners, though publically funded, also provided private policing services and the Principal Officers of the Bow Street Police Office hired out their services to private and public entities. Supra.
157. Established in Buffalo, New York, March 18, 1852, by Henry Wells and William G. Fargo
158. Established as a parcel company by Washington Perry Brink in Chicago, 1859.
159. Famous for allegedly providing personal security to President Abraham Lincoln, the agency was started by a Scotsman, Allan Pinkerton, and a Chicago lawyer, Edward Rucker. Originally named the North-Western Police Agency, they changed the name to The Pinkerton National Detective Agency in part to secure federal contracts. By 1871, the newly formed Department of Justice had hired Pinkerton's to detect and prosecute those committing federal crimes. The relationship lasted until enactment of the Anti-Pinkerton Act of 1893, which no longer allowed private agencies to be employed by the government.

160. This agency was established by William J. Burns in 1909. Prior to starting the William J. Burns National Detective Agency, he had worked as a Secret Service agent. He returned to federal employment in 1921 to become head of the Justice Department's Bureau of Investigation, which on retirement he handed over to J. Edgar Hoover as Director of the FBI.
161. See John Reid, Dividing the elephant; The separation of mess and joint stock property on the overland trail. *Hastings Law Journal.* 1977; 28(3). Jones, supra. The continent was sometimes referred to as the Elephant by pioneers.
162. Written in 1922. Frederic F. Van de Water, author of *Grey Riders: The story of the New York State Troopers,* New York: Putnam's Sons; 1922. Page 16 stated, "In America to-day, the countryside for the most part still turns for protection against marauders to the constable and the sheriff's posse that came into being under English law in 1295, as part of the militia system. These no longer carry the long bow or go about jingling in chain mail. Otherwise there is little to distinguish them from the keepers of the King's law in Merrie England of the Thirteenth century." The American militia system that Van de Water refers to "... grew out of the English Assize of Arms which, dating from the reign of Henry II, required all free men to provide arms and submit to training." Robert Reinders, Militia and public order in nineteenth-century America. *Journal of American Studies.* April 1977; 11(1); 81–101 at 82.
163. Little and Sheffield, supra, p. 806.
164. Jones, supra, p. 245.
165. Ibid.
166. Ray, GW. From cossack to trooper: Manliness, police reform, and the state. *Journal of Social History.* Spring 1995; 28(3); 565–586. Weiss, RP. Private detective agencies and labour discipline in the United States 1855–1946. *The Historical Journal.* 1 March 1986; 29(1); 87–107.
167. The Replies to Representative Maurer's Questions Reveal Distressing Conditions in Nearly Every Locality Where the Cossacks Were Located. Madison (Darrah P.O.), Pa., Feb. 22, 1911. Hon. James H. Maurer, House of Representatives, Harrisburg, Pa. 1911. It appears that the terms, 'Cossacks', 'Yellow Dogs' and Hoodlums' were in use against the Coal and Iron police as well as the Pennsylvania State Constabulary.
168. $20 per ton. The equivalent of paying $12 per gallon for gasoline today.
169. "It was a grime joke. The Coal and Iron Police were actually the mercenaries of the great industries." Van de Water, supra, p. 24.
170. E.g. The Lattimer Massacre that occurred near Hazelton, PA on 10 September 1897.
171. *A history of the Michigan state constabulary.* Detroit, Michigan State Con. stabulary Association; 1919. Chapter 2, p. 31.
172. Captain Groome was apparently promoted to the rank of Major once he took responsibility for the Pennsylvania State Constabulary. There are

also a number of later references to Groome as Superintendent and also to Commander Groome. The congressional hearing, supra, consistently refers to him as Major Groome.

173. May 6, 1915. The Commission on Industrial Relations created by the act of Congress on 23 August 1912, held at the Shoreham Hotel, Washington DC.
174. Groome took responsibility for a broad range of functions associated with the new force, including setting standards for recruits. During the Industrial Relations Committee Hearings, James Maurer, President of the Pennsylvania State Federation of Labor, was asked, "From what forces are the State constabulary recruited?" to which he replied, "The men are recruited from the ranks of ex-United States soldiers, and again many of them are recruited from the ranks or from the degenerate descendants of the middle classes, young men who are educated, but never amount to anything and no good for anything and generally hunt a job in the State police force." *Final Report and Testimony Submitted to Congress by the Commission on Industrial Relations.* 6 May 1915. Vol. XI. Document No. 415, p. 10932.
175. Williams, D. State police and the Irish "Black and Tans" in *The Bridgemen's Magazine.* January 1921; XXI(1); 77.
176. Ibid.
177. An interesting lack of geographical knowledge is displayed by Chairman Walsh, who at one point asked, "Does the constabulary in Ireland have authority in the large cities like Glasgow and Dublin?" Williams, supra, p. 78. A more pertinent question followed: "You spent, you say, three weeks at the barracks?" Major Groome. "Yes, and got their ideas and their rules and regulations." Ibid.
178. It is variously described as the Pennsylvania State Police and the Pennsylvania State Constabulary. Williams, supra, *Munsey's Magazine,* supra, Van de Water, supra.
179. Describing the officers employed by the new constabulary, Major Groome stated, "My instruction to each trooper leaves a great deal to his discretion. If he starts out to get his man, he must get him, even if he has to butt into the middle of a mob to find him. The troopers are advised not to use their guns unless they have to." *Munsey's Magazine,* supra, p. 448. This makes an interesting contrast with Peel's policing principles.
180. Jones, supra, p. 234.
181. When introduced the police were mocked. See Monkkonen, supra, p. 551.
182. See further: Vila and Morris, supra, pp. 36–39.
183. Miller, supra, pp. 345, 346, 347.
184. Miller, WR. Police authority in London and New York City 1830–1870. *Journal of Social History.* Winter 1975; 8(2); 81–101. This posits that the fundamental difference between the two jobs is that the authority each officer

possessed was different. The London "Bobby' had impersonal authority and the New York 'Cop' had far greater discretion. He cites the example of carrying firearms and how the American officer took to taking a firearm to work and as such became a more powerful presence than his London colleague.

185. "Throughout most of the 19th and into the 20th century, the basic qualification for becoming a police officer was a political connection, rather than demonstrated ability." Scaramella, supra, p. 9.
186. This relationship lasted until 1870 when a second municipal force was created. In the same year, 1857, Boston, having rejected a London police model in 1832, decided to move forward with the creation of an amalgamation of night watch and day police to form a full-time police force.
187. Jones, supra, pp. 234–5.
188. See: Vila and Morris, supra, pp. 35–37.
189. Scaramella, supra, p. 9.
190. Monkkonen, supra, p. 554.
191. Ibid.
192. Jones, supra, p. 108 and 219.
193. It can be further suggested that the London police were a centralized force due to the sole reporting line directly to the Home Secretary. This is true also of the Paris police, but not so of the New York police who were decentralized by the Municipal Police Act. It is recognized that local town policing in England became de-centralized by the formation of countrywide forces in the 1856 Act, supra.
194. Monkkonen, supra. Notes four important innovative features of the new police in the US. The second of these is that the US police located the police under the executive rather than the judicial branch. This differed from London where the police ran courts for many years. "This shift also sent the American police down a different developmental path from the English police, who long remained much more active and involved in preparing and prosecuting criminal cases than did their American counterparts." P. 550.
195. Monkkonen, supra, p. 553.
196. By the early 1900s, most major cities in America had established police forces that prioritized crime fighting as a primary role. The issue of political influence remained prevalent, however, until the 1920s. Commentary on this and upon the impact of August Volmer as a voice in establishing policing priorities supra, note 134.
197. Miller, supra, p. 347.
198. C.f. Roberg et al, pp. 36–37 and Jones, supra, pp. 242–243.
199. Fuller, supra, pp. 151–152.
200. Brophy, supra, relates a fascinating event when two R.I.C. officers were on vacation in Paris at a military parade. They both wore their green R.I.C.

uniforms at the time. Apparently Napoléon III saw the officers and questioned their origins. He then invited them to join in the parade and later referred to them as "*Officers de la gendarmerie Irlandaise.*" Pp. 22–23.

201. I presented a version of this chapter as a paper at the International Police Executive Symposium in New York, August 5–10, 2012. I am grateful to the conference organizer, Professor Dilip Das, for his permission to re-use the materials here.

POLICING AROUND THE WORLD

How we police crimes varies enormously depending upon the country that we are in when the crimes occur. Although there is a general consensus among all humans that the unjustified killing of another person is a criminal offence or that stealing from one another is wrong, the manner in which we investigate those offences is located within a complex set of customs, rules and societal values. Although police officers of the world may have an affinity with each other as they view the work undertaken as bonding across national barriers, the reality is that policing is not common and who is recruited into the police, how they are trained and what levels of discretion they have when once operational can differ within the same country as well as across other countries.

Policing is often regarded as being either a military or a quasi-military occupation or a distinctly civilian profession that more closely resembles public service, such as social work, nursing or teaching. But these views are limited by Western interpretation, and in fact there are far more models of policing taking place than these two extremes. For example, in Japan the policing style is strongly geared towards serving the community, with individual officers establishing relationships with citizens within small geographical areas. In China, policing is military and highly centralized, with officers having little discretion. In many countries of the Middle East, religious laws govern policing and officers are charged with upholding civilian and religious laws alongside of each other. In Scandinavia, police officers have wide levels of discretion even though many of the forces are centralized. In the USA, there are almost 20,000 law enforcement agencies and collectively they are highly centralized and highly decentralized. Some local small town police forces have as few as two sworn officers who possess considerable latitude in how they apply the law. State policing is typically a very centralized model with officers answerable to the state governor. Large city forces tend to be decentralized and are possibly the closest resemblance to the model espoused by Robert Peel back in the early 19th century in London. Federal forces are fairly unique. They are, *de facto*, centralized, but so too are forces in numerous European nation states; and more countries in Europe are looking at further levels of national centralized policing for the future. Also, there is the issue of training and qualifications. In some countries entrants into the police must hold a baccalaureate degree; in other countries not even a high school diploma is required. Every country has some degree of initial training for police officers, which again can be local and as little as a few weeks spent with a veteran officer or involve up to two years of initial training conducted in an academy, such as in Sweden where new recruits spend two years in training before individual patrol commences. Age and gender are also factors is policing. Some countries permit entrants into policing at 18 years of age; in others it is 21 years. Mandatory retirement exists in a number of countries so that once an age or length of service is reached, that police officer must retire. In other countries, it is feasible if not realistic to have patrol officers working the streets until they are 65 years of age. In other countries, there is no legal retirement age whatsoever. Women are now represented in most police forces of the world. Embracement of equality in policing has taken many decades to achieve and there still exist considerable discrepancies between conditions of service, pay and uniforms and training in some police forces.

Uniforms and the carrying of firearms are also features of contemporary policing. Some forces require all officers to carry firearms; some forces do not permit any officers to carry firearms. Some forces only permit men to be firearms licensed, whereas others supply the same training and weapons to all recruits, male and female. It is interesting that the word uniform means the same and yet police uniforms are most definitely not uniform. Some are totally military; some are more like civilian clothing. Some forces permit all officers to wear the same uniform and others have different dress wear for different ranks or different tasks or different genders. Some require headwear; some do not. Some require protective clothing to be worn on all occasions; other forces have no protective body covering or headgear. Policing is a multi-variable entity with great discrepancies existing within nation states and between nation states. What it means to become a police officer is not a constant; the recruitment, training and job are not the same across boundaries even if the types of criminality are remarkably similar—murder, theft, abduction and drug offences exist in every country of the world. But how we police those crimes is as variable as the *modus operandi* of the crimes themselves.

In this chapter, I am going to look at policing in a range of countries that represent policing models that differ from those in the USA, or at least that appear to differ at first blush but which may in fact be recognizable in the US with a little probing. The police forces chosen are those of South Korea, Saudi Arabia, Scandinavia (Sweden, Norway and Finland) and the RCMP of Canada. There are currently 196 countries[1] in the world and each one has some form of law enforcement provision. This book is not the venue to discuss all of the police forces on Earth, but a sample of forces that approach recruitment, training and roles and functions in different ways should provide the basis for lucrative discussion and set the scene for a more in depth look at police within the US covered in the following chapter.

South Korea is a nation with more than 4,000 years of history. It is a country that has always been a fusion of cultures and peoples, some transient others resident. Due to its geographical location, Korea has been a center point for military as well as for cultural influences. Four hundred years ago, Korea was invaded by Japan. It was occupied by Japan between 1910 and 1945. Later in the 20th century, it was at war again; this time it was a civil war between the Republic of Korea and the Democratic People's Republic of Korea, resulting in the 38th Parallel division between North and South Korea. Seoul is the capital of South Korea and has a population of more than 10 million people. Pusan is the second largest city, with a population of more than 4 million inhabitants. At the cessation of the Second World War, the US assisted Korea in establishing a civilian police force. Initially, policing came under the direction of the Ministry of Home Affairs when the military and civilian policing operations for the country were fused together into one paramilitary police force for the entire nation. By 1989, the Korean National Police comprised 105,000 officers that policed 13 metropolitan districts, numerous provincial regions, a Combat Police Unit, the National Maritime Police, the Anti-terrorist Police and the National Police Training Academy. All of these entities answer to the National Police Headquarters. Individual police officers operate on a strict 'beat system' within major cities, so that officers patrol a regulated area with the intention of providing a strong community presence for the citizens. Recruitment into the police has been challenging for South Korea and it has one of the lowest police/citizens ratios of any non-communist major industrialized countries. The Combat Police is an alternative option for males in South Korea who did not wish to participate in compulsory military service. Women are not required to perform military service. All new recruit training is conducted at the National Training Academy in Seoul. Like many Civil Law countries that operate a national police force, South Korea has different levels of entry into the police service so that, for example, a recruit who has a baccalaureate degree may enter the police as an officer at the rank of lieutenant or inspector. By 1991, the KNP was no longer subordinate to the Ministry of Home Affairs, as a police committee was established to create policy, training and development standards for the entire KNP. In 1991, the police became an independent government entity, the National Police Agency, headed by a commissioner general. In 2007, as a result of internal reorganization, the KNP established a Women and Youth Division. The KNP has six broad policies that direct policing efforts across the country. These are: guarantee for safe environment against crimes and accidents, assure social stability to support government administration, realization of police for human rights supporting people's rights and interests, expansion of basis for security services that meets the needs of the people, creation of healthy and active structure culture and security of police competitiveness to respond to the changing security environment.[2]

The Korean National Police University is open to any Korean national who has graduated from high school. It accepts approximately 120 students each year into a four-year officer entry degree program. Ten percent of applicants accepted are women. Married applicants are not permitted.

All recruits live in dormitory accommodation on campus for the four years and all recruits wear a police uniform throughout the duration of their studies. The main areas of academic study are law or public administration. Upon graduation, the degree-holding participants are assigned to police management duties at the rank of inspector.[3]

Basic training for new police recruits that are not attending the police university is conducted at the central police academy. Training comprises 8 months of coursework at the academy followed by practical training in the field. The academy syllabus comprises 3 weeks of close order drill followed by 25 weeks of preliminary education in law, physical education and knowledge and skills based training. During this 25-week period recruits will spend 6 weeks at a police station working alongside police officers. All new recruits live in academy dormitory accommodation and wear uniforms daily. The academy can accommodate up to 4,500 new recruits each year. Admission to the academy is dependent upon age—not less than 18 years and not more than 30 years of age—and possession of a high school diploma. All participants must hold a valid driver's license, have proportionate height and weight and pass a medical and aptitude test. Upon graduation, all students must have achieved 'masters' level competency in martial arts and self-defense alongside the usual array of competencies in the law, search and seizure, firearms training and crime scene investigation. Classes commence at 6 a.m. each day and conclude at 17.30. Rigorous weekly testing is conducted at every level to ensure competency of recruits in all examined areas. An integral part of the curriculum is "culture-based" training, which incorporates "police spirit, understanding human rights, gender equality and health management."[4] A comprehensive range of evening classes is offered to new recruits, including English conversation classes, yoga and advanced level martial arts.

The Kingdom of Saudi Arabia is the largest nation on the Arabian Peninsula.[5] Saudi Arabia is surrounded by water, but the interior is dry and arid and known as *Rub al-Khali,* the Empty Quarter. The nation has massive natural resources in oil and gas. Saudi Arabia is a country with a large growing population of which 92% are Sunni Muslim and 8% are Shii Muslim. The country has a monarchy founded in 1932 by the victorious tribal chief Abdul Aziz bin Abdul Rahman al Saud. The basic principles of law are that the Kingdom is based upon Islam's Sacred Law, which is based upon the principles of the prophet Muhammad. Islam is the official religion of Saudi Arabia; laws passed by the Saudi state are therefore considered Koranic laws and binding upon all citizens within the country. The state is responsible for ensuring compliance with Koranic values and teachings and disseminating Islamic and Arab values through Islam's sacred law, the sharia. The king is legally the ultimate source of all state authority and he possesses full executive powers. The judiciary is independent of the monarch though and considered answerable solely to sharia law. The country is divided into 13 provinces. Each province has a governor that carries the same rank and status as a Minister of State. Policing and security provision within Saudi Arabia are governed entirely by the provisions of sharia law. Saudi Arabia is the birthplace of Islam and the home to the two holy cities of Mecca and Medina. What this means in practice is that the primary function of the police is to protect Islam and its values. The police work under the Ministry of the Interior, which is also the body charged with investigating crimes, apprehending suspects and bringing those suspects before a court. Sharia courts then hear cases brought to them by the Ministry of the Interior. There is very limited information about the recruitment and training of police officers within Saudi Arabia. It is a centralized system that appears to be militarized and to operate as part of the internal defense forces. Members of the Saudi Police participate in international police conferences and the Association of International Police Officers and appear to wish to participate in a modernization of policing efforts within the country. Helicopters, cars and radios are now a common feature of policing within Saudi Arabia, and a centralized Public Security Service now supplies much of the internal security provision. Uniforms for police personnel are very similar to army uniforms. The distinguishing feature is the red beret worn by the police. Officers are armed with pistols, no longer the standard old style single shot rifle. There is a regular, uniform police division and, more recently a special investigation division, the General Directorate of Investigation, the *mubahith* or secret police. The Directorate of Intelligence is responsible for the collation and dissemination of all intelligence, police and military. There is also a SWAT, the Special Security Force. Compliance with religious living and practices is the responsibility of the *mutawwiin*, the religious police. The primary role of the mutawwiin is to ensure the observance of religious requirements, for example, prayers five times every day, fasting during Ramadan,[6] the ban on consumption of alcohol and the requirement that women dress modestly. The vigor and enthusiasm for application of sharia law by the mutawwiin has been subject to much Western criticism over the past 30 years, as well as some internal commentary also. At one time the mutawwiin had authority to detain suspects for up to 24 hours before handing them over to the 'regular' police. In some instances there have been allegations of brutality and the infliction of torture and beatings by the mutawwiiin. It was estimated that in 1990 there were in the region of 20,000 mutawwiin operating within Saudi Arabia. The current number is thought to be significantly fewer. Members of the religious police wear the traditional white *thaub.* In February 2012, an article titled "Saudis split on admitting women into Islamic police"[7] reported that citizens of the kingdom are split over whether or not women should be permitted to join the religious police. Apparently the new director of the Commission for the Promotion of Virtue and prevention of Vice stated that he was considering the recruitment of women into the often feared and secretive mutawwiin. Saudi society is clearly divided on the subject, and one commentator stated "No and 1,000 no's . . . The women's society is uncontrollable and admitting them into the Commission will only increase problems and disasters."[8] Another citizen stated "Yes and 1,000 yes's . . . But there must be conditions for this, including that a female recruit must be a university graduate and must be above 35 years of age."[9] The training of regular police officers, members of the Public Security Forces, is conducted through a police academy.[10] The actions of the regular police in Saudi Arabia do not attract the levels of international interest that the religious police achieve, mainly due to the interest held for policing methods that are not easily identifiable with Western policing models. There are no religious police units in any countries other than those that follow Islam, and consequently there is some reticence by the Saudi authorities to divulge details of police recruitment, training and operations. The Crime Prevention and Criminal Justice Division of the United Nations Office in Vienna is responsible for compiling information about the criminal justice systems of all nations; and this also involves commentary about police practices and issues, such as compliance with regulations and how matters pertaining to incidents involving police use of force are recorded. In every aspect, Saudi Arabia is compliant with recognized international criteria for the training and conduct of police officers and the manner in which complaints and the use of force are investigated.[11] The 20,000 or so religious police still manage to attract considerable international attention for alleged abuses of fundamental human rights. On February 15, 2012, ABC News reported that the mutawwiin had arrested more than 140 people for celebrating Valentine's Day. "In a six page statement, the religious police stated that they were saving women from 'deceiving men', who used the day [Valentines] to give the fake impression that they loved a woman while pretending to be a 'harmless lamb'."[12] Authorities reported that Muslims who participate in Valentine's Day are "weak, lacking imagination, and far removed from the 'sublime and virtuous' objectives of their religion."[13] In addition to making hundreds of arrests, the religious police also confiscated red roses from florist shops. Dancing, playing music and showing movies in public are also all religious crimes in Saudi Arabia. Mingling between the sexes is discouraged and may be viewed as an offence punishable as a crime, *khulwa.* Women who are arrested for socializing with men who are not relatives or husbands are liable to be charged with prostitution.

Finland is one of a number of countries that may be referred to as Scandinavia. There is some debate as to whether or not Finland joins Sweden, Norway and Denmark in making up "Scandinavia." The ambiguity extends further as the Faroe Islands and Iceland are also sometimes referred to as Scandinavia. For the purposes of discussing the policing of the northern European region of Scandinavia, I am including Finland with Norway and Sweden. It might be easier to talk of the Nordic countries, but this too is problematic as generally this term includes Denmark as well. Linguistically, the Swedes, Danes and Norwegians have similarities that do not apply to the Finnish, but the term Nordic Countries appears to be more inclusive than Scandinavia. That said, I am still using the term Scandinavia to include Finland, Norway and Sweden, and I leave you to thrash out the niceties at another time.

Finland shares borders with Sweden, and it was part of that country until 1809 when it became a duchy within the Russian empire until its independence in 1917. It is the eighth largest country in Europe and the least densely populated. Immediate neighbors are The Russian Federation, Sweden and, to the extreme north, Norway. Helsinki is the capital and largest city with a population of around 600,000 inhabitants. Finland operates under the Civil Law judicial system. Both Finnish and Swedish[14] are official languages of the country. Finland has a centralized police model with officers appointed to serve anywhere across the country. The first comprehensive police law came into effect in 1967[15] (as amended) and brought into effect the creation of police advisory units that bring citizens and police officers together to agree upon strategies and policing initiatives. The Ministry of the Interior is ultimately responsible for the police in Finland. The Police Department, the Supreme Police Command, reports to this ministry and has the day-to-day policing responsibility for the nation. Policing is divided into five main regions and 24 police departments and the Aland Islands. Since Finnish police provision is national, there are national centers for training, a National Bureau of Investigations, Security

Police, Mobile Police and a National Technical Center. New recruits are trained at the Police School in Tampere, POLAMK. Until January 1, 2008, entrants trained at the Police College of Finland in Espoo. The two colleges have now merged and are jointly referred to as The Police College of Finland. Typically the Tampere school trains in the region of 300 new recruits every year. All police officer recruits are trained to university level and must achieve the Diploma in Police Studies before graduating from the police college. Senior appointments in the police service ordinarily require candidates to hold at least a master's degree and increasingly a doctorate. Previous military service is considered an advantage for entry to the police service and a reduction in the basic training program is possible for military veterans. The Diploma in Police Studies takes 30 months to complete. It consists of practical and academic courses, similar to many aspects of all police academies, but the timeframe is considerably longer than initial training in the USA or the UK, for example. Courses are offered in Finnish and Swedish. The national training school accepts approximately 200 to 400 recruits from the 1,600 applications it receives each year. Typically, 25% of applicants to the national police force of Finland are women. There are in the region of 8,000 sworn officers in Finland, which represents one police officer per 681 citizens. The Police Act of Finland requires that "Police discharge their duties in an appropriate and impartial manner and seek to promote a conciliatory spirit. The actions of the police must not cause any more damage or inconvenience than is necessary to carry out the duty at hand. Measures taken must be justifiable in relation to the importance and urgency of the duty and the factors affecting overall assessment of the situation."[16] In the majority of Civil Law jurisdictions, police investigations are divided into degrees of seriousness so that less serious crimes will be investigated exclusively by the police and more complex crimes will have a judge or Examining Magistrate appointed to help direct the investigation, interview witnesses and suspects and prepare the file for prosecution. In Finland, the pre-trial investigation conducted by the police establishes whether or not a crime has been committed and who should take responsibility for further investigations. However, in Finland it is extremely rare that any authority other than the police will conduct the entire investigation into a criminal matter, and it is only in instances where a police officer is the suspect that a state prosecutor will take responsibility for the investigation. In Finland, the National Bureau of Investigation (NBI) investigates organized crime, domestic and international. Unlike the FBI is the USA, members of the NBI are sworn police officers rather than federal agents.

In March 2012, police sergeant Marko Forses, 'Fobba', was named Finland's police officer of the year for his pioneering work in crimes against youths committed via social media networks on the Internet. Fobba noticed that many crimes against young people were occurring on the social network IRC-Galleria, a network that typically attracts around 60% of young people who are social networking in Finland. Initially on a part-time basis, and then recently full-time, Sgt. Forses opened a profile to patrol the site online. He found that his profile received in the neighborhood of 5,000 visitors a week and at one point as many as 35,000. On his profile he posted a large number of user questions resulting in the official police page having 46,000 hits in the first 9 months. Eventually, and in part due to a school shooting incident leaked online, the Ministry of the Interior agreed to fund three officers to work permanently on the social networking site. Social network sites are a prime recruitment tool for pedophiles and traditional methods to encourage reporting are generally low in most countries due to the nature of the crime and the age of the victims. Encouraging young people to report offences through the non-visual and indirect medium of the Internet has already paid off for numerous police agencies. Cyber bullying is also increasing significantly and, according to Forses, "It's sometimes enough to give the buller, youth or adult, a virtual warning. Usually that stops the bullying because normal people want to avoid police investigation."[17]

Sweden is an immediate neighbor to Finland. It is the fifth largest country in Europe and, like Finland, it too has a small population—9.5 million of which 85% of the population lives in the southern part of the country. Stockholm is the capital and has a population of around 2 million. Sweden has a constitutional monarchy as well as a democratic parliament. Prior to 1965, policing was municipal and regional. Since then it has become a national force with the National Police Board as the governing body. There are about 17,000 sworn police officers representing a ratio of less than 2 police officers per 100,000 population.[18] Policing is divided up into counties (districts); there are 21 in total, the largest being Stockholm with 4,500 officers.

Each county typically has operations, criminal investigations, drugs and technical support divisions. The overall responsibility for the police rests with the National Police Commissioner who answers to the Ministry of Justice. In addition to district police responses, there are a number of national level departments, such as the anti-terrorist unit, the National Security Service, criminal investigations, the National Criminal

Investigations Department and the National Police Academy responsible for initial recruit training and specialized courses. There is also a national forensics laboratory service, the National Laboratory of Forensic Science. The police receive their powers under the Swedish Police Act 1999. Basic training consists of attending a police academy—Stockholm, Umea or Vaxjo. The institution at Solna, Stockholm is exclusively a police academy. The other two police academies are part of universities. Basic training lasts for two years, and after passing university level courses graduates leave with a diploma that permits them to apply for a probationary working position within a police county. This second phase of training lasts six months. Basic training places a strong emphasis on behavioral science and knowledge of the law. Classes are structured around participant discussions that emphasize human rights and the 'science' of policing ethically in a diverse society. Having successfully completed the academic training and the practical training, the recruit is now considered a constable/patrol officer. Entry into the national police service is highly competitive. Sweden operates an examining magistrate system so that serious crimes are investigated under the direction of an investigating judge who directs the police in terms of the detention of suspects, what and when charges should be brought and overall responsibility for the preparation of the case prosecution.

Norway is a country that has the most northern border in Europe and a population spread of just 14 inhabitants per square kilometer. It is one of the least populated countries in Europe. Norway shares borders with Sweden, Finland and Russia. Norway has two official languages—Dano-Norwegian, *Bokmal,* and New Norwegian, Nynorsk. Both languages have equal status in the country. There are 19 counties in Norway and one national police force divided into 27 police districts.[19] Each district has a Chief of Police. Overall, the police report to the Ministry of Justice. Legal procedure in Norway is adversarial in nature, rather than inquisitorial, and the courts operate the principle of binding precedence with decisions of the Supreme Court binding all lower courts. Senior police officers in Norway are part of the Prosecuting Authority and consequently Chiefs of Police are also qualified lawyers. Norway is a constitutional monarchy like Sweden, and if a chief of police decides to prosecute a senior government official for a criminal offence it is a matter for the king to decide on the appropriateness of proceeding with the matter. Apart from the 27 semi-autonomous police districts, there is centralized training and special services, such as the National Criminal Investigations Service, the National Economic Crime Unit, OKORIM, the Central Mobile Service, the National Police

Immigration Service, the National Police Computing and Material Service and the Security Service. Although the origins of policing in Norway are attributable to the French gendarmerie model, today the force is a mixture of relatively independent district forces operating under one chief of police, as well as a centralized system for national services and training. Norway represents a hybrid model of policing that is neither exclusively centralized nor decentralized. Entry into the Norwegian police service requires acceptance into the National Police Academy in Oslo, the Norwegian Police University College. The program is a university level program and all successful graduates are awarded a baccalaureate degree, the bachelor's degree in police education. The three years are divided up into academic and practical training where, after the completion of year one, recruits spend 12 months in the field at one of the 27 police districts before returning to complete academic studies and final exams. Law and sociology are required classes in year one. 'The purpose of the bachelor's program is to educate thoughtful and vigorous police officers who are able to prevent crime, enforce the law, and provide assistance in a manner that attends to the legal protection and safety of the citizens, as well as to the interests of society at large.'[20] Admittance into the degree program requires Norwegian citizenship, a minimum of 20 years of age, character and background checks, aptitude tests and "required personal maturity and character to serve as a police officer."[21] In 2011, there were 2,760 applicants to the police university college. Of these, 720 were accepted and 36.1% of the accepted applicants were female.[22]

Canada is the second largest country in the world. It has a population of 34.5 million people.[23] Life expectancy is 80 years on average and education and healthcare are free for all citizens. More than one million of the working population holds a doctorate or a master's degree. Eighty-five percent of all Canadian exports go to the USA. Canada is a federal state as well as a constitutional monarchy headed by Queen Elizabeth II, represented within Canada by a governor general. Canada is a federation comprised of 10 provinces and three territories. Canada has two official languages, French and English. The legal system is the Common Law other than in French speaking Quebec where it is the French Civil Law for civil matters. The Supreme Court of Canada is the ultimate authority for both Common Law and Civil Law matters. There are in the region of 500 different police and criminal justice organizations in Canada,[24] and the largest by far is the Royal Canadian Mounted Police, the *Gendarmerie royal du Canada* (RCMP), which is a national force. Policing provision is provided at the local municipal level, the province and territory level and at the federal level. Overall, there are in the neighborhood of 185 police officers per 100,000 population. This is less than either the USA or the UK, which both have more than 200 officers per 100,000 population.[25] In 2011, there were a total of 69,438 sworn police officers in Canada,[26] the largest single number being in Ontario with 26,387 sworn personnel.[27] The highest density of officers per 100,000 population is in the Northwest Territories with 451.1 of the province, and the fewest is Prince Edward Island with 167.3.[28] The National Police Services (NPS) is a business arm of the RCMP that provides information and training to all of the various agencies and organizations. Services provided by the NPS include the Centre for Missing and Exploited Children, the Canadian Police College, the Canadian Police Information Centre, the Criminal Intelligence Services Canada and the Forensic Science and Identification Services. The Canadian Police College is not responsible for basic training due to the diversity of police services provided across the nation besides which much is policed locally and at the state level. What the NPC provides is executive level courses for senior officers from the various national, provincial and municipal forces. The RCMP is a world-renowned police force that is unique in that it is a national, federal, provincial and municipal police force. Easily distinguishable by the famous red tunic known as "The Red Serge," the RCMP has been a feature of Canadian policing since 1873. Today the RCMP policies three territories and eight provinces; it does not provide municipal policing to Ontario or Quebec, to 190 municipalities, to 184 Aboriginal communities and to three international airports. The RCMP is organized under the RCMP Act and reports to the Minister of Public Safety. The current total strength of the RCMP is 29,235.[29] Unlike most other police forces in Canada, the RCMP is not unionized. Training of recruits into the RCMP is conducted at 'Depot', the RCMP Academy in Regina, Saskatchewan. Initial training lasts for 24 weeks. It is called the Cadet Training Program and is geared very much towards adult learning and community policing with problem solving scenarios and discussions. Application to the RCMP requires Canadian citizenship, a minimum age of 19 years, a high school diploma, a current valid Canadian driver's license and proficiency in either French or English. As is the case in the USA and the UK, there is no officer entry into the police service; all recruits join at the constable level regardless of academic qualifications upon entry. Entry requirements also include the statement, "You should possess the following values: integrity, honesty, professionalism, compassion, respect and accountability. Our selection process will determine if your personal history, traits and characteristics are suitable for a career in policing."[30] In addition to the RCMP, there are hundreds of police forces across the country that provide a response to local policing needs. Many of these forces are very small in size and in order to defer training costs they encourage new recruits to obtain the academic stages of training from a community college before being accepted into the force for practical training. Within the more populated provinces, there are also sheriffs in addition to city police forces; for example, the British Columbia Sheriff Service. In addition to supplying police services to the entire province, the sheriff's department also continues to provide services to the courts system of the province in very much the same way as was established back in the Dark Ages in England. As you will recall from Chapter Six, in the UK the office of sheriff is now largely ceremonial. In Canada it is more similar to the USA's model where sheriffs are engaged in every aspect of policing as well as the additional role of protecting Provincial, Supreme and Appeal Courts of BC, judges and Crown Prosecutors. The BC Sheriff's Department also runs the court detention cells (not the city jails) and escorts prisoners. The Vancouver Police Department is one of a number of police forces within the Vancouver metro area. It was the first municipal police force in Canada to appoint a female officer. The VPD started with the appointment of one officer in 1886 and is today a force of 1,700 civilians and sworn officers. In addition to providing police services to the City of Vancouver, the force also has a separate department that employs jail guards for the city jails. Jail guards are not sworn officers though many become sworn police officers after serving in this department. Training to become a jail guard is of one-month duration and takes place during evenings and weekends. The VPD also employs non-union sworn officers as special constables in the Traffic Authority. These officers have limited authority, such as directing traffic at major events. It is a paid, part-time position. Training involves completion of an 85-hour program over evenings and weekends and includes such issues as legal studies, use of force and traffic control. Police officers are selected through an assessment center process where all applicants spend one day at the police academy engaged in role-play scenarios. If successful and all other entry requirements are completed, initial training consists of attendance at the Justice Institute of British Columbia (JIBC) on Vancouver Island. Training is divided into three blocks: basic training 11 weeks, field training (on patrol under supervision) 13 weeks and then advanced training back at JIBC for a further 11 weeks. There is no officer entry into the

VPD. Two provinces have a statewide police responsibility; the Ontario Provincial Police, OPP, and the *Sûreté du Quebec.* Basic training with the OPP involves completion of a 12-week academy at the Ontario Police College. This is followed by a period of field training and then a further 5 weeks back at the academy. The first 12 months of employment as a sworn officer, once all initial training is complete, is considered a probationary period. After completion of this probation, a constable officer is confirmed in office and rank. The *Sûreté du Quebec,* referred to in English as the QPP, was formed in 1870 and is responsible for providing police service to the entire province of Quebec. Entry into the QPP requires recruits to obtain a Diploma of Collegial Studies from one of the 12 colleges located within the province and then to have completed the basic Patrol Officer Program at the QPP academy. After successful completion of the first stage, officers must have an offer of employment from the QPP and then attend and complete the 15-week initial training program at the Quebec police academy, the *Ecole Nationale de Police du Quebec.* Upon completion of the second stage of training, ". . . the school issues a report indicating the degree to which the candidate has mastered the competencies learned. This attestation is the result of a continuing formative and summative evaluation process based on instructor supervision as well as the observations of all the contributors encountered by the candidate during his stay at the *Ecole nationale de police du Quebec.* A diploma in police patrolling is awarded in recognition of the successful achievement of the requisite criteria for each of the competencies making up the program."[31] The cost of operating the program per recruit, excluding salary, is $6,615 Canadian dollars for the 15 weeks.[32] The language used at the academy is French and all recruits must pass examinations in French to graduate.

The RCMP was modeled on the Royal Irish Constabulary, which I have argued in Chapter Six is a manifestation of the French gendarmerie disguised as such by Robert Peel. The police of French speaking Quebec are not direct copies of the French gendarmerie though; in fact, they are closer in nature and form to a city force structure that might have originated in London with the Metropolitan Police. Both models are indicative of the diversity of policing seen in Canada. There are national, provincial and municipal forces and there are sheriffs. Additionally, there are Aboriginal police forces that specialize in policing under the First Nations Policing Program.[33] Policing in Canada is truly diverse and complex with a number of apparent police models—centralized, decentralized and hybrids. Together they provide a police response across a massive landmass to a population of numerous multi-cultural origins. There are few countries of the world that have as diverse an arrangement of police provision as Canada. Even in the United States, which has in the neighborhood of 20,000 different law enforcement agencies, there is nothing similar to the RCMP; and when you add to that the state, local and sheriff provision, it represents more models of policing encompassed within one nation than any other country.[34]

As seen by the differences above, the recruitment and training of police officers varies greatly between different countries and even within those countries between states and municipalities. What it means to police is a vexing question without one uniform answer. Policing can be centralized and viewed as an arm of the government or decentralized and answerable to a body of elected local citizens. It can be military and serve the whim of a dictator rather than the citizens at all, and it can be religious. In between all these variations there are further layers that have developed over time in response to cultural and societal developments. The crimes discussed in the first part of this book are common occurrences throughout the world, and in the vast majority of cases these crimes are investigated by local or national level police agencies as determined to be offences within a particular nation state and that nation state, that country, invariably has jurisdiction over all criminal offences committed within that country's borders. As we have seen, however, some crimes are deemed so offensive to all of humanity that we classify them as crimes against humanity or war crimes. Drug trafficking is such a crime, and so too is human trafficking. Consequently, although the majority of murders, assaults, abductions and drug trafficking cases will be local, it may be that they could be international crimes that could be dealt with by any nation state. It would follow that if we have a bank of crimes that are international and any country in the world can arrest and prosecute the criminals committing those crimes, then perhaps we would want or need an international police force to conduct those investigations—a police force that is not restricted by national laws or national boundaries and borders. Perhaps policing international crimes requires an international police agency with powers of arrest and detention anywhere, eventually even into space. Well, we are certainly not there yet, and what international 'police' type agencies we have are restricted in their scope and powers. In fact, the majority of global responses are not a police force at all but more of an intelligence collating response that provides support to local forces to effect arrests. As yet, we do not have a mobile international police force. What we do have, and the direction we are heading in, is the subject of the last part of this chapter—international police responses.

Today it is not uncommon for a police officer from one country to spend a period of time serving abroad. This might be for the United Nations as part of a UN police keeping mission, working for the D.E.A. in Peru providing assistance and training to the national federal police. It could be on secondment to EUROPOL or working for Interpol gathering evidence to prosecute war criminals before the International Criminal Court in The Hague. Whereas all of these police responses are necessary and undoubtedly attempt to provide a more secure world for us, there are issues about accountability that should be borne in mind. So far we have established that nation states generally write and enforce their own criminal laws. We have also established that some crimes are international. The potential for problems is that if our police forces are locally appointed and locally accountable then who is watching them on the international platform? At the moment, most citizens have a pretty good idea of what it means to be policed, locally. But what does it mean to be policed internationally? What laws do and should govern international criminal investigations and what powers do we want police officers to have to effect arrests or to conduct investigations in another sovereign state? Most citizens of the US would be surprised if they were to answer their door and a police officer from Finland started making enquiries of them. This is not to say that we do not have rules and protocols, and we certainly have bi-lateral and multi-lateral agreements that are aimed at providing the appropriate parameters for the powers of international police agencies. The problem though is that the general citizen's awareness of international policing is little if anything, so established limitations on the abuse of power could be compromised with the best of intentions. On the issue of international policing, one question should be who is policing the police? A second issue is whose criminal justice system will dominate, as surely one will? Alternatively, some people will be of the view that these are issues unlikely ever to be a serious problem as a truly international global police force is never likely to happen; but transnational police certainly are a reality and already do exist. One definition of transnational policing is that it is ". . . any form of order maintenance, law enforcement, peacekeeping, crime investigation, intelligence sharing, or other form of police work that transcends or traverses national boundaries."[35] This is helpful as it causes the reader to look beyond the better-known entities and also consider agencies such as the Financial Action Task Force (IACP)[36] and the UNODC[37] under the framework of international policing responses.

In 1914, the world's first international policing congress was held in Monaco. As a result of this, there was a consensus of agreement to form a police support agency that would act as a conduit to help police forces across the world to share information. INTERPOL is now an organization of 188 countries that collectively contribute to maintain a headquarters in Lyon, France, and seven regional offices, (NCBs) around the globe. Each member state has one vote at the annual general assembly. The secretary-general holds office for a renewable four-year term and acts as the chief executive officer. In addition to providing support services to member countries, INTERPOL also tests technology and will assist national agencies in missions. INTERPOL is also the primary agency for circulating wanted persons across the globe; this is achieved through the 'Red Alert' system. As with all information systems, the information is only as good as what is put in; and there have been a few unfortunate instances of innocent civilians[38] being arrested and detained due to faulty or outdated data input. The 'Red Alert' is not a warrant of arrest though. INTERPOL is not a police force and has no powers to arrest or to conduct international crime investigations, but it will send an Incident Response Team (IRT) into a country at the request of that country to provide immediate assistance during a major crisis. IRTs are highly mobile and typically are deployed within 24 hours anywhere across the world. The first use of an IRT was in Bali, Indonesia, in 2002 in response to a request for assistance dealing with a terrorist bombing. INTERPOL assisted in more than 30 police operations in 2011.[39] It is perhaps inevitable that as the nexus of drugs trafficking and organized crime extends across terrorism also, agencies such as INTERPOL will be drawn into a more quasi-operational role where it conducts more and more operations alongside national police forces. Whether this transgresses the concept of national sovereignty in matters of criminal law remains to be seen, but certainly there is a trend towards greater internationalization of policing and INTERPOL is placed to be at the forefront of this discussion. Over the past 10 years, the amount of involvement in drug trafficking operations by INTERPOL has increased significantly, especially in the area of cyber-trafficking in drugs and humans where it can provide expert services without being 'operational'. The issue though is where will the divide fall and at what point is INTERPOL *de facto* an international police agency? In its 2011 annual report, INTERPOL reported that, at the request of SEPCA,[40] INTERPOL designed, implemented and *managed* a project targeted at organized crime groups. Under project BESA, more than 200 arrests were made.[41] It may be a matter of semantics, but when an organization is 'managing' a major police operation to disrupt organized crime and drug trafficking resulting in the arrest of 200 individuals, that sounds very much like a police operation.

In 1994, the European Drug Unit was formed. It consisted of police officers drawn from every contributing European Union member state. By 1999 this unit had morphed into EUROPOL. The main business of EUROPOL is similar to that of INTERPOL but exclusively for nation states within the EU. In reality, the scope of its work has grown to be that of an operational police unit that can move across borderless Europe in pursuit of organized criminal enterprises. Additionally, EUROPOL works increasingly with law enforcement agencies outside of the EU and a number of national agencies have law enforcement personnel working with EUROPOL on a secondment basis. Within Europe, there are a number of bi-lateral agreements between nations that share borders so that officers may have a limited level of 'hot pursuit' capability. In 2008, an arrangement between France and Spain was formalized to allow officers on either side of their borders to operate together as one force. This was specifically designed to counter the work of the Spanish separatist organization ETA. Recently ETA announced a cessation of its campaign,[42] but the original anti-terrorist capacity has been formalized into GEAD, a combined dual-nation anti-drug force. Most of the countries of continental Europe have a military gendarmerie as well as a civilian police presence. In January 2006, EUROGENDFOR[43] (EGF) was established as a European gendarme force. It currently has 30 staff and 900 officers that are on detachment from their home countries of France, Spain, Portugal, The Netherlands, Belgium and Romania, to the unit. A challenging question for the future of this police unit is, will it have a remit to operate in those countries that do not have a military police force, if perhaps those countries do not want military style policing within their borders.

The United Nations has a number of policing roles, such as the work of the UNODC and UNPOL. UNODC has the mission of "making the world safer from crime, drugs and terrorism."[44] UNODC is not a police unit of the UN. It achieves its mission by working alongside individual countries as well as global agencies, such as INTERPOL, to achieve new levels of crime prevention and criminal justice reform. UNODC has made significant contributions towards opening up dialog between national policing agencies and it is a major voice in encouraging transparency between police forces across the world. UNODC provides expert advice in a number of areas of criminal justice, which is disseminated through its website and also its regional and country programs. UNODC is also responsible for the collation and distribution of crime data and the compilation of annual reports about trends in crime and the ability of nation states to work effectively in preventing human trafficking, drugs trafficking and other crimes against humanity. Scientific and technical support is also offered by UNODC through its Laboratory and Scientific Section. This section provides expert services through manuals, guidelines and publications pertinent to drug analysis, forensic science and the needs of national law enforcement agencies, as well as the UN Commission on Narcotic Drugs and the International Narcotics Control Board.

"The United nations has been deploying police officers for service in peace operations since the 1960's. Traditionally, the mandate of police components in peace operations was limited to monitoring, observing and reporting. Beginning in the early 1990's, advisory, mentoring and training functions were integrated into the monitoring activities in order to offer peace operations the opportunity to act as a corrective mechanism with domestic police and other law enforcement agencies."[45] There are currently more than 17,500 United Nations Police Officers serving across the world. The first UN police unit deployed was to the Congo in 1960. By 1994, the number of officers in CIVPOL (the name changed to UNPOL in 2005) had grown to 1,677. A large number were at this time deployed in the former Yugoslavia. The first 'formed police unit' (FPU) was established in 1999. An FPU consists of 140 officers working as a single unit in crowd control and riot situations. There are now more than 600 FPUs employing more than 6,000 officers.[46] By 2009, there were 11,000 UN police officers deployed in more than 100 countries. The number of female officers has steadily increased also and there is now an initiative to get the strength of female officers up to 20% of the force by 2014. Ordinarily, UNPOL officers are sent into a country alongside UN peacekeeping missions and military personnel. Their primary function is to assist local police efforts, in an advisory capacity, with public order, crime fighting and technical advice and training. In some cases throughout the past 50 years, UNPOL has acted as the police force for a nation state while that state rebuilds itself. In these cases, the UNPOL officers have full rights of arrest, search and seizure in the same way as the domestic police. This was the case in Kosovo and is currently happening in the Cote D'Ivoire, the Democratic Republic of the Congo, Haiti and Liberia. Another function of UNPOL is to provide protection to UN personnel within a nation state. Recruitment to UNPOL consists of a Selection and Assessment and Assistance Team (SAAT) interview process that starts in the applicant's home country. Members of UNPOL are all existing police officers in their home nations who serve with UNPOL for an initial six months. Upon acceptance to UNPOL new recruits undergo UN training before deployment in the field. Entry into an FPU starts in the same way but involves a different training program with the UN that consists of a six-week training program in public order control.

In addition to the various international police responses that are now in existence, many nation states send attaches and liaison officers to work in other countries alongside the domestic police. The UK has more than 180 officers serving overseas; France a similar number.[47] The US has hundreds of CIA, FBI, Federal Marshalls Service and DEA personnel serving in a variety of capacities in missions and embassies throughout the world; so too do Canada and Australia. [48] The International Criminal Court in The Hague has no police force of its own to make arrests and secure the attendance of criminals suspected of crimes. The ICC can issue arrest warrants, but without the efforts of other police agencies to make arrests, these actions would be hollow. It is therefore and currently solely reliant upon the resources of member states to provide the local law enforcement services to make arrests. "When the Court's jurisdiction is triggered by the Security Council, the duty to cooperate extends to all UN Member states, regardless of whether or not they are a Party to the Statute. The crimes within the jurisdiction of the Court are the gravest crimes known to humanity and as provided for by article 29 of the Statute they shall not be subject to any statute of limitations. Warrants of arrest are lifetime orders and therefore individuals still at large will sooner or later face the Court."[49]

How the enforcement of arrest warrants develops in the future, as more global criminals are indicted and brought before the international tribunal, will be interesting as there will surely come a time when either UNPOL or another existing, or created, agency will take responsibility for enforcement of ICC warrants. The ICC is currently investigating alleged crimes against humanity[50] in Afghanistan, Colombia, the Republic of Korea, Georgia, Guinea, Honduras, Nigeria and Palestine.[51] There are 108 members of the ICC; the USA has not re-joined the Court since President George Bush 'unsigned' the joining treaty in May 2002.[52] Alongside the US, China is also a country that has refused to accept the jurisdiction of the ICC over its nationals.

Policing the world is a huge undertaking—that is, if it should be undertaken at all. The fundamental right of nation states to police themselves is inviolable for many citizens and the idea that a 'superjurisdiction' could or should take responsibility for bringing world criminals to justice is offensive to many citizens (and leaders). But in many ways we are already there. National police forces supply expertise and personnel to a wide range of law enforcement agencies that have supranational reach. Models of policing are shared and copied so that EUROPOL looks like a European DEA. The new National Crime Agency in the UK has already been dubbed the UK's FBI, and France has unified the police of two countries into one force on its southern border with Spain. Gendarmes across Europe have grouped together to provide a military police agency to those that have this policing model (and maybe those who do not). Federal agents from the US, Canada, Australia and many other nations share colleagues across virtual and real borders; and the UN has a multi-national police response that now assists in public order matters as well as investigating and assisting in prosecuting terrorism and a wide range of other crime—the very crimes discussed in previous chapters of this book: murders, abductions, networked thefts and drug trafficking. Our international police responses are no longer restricted to investigating gross human violations as they were 40 years ago. Today we internationally police the entire plethora of the criminality. Perhaps a discussion about what model of policing will 'WorldPol' assume is otiose after all.

In this chapter we have considered a range of policing models and we have seen that 'becoming a police officer' varies greatly from country to country. It is quite possible that many citizens across the planet have come to view policing as a generalist task that is very similar regardless of where it is taking place. The reality is that policing is not 'one size fits all' and what the police are expected to do is very much a reflection of national and local laws and domestic cultural influences set against a backdrop of increasingly globalized criminal endeavors. In some countries, a person may become a police officer at 18 years of age with little more than a high school diploma; in others, the minimum entry age is 21 and a degree is required. Initial training can be as brief as six weeks[53] or as long as three years. Some forces are highly centralized with a government department taking a significant role in how the police are trained and operate; other countries have devolved the policing function to local accountability with considerable local civilian input. In some countries police training is very similar to a military boot camp, whereas in others the emphasis is upon gaining social skills, understanding human rights and group discussion. The police are civilian, military and religious. They are local, municipal, tribal, state, provincial, national and international. And there are also private police agencies and a range of police 'family members' such as: ISD police, parks police, housing police, special jurisdiction police, customs and immigration. We have joint forces, joint operations, formal and informal agreements—lateral, bi-lateral and multi-lateral. We are not constrained by real or virtual borders and the police are not either.

If this portrayal is accurate, then the likelihood of a police officer in a rural location managing to complete an entire career without exposure to international crime or criminals is extremely unlikely. It would follow that being aware of 'who' 'what' and 'how' international crime impacts domestic policing would be vital to all sworn officers. The USA has more police officers and police forces than any country on Earth; there are 65 federal agencies, 27 offices of inspector general, 50 state police agencies and more than 19,000 local agencies, some with as few as one sworn officer.[54] In the following chapter we will investigate how the diverse medley of US police officers is trained and prepared for dealing with the challenges of policing contemporary society and investigating the crimes that were presented in the first part of this book. As you the reader may appreciate, crimes often appear local but in reality can transcend county, state, national and international borders. How well prepared our police officers are to deal with these challenges is itself a challenge for policing in the 21st century. In the following chapter we will look at these challenges as well as what support mechanisms are in place to assist officers to be effective, ethical police.

Endnotes

1. There are 193 member states that comprise the United Nations. The Vatican City and Kosovo are independent countries and currently not members of the UN. Taiwan meets the UN requirements to be classified as a country but currently does not do so due to its tense political situation with China. Puerto Rico, Bermuda, Palestine, Northern Ireland, Scotland and Wales are frequently referred to as countries. They are not at this time and are not counted as part of the global total of 196.
2. www.police.go.kr
3. See further: www.police.ac.kr
4. www.cpa.go.kr
5. Others include: Yemen, Oman, Bahrain, UAE, Kuwait, Iraq, Jordan, Syria and Lebanon.
6. Interestingly, there was a time when the original police of Paris in the 17th century were required to ensure compliance with the rule not to eat meat on Fridays, once required of all Catholics, and the observance of Lent. Butchers

found transgressing the no meat on Friday laws were subject to arrest and financial penalties.

7. Nadim Kawach. February 29, 2012. www.emirates247.com
8. Ibid.
9. Ibid.
10. The Royal Saudi Arabian Police Academy, Riyadh.
11. Details available at www.uncjin.org ksuadi.pdf
12. Religious police swoop on Valentine's Day lovers. ABC News. 15 February 2012. www.abc.net.au/news
13. Ibid.
14. Six percent of the population speaks Swedish.
15. No 84/1966
16. 'General Principles of Operation' at www.poliisi.fi
17. Stevens, L. Online patrols: How one Finnish cop tracked youth crime. 27 March 2012. www.policeone.com
18. A similar ratio to neighbor Finland at 1 officer per 681 citizens.
19. The Norwegian Police Directorate was established in 2001 to coordinate central and regional policing efforts.
20. National Police Academy information webpage "Bachelor-Police Studies." www.phs.no
21. Ibid.
22. Ibid.
23. Source: World Bank 2011 Public data
24. www.rcmp-grc.gc.ca
25. www.statcan.gc.ca
26. Ibid.
27. Ibid.
28. Ibid.
29. www.rcmp-grc.gc.ca
30. Ibid.
31. www.enpq.qc.ca
32. Ibid.
33. Provides policing services to 408 First nation and Inuit communities with a total population of 327,430 people by 1,240 officers. Source: www.publicsafety.gc.ca
34. The closest resemblance would be in Australia where there are federal police, state police, municipal police, sheriffs and bailiffs. However, the range of responsibilities assigned to the RCMP is greater in scope, and the RCMP, in some instances, provides the only local municipal policing response in remote parts of the country.
35. Bowling, B. and Sheptycki, J. *Global policing.* Los Angeles: Sage; 2012. P. 3.
36. International Association of Chiefs of Police

37. United Nations Office on Drug Control and Crime
38. See for example the incident involving Derek Bond, a UK citizen on vacation in South Africa in 2003, who was detained erroneously for three weeks on a 'Red Alert'. It was believed Bond was Derek Sykes, alias Bond, wanted in the USA for fraud. The Red Alert information circulated by the FBI was found to be inaccurate and incomplete.
39. www.interpol.int. Annual Report 2011.
40. Southeast Europe Police Chiefs Association
41. Source: 2011 Annual Report. Supra.
42. October 2011
43. www.eurogendfor.eu
44. UNODC website home page. www.unodc.org
45. www.un.org/en/peacekeeping/sites/ploice. United Nations Policing 'A crucial part of UN peace operations'.
46. Ibid.
47. See Bowling and Sheptycki, supra, pp. 4–6.
48. Ibid.
49. www.icc-cpi.int
50. The ICC has jurisdiction over genocide, crimes against humanity and war crimes. It does not currently have jurisdiction over drug trafficking or terrorism cases unless these fall under within the previous three, even though both of the latter are considered 'global' crimes. Crimes of Aggression (invasion, annexation by force, blockades and military occupation) may be included after a planned vote is taken in 2017.
51. www.icc-cpi.int
52. For a thorough discussion of the issue see: US policy toward the International criminal Court: Furthering positive engagement. Report of an Independent Task Force convened by The American Society of International Law. March 2009. Available at www.asil.org. The US did eventually sign the Rome Statute in 200 but President George Bush 'unsigned' the US in 2002. And he followed up this removal by threatening military action against the ICC if any US nationals were held at The Hague; see: www.globalissues.org. United States and the International Criminal Court and the American Servicemembers Protection Act 2002 (The Hague Invasion Act).
53. In the USA, some 'academies' are of less than six weeks duration. See: www.bjs.ojp.usdoj.gov. State and law enforcement training academies 2006. Published February 2009. NCJ 22987
54. www.discoverpolicing.org

LAW ENFORCEMENT IN THE USA

Why we need to have the police in contemporary society will have a different response depending upon where we are when we ask the question. As seen in the previous chapter, some countries prioritize the social service aspects of policing so that in many ways the police appear more closely aligned to social workers than to crime fighters and the emphasis is often placed upon community response policing and human rights. In other countries, such as the US, the primary task of the police is to prevent crime. Now there are probably a number of academics who will immediately disagree with this statement and cite the emphasis that was placed upon community policing in the 1990s and the huge amounts of money the federal government made available to support Community Oriented Policing (COPS). In my view, this is no longer an accurate portrayal of policing in America today, as I believe that we have moved progressively towards a quasi-military style of policing with increased emphasis on security and then a focus upon preventing and detecting crime. Many serving police officers are very happy with this shift, as they have always held the view that

policing is about fighting battles,[1] either terrorists or crime (thief taking). Some members of the public are less enthusiastic as they feel that community priorities have been traded out for 'hot spot' crime targeting or a military looking officer (and vehicles) that provide 'enhanced security'. What is really needed, and sometimes achieved, is a balance. How we achieve that balance depends upon a large number of factors and whatever is deemed to be the right balance for one country will not be the same balance for another due to the make-up of each individual country. At this point, you might want to question for yourself how it is that for so many developed countries that have similar GDPs and quality and standards of living that we can invest such completely different amounts of money and training on the police—three years training and a degree or five weeks. And yet we call the product the same thing, a police officer. As you now know, these differences are not between developing and developed nations; they are between nations that have the same standards of living, wealth, education and human rights.

In the United States the current emphasis is on 'less is more'. It spends less time training new recruits than many other countries, and it focuses more on the practical aspects of training and far less on the academic training than other similarly placed nation states. If it is true to say that the police perform a multitude of tasks within society, then why would it be the case that so little time is spent on academic achievement and relationships with the community in lieu of driver training, firearm training and self-defense? After all, if the main thrust of police work is crime prevention and crime detection, then surely these issues would be the most important aspect of new recruit training. But it is not—general patrol is the area most covered, the argument being that this is what most officers do most of the time. This may be accurate, but it depends upon what you call 'general patrol' and whether or not this includes identifiable crime prevention and detection. So, before we get too much further into the chapter you may want to pause and consider: Is policing about 'Protect and Serve' or 'Prevent and Serve'? New recruits rarely investigate murders,[2] but they attend a very large number of domestic disputes where there are assaults. New recruits may not investigate kidnapping, but child abduction is one of the most prevalent crimes in America, and this is most definitely a crime reported to patrol officers. New recruits may not investigate bank robberies, but they do deal with thousands of thefts, the key ingredient in robbery; and new recruits may not deal with drug trafficking organizations but they do deal with the product, illicit drugs, on a daily basis,[3] as well as with street level dealers that directly or indirectly are employed by the traffickers. So there are significant links between very serious crimes and the work conducted on the streets, and if this is what is now prioritized in police work that may be valid and meaningful and of great benefit to society. If we have diverted attention (and funding) away from community focused policing to prevent and detect more less serious crimes, that too may be justifiable and of value. If we have compromised both community policing and crime prevention and detection in order that the focus on training police officers is to achieve practical skills related to public order, self-defense and the use of weapons, and yet these represent a minor part of the working life of the majority of police officers,[4] then perhaps as the century progresses the US may want to look further afield at training models in other developed countries to see whether or not there is an alternative model that might better serve the citizens of the country. Against this backdrop, it should be remembered that with around 19,000 different law enforcement agencies in the US there are naturally large differences in terms of policing priorities, recruitment and training. On this note, it is time to look at how people are recruited into the police in the US and what basic training they undertake.

The New London, Connecticut, Police Department gained notoriety in 1999 for preventing Robert Jordan from joining the department on the basis that he was too intelligent. Jordan subsequently sued the department after he had scored 33 out of 50 on the initial screening test. His score of 33 was considered to be 6 points *above* the level sought for police recruits and therefore he was not invited for interview. Deputy Police Chief William C. Gavitt stated that "Bob Jordan is exactly the type of guy we would want to screen out . . . Police work is mundane. We don't deal in gunfights every night. There's a personality that can take that."[5] Robert Jordan was subsequently interviewed by CNN, and he stated that in a conversation he had with the personnel department at the New London PD he was told, "Listen, Mr. Jordan, we don't like to hire people with too high an IQ to be a cop in this town."[6] Jordan was unsuccessful in his suit at the District Court and at the U.S. Court of Appeals where both held that his constitutional rights had not been abrogated by the New London hiring policy as its policy was rational and designed to prevent high job turnover.[7] The US Appeals Court stated that "New London's use of an 'upper-cut' did not violate the equal protection clause' and it upheld the judgment of the district court."[8] It was also noted that "Plaintiff presented some evidence that high scorers do not actually experience more job dissatisfaction, but that evidence does not create a factual issue, because it matters not whether the city's decision was correct so long as it was rational."[9] Most would agree this is a low point in the discussion about what the requirements are for entry into the police service in the USA, but it does demonstrate a sharp difference from the view taken by some countries that you need to hold a baccalaureate degree at a minimum to be an effective police officer, and in some instances in the USA where an above average IQ is a bar to appointment due to the likelihood that bright people will get bored by the mundane nature of police work. Clearly there is some significant discrepancy between the view of what police work entails in some parts of the US and in a number of countries in Europe. This should be borne in mind as more and more criminal investigations involve transnational crime groups and necessitate police forces from a number of countries to liaise and work together despite any linguistic or academic abilities individual officers may have to have.

As a general statement, police recruits must be physically fit, not have a criminal record and be at least 21 years of age. Some forces have an upper age limit, but this is liable to challenges of age discrimination (the Washington State Police Academy graduated a student of 52 years of age).[10] In 2003, more than 50% of US police forces did not have an aptitude test.[11] Twenty-five percent held a polygraph test and just 1% required second language ability. Only 67% of forces required psychological evaluation.[12] Candidates must be US citizens. Whether or not the recruits need to be local, city or state residents, or from out of state, varies with each hiring department. State and local law enforcement employ more than 1.33 million full-time personnel of which 765,000 are sworn officers.[13] Forty-nine percent of all agencies employ fewer than 10 full-time sworn officers and 64% are employed in agencies of fewer than 100 officers.[14] One in 8 new recruits is female. And 1 in 10 is Latino.[15] There are more than 650 state and local law enforcement academies across the nation that provide basic entry level training to new recruits into police departments. On average, 86% of new recruits successfully complete basic training.[16] Ninety percent of basic training academies now provide terrorism training to new entrants.[17] According to the US Bureau of Labor Statistics, police applicants "need to meet the minimum educational requirements, which usually include a high school diploma or its equivalent and many law enforcement agencies require some level of college-level courses to be completed before attending a police academy." The key skills for police listed on the Bureau of Labor Statistics website[18] are: ability to multi-task, communication skills, empathetic personality, good judgment, leadership skills, perceptiveness and strength and stamina.[19] Many police departments have their own training academies. For example, Arlington, Texas, has a 26-week academy with classes in law, procedure, patrol and investigations, as well as driving and fitness training. Classes are based on a 5-day week. In keeping with many forces across the nation, attendance is daily and non-residential.[20] Following successful completion of the initial academy, officers are assigned to patrol under the direction of a Field Training Officer (FTO) for a further 14 weeks.[21] As a Texas police force, Arlington is required to adhere to the Texas Commission on Law Enforcement, Officer Standards and Education (TCLEOSE). There are currently 2,644 agencies, 105 training academies and 174 contract training providers in the state of Texas.[22] After initial training, Texas police officers are required to hold a basic Police Officer Certificate, which is obtained after one year in service. It is possible for citizens who are not employed by a police department to participate in basic training and then to approach a department for employment opportunities. One example of this is the academy run at the Central Texas College 'Basic Peace Officer Academy', a part-time class run during days or evenings that prepares candidates for the Texas Police Officer Licensing Examination. TCEOSE requires a minimum of 618 hours of training before candidates are eligible to sit the licensing examination.[23] College based training programs are eligible for college credit that may count towards a degree later. Typically completion of the Licensing Exam will attract in the neighborhood of 22 hours of potential associate degree credit. Participation in basic training is not precluded due to a candidate having a criminal conviction, and this is true with regard to many police departments across the nation. The issue is: What is the conviction for? Felons are excluded from employment as police officers, but conviction for a Class B misdemeanor within the past 10 years would not necessarily prohibit appointment.[24] The Tulsa PD application information states that, "All applicants will undergo a police background check before being hired. Any person with a felony conviction or a conviction for a crime of moral turpitude is ineligible for employment with the Tulsa Police Department."[25] Arlington PD[26] and Tulsa PD are two of 36 police departments nationwide that now require all applicants to hold a four-year degree from an accredited university.[27] As a comparison, it is of note that only 11% of police training academies require their instructors to hold a four-year college degree and 8% require a two-year associate degree.[28] Overall, 98% of all hiring departments conduct personal interviews with candidates; 73% conduct a drugs test; and 43% have a written aptitude test.[29] In forces with fewer than 2,500 personnel, sworn and unsworn combined, 31% required a physical agility test, 20% required a written aptitude test, 11% had a polygraph test and 63% required a drug test.[30] Overall, 1% of US police forces require applicants to hold a four-year university degree.[31] This figure equates to the 36 departments that now require a bachelor degree, but the type of degree or the major is rarely specified or perhaps even important.[32] Nine percent of forces require a two-year degree.[33] Thirty-two percent of recruiting departments offer incentives to candidates who hold higher education qualifications.[34] This figure rises to 75% in those large city departments serving populations of greater than 1 million citizens.[35] Ultimately, no matter how a person is recruited into the police force once he has passed the interview procedures and been offered a position at an academy, he will undertake an average of 19 weeks of basic training that will involve the following: law, weapons, self-defense, human rights and investigations training to equip him with the minimum level of preparedness necessary to then undertake street patrol under the supervision of an experienced officer. During the first few years of employment, the officer will have to undertake a number of specialist training courses and then throughout the career mandatory yearly training. Those academies that have a more academic and stress-free philosophy appear to achieve better overall retention and passing rates (89%) than the academies that are more militaristic in approach and para-military in shape and form (80%)[36] where the 'shock' of initial military style training is a major deterrent to some applicants and in some instances has led to a significant withdrawal from the program in the first two weeks.[37] Notwithstanding this observation, overall 43% of state academies report their training programs are stress-based; 89% of county police academies are stress-based, and 66% of municipal police academies are stress-based.[38]

The controversy over whether or not all police recruits should hold a college degree has been taking place for the past 40 years. Generally, the move has gone towards requiring degrees, but this has to be considered in the light of recruitment shortages, officers being called up for military service and regrettable incidents of police corruption that tarnish the image of the police across the entire nation and often result in a lull in applicants. The Police Association for College Education (PACE)[39] is a non-profit organization that encourages and facilitates a minimum education level of a four-year degree for all police officers, and it has worked closely over the past decade to encourage PDs and advisory bodies to promote police degree requirements. The Commission on Accreditation for Law Enforcement Agencies (CALEA) issued the following standard in July

2011: "A written directive establishes the agency's commitment to higher education through one or more of the following: a. a requirement of all candidates for full-time sworn positions to possess at a minimum a bachelor's degree; . . .".[40] As the author of the report stated, "In summary, an educated workforce is more empowered, diverse in thought, and prepared. Hiring college-degreed candidates into the law enforcement profession does not guarantee they will be good officers. However, better educated officers will have a greater likelihood of creating sound solutions to today's public safety issues."[41] I started this chapter commenting on the growth of military style policing particularly since 2001. It is not uncommon today for local police departments to undertake paramilitary training with other agencies and to receive specific training from military personnel. That is not to say that many of the skills learned by the military, to release hostages for example, are not of enormous value to civilian police operations; but in case you remain unconvinced of the influence that causes some commentators concern, it is worth looking at the Tampa Police Tactical Response Team[42] website and view the array of vehicles they have. If you had any doubts whatsoever as to whether civilian police forces are equipped to deal with a war, this site will convince you otherwise. Not only does this force have an "amphibious tank type vehicle that can reach speeds up to 60 mph,"[43] it also boasts ownership of a 12-ton Armored Personnel Carrier that is, "bullet resistant, can hold 13 passengers and is virtually unstoppable . . . this one of a kind APC was purchased from the military. . . ."[44]

If you think back to Chapter Six, you will remember that I talked through some of the history of municipal police, county police and state forces. Soon in this chapter we will discuss federal law enforcement agencies and some of the specialist skills they have to deal with certain murders, thefts, kidnappings and drug trafficking. But before we do so, it is important to pay some attention to the role of sheriffs and the role of state law enforcement officers. Sheriffs' departments play a major role in policing across the US, particularly at the county level. Additionally, they provide the corrections element of criminal justice in running county jails. Just like municipal forces, sheriffs' departments may be small and consist of a few sworn officers or very large, such as the Los Angeles County Sheriff's Department. LACSD, sometimes also known as the Los Angeles Sheriff's Office (LASO) is the fourth largest local police agency in the US and the largest sheriff's department in the world.[45] Since its creation in 1849, LASO now employs more than 18,000 personnel, of which more than 10,000 are sworn officers. The Court Services Division is responsible for security, providing bailiffs and local custody provision inside the courts to 48 courthouses within the county. The LA County jail system is the largest in the US, and the sheriff's department is responsible for correctional services provision to more than 200,000 inmates each year. The Inmate Reception Center (IRC) is the main intake point for the 18,000 prisoners being held in the county jail system at any point in time. From the IRC, prisoners are then allocated to a county facility such as 'Twin Towers', a downtown location spread across 10 acres consisting of more than 1.5 million square feet of prison facility.[46] The IRC central intake point employs 800 people, 450 of which are deputy sheriffs. The Court Services Division employs 1,100 sworn officers and more than 500 civilians. In addition to court security and judicial protection services, recall that sheriffs also serve criminal and civil process.[47] Patrol is part of Field Operations and is divided up into three regions that together operate 176 sheriff stations across the county. Detective investigations are conducted through the Detective Division, which has six bureaus: Homicide, Major Crimes, Commercial Crimes, Special Victims, Narcotics and the Taskforce for Regional Autotheft. In 2002, the LASO created the Homeland Security Division with this task: "Our mission is to prevent, intervene, disrupt, mitigate, and provide specialized response capabilities to acts of terrorism and Homeland Security threats, whether[48] natural or caused by man." In addition to the above, the LASO is the second largest transit police agency in the nation. It provides a police response to the entire Metropolitan Transit Authority system of Los Angeles. Due to the size of the force, it runs its own basic training academy for deputy sheriffs and custody assistants. Applicants who hold an associate degree are offered an enhanced monthly salary, and those holding a four-year degree are paid an increase above this.[49] Initial deputy sheriff recruits follow an 18-week training program. Deputy sheriffs must be 20 years of age and participate in a written examination and pre-employment physical. Applicants who fail the written test three times may not re-apply for six months. Once selected, the academy operates five days per week and is non-residential. Many aspects of the work of a deputy sheriff are the same as those of a patrol officer in a police department[50] where they differ in the provision of custodial and protective services. As stated by the LASO, "The Los Angeles County Sheriff's Department differs from other police agencies in several ways. The most significant is that the Sheriff's department provides staffing for 8 custody facilities and security for 48 courthouses throughout the County. The Sheriff's department also provides patrol and investigative services to 40 contract cities and unincorporated areas of Los

Angeles County. This difference creates more assignment diversity than any other police agency in the Southern California basin."[51]

Every state in the US has some form of statewide police provision—state troopers, a constabulary, a state bureau, a highway patrol or a department of public safety. The Pennsylvania State Police were the first statewide police response in the US and their history is mentioned briefly in Chapter Six. Hawaii is the only state without a designated force in name, but it operates a Department of Public Safety,[52] and under this body the sheriff's office provides statewide policing. The Maine State Police, motto *Semper Aequus*,[53] also operates under the Department of Public Safety; and it consists of 341 sworn trooper officers under the command of a colonel. It is a 'full-service' state police force that patrols all the state's highways and provides police services across the state. These include criminal investigation and forensic services. The original 1921 requirement that all troopers be proficient horsemen has now been dropped, but wearing a military style uniform remains. New recruits undertake a basic 18-week training program including Basic Law Enforcement Training (BLET) that all law enforcement personnel in the state of Maine must undertake. In addition to the usual requirements of honesty, not being a felon and being fit, applicants must be at least 21 years of age unless they possess an associate degree in which case they may enter at the age of 20 years. Total curriculum hours at basic training amounts to 720. The largest single most hours are spent teaching 'Testing and Critiques', while second is 'Lifetime Fitness'.[54] Upon completion of the academy, troopers are assigned to patrol. At this point they are now referred to as Field Troops. "The Troopers who work in the field troops patrol all municipalities in the state of Maine who do not have their own police departments. They enforce criminal and traffic laws through investigation and patrol work. Filed Troopers investigate traffic accidents and respond to a wide variety of criminal complaints including domestic violence, burglary and assault."[55] The state troopers under the responsibility of the Special Services Division conduct a large number of special operations. These include: an air wing, a bomb team, criminal investigation and forensics and a tactical team. The investigation unit provides a nationally accredited forensic science laboratory service to all law enforcement agencies in the state of Maine. Members of the tactical team provide support to federal agencies for homeland security issues, and they work closely with a number of state and local agencies. The titles and ranks of officers serving with the Maine State Police are military and their dress uniform is styled on an original military uniform. The 23 members of the tactical unit continue this tradition by wearing army combat uniforms and not civilian police attire. Currently, 42 of 50 state police agencies have a specialized SWAT provision.[56] In common with most state enforcement agencies, the Maine State Police provide protective services to the governor of the state and his family.[57]

Many law enforcement applicants are attracted to working for a federal agency. There are the kudos, the opportunity for travel and the attention paid to federal agencies by the film industry—they are usually heroes—and the repute of the agency at home and abroad. And there is the pay. Federal agencies typically pay far more than local and state agencies. According to Kenneth Peak, the three-year salary range offered by the US Department of Homeland Security is between $100,502 and $118,589 if you hold a master's degree.[58] But since most applicants will not know this, it is probably not the salary that attracts them; it is the variety and caliber of the work. Federal law enforcement agencies have grown in number significantly over the past one hundred years and their focus has also moved towards a general embrace of more national law provision across the US. Federal agencies have seen their sphere of responsibilities progressively increase and the sense of 'protection' from a federal agency has been manicured successively in the latter part of the last and early years of the current century. National law enforcement and national prison systems are a growth industry. Many agencies have been reformatted or merged into 'superagencies' since 9/11, so that today there are 73 agencies with federal arrest authority that are authorized to carry firearms while on duty.[59] Of the total 120,000 sworn personnel, the four largest agencies—Customs and Border Protection, US Immigration and Customs Enforcement, the Federal Bureau of Prisons and the Federal Bureau of Investigation—account for the employment of four of every five federal officers.[60] Customs and Border Protection and US Immigration and Customs Enforcement (ICE) are part of the Department of Homeland Security, which employs 55,000 officers (46% of the total number of federal officers). Between 2002 and 2008, the US Customs and Border Protection service grew 33.1% in size, and during the same period the US Postal Inspection Service decreased in size 23.1%.[61] However, it was the Pentagon Force Protection Agency that grew the most over the period. It expanded its personnel strength by 50.4%.[62] The other large federal law enforcement employer is the Department of Justice (DOJ); the FBI and federal prisons come under this department. The Bureau of Prisons (BOP) is the larger of the two and employs nearly 17,000 correctional officers. There are currently in the region of 165,000 BOP inmates.[63] The FBI employs

12,760 full-time weapons carrying sworn agents, 500 more than in 2004 when the last census was conducted. Also within the DOJ are the Drug Enforcement Administration (DEA) (down 2%), the Marshals Service (up 2%) and ATF (Alcohol, Tobacco, Firearms and Explosives) (up 7%).[64] Other large increases in personnel between 2004 and 2008 happened in the Bureau of Diplomatic Service, which now employs 1,049, an increase of 27%, and the Veterans Affairs law enforcement and protection provision that saw an increase of 29% in officer numbers. There are 16 federal agencies that employ fewer than 250 personnel with arrest powers. The smallest is the Bureau of Reclamation with 21 special agents. The largest employer of federal agents outside of the executive is the Administrative Offices of the US. Courts. It employs 4,696 probation officers with arrest and firearm powers. This unit grew by 14% between 2004 and 2008.[65] The US Capitol Police also grew 7% in size to 1,637 sworn police officers. Offices of the Inspector General employ 3,501 officers with arrest and firearm authority, which is 12% more than in 2004. IG officers investigate cases of fraud, bribery, waste and abuse related to federal programs. Five IG offices employ more than 250 arrest and firearm officers. Despite the labor cuts, the US Postal Service is still the largest of the IG agencies, with 508 special agents.[66] Currently one-sixth of all federal special agents are women.[67] The largest single percentage of arrest and firearm female special agents is with the Administrative Offices of the US. Courts, 46.2%. Of the officers employed by the Pentagon Force Protection Agency, 51.2% are members of a racial or an ethnic minority.[68] The highest number of assaults upon federal officers happened against the Bureau of Indian Affairs police where 37.9% of officers were assaulted between 2004 and 2008. The least, with 0.0%, were the special agents of the US Postal Service. Perhaps not surprisingly one of the largest concentrations of federal agents is in Washington DC—10,222 agents and police. The largest total number of federal agents, arrest and non-arrest power, working in any one state is Texas, where there are 18,322 special agents deployed. The highest concentration of arrest and firearm special agents per 100,000 population is in Washington DC, by a considerable margin, at 1,732. The state with the highest ratio of agents per 100,000 population is New Mexico at 130. The overall average number of federal arrest and firearm officers per 100,000 population is 40. Overall, the number of federal officers employed in the US grew by 14% between 2004 and 2008. Twenty-three percent of all federal officers are involved in some form of police patrol; 15% perform immigration and customs functions and 14% are employed in prisons and detention services.[69]

The Department of Homeland Security (DHS) was established under the Homeland Security Act 2002 in response to the terrorist attacks upon the US in 2001. DHS brought 22 existing agencies into one new entity.[70] Two of the numerous functions the agency undertakes are passenger and cargo screening at airports and the air marshal's service. The passenger screening program of the Aviation Security Unit employs 50,000 officers to screen more than 1.7 million airline passengers every day and more than 700 million each year.[71] Federal Air Marshals are armed agents who are deployed on national and international flights to protect passengers and crew in the event of a hostile attack on board a flight. Applicants to the agency must be between the ages of 21 and 37 and successfully complete a 30-week training program broken down into two 15-week segments. Part one is basic law enforcement training, BLET. Phase two[72] is specific to the marshal's role and includes training in international law, arrest procedures pertinent to the aircraft industry and on board flights, international communication and advanced firearm tactics. Air marshals have the most stringent pistol firearms qualification score requirement of any police agency in the US. This was shown in action when in 2005 a passenger who claimed he had a bomb was shot and killed by air marshals as he attempted to board a plane in Miami. The 44-year-old US citizen, Rigoberto Alpizar, was on route to Medellin, Colombia, when he claimed to have a bomb in his backpack. When air marshals attempted to engage Alpizar in conversation, he reached into his backpack, at which point he was shot dead.[73] Starting pay is in the region of $40,000 per annum depending upon entry level and previous employment qualifications. Federal air marshals ordinarily work in teams of two on flights.

The Bureau of Alcohol, Tobacco, Firearms and Explosives is one of the agencies that were reconfigured after 9/11. On January 24, 2003, ATF was transferred from the Treasury to the Department of Justice—well, some of it was. The law enforcement part of ATF is now under the DOJ, and the tax and trade side of ATF is still with the Department of the Treasury but renamed the Alcohol and Tobacco Tax and Trade Bureau. ATF describes itself as "The Violent Crime Bureau," which is an interesting title. You have to ask how closely this would mesh with the idea the general public has of the agency and what it does. Also, I doubt whether many agencies from outside of the US think of ATF when they think of the primary US domestic agency tasked to deal with violent crime. I suspect the response would be the FBI. Perhaps there is a study in here for a student? ATF is "A unique law enforcement agency in the United States Department of Justice that protects our communities from violent criminals, criminal organizations, the illegal use and trafficking of firearms, the illegal use and storage of explosives, acts of arson and bombings, acts of terrorism, and the illegal diversion of alcohol and tobacco products. . . ."[74] The rhetoric gets even more dynamic and emotive: "A dedicated team securing America's future by accomplishing a critical mission today." "Combating violent crime is our specialty, our niche." "The profession of special agent is exciting and rewarding. Special agents must be tough—both physically and mentally. They must be able to handle rigorous training, personal risks, irregular hours, and extensive travel. . . ."[75] In order to be considered for employment as a special agent in ATF, applicants must be US citizens, a minimum of 21 and a maximum of 36 years of age and hold a four-year degree.[76] Basic pay for a new entrant is $33,829 plus 25% law enforcement ability pay (LEAP) and locality pay.[77] Applicants that hold a master's degree enter at a salary point of $42,948, plus the enhancements applicable to all entrants. Applicants who have proficiency in a foreign language are eligible for cash awards. Having successfully passed the entrance examination and interview stages of recruitment, new recruits enter the academy. There are two stages to initial training. Part one is held at the Federal Law Enforcement Training Center (FLETC), Department of Homeland Security, Glynco, Georgia. This stage includes firearms training, driving, making arrests, basic crime investigations, surveillance techniques and federal court procedures. This is a 12-week class. The second stage of training is Special Agent Basic Training (SABT). This is a 15-week course geared specifically towards the needs of federal agents and includes such issues as field operations, undercover work, report writing and ATF investigation issues.

The nexus between drug trafficking and terrorism has now been clearly established,[78] and these crime organizations use a multitude of criminal operations to create a diverse source of illegal incomes. The idea that cigarette smuggling is not a major crime and that it may only entail a limited amount of tax avoidance is fiction. Cigarette smuggling continues to be a significant criminal enterprise for numerous international crime organizations and much of the wealth produced is then siphoned off into paying for violent criminal attacks upon citizens across the globe—terrorism. According to the ATF, at one time the Real IRA were generating $100 million of terrorist funds through illicit cigarette smuggling every year.[79] On March 31, 2010, President Obama signed into law the Prevent All Cigarette Trafficking Act, a law that amends the Jenkins Act[80] beyond the collection of taxes and illegal trafficking in cigarettes to now impose additional requirements for registration, reporting and recordkeeping, as well as prohibiting the sale of cigarettes through the mail.[81] Violation of PACT is punishable with up to three years imprisonment and a fine, both criminal and civil.[82] It is important to recognize that although cigarette smuggling may not appear to be a significant problem and does not immediately attract the level of media attention that a bombing or a major firearms incident will, the impact of this type of crime is widespread and does undoubtedly provide a significant revenue stream for a number of diverse crime groups across the globe. More sensational, however, are such investigations as "Operation Anything For a Buck," a joint operation between the ATF, the Escambia Sheriff's Department and the Pensacola Florida Police Department. The case resulted in the indictment of 22 defendants with federal firearms charges and an additional 53 defendants with state offences. In the federal matters, the defendants had sold undercover agents 270 assorted firearms and engaged in more than 100 drug deals for marijuana, cocaine, heroin, Xanax and Oxycodone.[83] As seen by this operation, a major part of ATF work involves checking on the sale and possession of firearms;[84] there are more than 2.4 million handguns in the US and more than 3 million rifles and shotguns.[85] Compliance with the laws, sales licenses, purchasing and ownership are the responsibility of ATF; so too is enforcement of the laws relating to the use of firearms and the elimination of illegal firearms trafficking in the US. There were also 7,367 applications to import firearms into the US in 2010.[86] The unfortunate events surrounding operation "Fast and Furious"[87] have adversely tarnished the image of ATF for now; but in the long term history, the agency that started with just three detectives back in 1863 will recover and continue to make a meaningful and valuable contribution to the prevention and detection of criminal offences involving alcohol, tobacco, firearms and explosives.

The United States Secret Service was formed in 1865 and today consists of more than 150 offices across the US and worldwide, as well as its headquarters in Washington DC. The Secret Service has two responsibilities: the protection of designated national and international leaders and criminal investigations. The service was originally established to prevent the counterfeiting of US currency. It still undertakes this responsibility today by safeguarding the "financial infrastructure and payment systems to preserve the integrity of the economy. . . ."[88] During the American Civil War, it was estimated that up to one-half of all the currency in circulation was counterfeit. The Secret Service was established to counteract this problem, and it continued with this sole responsibility until the attack upon President William McKinley's life in Buffalo, New York, in 1901. Since that time a protection service for the President,[89] and then later for designated dignitaries, has been a major function of the service.[90] Since 1965, former presidents and their spouses[91] became eligible for lifetime protective services, but they may decline. In 1997, this was reduced to 10 years of protection upon leaving office unless they were in office before January 1, 1997. President George W. Bush will be the first president to have protection for a maximum of ten years upon leaving office. So if we now return to the two responsibilities—protection and criminal investigations—these are achieved through the protection of designated persons and the investigation of threats against the protected and the investigation of financial crimes. Approximately 3,200 officers are employed in the Secret Service, of which 1300 are uniformed[92] and the remainder are Special Agents. Established as the White House Police Force in 1922,[93] today the "Secret Service Uniformed Division Officers provide protection for the White House complex, the Vice President's residence, the main Treasury Building and Annex, and foreign diplomatic missions and embassies in the Washington, D.C., area. Additionally, Uniformed Division officers travel in support of presidential, vice presidential and foreign head of state government missions."[94]

Due to the nature of the work, all Secret Service positions require a comprehensive background check and security clearance. Applicants must be a minimum of 21 years of age. Secret Service Uniformed Officers, the uniformed branch, are initially sent to Glynco, Georgia, to complete Federal Law Enforcement Training. Upon completion of this 12-week course, they are sent to the James J. Rowley Training Center for completion of law enforcement training. This lasts 14 weeks. Special Agents employed in the criminal investigations side of the Secret Service attend the Criminal Investigator Training Program (CITP) at Glynco and upon successful graduation attend an 18-week Special Agent Training Course at James J. Rowley. Although most agents are employed within the US, there are offices in 15 countries, as well as at INTERPOL in Lyon, France. On March 16, 2012, the US Department of Homeland Security issued a press release titled "US Secret Service's Operation Open Market Nets 19 Arrests." The operation was a case of cybercrime fraud and identity theft involving the purchase and sale of financial information by international organized crime group members. The operation was conducted by the Secret Service's Electronic Crimes Task Force in association with members of ICE. The 19 suspects have been charged with racketeering, conspiracy, production and trafficking in false identification documents and access device cards. In total 50 people have been charged and further arrests are expected. The investigation established a network of criminal enterprises exchanging financial information and identities to buy and sell money laundering services, fraudulent debit and credit cards and stolen PayPal account information. It has yet to be established exactly how many identities have been compromised, but if a previous investigation, Operation Firewall, is indicative of the numbers, then this operation will amount to millions. Firewall was successfully concluded in 2004 after the Secret Service arrested 28 individuals from six countries for trafficking 1.7 million stolen credit card numbers and false identification documents under websites named "Shadocrew," 'Carderplanet" and "Darkprofits."[95]

The oldest federal agency in the United States is the US Marshals Service. It was formed by President George Washington on September 24, 1789, when he appointed 13 marshals. One of the many tasks this agency undertook was to perform the execution of federal convicts sentenced to death; another was to investigate matters of counterfeiting until the creation of the Secret Service. There are 94 marshals, each representing one federal court district. They are all appointed personally by the President. The marshals are assisted by 3,950 deputy marshals Their principal roles are protection services to judges, federal DAs, jurors, members of the public[96] using the courts and defendants. The service also houses and transports federal prisoners, operates the Witness Security Program,[97] apprehends federal fugitives, seizes and distributes property taken under the Department of Justice Asset Forfeiture Program[98] and assists other federal, state and local law enforcement agencies in fugitive operations. The Service also provides protection to the 'Drug Czar', the Director of the Office on National Drug Control Policy, when he travels, as well as to Supreme Court Justices when they travel, and protection to foreign officials when the United Nations assembly is in session. In 2010, the US Marshal Service (USMS) apprehended 36,100 federal fugitives and assisted local agencies in the arrest of 81,900 state and local fugitives in the execution of 108,200 state and local warrants. The Service also coordinated 805 extraditions and deportations from 67 countries.[99] The USMS has field offices in Colombia, the Dominican Republic, Jamaica and Mexico. The USMS is responsible for the safe conduct of all federal prisoners from the point of entry until acquittal or conviction. Upon conviction, the agency is responsible for the delivery of prisoners to a federal penitentiary. In 2010, the service received 225,329 prisoners. It has more than 53,000 detainees in custody every day.[100] The

Service operates a Special Operations Group for use in high-risk or sensitive enforcement situations or for deployment to assist in national emergencies. Appointment to the USMS requires US citizenship, being aged between 21 and 36 years, a four-year degree and a personal profile assessment. Upon acceptance into the Service, candidates must complete the initial 17.5 week USMS training course at Glynco, Georgia.

Operation Falcon was a nationwide fugitive apprehension operation coordinated by the USMS that involved dozens[101] of other agencies across the US. The first phase was completed in 2005, and since then there have been a number of continuing operations. It is now so famous that there are TV documentaries about the various stages of the operations. Phase 1 took place between April 4 and 10, 2005; Phase II was in April 2006, and Phase III was in October 2006. Phase I resulted in the largest total number of arrests made during one operation when 10,340 fugitives were apprehended over seven days. Operation Falcon[102] continued into 2009 as a national fugitive arrest program with regular statewide arrests[103] being made of large numbers of wanted persons. To date, more than 91,000 arrests and 117,000 warrants have been executed since Falcon commenced in 2005. The last year of reported operations, 2009, resulted in the arrest of 35,190 fugitives and the execution of 47,418 warrants. This last reported operation involved 42 federal agencies, 209 state agencies and 1,973 local sheriff and police departments.[104] The USMS has not operated Falcon since 2009. Instead, in 2010, the USMS Investigative Operations Division focused on a joint initiative with state agencies to implement a gang participation reduction program. "Statistically, the gang surge numbers show great success. The Gang Surge realized a 288% increase in gang member arrests compared to the previous three month average."[105] The USMS is unique in that it has federal and state powers; this means that when the Service is operating within any state, marshals have exactly the same powers as a sheriff of that state, in addition to the federal powers they hold.

The nature of the crimes discussed in the first section of this book is such that they often require local and state agencies to request assistance from federal units. This is not to say that all murders, assaults, thefts and drug trafficking are of such a scale that additional resources are always needed, but federal agencies are well placed to provide support, resources and expert services for the more complex and organized of these crimes, as well as for their impact, locally, nationally and sometimes internationally. In response to this growing need, the Federal Bureau of Investigation (FBI) has created a number of specialist units—Behavioral Analysis Units

(BAU)—that focus on some aspects of these crimes, for example: serial killings, mass killings, killings and attempted killings of particular persons. The mission of these units is to provide operational and specialist support to state and local agencies for specific and often sensitive crime investigations. Members of BAU are specialists in observing and interpreting offender behavior patterns and the factors behind specialty crimes, such as motive and frequency. All members of BAU hold advanced degrees and are drawn from the supervisory ranks of the FBI, or they are previously serving police officers with a considerable degree of experience in the specialist field. Criminologists and clinical psychologists also serve as members of BAU, as do research and crime analysts. As the FBI website states, "Spies. Terrorists. Hackers. Pedophiles. Mobsters.[106] Gang leaders and serial killers. We investigate them all, and many more besides." Authority to investigate federal crimes is through a number of statutes, the primary being US Title 18. Assisting and investigating state crimes is at the request of the state, so that the state will make a formal request in such cases as a felony murder of a state law enforcement officer, violent crimes against interstate travelers or serial killers, but the authority to investigate is vested in the FBI through federal legislation.[107] The FBI will take over the investigation in instances of kidnapping or a 'missing child' under the age of 12 years. In other instances of abduction and kidnapping, the FBI will provide support and assistance and monitor the crime developments.

There are four BAUs: Counterterrorism and Threat Assessment, Crimes against Adults, Crimes against Children and Unit 4, ViCAP, Violent Criminal Apprehension Program. Behavioral Analysis Unit 2, (crimes against adults) works on cases of serial killing, spree killings, mass murders, other murders that are particularly complex or sensitive, sexual assaults, kidnappings, missing adults and any other cases of violent crime that involve adult victims. Unit 3 covers the same range of offending that targets children as the victims. Unit 4, ViCAP, focuses on specific murder cases that have involved an abduction or are of a sexual nature or appear to be random or motiveless or stranger killings. They also investigate human remains where cause of death is unknown, and this Unit holds the national database for unsolved cases within the above criteria. ViCAP is also the Unit that provides support to state agencies that are investigating violent crimes committed on major highways; and it is the repository of all information held about homicides, missing persons and sexual assault victims associated with highways across the nation. Contrary to much television and cinema portrayal, the FBI very rarely takes over a local investigation.

What this agency does is supply expert assistance and resources as well as research, analysis and experience to a range of crimes that often test the physical resources and experience base of smaller local and state agencies. In some instances, there will be concurrent jurisdiction, for example, in a case of drug trafficking that involves local, state and federal violations; but unless the offence is one of the few crimes designated exclusively as a federal crime, such as murder of a federal agent or murder committed on federal property, in most cases the local law enforcement response will take lead responsibility for the investigation.

As seen throughout this chapter, the multitudes of law enforcement agencies in the US means that effective collaboration between them is crucial to the successful investigation of a broad range of crimes. Most people who join a law enforcement agency do so at the local or state level. Few of these agencies currently require a four-year degree. Their training programs are ordinarily around 12 weeks in duration and once in the field, officers are monitored and trained for varying periods of time by a more experienced colleague. In the US, entry level policing is very much like an apprenticeship where new recruits cover basic material together and then learn the job by practice under the tutelage of a more senior practitioner. If contrasted with a number of police training programs outside of the US, it is clear that there is a wide discrepancy in some instances and great similarity in others. Compare for example three years of academic and practical training in the Scandinavian countries with three months of training in the US and the UK. Compare flat level entry for the US and the UK, Canada and Australia with multiple entry levels into the police service in France, depending upon how much higher education you have received, or officer entry for university graduates in South Korea. Over time, some of the local US police officers will develop a portfolio of experience and academic achievement so that they are well placed to apply for employment as a federal agent. Once accepted, they will embark upon extended periods of training, field supervised development and continuing education. Most of the federal agencies now require applicants to hold a four-year degree and enhanced pay is available for those with a masters and/or foreign language proficiency. Federal law enforcement work will be more specific and agents have the chance to work in highly specialized fields, nationally and internationally. Whether or not learning the craft of policing at a local level, so that hands-on experience is gained in dealing with dozens of minor theft allegations, assaults, low level drug dealing and missing persons reports is *sine qua non*[108] for investigating complex major crimes is, and perhaps always will be, debatable. For those specialist agencies that recruit directly, apparently street experience is not a relevant criterion, although a number of agencies make specific reference to applicants who are currently employed by a local law enforcement agency. For those countries that require their police officers to attend university as part of basic training, well, they tend not to have federal agencies that supplement the work of the police. Typically, the police in these countries investigate the complex national and international crimes as well as the routine. But there is movement; the UK is creating a super-agency, vigorously claimed by politicians not to be a UK FBI but a National Crime Agency. Member states of Europe have moved beyond a Euro-wide drug unit to a Euro-wide police force, and its sphere of responsibility is growing. The military gendarmes of Europe are following closely behind. Australia already has federal police and the RCMP; well, it is truly unique as it provides national, state and local police, as well as federal style specialist services and support to smaller forces. The UN has a police force. One thing is clear—contemporary policing responds to levels of interstate and inter-country criminality on an unprecedented scale. And although minor assaults, thefts and drug deals may be the 'bread and butter' of policing, they are no longer the only carbohydrates on the table. However technology assists or shapes the way forward, it will most definitely have a role in every aspect of policing at every level. Even the most routine theft investigation is now driven by technology, as are reports of missing persons, the pattern of drug dealing in small cities and the frequency of assaults. Even 'bread and butter' policing cannot survive without some technology input any longer. Global policing arrived the day the first cybercrime was committed. There really never was 'business as usual' for policing, it has always been dynamic; we just added virtual and global policing to the mix. And, therefore, in the final chapter we are going to look at some history and then some current and even a little future use of technology in policing. Upon concluding the final chapter, you will then have a more informed dialog about the issues of *Crime and Policing Crime.*

Endnotes

1. Gaines, L. and Keppler, V. *Policing in America.* 6th ed. Newark, NJ: LexisNexis; 2008, infra, cite the findings of Manning 2006 stating that many police officers view themselves as crime-fighters or crook-catchers, p. 16.

2. However, 92% of all local forces investigate crimes of which 64% investigate homicides themselves. Source: *Local Police Departments 2003.* Law Enforcement Management and Administrative Statistics. US Department of Justice report prepared by Mathew J. Hickman, Ph.D. and Brian A. Reaves, Ph.D. May 2006. NCJ 210118. P. 15.
3. Nine out of 10 local police departments in the US perform drug enforcement functions. Source: *Local Police Departments 2003.* Op. cit. p. 16.
4. For commentary on the role of the police in American society, see: Gaines, L. and Keppler, Op. cit. Chapter 1.
5. Allen, M. Ideas and trends; Help wanted invoking the not-too-high-IQ test. 19 September 1999. www.expertlaw.com
6. Transcript of interview with Robert Jordan, September 12, 2000 at www.postroad.com
7. Ibid.
8. Robert Jordan v City of New London No. 99-9188. 2000 U.S. App. Lexis 22195. Decided 23 August 2000.
9. Ibid.
10. Source: Recommendations for the North Carolina Highway Patrol. Produced by Ervin, A., Flores-Macias, G., Lee, H., and Taylor, B. May 2002 for the Terry Sanford Institute of Public Policy, Duke University, NC. Chapter II. Available at www.sanford.duke.edu
11. *Local Police Departments 2003.* Law Enforcement Management and Administrative Statistics. US Department of Justice report prepared by Mathew J. Hickman, Ph.D. and Brian A. Reaves Ph.D., May 2006. NCJ 210118. P. 8.
12. Ibid.
13. Bureau of Justice Statistics. This is 2008 data. The information is supplied every four years and 2012 figures are not yet available. www.bjs.usdoj.gov
14. Ibid.
15. *Local Police Departments 2007.* Bryan A. Reaves. December 2010. NCJ 231174 at www.bjs.ojp.usdoj.gov
16. www.bjs.ojp.usdoj.gov
17. Ibid.
18. www.bls.gov
19. Ibid.
20. Many municipal forces now participate in Regional Training Academies, such as the North Central Texas Council of Governments Regional Police Academy in Arlington, TX.
21. Further information at www.arlingtonpd.org
22. www.tcleose.state.tx.us

23. The total number of course hours varies between colleges. For example, El Paso Community College offers 704 contact hours of training.
24. In Texas, a class b typically incurs a fine not exceeding $2,000 and up to 180 days in jail. Examples include: shoplifting, prostitution, criminal trespass, minor drug possession and first offence DWI.
25. www.tulsapolice.org
26. Three Texas forces require a four-year degree: Arlington, Sugarland PD and Deer Park PD. The largest forces in the state, Houston and Dallas PD, do not have such a requirement.
27. "Applicants must have completed a bachelor's degree with a C+ average or better at an accredited college. No military hours or credits are accepted unless they are received from or converted through an accredited college." www.tulsapolice.org
28. State and Local Law Enforcement Training Academies, 2006 (Revised 4/14/09). Bryan A. Reaves. February 2009 NCJ 222987 at page 3. www.bjs.ojp.usdoj.gov
29. *Local Police Departments 2003.* Op. cit., p. 7.
30. Ibid.
31. *Local Police Departments 2003.* Op. cit., p. 9.
32. For further discussion see: Reflections from the one-percent of local police departments with mandatory four-year degree requirements for new hires: Are they diamonds in the rough?" Diane Bruns, Bacone College. bruns@bacone.edu
33. Ibid.
34. Ibid.
35. Ibid.
36. Source: State and Local Law Enforcement Training Academies, 2006 (Revised 4/14/09). Bryan A. Reaves. February 2009 NCJ 222987 at www.bjs.ojp.usdoj.gov. This was confirmed in Recommendations for the North Carolina Highway Patrol Produced by Ervin, A., Flores-Macias, G., Lee, H., and Taylor, B. May 2002 for the Terry Sanford Institute of public policy, Duke University, NC. Available at www.sanford.duke.edu
37. Ibid.
38. State and Local Law Enforcement Training Academies, 2006 (Revised 4/14/09). Bryan A. Reaves. February 2009 NCJ 222987 at www.bjs.ojp.usdoj.gov
39. www.police-association.org
40. Is policing a job or profession? The case for a four-year degree. CALEA Update Magazine Issue 108. The author of the article is the Chief of Arlington PD, Texas. Theron L. Bowman, Ph.D. Available at www.calea.org
41. Ibid.
42. www.tampagov.net/dept_Police
43. Ibid.
44. Ibid.

45. The NYPD is the largest, then Chicago PD. The Los Angeles PD is third.
46. Other facilities are: Pitchless East, Pitchless North, North County Correctional facility, Mira Loma and Men's Central.
47. Civil process includes matters such as a writ of possession, summons and complaints, and restraining orders. For a complete list see the LASO website. www.civil.lasd.org/CivilProcess
48. www.lasdhq.org/divisions/homeland
49. Basic monthly pay is $4,702.45, which rises to $464.73 for those with a 2-year degree and $5,242.00 for those applicants holding a 4-year degree. Source: www.lasdhq.org/recruitment
50. For a comparative perspective see Peak, K. *Policing America: Challenges and best practices.* 7th ed. Upper Saddle River, New Jersey: Pearson. Pp. 82–86.
51. www.la-sheriff.org
52. State of Hawaii Public Safety Sheriff. This is one of two law enforcement divisions within the Department of Public Safety.
53. Always Just
54. 68 and 57 hours respectively. Source: www.maine.gov/dps/mcja/training
55. www.maine.gov/dps/msp/field_troops
56. Source: Peak, K. Op. cit., p. 62
57. And anybody else designated for protective services by the governor's office
58. I have not been able to verify these figures. His source is cited in Peak, op. cit., p. 65.
59. Source: Census of Federal Law Enforcement Officers 2008. www.bjs.ojp.usdoj.gov produced by Brian Reaves, Ph.D. 26 June 2012 NCJ 238250. This census does not contain details of the CIA or TSA (Air Marshalls) as it is 'classified information'.
60. Op. cit., Census 2008
61. Ibid.
62. Ibid.
63. Ibid.
64. Ibid.
65. Seven Federal Courts do not permit their probation officers to carry firearms.
66. The others are: Department of Health and Human Services, Department of Defense, Department of the Treasury and the Social Security Administration.
67. Op. cit., Census 2008.
68. Ibid.
69. Ibid.
70. For a list of the 22 see: www.dhs.gov/xabout/history
71. www.dhs.gov
72. Conducted at one of the FAMS training centers: New Jersey or New Mexico
73. Man killed after bomb claim at airport. 7 December 2005. www.cnn.com/2005/us/airplane.gunshot

74. www.atf.gov/careers
75. Ibid.
76. Applicants who do not hold a four-year degree may apply if they have 3 years of work experience and an associate degree or are currently serving in a law enforcement agency or are currently serving as an investigator in another federal agency. Applicants with a 4-year degree who achieved a grade point average of 2.95 or above are eligible for enhanced entry and pay.
77. Locality pay varies between 14.16% and 35.15%.
78. See Johnstone, P. *Drugs and drug trafficking.* Dubuque, IA: Kendall Hunt; 2012. Chapter 5.
79. Ibid.
80. 15 USC Chapter 10A
81. Cigarettes and non-smoking tobacco products. Cigars are exempt.
82. Under title 18 USC
83. See: "75 Defendants Charged on Firearm, Drug Distribution, or Related Offenses Following 8-Month Undercover Investigation". www.atf.gov/press/releases/2011
84. The state with the highest number of registered guns is California 242,766; the second highest is Texas with 224,200 license holders. Source: ATF 2011 infra.
85. www.atf.gov/publications/firearms/121611-firearms-commerce-2011
86. Ibid. 63% of imported firearms are handguns; 19% are rifles and 18% are shotguns.
87. There was massive media coverage of this incident. See for example, The truth about the Fast and Furious scandal. 27 June 2012. Fortune magazine. www.fortune.cnn.com. Exclusive: Fast and Furious IG slams ATF Phoenix personnel. 27 August 2012 by Sharyl Attkisson. www.cbsnews.com
88. www.secretservice.gov
89. There have been 7 direct assaults upon the president since 1950, one resulting in death, President Kennedy. Only one president has been assaulted twice, Gerald R. Ford, twice in September 1975. Source: The U.S. Secret Service: An Examination and Analysis of Its Evolving Mission: Shawn Reese. 16 December 2009. Congressional Research Service at www.crs.gov RL 34603
90. By law, the Secret Service protects the President, the family of the President, the Vice President, the President elect and the Vice President elect, former Presidents and their spouses, children of former Presidents until they are 16 years of age, other individuals next in line to be President, e.g. the Speaker of the House, the House Minority Whip, major presidential candidates (within 120 days of a general election—this was extended to 6 months for the presidential candidate Barrack Obama, the first time in history that there was such an extension for a candidate); visiting heads of state and their spouses travelling in the US. Also, individuals designated by an Executive Presidential order and National Special Security Events when designated by

the Secretary of the Department of Homeland Security, such as a State of the Union Address, a presidential inaugural celebration or even the SuperBowl.

91. Jacqueline Kennedy and her children were provided with 2 years of protection after the assassination of President John F. Kennedy. This has not happened since and ordinarily the widow of a former president is not provided with protective services upon becoming a widow.
92. Previously known as the White House police, they were renamed The Executive Protective Service in 1970 and then received the current name: The Secret Service Uniformed Division in November 1977.
93. 1 October 1922 at the instigation of President Harding. It became part of the Secret Service in 1930.
94. www.secretservice.gov/careers
95. See: 28 October 2004, US Department of Homeland Security press release, US Secret Service's Operation Firewall nets 28 arrests. The role of the Secret Service in investigating cybercrime was expanded under the Patriot Act (107-56), which included the establishment of a nationwide electronic crimes taskforce. This unit grew again in 2006 from 15 to 24 nationwide 'taskforces'. Since 2003, the Secret service has made more than 29,000 arrests for cybercrime, counterfeiting and financial crime offences. Source: www.secretservice.gov/history
96. There are in the region of 1,400 threats against the judiciary every year. Source: www.usmarshals.gov/duties/factsheets
97. Started in 1971, more than 8,300 witnesses and 9,800 family members have participated in the program since its inception.
98. Currently 18,000 assets valued at $3.9 billion. Source: www.usmarshals.gov
99. www.usmarshals.gov/duties
100. The USMS rents local jail space from other prisons and jails around the country to provide daily facilities for federal prisoners.
101. 25 federal agencies, 206 state agencies, 302 county sheriff departments and 366 police departments. Source: www.doj.gov
102. Federal And Local Cops Organized Nationally. FALCON
103. E.g. 9 July 2009, 86 arrests under falcon were made in Madison, WI. www.doj.state.wi.us
104. www.usmarshals.gov/falcon
105. USMS FY 2012 Performance Budget President's Budget. February 2011. Department of Justice Publication. Page 34 available at www.justice.gov/jmd/2012justification
106. www.fbi.gov/about-us/investigate
107. 28 USC 540, 540A and 540B
108. Meaning an indispensable action or requirement. Often something that is required in advance.

FORENSICS AND TECHNOLOGY

Forensic science is science that is used in a public forum, the courts. Today we associate the term with those scientists who attend crime scenes or work in laboratories for law enforcement agencies that help to establish the perpetrator of a crime. What was once a behind the scenes type of employment, where a specialist police officer investigated the crime scene and scientists conducted the 'lab work', today, with a large input from Hollywood, the role of the CSI or 'Bones' has become glamorous and active and no crime is ever solved without one. The reality is that crime scene analysis—establishing what happened at a crime and who did what—has become increasingly scientific and technology driven. We have always wanted to know how a person died. When Julius Caesar was murdered or assassinated by his peers, his body was examined after death, a

post-mortem, and it is believed that of the 23 stab wounds he received the second wound to the chest was the fatal blow.[1] Today a 'forensic science' search reveals 8.9 million hits with dozens of categories and sub-categories. Scattered throughout history further back than Caesar there are references to fingerprints and palm prints in blood, and in 250 BC Erasistratus allegedly found that his patients' pulse rates increased when they were lying to him. In 1235, and again in 1248, there are specific references to work being conducted in China relating to the identification of murderers. In one instance, a peasant was killed; the murder weapon was a sickle. In an early form of death scene investigation that has led to forensic entomology, the crime investigator called upon the entire village folk to bring forward their sickles. Eventually flies settled on the murder weapon, as they were attracted to the residue of blood and human tissue left on the weapon from the victim. Later, in 1248 Sung Tz'u wrote "The Washing away of Wrongs" where he recorded the incident of 1235 and other examples of how to use medicine to solve crimes.[2] By the middle of the 16th century, establishing the cause of death by autopsy, or forensic pathology, was gaining popularity among the surgeons of Europe working with dead soldiers on the battlefield. Leading this movement was Ambroise Paré who served as a surgeon and barber[3] to two kings, Charles IX and Henri III, as well as to Queen Catherine de Medici. Among his successes, Dr. Paré established that pouring boiling oil into a gunshot wound was not beneficial and that ligatures rather than cauterization were beneficial in amputation cases. Having served as a military doctor, he was particularly interested in the effects of violent wounds to the internal organs and the possibility of treating the injury at the same time as relieving the pain and suffering of the victim. He is attributed with being the father of modern surgery and for establishing modern forensic pathology.[4] In 1784 in Lancaster, England, physical matching was used to secure a prosecution against a murder suspect. The case involved the murder of Edward Culshaw. Culshaw was shot in the head and died as a result of his injuries. In the 18th century, it was common practice to pack down the lead shot with paper. Upon discharge of the pistol, the paper packing would discharge with the shot. In Culshaw's case, part of the paper, which was from a newspaper, was retrieved from his brain. John Toms was a suspect in the murder and when arrested he was found to have a piece of newspaper on him that matched the torn piece of paper used to make the paper wad found in the victim's head. Toms was subsequently charged and convicted of the murder.[5] Mathiew Orfila[6] is viewed as the father of forensic toxicology due to his work with poisons and the effect they have upon the body. During the 18th and early 19th centuries, arsenic was widely used as a poison as it was not possible to detect the substance in the body. Thanks to the work of Orfila, this changed. He was responsible for making chemical analysis normal procedure in forensic medicine. He studied asphyxiation and body decomposition and was one of the first to use microscopic[7] traces of blood and semen stains. In 1840, he was an expert witness for the defense in a murder trial involving Marie Le Farge who was on trial for arsenic poisoning of her husband. The method developed to detect arsenic poisoning at the time was the Marsh Test, a method developed by an English chemist, James Marsh. The body of the deceased was exhumed and, unfortunately for the defense, Orfila did not disprove or discredit the Marsh Test, simply that it had been administered incorrectly. Marie Le Farge was convicted and executed. The result of this famous trial was to be a boast to the science of toxicology generally and for Orfila specifically, and the occurrence of arsenic poisoning reduced dramatically after this trial. Lambert Adolphe Quetelet was an astronomer, statistician and mathematician whose interest in mathematics and probability calculus led him into the establishment of the cartographic school of criminology. In 1835, he presented the idea that human traits could be identified through the process of scientific body measurement, or anthropometry.[8] He then extended his thesis to consider the demographic and anthropomorphic characteristics of man and applied his mathematical genius to the probability of man's behavior related to issues such as moral behavior and propensity to commit crime. Quetelet is a great among scientists; he was hugely influential upon those seeking to explain crime and criminals and he was highly regarded by Charles Darwin's cousin, Francis Galton, who went on to become one of the leading voices in fingerprint evidence.[9] Ballistics[10] was developed by a former 'Bow Street Runner' and member of the new London Metropolitan Police, Henry Goddard. "In relation to examining ammunition, the Bow Street officer, Henry Goddard, described one of his cases, in 1835, when he solved a case at the home of a Mrs. Maxwell of Southampton whose butler, Joseph Randall, had apparently had an exchange of gunfire with burglars. Goddard was suspicious of Randall's story, and when he examined his guns and ammunition he found an identical pimple on all the bullets, including the one which had allegedly been fired at Randall. He then found a corresponding pinhead-sized hole in the mold from which the bullets had been made. This indicated that the bullet fired at Randall was in fact part of his own ammunition. In prison, Randall confessed to making up the story with a view to obtaining a reward from his mistress for his bravery in protecting her property, and was eventually released with a sharp warning from the court. Goddard's keen observation had linked a series of bullets together."[11] The first time that fingerprint evidence was used to identify a murder suspect occurred in Argentina in 1892.[12] It was first used to secure a conviction in court in London in 1905.[13] However, the history of fingerprints started many years earlier and involved a number of disputes and claims that remain unresolved today. The claimants in the fingerprint dispute are William Herschel, Henry Faulds and Francis Galton. In 1858, William Herschel[14] was working as chief magistrate in a rural subdivision in the province of Bengal, India. During the course of his work he needed to get locals to sign for employment and contracts and since many could not write he started to take an imprint of their hands and then just fingers, in ink. Herschel then started to keep the ink prints and to sort and order them. Eventually he recorded his findings in *The Origin of the Fingerprint.* By 1877, Herschel had been promoted to Chief Magistrate for Hoogly, Jungipoor near Calcutta; and he was able to require the implementation of his fingerprinting system to record the details of farmers, tenants and locals who had disputes between each other and also with the British Government. Looking back, what is clear is that Herschel understood the process of fingerprinting but he probably never perfected its use to be conclusive evidence of unique identity. As author Colin Beavan writes, "Even if Herschel understood the technical nuances of fingerprinting it is clear that his subordinates did not. Under Herschel, fingerprints were more effectively used as a means of intimidation than for real scientific purposes."[15] Although Herschel had left India by the time of implementation in 1897 the Governor General of India approved the use of fingerprints for the classification of criminals alongside use of the Bertillon identification system to be utilized by the Calcutta Anthropometric Bureau. It was within thi Calcutts Bureau that two Indian officers—Rai Bahadur Hem Chandra Bose and Azizul Haque—that Herschel's system was refined and used effectively as a forensic identification method. Their boss in Indi, Edward Henry, was later to return to England and help establish the fingerprint bureau at Scotland Yard. Sir Edward is credited with establishing the Henry Classification Method for sorting fingerprints by physiological characteristics.

Henry Faulds was born in Scotland in 1843. He studied mathematics and logic and then medicine. He served at the Glasgow Infirmary under the famous Joseph Lister before becoming a missionary. As part of his work in Japan, Faulds lectured medical students. During the course of teaching he became fascinated with the imprints left by fingers in ancient Japanese pottery. He then spent some time working alongside Japanese potters and established that every potter had a unique set of fingerprints left in the clay. He then started a collection of prints taken in clay and wax and started recording the similarities and differences. Ironically, Hershel was doing the same thing thousands of miles away in India. By 1880, Faulds was convinced of the uniqueness of every fingerprint and he wrote to Charles Darwin for support. Darwin, who by then was 71 years of age, declined but did offer to solicit support from his cousin, Francis Galton.[16] Galton was not so responsive and by the end of the year Faulds decided to go ahead and publish his findings in *Nature.*

Francis Galton came from a privileged family and he was extremely intelligent. By the age of two he was reading and by five had consumed Homer's *Iliad.* He was fortunate enough to have sufficient family wealth that he never had to work. By all accounts he was self-opinionated and condescending towards those he considered his 'inferiors'. With such an ego it was hard for Galton to recognize that Fauld's was really the leading voice in the development of fingerprints and that he had missed an opportunity when he snubbed Faulds in 1880. Ironically, Galton shared a train ride with William Herschel in 1888 and during that journey they exchanged ideas about fingerprints.[17] Galton had his interest awakened by Herschel and he immersed himself in the literature on the subject, including the article written by Faulds in *Nature* in 1880. If Faulds were correct, then fingerprint ridges may be hereditary and an indicator of intelligence and physical attributes. Given the contemporary European discussion taking place about body measurements and a 'criminal type', Galton believed that fingerprints might be the key to predicting criminal behavior. Galton then proceeded to work with Herschel to claim ownership of the invention of fingerprinting. Given his temperament and attitude towards those he considered inferior, Galton was never prepared to accept the work of Faulds and he committed himself to proving Herschel and himself as the originators of fingerprinting. It should be said that Galton did make a number of meaningful contributions to the field. He significantly advanced the interpretation of ridge patterns and established that even identical twins had individual fingerprints. In 1892, Galton published his book *Finger Prints.* It was moderately well received, but it did not shake the ground from beneath the scientific community as he had expected. He made no reference to the work of Henry Faulds.

The 19th century was a very busy time for developments in forensic science. This was true not only in Belgium, India, England and Argentina, but also in Austria where Eduard von Hoffman discovered that persons burned alive had soot in their windpipes and lungs and carbon monoxide in their blood. German physician Paul Uhlenhuth was on the verge of distinguishing one type of animal blood from another, which led to the identification of human bloodstains as distinguished from animal blood. Another German, Karl Landsteiner, discovered that human blood cells could be grouped as *A, B* and *O* types (he went on in the early 20th century to isolate the *Rh* factor). In France, Albert Florence developed a chemical test for identifying human semen in 1870 and Ambroise Tardieu had discovered spots under the pleura characteristic of death by rapid suffocation. The city of Paris had now had a uniformed police force since the 17th century and Napoleon had increased its powers and that of the military gendarmerie during his emperorship. He had also instigated the creation of a detective force, the *Brigade de Sûreté,* in Paris, which ended up under the directorship of a former criminal, Eugene Vidocq.[18] Now Vidocq was a great 'thief taker', but he was no scientist. However, he did give Paris and to some extent the world[19] a model for establishing a detective bureau though it was a much quieter minor official who led the development of forensics in France. Alphonse Bertillon was born in Paris in 1853. He had a modest education and managed to get himself expelled from school after an unfortunate incident where he 'accidentally' lit a fire in his desk. He drifted for a few years until he joined the French army; then on discharge he joined the police as a clerk. His father was a statistician and his influence may well have shaped Bertillon's interest in order and method. Once in the police, Bertillon soon realized that a number of criminals were returning to the courts and claiming to be first time offenders because no effective method of identification existed to establish their true identity. Fortunately for the Paris police, Bertillon was working in the records department and had the opportunity to see firsthand how chaotic the system was and how many recidivists were escaping justice. "In 1879, he decided, on the basis of his observations and knowledge of science, that no two people could have exactly the same physical measurements. If enough measurements were taken, a high degree of individuality could be developed for each person contained within a police agency's files."[20] At the moment, a search for just one name could yield hundreds of results, as there were no distinguishing features by which to narrow the search. By 1883, Bertillon's 11-point anthropometric method of body measurement taking, '*Bertillonage*', proved successful after he identified a repeat offender using the alias of Dupont. By the end of the year, Bertillon had successfully identified 26 recidivists, and by the end of one full year of operation he had achieved 241 successes.[21] By 1887, the Bertillon system was in widespread use across Europe and by the end of the year had arrived in the US. Eventually the reliability of the Bertillon system came into question when it was shown that different results could be achieved depending upon how the measurements were taken. Unfortunately for Bertillon, he was also implicated in the Dreyfus scandal when an innocent man was wrongly convicted and sentenced to life imprisonment on Devil's Island. Bertillon had supplied 'expert' handwriting testimony at the infamous miscarriage of justice trial.[22]

In 1902, a forensic anthropologist named R. S. Fisher started to produce work that showed every human's lip prints to be unique.[23] Forensic cheiloscopy[24] has now gained in use and validity, and it is recognized that today lip prints are a valuable and credible way of making a unique identification of a person. Over past centuries, the development of forensic pathology, fingerprint analysis, blood sampling, anthropometry, odontology,[25] toxicology, otoscopy,[26] ballistics and, more recently, D.N.A., have all made huge contributions towards the identification of victims and offenders. The world's first crime laboratory was opened in Lyon, France, in 1910 by the forensic anthropologist Edmund Locard. He was responsible for taking Fischer's cheiloscopy idea and making it work for police identification purposes. It was Locard who turned the phrase "Every contact leaves a trace."[27] He is also credited with introducing the 12-point fingerprint identification method. Dr. Locard was a founding member of the International Academy of Criminalistics in 1929. In the US, a Bureau of Identification had been created in 1904; and in 1911 Thomas Jennings[28] was the first person in America to be convicted of murder through fingerprint evidence. Jennings forcibly entered a Chicago house at nighttime on September 19, 1910. The house owner, Clarence Hiller, disturbed him. After a struggle, Jennings shot and killed Hiller. Later that night Jennings was stopped by police and found injured and in possession of a handgun; he was arrested. At the crime scene a fingerprint was found at the point of entry and this was matched with Jennings', who had recently been released from federal prison. The fingerprint evidence was submitted at trial and Jennings was found guilty and received the death sentence. He was executed February 16, 1912. Three of the four fingerprint 'experts' who gave evidence at the trial had been trained a few years previously by the fingerprint bureau at Scotland Yard in England. In 1923, August Vollmer established the first US crime laboratory[29] in Los Angeles, California. This was followed by the creation of the FBI crime laboratory in 1932. Britain followed with the creation of the Metropolitan Police Forensic Laboratory in Hendon, London, in 1935. Around the same time as Vollmer was professionalizing policing across the US through the implementation of forensic laboratories, Calvin Goddard was making considerable progress with forensic ballistics. Goddard, a former US Army colonel, is credited with introducing the term forensic ballistics. He was responsible for the establishment of The Bureau of Forensic Ballistics at Northwestern University[30] in part due to his expert ballistics testimony at the infamous St. Valentine's Day Massacre trial.

Today forensic technicians arrive at a crime scene with a vehicle full of equipment. Years ago regular detectives would arrive with little more than a notebook. Crime scenes were often compromised due to the transfer of material brought to the scene by the police. Methods of trace material collection were primitive and the sheer number of officers who would trample across a crime scene would make it very challenging to later establish who and who not had been into the premises where the offence occurred. Although a number of great successes were recorded throughout the early part of the 20th century, one problem many forensic scientists encountered was the lack of care taken in collecting and preserving evidence from the scene. In the UK, Sir Bernard Spilsbury, Home Office pathologist, was about to remedy this by inventing a 'Murder Bag'. Spilsbury was an experienced pathologist and when he arrived at the crime scene known as 'The Crumbles' in 1924, he knew that there would be many challenges. Patrick Mahon was a married man who had taken a number of mistresses throughout his lifetime. Emily Kaye was another. Kaye was 38 years of age and a spinster. She was also pregnant by Mahon. He arranged for them to meet at a remote cottage in an area of Sussex known as 'The Crumbles'. She was accepting an invitation to her own death. Mahon brutally murdered Kaye and then chopped up her remains and set fire to them. Her bloodstained clothes he took home in a leather Gladstone bag, which he left in the Left Luggage department at waterloo station. Eventually staff at the station noticed the locker smelled bad and upon opening it called the police. They waited until the bag was collected and then arrested Mahon. Mahon did not admit to murder but said that Kaye had fallen and hit her head on a coal bucket while at The Crumbles cottage. He panicked as she was dead, removed her clothing, destroyed the body and left her clothes in the bag the police now had possession of. The crime scene at the cottage was chaos. There was blood and debris scattered all over the few rooms. The premises had no toilet, so Spilsbury surmised that the body butchering had taken place on the kitchen table and some parts had washed down the sink. The police officers that had initially attended the scene had, as usual, inadvertently compromised the crime scene and evidence had been transferred between different rooms and from the inside to the outside of the premises. Spilsbury eventually removed more than 1,000 body parts and samples and Mahon was tried for murder. He denied the charges and entered a not guilty plea. Kaye's head was never recovered from the crime scene and therefore the alleged injury causing death could not be examined. Spilsbury testified with regards to the remains he had found; many were boiled and torn apart. The sink and waste pipes were clogged with human fat and there was head and body hair scattered around the premises. Officers at the scene had picked up large chunks of human flesh by hand and placed it into buckets found at the scene. No police officer had access to rubber gloves. It was truly a task for Spilsbury to piece together what had happened and be able to present this in a manner that was acceptable to the trial judge and jury. Spilsbury's reconstructed skeleton, minus the head and upper neck, was able to show without any doubt that she had been brutally murdered and literally hacked to death then pulverized and crushed to pieces before being burned. The jury was convinced and Mahon was sentenced to death. Soon after this, in association with the head of the Metropolitan Police CID, Spilsbury created the "Murder Bag" so that in the future detective officers would have a guide and the basic equipment necessary to take samples from a crime scene and to preserve evidence. The initial bag comprised of fingerprint taking equipment, test tubes, magnifying glasses, rubber gloves, a rubber apron, scissors, forceps, disinfectant, towels and soap, a flashlight, tape measure, a two-foot ruler, a compass and a pair of handcuffs. Over time the contents varied and increased in number, but the basic 'go bag' for CSI investigations was now a standard issue item for all police investigators available at the police station. Just as August Vollmer would do, Bernard Spilsbury committed suicide; he too was sick and knew that it would soon be impossible for him to continue in his career. Therefore, he took his own life by gas poisoning in his own laboratory in December 1947.[31]

James D. Watson and Francis Crick published their article "Molecular Structure of Nucleic Acids: A Structure for Deoxyribose Nucleic Acid" in *Nature* on April 25, 1953.[32] Often described as the "pearl" of science, the article unpacked the mystery of how organisms send on genetic data for future generations. Although sometimes referred to as the "cracking of the genetic code," this is not accurate as it happened some years later. Although the glory goes to Watson and Crick for moving forward the entire genetics discussion, much of what they discovered was a result of the work on the chemical structure of DNA by Rosalind Franklin and her colleagues at Kings College, London. Familiarity with the term DNA is now such that there is unlikely to be a reader of this book who is not familiar with the diagrammatical representation of the DNA double helix. DNA (deoxyribonucleric acid) matching is close to blood typing in terms of its uses in forensic science. But it is considered of greater value, as DNA is unique whereas type blood is not. DNA is found in all human cells and its pattern is hereditary. Originally DNA testing was used to establish paternity. Any human tissue or cellular material may be used as a sample although blood is still the most commonly analyzed, as it is frequently found at crime scenes. To identify an individual, scientists can scan 13 DNA regions of the suspect and from that create a unique 'profile' or DNA 'fingerprint'. Ordinarily a blood sample will only tell you that, for example, blood found at a crime scene is type 'O'. Of itself, that is of little value given that 45% of the population has O blood type. However, if other evidence from the scene is obtained, such as saliva from a cigarette butt or lip prints from the rim of a glass, hair from the suspect and shoe print evidence from the scene, then collectively these create a picture of the offender that can be measured against a suspect when apprehended. DNA has advanced this situation by a considerable margin, as the DNA makeup of each of us is unique. Those of you reading this book do not have the same body images through fingerprints and body secretions as me, so that as you turn each page you are leaving a unique calling card on the book different from mine as I proofread it. The more DNA probes a scientist is able to establish, the more distinctive is the pattern of that person's DNA. If that DNA is then found again, at another crime scene, we can say with a very high degree of probability that the same offender committed both crimes.[33]

The University of Leicester website for Professor Sir Alec Jeffreys has the following quote by him: "My life changed on Monday morning at 9:05 AM, 10 September 1984. What emerged was the world's first genetic fingerprint."[34] What Jeffreys discovered was that it was possible to view Variable Number Repeat Tandems, VNRT, as a bar code. Most importantly for criminal investigations, these VNRTs were virtually unique, so that when viewed on a type of X-ray machine the 'bar codes'[35] could be used to determine the exact identity of one individual human being.[36] The work of this scientist truly revolutionized forensic science and has continued to do so since 1984. The first use of the DNA genetic fingerprint in a murder case was during the investigation into the killing of 15-year-old schoolgirl,

Lynda Mann. Lynda was found raped and strangled on the grounds of a psychiatric hospital in Leicestershire, England, in November 1983. Two years later a similar rape and murder occurred. The victim was another 15-year-old schoolgirl, Dawn Ashworth. Soon after the second murder, a 17-year-old male with learning disabilities, Richard Buckland, was arrested. Buckland worked at the hospital where the first murder had taken place. Semen had been obtained from the victims of both murders and these were analyzed using Alec Jeffreys' DNA technique. To the surprise of the police and to the suspect Buckland—for he had admitted to killing Dawn Ashworth—he was found not responsible for either crime, as his blood and semen did not match those found on the victims. So, in fact, the first use of DNA sampling in a murder trial actually proved that the suspect did not commit the crimes. The police now returned to the investigations and in 1987 conducted a mass, voluntary, DNA screening of all males between 17 and 34 years of age who lived in the Leicestershire villages of Enderby, Narborough and Littlethorpe. Ninety-eight percent of the males from these villages consented to supplying a saliva or blood DNA sample. The screening did not, however, produce a suspect. Then in August 1987 a man from one of the villages, Ian Kelly, was heard telling some villagers that he had given a DNA sample on behalf of a friend of his, Colin Pitchfork. Pitchfork had told Kelly that he could not give a sample as he had already given a sample himself on behalf of another friend who had a conviction for sexual indecency. It was Pitchfork himself who had the convictions for indecency by exposing himself to schoolgirls. As a result of the information given by Kelly, the police arrested Colin Pitchfork in August 1987. He provided a positive DNA match with the semen found in both murder victims, and on January 22, 1988, he was sentenced to life imprisonment for double murder[37] with a recommendation he serve a minimum term of 30 years.[38] The very first use of DNA 'fingerprinting' in a criminal case was not a murder trial though but one for rape. The trial of Robert Melias took place a few months before the Pitchfork murder trial. Melias was convicted on November 13, 1987, at Bristol Crown Court, England, for raping and paralyzing a 43-year-old woman. The court heard how the chance that the semen found on the victim did not belong to Melias amounted to 1 in 4 million. Since the early flush of enthusiasm, there have been a number of challenges to the validity of DNA evidence. Initially, DNA evidence was seen as an exclusive tool for the prosecution. Then it was utilized by the defense, occasionally to the objection of the prosecution.[39] "Prosecutors are enthusiastic about using DNA to imprison people, but resist having the tables turned."[40] In the US, there have been 297 post-conviction exonerations due to the use of DNA to date.[41] The Innocence Project is a source for information about cases involving invalidated or improper forensic science and 49 states now have laws permitting inmates' access to DNA testing.[42]

As the 20th century progressed, more and more advances were made in almost every sphere of forensic science. William Bass pioneered the development of the "Body Farm" at the Forensic Anthropology Research Facility at the University of Tennessee. The name Body Farm was used by criminal fiction writer Patricia Cornwell in one of her novels and it has stuck. Professor Bass himself is not only a world authority on body decomposition and human osteology, he is also a crime writer publishing under the name Jefferson Bass. For many years, scientists grappled with the idea of lifting fingerprints from human flesh. It is often the case that victims of violent murder have been touched directly by the offender. The question has been, are these fingerprints recoverable for the purposes of identification. In 1978, the Miami-Dade Police Department successfully recovered fingerprint samples from human skin resulting in a murder conviction. On July 23, 1978, three victims were shot and killed inside the World of Health Spa, North Miami Beach. One of the deceased, a female, was found naked and had been sexually assaulted. Three fingerprints were successfully lifted from her left ankle using a latent print method involving black magnetic powder. Stephen William Beattie was identified as the killer and was sentenced to death on 31 January 1979. He committed suicide in prison before the death sentence could be carried out. Since then hundreds of cases have been prosecuted where latent fingerprints have been lifted from a cadaver.[43] As one forensic investigator noted, "The bottom line is that success is possible so long as the skin is intact and the temperatures and humidity are in correct ranges. More well-trained people are needed and body processing should be attempted much more often than it has been."[44] Towards the end of the 20th century, mitochondria DNA[45] evidence had been used in court;[46] the FBI had developed a DNA database, NIDIS;[47] and the British Forensic Science Service created an online footwear identification and coding management system for footwear identification from crime scenes called Footwear Intelligence Technology.[48] Electronic communications are now a source of benefit to local, national and international criminals that has moved far beyond the idea of making an international phone call to the point where communication devices can serve as payment systems for drug deals, counterfeit goods and illegal services. Disposable pay-as-you-go phones make it possible for criminals to make bulk purchases of phones and literally throw them away after each call is made in order to further obfuscate the trail of criminality. The analysis of an individual's electronic communications equipment over time is an effective way of ascertaining interest, contacts, activities and behavior. Social groups are also very telling, and these too can be analyzed over time to show a pattern of activity and affiliations. Columbia University developed the Email Mining Toolkit (EMT).[49] which has the capacity to automatically mine large email collections for patterns of activity. Rolling Histograms and Social Mining are other methods of user profile identification and user pattern identification.[50] Tactical crime analysis is now a term used to describe the constant review of crime data by drawing upon multiple sources of crime data collection, including some or all of those mentioned above. Linkage Analysis is the process of connecting a suspect to a series of criminal events. Target Profiling uses data to determine offense pattern areas, and GIS—Geographic Information Systems—is a system to store, retrieve, analyze and display data that employs the use of computers, maps, microscopes and visual identification[51] to display crime pattern data, commonly referred to as Crime Mapping. Crime mapping results in a visual display of criminal activity in locations and over time so that a police officer or manager can see the number of incidents over space and time. It is the contemporary (and more sophisticated) version of a map on the wall with pins stuck into it to show where crimes are happening. Geographic Profiling is a system that seeks to identify the likely location of an offender based upon geography, psychology and mathematics. The Rigel Profiler is: "The world's most advanced geographic profiling application, developed specifically for Geographic Profilers who have advanced training on special analysis techniques for violent crime investigation. It builds on the functionality found in Rigel Analyst, with an expanded set of expert analysis tools needed to address the unique nature of violent serial crime."[52] It is a computer-based information sorting system that enables large amounts of data to be sifted into priorities based upon theoretical profiling models, for example, DNA mass screening based upon the geoprofile of the offender.

Forensic science in the 21st century is likely to be more closely aligned with technology than in the past. Already we have seen the introduction of Biometrics that incorporates voice recognition, fingerprint identification, eye pattern analysis (retina scanning) and lip movement and pattern identification. Facial recognition software is now utilized to improve the image creation of suspects seen by eyewitnesses, and it is also used as a security device to ensure that authorized personnel access premises.

CCTV has been used extensively in Europe for the past 40 years. It too is now crossing to the US with some frequency, and despite concerns over 'citizen spying', the reality is that most citizens are happy to give up a little freedom in exchange for the perceived advantages of better security and easier criminal identification. Under the auspices of the Department of Homeland Security, the Homeland Security Information Network (HSIN) is "a national secure and trusted web-based portal for information sharing and collaboration between federal, state, local, tribal, territorial, private sector, and international partners engaged in the homeland security mission. HSIN is made up of a growing network of communities, called Communities of Interest (COI). COIs are organized by state organizations, federal organizations, or mission areas such as emergency management, law enforcement, critical sectors and intelligence can securely share within their communities or reach out to other communities as needed. HSIN provides secure, real-time collaboration tools, including a virtual meeting space, instant messaging and document sharing. HSIN allows partners to work together instantly, regardless of their location, to communicate, collaborate, and coordinate."[53] Voice encryption, interoperability communications,[54] VPN's[55] and content scramble systems are all now in common use by law enforcement and by illicit communities. Even the Smartphone, once thought revolutionary is already passé for criminals and crime fighters. Automatic fingerprint recognition systems are likely to be in common use over the course of the next 10 years. Enhanced use of digital personal recognition systems seems inevitable. Further sharing of information held on electronic databases will continue, whether civil libertarians approve or not it seems. Vehicle identification systems will be employed more often, so that every vehicle movement is recorded as we move across cities and towns throughout our daily lives. GIS and computerized crime mapping will become more effective as we become more efficient at manipulating the data. Gunshot Locator Systems will no doubt be installed in some cities across the US so that a computer enhanced microphone system can accurately pinpoint gunshot by radio wave movement. Forensic science will continue to attract serious and not so serious attention as the media bends the truth of crime scene investigation to suit a 40-minute media slot. The myths of forensic science will live on despite the best efforts of real scientists. Every piece of evidence will never be perfect and the technician at the scene will never be a scientist equipped with a fully functioning laboratory, and of course the analysis of data will get quicker but never the 15 minutes it currently takes for an episode of CSI to identify a weapon, a cause of death and an offender. And hopefully we will never reach a point in time where there are five murders every episode.

The future of forensic science looks very bright. Advances in technology look set to continue and add further tools to the on-scene investigations that are so crucial to effective crime analysis. Hand-held DNA recorders are a distinct possibility so too will be the greater use of computers to make precise crime scene drawings that will further assist juries in seeing the crime scene as it first appeared to the police. Fingerprinting revolutionized one century and DNA another. It is exciting to wonder what the contribution will be to the 21st century.

Professor Paul Knepper[56] concludes his book *The Invention of International Crime: A Global Issue in the Making 1881–1914* with the following comment, "In Britain, government authorities shared with critics of government authority concerns about the impact of an interconnected world, despite their disagreements about what needed to be done in response to these impacts. Collectively, governments, voluntary organisations and individuals made crime an international issue of some significance. The people who lived in the decades between 1881 and 1914 were the first to grasp crime as an international issue, and they introduced ways of thinking and responding that continue into the present era."[57] The central focus of the discussion shifted from Britain to the US over the course of the last century, but the words are even more pertinent as we have seen in this book, as local and state police are facing increasing pressure to be the responsible agencies for the prevention and detection of crimes that can appear locally innocuous but are often internationally impactful. We remain, in the early years of the 21st century, incredibly capable of manipulating or outright avoiding culpability for a broad range of behavior that is thoroughly offensive to every human on the planet. Despite lofty protestations that we are sophisticated and capable of self-policing, apparently we are no more able to do this than at many stages in our history. We continue to need a body of men and women to detect the few of us and to prevent most of us from being criminal. In my view, the people writing about crime and policing crime at the end of this century will be commenting on the mid-century introduction of the world's first global police force, the use of wrist worn forensic 'superscanners' that identify what at a crime scene should be taken for analysis on the basis of a general scene scan that instantly records a number of sample possibilities. And it is possible, perhaps, that the officers dealing with those crimes will be policing them in a uniform and using equipment that resembles civilian life and not military.

Whatever shape or form the policing of crime takes over the course of the next hundred years, it should be our collective passion for policing and not crime that drives the agenda forward.

Endnotes

1. American College of Forensic Examiners. First recorded autopsy at www.historyofforensics.com
2. The most recorded example is of how to distinguish between a drowning and strangulation. There are a number of reports on the work of Collected cases of injustice rectified by Xi Yuan Ji Lu. Most sources agree that this work was incorporated into the better known work, *His Duan Yu*, The washing away of wrongs, authored by Sung Tz'u (also written as Song Ci).
3. It was the case throughout all Europe during this period that surgeons were also barbers. The professions did not part company until the 17th century.
4. Drucker, CB. Ambrose Paré and the birth of the gentle art of surgery. *Yale Journal of Biology and Medicine.* December 2008; 81(4); 199–202.
5. There are numerous, short, references to this incident. E.g. *The encyclopedia of forensic science, forensic science timeline and history of forensics* (compiled by the American College of Forensic Examiners. Op. cit.)
6. Also written as Mathieu. Born in Spain in 1787, Mathiew Joseph Bonaventure Orfila went on to become professor and dean of medical chemistry at the University of Paris, Athénée. He was elected President of the Academy of Medicine in 1851.
7. The microscope was developed in 1674 by Dutchman Anton van Leeuwenhoek.
8. Quetelet created the 'Quetelet Index', a forerunner to the Body Mass Index used today.
9. Eknoyan, G. Adolphe Quetelet (1796–1874)—the average man and indices of obesity. *Nephrology Dialysis Transplantation.* 2008; 23(1); 47–51.
10. The term was introduced by the American Calvin Goddard and in correct use means the study of the projection of a bullet upon discharge from the firearm. Common usage is for 'bullet matching'.
11. The development of ballistics. www.historybytheyard.co.uk/pc_gutteridge. It is of note that this case is frequently mis-reported as a murder investigation, including in the entry made by the American College of Forensic Examiners at www.historyofforensics.com 1837 bullet matching and Forensic Science Central, which also incorrectly states the case facts. www.forensicscience central.co.uk
12. In Argentina, Jaun Vucetich took fingerprint evidence left in blood on a door at the crime scene and compared this with the prints of the mother of the two

victims, whereupon she confessed to the double killing. The evidence was not used at trial due to her confession. Vucetich was a police employee, in the Identification and Statistics Department in La Plata, who successfully devised a system of fingerprint identification. His work was informed by the work of Francis Galton, *infra,* and he would most likely be credited further with his work were it not for developments in the UK that attracted greater interest and also due to the fact that his success in the murder case in Argentina took years before the news reached Europe. He is certainly responsible for spreading the word about fingerprints, especially after his publication in Spanish of *Dactiloscopia comparada* in 1904. Vucetich was convinced that 10-finger sets of fingerprints were sufficient to make an identification of a suspect. He was right, and in many ways his work led to the demise of the Bertillon, *infra,* system. For a more detailed discussion, see Colin Beavan, *infra.* Chapter 7.

13. March 27, 1905 was the date that Alfred and Albert Stratton were convicted of the murder of Mr. and Mrs. Farrow, having broken into their paint shop in London and stolen a cash box. They brutally murdered the victims at the scene. The cash box was recovered from the home of one of the defendants and the fingerprints found on the box were used to identify the defendants. The fingerprint evidence was then admitted into evidence at trial. The Stratton brothers were hanged on May 23, 1905.
14. Born 9 January 1833, he was son of John Herschel, credited with inventing sensitized paper for photography, and grandson of William Herschel, the astronomer who discovered the planet Uranus.
15. Beavan, C. *Fingerprints: The origins of crime detection and the murder case that launched forensic science.* New York: Hyperion; 2001, 47–48.
16. Darwin wrote such a letter of support and introduction in April 1880. See: Beavan, op. cit., pp. 73–74
17. Beavan, op. cit., p. 102
18. Jones, M. and Johnstone, P. *History of Criminal Justice.* 5th ed. Waltham, MA: Andersons; 2011, 223–225.
19. Allen Pinkerton, founder of the U.S. private detective agency. "Pinkerton's called himself 'The Vidocq of the West'."
20. Jones & Johnstone, op. cit., p. 321.
21. Beavan, op. cit., p. 90.
22. The 'Dreyfus' scandal involved an army captain, Alfred Dreyfus, who was wrongly convicted of selling secrets to Germany in 1894. Much of the testimony was found to be biased and faulty, including Bertillon's 'expert' handwriting testimony. Eventually Dreyfus was exonerated, but not until he had served five years hard labor in the infamous prison, Devil's Island, *île du diable,* off the coast of French Guiana, South America.

23. Kasprzak, J. Possibilities of cheiloscoy. *Forensic Science International.* May–June 1990; 1–2 (46); 145–151, and Kasprzak, J. Cheiloscopy in *Encyclopedia of forensic science.* Vol. I. Siegel, JA, Saukko, PJ, and Knuper, GC, editors. London: Academic Press; 2000; 358–361 at 358. http://dx.doi.org/10.1006/wifs.2000.0436 See also: Marc Abrahams' article The research that's on everyone's lips. *The Guardian Newspaper.* Monday June 18, 2012. Available at www.guardian.co.uk
24. There is a considerable body of information about contemporary use of lip prints but very little information about R. Fischer, the man responsible for originally investigating the uniqueness of human lips. Many sources state that the application of lip identification became viable due to the work of French forensic anthropologist Edmund Locard in 1932. For example, see: Prabhu RV, Dinkar AD, Prabhu VD, and Rao PK. Cheiloscopy: Revisited. *J Forensic Dent Sci.* 2012; 4; 47–52.
25. Dentistry, forensic odontology, has been recognized as an identification method for centuries. Teeth age can be determined by the specific gravity of the tooth and therefore the age of a corpse can be established. The size, alignment, color and distribution of teeth are unique and contained in dental records; consequently, bite marks too are unique. It is therefore possible to identify corpses and also live suspects through teeth identification. Jones, G. & Johnstone, P. *History of Criminal Justice.* 5th ed. Waltham, MA: Andersons; 2011; 323–326. The first application of 'bite marks' evidence in the US was in Texas in 1954. Doyle v State No. 26761, Jan. 20, 1954. 159 Tex Crim. 779. 310,263 S.W. 2d. Court of Criminal Appeals.
26. Ear prints. Much recent work in this field has been headed up through Dr. Jerzy Kasprzak at the Military Forensic Laboratory, Warszawa, Poland. He is also the person responsible for introducing the work of anthropologist R. S. Fischer, *supra,* and lip prints (cheiloscopy).
27. Known as Locard's Exchange Principle.
28. People v Jennings 252 ILL 534. 96 NE 1077 (ILL 1911)
29. Known as The Scientific Investigation Division. Vollmer is remembered every year for his pioneering work as a police chief and his belief in forensics by the International Association of Chiefs of Police "August Vollmer Excellence in Forensic Science Award."
30. Goddard had previously created the Bureau of Forensic Ballistics in New York in 1925 with C. E. Waite, Philip O. Gravell and John. H. Fischer. The laboratory at Northwestern was the first independent entity, and it was headed by Goddard, who was Professor of Police Science at Northwestern University.
31. Evans, C. *The father of forensics; The biography of Bernard Spilsbury.* London: Berkeley; 2006.

32. JD Watson and FHC Crick. A structure for deoxyribose nucleic acid. (1) April 25, 1953 (2), *Nature* (3); 171, 737–738.
33. For further information see: Human Genome Project Information at www.genomics.energy.gov or www.ornl.gov
34. www.le.ac.uk/discover/dna
35. The term 'bar codes' was used due to the similarity in appearance of the profile to a pricing bar code found on items in stores.
36. Identical twins do have the same DNA.
37. Pitchfork appealed his conviction in May 2009, and as a result of this he was given a two-year reduction in sentence. Whilst in prison he has taken a degree and is working on translation work into Braille. He will be released in 2016.
38. Crime-fighting successes of DNA at www.news.bbc.co.uk. At this same site are details of other major breakthroughs using DNA to solve crime, including the first ever successful use of *famial* DNA to convict a man for manslaughter.
39. Gianelli, P. Impact of post-conviction DNA testing on forensic science. *New England Law Review.* 2001; 35(3); 627–638.
40. Krajick, K. Genetics in the courtroom. *Newsweek.* January 11, 1994 at 64 cited by Gianelli; supra at p. 627, Note 3.
41. As per data provided by The Innocence Project up to September 3, 2012. www.innocenceproject.org
42. Oklahoma does not permit DNA testing by inmates. Source: Innocence Project.
43. See further Sampson, W. and Sampson, K., Recovery of latent prints from human skin. *The Journal of Forensic Identification.* May/June 2005; 55(3). Available at www.crime-scene-investigator.net
44. Ibid.
45. Generally DNA is located in chromosomes within the nucleus. However, mitochondria have a small amount of their own DNA. This mitochondria DNA has 37 genes.
46. One of the most famous cases is still pending appeal, the case of Army green beret and surgeon Jeffery Macdonald who allegedly brutally murdered his wife and two daughters in 1979 at Fort Bragg. MacDonald has always maintained his innocence, and its looks as though he will finally have a chance to test the DNA evidence against him in September 2012 using a new technique known as KFiler Kits. See: Fran Norton, Convicted Bragg murderer has evidence appeal delayed. Friday, 6 April 2012. Star News On-Line at www.starnewsonline.com
47. The National DNA Index System, NIDIS. "The DNA Identification Act of 1994 (42 U.S.C. §14132) authorized the establishment of this National DNA Index. The DNA Act specifies the categories of data that may be maintained

in NDIS (convicted offenders, arrestees, legal, detainees, forensic (casework), unidentified human remains, missing persons and relatives of missing persons as well as requirements for participating laboratories relating to quality assurance, privacy and expungement. www.fbi.gov

48. See: Paula Dear, Tread carefully to fight crime. 15 February 2007 at www.news.bbc.co.uk
49. www.sneakers.cs.columbia.edu
50. See: Creamer, Germán G., Stolfo, S. and Hershkop, S. A Temporal based forensic analysis of electronic communication. San Diego, CA: Digital Government Proceedings; 2006. Available at SSRN: http://ssrn.com/abstract=2028734
51. Any information that can be "geocoded" can be put into the GIS for analysis. As with all systems, the output is entirely dependent upon the quality of the input.
52. Environmental Criminology Research Incorporated, inventors of the Rigel profiler System at www.ecricanada.com
53. www.dhs.gov/homeland-security-intelligence-network
54. AGILE, Advanced Generation of Interoperability for Law Enforcement, at www.rkb.us and www.safecomprogram.gov
55. Virtual Private Networks. Encryption scrambling software.
56. Paul Knepper is Professor of Law, the University of Sheffield, UK and Visiting Professor at the Institute of Criminology, University of Malta.
57. Knepper, P. *The invention of international crime: A global issue in the making.* London: Palgrave; 2010; 193.